COLLECTING
RHINESTONE
& COLORED STONE JEWELRY

An Identification & Value Guide
3rd Edition

by
Maryanne Dolan

ISBN 0-89689-099-6

BOOKS AMERICANA
INC.

P9-DTL-738

DEDICATION:
For My Grandmother - A Jewel

TABLE OF CONTENTS

ACKNOWLEDGEMENTS

Jewelry from the collection of the author and these special friends:

Yvonne Brooks
Donna Charkowicz
Virginia Cox
Deanna Doering
Virginia Keefauver
Bill and Jan McLorn
June Richwine
Dorothy Senger
Bess Ryon
Shirlee Thompson
Ann Thatcher

With particular thanks to Karl Eisenberg of Eisenberg Jewelry and Bruce Hobe' of Jewels by Hobe' for their cooperation.

To Franc M. Ricciardi of Richton International Corp., Diane Hornberger of Krementz & Company, Maybeth Mooney of Hallmark Cards, Inc., and Charles Richter of Richter's Fifth Avenue, my gratitude. To William J. Slattery of Sarah Coventry and Sanford G. Moss of Haskell Jewels Ltd., my thanks.

For their contributions to this edition my deepest gratitude and affection:

Rita Sachs of New York City
Elsa Houle of Yuba City, California
Deanna Doering of Berkeley, California
Susan Fischer of Kingsley, Iowa
Karl Eisenberg of Eisenberg Jewelry, Chicago
Stefania Sakiotis of Richelieu, New York
Beth Miller of Napier, New York
Pat Hill of Ciner, New York
Kerry Prill and Jan Sandstrom of Nordstrom, Seattle.
Elaine Yeary, Pleasant Hill, California

AUTHOR'S NOTE

Sapphires couldn't have done it; emeralds or rubies — certainly not; probably not even diamonds - but rhinestones, that's another story - this story.

Since the first edition of this book was published I have received over 12,000 letters and telephone calls from all parts of the world. To all of you whom I have met, long distance, I wish to express my profound appreciation for your kind comments, your wonderful sense of sharing and your deep love of this unique jewelry.

You have enriched my life.

PREFACE

The rhinestone world is alight with developments. Prices have changed, specific collections have been defined and refined, marks from the 1950s, 60s and even the 1970s are becoming collectible and generally a more sophisticated attitude has emerged since the first edition of this book on rhinestone jewelry was published. The jewelry is now appreciated for what it is - a stunning, well-made representation of an American period and a particular culture.

The greats of the rhinestone world continue to command very high prices and attention. Eisenberg, Trifari, Coro, Hobe', Kramer, Haskell, among others, continue to hold intense interest among wise collectors and prices continue to rise on select pieces. Large collections have now been made and logically fewer desirable pieces at reasonable prices will be available.

New names have surfaced, wonderfully bizarre examples have tumbled out of drawers and boxes; rhinestones have been included in other books; elegant shops can now be found which sell nothing but this jewelry; younger people continue to be attracted to the field and one whole segment of our world is undoubtedly happier because of these bright and enticing bits of glass. Karl Eisenberg of the Eisenberg firm says "the continuing popularity of this jewelry is such that we can't keep up with orders."

Christmas trees with colored stones have become a large collecting item and in this area the intelligent collectors need to keep current by buying annual issues of companies such as Eisenberg and Hobe'. Powder compacts with stone accents are becoming popular and are still undervalued; shoe buckles are achieving status both as a wearable and collectible artifact; more costume rings are surfacing, but remain among the rarest of the old pieces; unmarked jewelry - the necklaces, bracelets and earrings of the 1940s with their razzle dazzle have stabilized, even come down, in price. Collectors though should never ignore an interesting, well-made, unmarked piece. Many of these are significant and worthy of any collection. The designer signed jewelry has established itself as a prime target in spite of the expensive price tag and is indeed moving toward museum status.

Younger collectors have already moved into the 1950s, 60s and there is some stirring among collectors into the 1970s production, since prices for these among dealers are somewhat lower and pieces more abundant. Nothing, however, will ever compare with the really monumental achievements from the early period of rhinestone jewelry production. Even a quick perusal of any fine department store jewelry section will prove that the innovative styles and types of jewelry from the 1930s and 40s are being copied with impunity by the contemporary designers, and such a look will also prove that in buying older pieces the collector not only owns a fascinating, wearable piece of America's past, but the price is apt to be equal, if not lower, than some of the newer pieces command.

Names from the 1960s and 70s which have not yet peaked are Ballau, Goldcraft, Famor, Sarah Coventry (which discontinued its Home Party Plan in the fall of 1984 and sold the inventory and equipment. The name will be retailed under licensing agreements), Kenneth Lane (who is already popular with some celebrities), Robert Fleischer, Monet, Real Art, Winaird and Avon. No collector should reject any marked piece if the price is right - it is all collectible and there are probably names still unrecorded. Mimi di N designed some lovely jewelry during this period and Robert whose nifty pieces from the 1940s are somewhat scarce was still producing some interesting jewelry in the 1960s. Beauty is in the eye of the beholder but good, signed jewelry is money in the bank.

This third edition is a tribute to your love of rhinestone jewelry and your acumen in collecting it. Vive la rhinestone.

INTRODUCTION

The most amazing situation exists in the exuberant world of rhinestone and colored stone jewelry. Interest continues so high that prices on good to choice pieces are going up all the time, new collectors are flocking to the field and the attitude of former unbelievers is enthusiastic if somewhat dazed, after all $3,000 for an Eisenberg Original at Trump Towers in New York - even a stone would be impressed.

There is a whole new philosophy abroad in the land which says SEEK YE CELEBRITY JEWELRY IF YOU WOULD BE A NABOB. The only flaw in this thinking is the neglect of lesser, equally beautiful pieces which are still available and reasonably priced.

Recently two absolutely stunning collections were brought to my attention. Both owners are also dealers, one of whom sells almost exclusively to people in the entertainment industry. The other sells to a rather upscale suburban clientele. Both dealers have no difficulty commanding high prices for any good signed piece or an unusually attractive or interesting 'jewel'. Both say "Good rhinestone jewelry sells itself". A fascinating aside is reflected in my mail - very seldom anymore does anyone mention price - value, yes, price, no. This is because of the status the jewelry has achieved. All is sanguine, even euphoric in this delightful, sparkling world. A world of great fun but a place where a wise investment can reap major rewards. It's a changing world though, competition is now so keen that even the empty boxes original to the jewelry, well-made themselves and carrying the manufacturer's name can be a source of rivalry. At a church sale recently two Carl Art boxes were sitting on a table, pretty boxes in odd shapes. My friend who asked about them was quoted a price but before she could react they were snatched up she says by a "furious woman" who paid for them instantly and stalked off. Always try to keep Miss Manners mandates in mind but also make your inner deliberations short if you see something you really want.

The great designers of this jewelry are the superstars. Schiaparelli has achieved amazing popularity and has become one of the foremost names - Boucher, Nettie Rosenstein, McClleland Barclay, Panetta, Pennini are now names which have become familiar where not so long ago they were known only to a select, smallish group of collectors. Not only names but situations have taken on a new dimension - in the way of a Great Masters or a newly unearthed antiquity, rhinestone jewelry is now the subject of an underground information network activated when a particularly fine piece becomes available, rather in the way of a Hope Diamond. Great pieces of rhinestone and colored stone jewelry have taken on a life of their own. It may very well be that in future reference may be made to rhinestone jewelry as 'fine' and true gemstone jewelry as 'privileged jewelry' or some other designation meaning 'for the few' although with current prices on some costume jewelry this too may be a misnomer. The jewelry world has certainly been confounded by all this. In 1985, for example a trade journal reported under the headline PEOPLE WANT FAKES, 'AMERICANS ARE IMPORTING FEWER GENUINE GEMSTONES AND FEWER SYNTHETICS' BUT THEY ARE IMPORTING FAR MORE 'IMITATION STONES'. Imports of imitation stones made of glass were up 43% that year. Naturally this made an impact on the genuine gemstone business and it was a surprising enough statistic to warrant space in such a magazine. So now it is official, (as anyone who collects seriously or deals in rhinestone jewelry knows) that the revival of rhinestones after the first edition of this book was published is not a fad, nor just a passing fancy. This is so not only because of the attraction of the jewels themselves but because of the history and the provenance connected with much of the older production. In actuality it is a lifestyle which we not only enjoy but which connects us to others. Recently a caller alerted me to a complete set of McClleland Barclay he was considering purchasing. A very intoxicating prospect that, we discussed it, we deliberated, talked of the man and his jewelry, solidified our thinking and generally felt pleased with the jewelry, the conversation, the exchange of knowledge and the camaraderie. What more could one ask of any given day?

Barclay himself, of course, represents a different approach, a more experimental, unusual, often 'arty' style which reflects the man himself. So when one of his complete sets surfaced it was worthy of cross country discussion. Calls from Asia and Europe confirm that this indeed is the high plateau this jewelry has reached and my international correspondence reinforces the incredible desirability and interest the jewelry has fostered. Still there are those who are surprised. Recently Skinners auction house of Boston was reportedly just so shocked when its 1992 auction of the contents of a costume jewelry and accessories shop brought unanticipated crowds and high prices. As I lecture across the country there are still stunned reactions to quotes of fully documented prices on some of this jewelry. The Skinner auction had many famous signatures on the jewelry so success was assured even though vast numbers of people were not aware of the sale. Enough collectors knew of it to be almost a surplus.

In 1987 Southeby's sold the collection of Diane Vreeland of *Vogue Magazine*. She was much given to wearing oversized jewels and to wearing many pieces at any one time. That auction certainly proved that while there was much that was beautiful, even the most ordinary pieces will sell well if there is a celebrity connection. This force is driving the market today.

Another powerful influence on contemporary buying is the "ethnic". It is a design motif which has peaked and waned over many decades and the early examples are sought after and expensive. Current designs are imitating these innovative, often startling conceptions but somehow lack the sheer emotion of the 1920s, 30s or 40s jewelry. This category is interesting as a specialty because it usually illustrates exotic design work and cultural influences in this country. The earlier examples of ethnic costume jewelry (Katz, Phillippe and Eisenberg) are rare and are cause for severe excitement when found but collectors should not hesitate to add any new, worthwhile piece to a collection. Wear it, enjoy it and leave it to your heirs, most of it has been based on earlier designs anyway. It will not have the same value as the old pieces, but its price will certainly appreciate.

As with the 'ethnic' motifs, most of the large manufacturers are 'adapting' new jewelry from the old designs and molds. Richelieu-Lisner, e.g. says it has not 'adapted' jewelry "but many of our styles have been reorderable for over 100 years". In 1989 Karl Eisenberg noted "The adaptation of this year's jewelry are exact copies taken from the original sketches of the old design. They are marked differently. Each piece has a small metal tab on the back inscribed with the words Eisenberg Ice. The earrings are not marked"; Pat Hill of Ciner says "From time to time we resurrect old designs if we feel they relate to current looks in jewelry. Old link bracelets and necklaces seem the most applicable. But this happens very infrequently". Other companies also seem to rework old designs from time to time. It is not something collectors need to stay awake at night worrying about. The companies intend no deceit and the marks are usually different.

Be aware too that some of the great makers are advertising collections geared to special events. The Spring Bridal Collections of Marvella are a good example, they often feature pearls and rhinestones and are exquisite; Eisenberg has moved into this orbit, they too combine pearls with pink or blue stones. Any pieces from such a coordinated collection are beautiful and certainly worth the price. We all want what is older with its fabled past and higher value but keep in mind such jewelry is now beyond its first renaissance. Much of it has disappeared forever into museums and private collections and that any good piece you buy now will have added value in 20 years. In a relatively short time there will not be many affordable signed older pieces for collectors to acquire. We probably have not realized how fortunate we have been to have begun collections when we did. We have so enjoyed the quest it's been akin to partying while watching our investment grow. It must be kept in mind though that appreciation of the jewelry for itself should always be the first consideration. A few years ago I was walking through an airport wearing a rhinestone pin spelling out PARIS on my jacket lapel and a smaller rhinestone pin spelling out ROME on my handbag. If I had a large rhinestone for every person who stopped to ask me where I had bought these pins I could make myself another one spelling out MISSISSIPPI. The excitement generated by these relatively inexpensive pins is one of the main attractions of this jewelry - it attracts attention. Clothing designers know this and act on it.

The 1980s saw Parisian designers loading their runway models with bold, fake gems. Designers here did the same thing, "glitter and sparkle wake up the audience" said one. Too true. Watch the Academy Awards ceremonies some time, you will be blinded by the dazzle of fake gems. A spectacular pair of my long dangling WEISS earrings made it to one of the awards evenings, in the 1990s these 1940s jewels were as sparkling as ever, as sensational looking as ever and as contemporary as the awards themselves. One of the greatest elements of good design was embodied in those earrings - good design which rendered them timeless.

The return of rhinestone jewelry made in period design is a factor all collectors should recognize. A 1959 *Life* magazine cover featured a model wearing a rhinestone choker with pearls and matching earrings. "Glittery comeback for chokers" trumpeted the story. But has there ever really been a time since the 1920s when rhinestones were not glittering somewhere? Photographs displayed the Edwardian dog collar, a flattering multi strand high choker favored by Royalty and actresses. In this country they were designed for use with casual wear, with sweaters or evening wear (never to be worn without your tiara). In 1959 these chokers would have cost you $30 (Trifari) slightly less than Queen Alexandria's cost in 1902. Lately several good collections of period type rhinestone jewelry have been made, the dog collars are especially impressive. Collecting in period is interesting and is most often done by Vintage Clothing lovers. Collecting in period leads to a study of history and can add depth to your jewelry pieces. The research of periods can be traced by perusing the pages of magazines such as *Harper's Bazaar, Vogue* and other immensely influential women's periodicals. In the past they have had a powerful effect refining the taste of the American woman. Their advertisements have pointed the way because the women who were (and are) interested in high, up-to-the-minute fashion who were willing to buy the magazines were also willing to be guided by the dictates of the editors. You can leaf through old issues of these magazines today, note the ads for genuine gemstone jewelry and think of your own collection of rhinestones. How many of your pieces resemble these expensive creations? For *Vogue* and *Harpers* were not the motivators for the original rhinestone buying frenzy but the jewelry pictured in their pages was often the inspiration for the very piece your mother may have bought in Gimbels or Woolworths.

But today the fact that some of today's costume jewelry manufacturers use these very magazines, once the province of fabled fine jewelers, to introduce their own new designs to the American woman points out just how far these 'brilliants' have come. It illustrates the heights to which such jewelry has risen. Advertising in such media does not come without cost so expect newer rhinestone jewelry to keep getting more expensive. A cursory tour of any big department store will allow you to view the new inventory and to check out prices. While you do this look at Christian Dior, the Carolee, Napier, Trifari, all the good names are still out and about and some of them are still doing masterful work.

Think about men's jewelry which is making a huge collecting surge. The older cuff links, tie clasps, tie tacs, many with pretty stones, are all in demand, and still inexpensive. Stick pins are already a big category and emblematic jewelry is attracting a quiet, steady audience. Some novelty jewelry has a special appeal for men, automotive pins, planes, pipes, musical instruments, have found a niche. Many manufacturers extended themselves into these areas and novelty jewelry with good signatures is still abundant. Some of the unsigned pieces date from the 1960s and 1970s when many of these little delights were made from rhinestone and colored stone jewelry kits which sold prodigiously during those years. Depending on the ability of the creator to follow directions accurately, this kind of jewelry can have either a professional or a primitive look. The American flag was one of the most dominant of this kind of jewelry.

"Estate Jewelry" auctions and sales have become an increasingly popular designation for sales of Vintage jewelry. From the turn of the century to the 1920s to Art Deco through the 1940s these sales are becoming the province of fashion setters and younger collectors. While the term "estate jewelry" can mean almost anything, the Vintage connotation is definitely there. It is at one of these sales a friend found an exquisite Mosell in a bag of what was labeled 'broken', true the pin is off its back, but the piece itself is intact and beautiful.

She also found many novelty pieces and while she is not a jewelry collector (she avidly seeks buttons and found some in the bag) she has been converted, she is impressed by the craftsmanship and as her teen-age daughter put it she too "is swept away" by the imagination of the designer of her vintage boat pin. Never neglect these estate auctions or sales. Everything depends on who is there, what they are seeking, even the weather plays a part. Always preview such auctions carefully and never skip an 'estate' sale even if you go late.

New collectors are flocking to this field every day, but one change must be noted - even the veriest neophyte is looking for "good marks" and thinking in terms of ultimate value. So what becomes of all the wonderful unmarked rhinestones. Some of it is selling for much less than it is worth and if by now you have learned to recognize the old or older pieces from the new it is only sensible to buy it if the price fits your budget. Some of the most exquisite pieces in my own collection do not bear prestigious signatures although they may have the characteristics of the great companies which made them. So we are at the point where people who are accepting the challenge of putting together an in-depth, valuable collection are on a quest which is being stimulated by the many speakers, dealers and writers who are now promoting this jewelry. It makes for very keen competition. The two previous editions of this book are so definitive not much new information has surfaced but some names mentioned in the earlier editions are now assuming tremendous importance - Barclay, Schiaparelli, Nettie Rosenstein, Mimi D'n, Pennino, Doctor Dress, Cardoro, and others - names to watch for now are Bauer, LaRel, S.A.L. Alexander Korda, Van. S. Authentics, early Monet, early Avon, Sarah Coventry, Pauline Trigere, Jo Copeland and of course any and all of the masters.

Train yourself by studying pieces in shops and at shows to recognize the work of the greats, almost always it has certain characteristics which help to identify it, Trifari and Krementz, for example, Eisenberg, Joseff and Haskell all have recognizable qualities, almost like fingerprints. Be alert, do some serious looking, handling and reading. The early work of Schreiner for example and the early Hobe' are prime examples of easy to recognize jewelry. Be watchful for some types made by Selro Co., ask the jewelry gods to direct you to a Mosell or Marcel Boucher. Above all, keep hunting. Keep your sense of humor in good working order, but be serious about this non-serious jewelry.

NOTE: My mail and telephone calls concerning this book and the rhinestone world in general have soared well above 12,000. To all of you who have written and called, to all of you who have shared your thoughts with me and to whom I have not been able to respond, I beg your indulgence - I have enjoyed knowing about you, I have sincerely wanted to expand our acquaintance (if even by mail) but it is not possible. I certainly appreciate it and I am sincerely grateful.

Pleasant Hill, California

RHINESTONE JEWELRY

It's a bit like a conjurer's trick — what you see is not what you think you see. Those diamonds glittering around the neck of that fashionably dressed beauty are really only rhinestones. Beautiful, dazzling rhinestones, long dismissed as 'garish' or 'worthless' but now back in vogue and commanding higher and higher prices. The colored stones, as many as 15 shades on one bracelet, are attracting audiences everywhere; this whole field is a collector's paradise.

It's all a kaleidoscope, a fury of color and brilliance to catch the eye and the pocketbook while it's still affordable. It's light-hearted and flattering and definitely not diamonds unless you know the nabobs who can afford the real thing in this giant economy size.

The rhinestone world has come into its own again and it's exciting and often quite lovely and those of you who have a fondness for the late 1920's, the 30's, the 40's and the early 50's, your time has come again. "If ever there was a season to light up the town with loads of rhinestone costume jewelry, this is it," said a fashion writer in 1983, "and if you can find the dangling earrings from the 40's, better still."

Well, those dangling earrings are certainly out there and the writer was merely echoing what collectors and dealers have known for some time. Not only are rhinestones one of the fastest rising collectibles, they're fun and still not prohibitively priced. And the Rhinestone story is worthy of the Brothers Grimm, it is a true Cinderella tale.

The rhinestone is, quite simply, hard, bright glass backed with foil. Glass does not reflect light from its interior as a real diamond does, so in order to throw the light back from the glass, it is backed with foil or tin. This prevents light from going right through the glass, instead the stone catches the existing light and acts in the same way a genuine stone would.

Even the name 'rhinestone' exudes a certain glamour, and it seems fitting that the origin of the rhinestone rests in the River Rhine where these small, water-smoothed pebbles of rock crystal quality were first found, or so goes the story.

In their various past lives, rhinestones have been known as strass and paste, which have been made for centuries. George Frederick Stras(s) is credited with inventing 'strass' a combination of flint glass and the 18th century development of brilliant cutting. This was very high quality, carefully done, but there are those who insist George Frederick Strass never existed and this jewelry simply evolved. The designation 'strass' lives on, although rarely used to describe rhinestones today.

Paste again is glass and has been used in jewelry since the days of the ancients. 'Strass' is actually 'Paste', a remarkably brilliant and clear glass, beautifully cut and polished with foiled backing. A myriad of colors could be made and tinting the foil backing could produce different shadings in the stones. Paste went out of fashion in 1870 when mass production entered the industrial picture.

Early paste jewelry was of such quality as to be in a class by itself. The stones were cut with great skill and embedded in costly settings by hand. Much paste has been lost because of those costly settings, the jewelry was broken up for the setting, not the stone. Paste jewelry was fashioned to create an impression of reality, in some cases a thin slice of diamond was put over the glass. Even experts were fooled, and many was the aristocrat who eventually tried to sell family jewels for a profit and found he was trying to sell glass.

The old 'paste' and 'strass' were not costume jewelry in the sense we use the words, but they certainly were made in imitation of diamonds. At all times the diamond has been coveted and those who could not have the real thing were willing to settle for less but only if it looked like the genuine article. It was only in the 1920's and 1930's that the advertisers were willing to take the risk of blatantly announcing 'imitation diamond' or 'brilliants'. They played heavily on the desire for diamonds, everybody wanted them but in the late 1920's nobody could afford them. Their risk paid off so well Horatio Algers were popping up all over the landscape. And it was this bit of glass with a bit of foil that made their fortunes. The very simplicity is ingenious, if not new, and it was the basis for the whole rhinestone industry.

Many sophisticated jewelers preferred to call it 'Fashion Jewelry' and it was their demand for better quality which led to the more expensive pieces being produced. To the collector with money to spend, this 'fashion jewelry' of the early years should be a primary goal, it can cost as much as $100 or more depending on who made it and where you buy it. The generally inexpensive costume jewelry has more pizzaz, more of a sense of fun and is still well underpriced.

Within the whole category there is that which is blatantly and proudly fake. It was deliberately crafted to look overdone, to be so startling in its brilliance no one could mistake the message. Its size, too, is often overpowering. Some of the pieces are too large for the timid, and are thoughtfully outrageous in their design. Indeed, it takes a certain type to wear these with flair because they are often so spectacular, even bizarre, but oh, what an addition to a collection.

The resurgence of this whole field of jewelry is misted over with a sense of 'deja vu' — where have I seen this happen before? — with Victorian jewelry, that's where.

Costume jewelry finds itself in the same position today as Victorian jewelry did in the 20's, 30's and 40's. Considered old-fashioned, out-of-tune, cumbersome, maudlin and impractical, these older pieces were thrust into boxes and cases well out of sight. Those who had foresight saved it and those who did not have given their heirs many a regretful moment. But once Victorian jewelry came back out of the closet and created a stir, it has never again lost favor. It is now considered charming and quaint, well-made and endearing. It has come full circle.

So it is with costume jewelry, particularly the rhinestones, of the 1920's, 30's and 40's. It is undergoing the same sort of renaissance, and there is genuine joy in seeking it, for here we are not dealing with gold and platinum or genuine stones which often characterized the Victorian. No, we are off on a chase for the once very inexpensive, light hearted jewelry whose purchase will not send us to the poorhouse. The lesser pieces can be collected with a clear conscience and a small budget and while the better examples will continue to cost more as knowledge is more widely disseminated, all are still within a sensible price range for what they are.

What they are, of course, are the bracelets, the necklaces, the dress clips, the brooch-pins (usually called pin nowadays), the shoe clips and buckles, the hat pins, the tiaras, the lorgnettes, even the rhinestones studded napkins. In their heyday very little escaped the rhinestone touch. The collecting field is wide open.

If you like this jewelry and intend to collect it, begin with any piece which strikes your fancy regardless of vintage, if the price is right. The necklaces or brooches, the dress clips and earrings are a true abundance of riches. It would seem as if every woman in the United States must have owned at least one of these types of rhinestone jewelry, and with slight variations from piece to piece, the more inexpensive ones are just sitting there waiting for an astute buyer to pick them up.

But for the collector the collection begins with one piece. There is much to choose from but the initial purchase should reflect what you like rather than a particular era or type. Give yourself time to choose a period, learn to recognize the look of the old rhinestones as compared with the new, familiarize yourself with the metals and decide if your budget runs to the marked or the unmarked pieces.

Do not let yourself be influenced by those who dismiss this jewelry as 'junk' and hurry past it, consider yourself fortunate to be among the growing numbers who appreciate it, think it beautiful or provocative and well worthy of collecting. In fact, consider yourself somewhat avante garde. If your predilection is for the 1920's and 1930's you are a conservator of what is left of these unparalleled ornaments. The Art Deco period already has its own cult and rhinestones alone or blended with other materials have long been the target of specific collectors or admirers of the period, it is the 1940's and 50's which are coming into their own.

In order to become an astute collector of this jewelry it is necessary to handle quantities of it. The older is heavier and often primitive in its details and basic metal. The more expensive lines are usually more carefully designed overall, are often made of sterling silver, or gold plate or wash over sterling, and adhere generally to the ideal of precious jewelry. For the most part it was more tasteful, made with an eye to elegance and a desire to fool most of the people most of the time. It is generally more restrained and did then, and does now, cost more than lesser pieces, although all rhinestone jewelry was inexpensive by today's standards.

Pieces which retailed for $2 or $3 in the 1940's can now begin at $25 and go from there, depending on their visual appeal, whether the stones are hand-set, whether the metal is sterling, or better, and whether it is marked with the manufacturer's name. Increasingly this will be a factor.

The truly dedicated collector of course, is not swayed by the obvious, if the piece appeals, other considerations become secondary. The fact that the jewelry was produced in vast quantities and was enormously popular gives any collector much scope, there is still so much around. It was so popular because it was affordable, it went well with the clothing, and it matched the mood of the female buying public. It was, and is, basically a fashion accessory as well as a definite kind of jewelry, and jewelry for personal adornment is as old as man, or woman.

When man first admired a shell, or saw the possibilities in a polished animal bone, he was thinking in terms of how it could be used or worn, what it would do for his image. Ten shells worn on a leather strap around the neck would surely proclaim his status, especially to those others who perhaps could find only five or six. This made our hero a better beachcomber, he was, in a small way, out of the ordinary. This has always been the primary function of jewelry, to adorn.

All the ancient cultures have yielded up fantastic unbelievable beauty in the jewelry taken from their burial grounds or tombs. Museums are chock full of it, travelling exhibits display it and the public is willing to wait in long lines to view it. Private collectors pay astronomical sums to buy it.

So jewelry as a wearable or collectible is not a new thing. What is new is the nature of the jewelry we collect. There are those who covet and hoard precious jewels of kings and queens, they, indeed, must worry quite a bit;

there are those who treasure uncut gems for the lure of the stone; many collect the metals, the gold and the platinum, but they are different from the collector of costume jewelry. Not only in money invested but in their very genes. Anyone on the trail of an early Eisenberg brooch of gigantic size or a fine, imaginative Hobe' necklace is bold and outgoing, no locking up jewels at night for them. It's the fire and glare for them, the almost over-powering display of the rhinestones which veritably scream 'counterfeit'. It's not diamonds, but glorious in its disguise. It is jewelry which often demands a sense of humor and if it is displayed properly so it catches the light, anyone who lives with such a collection will inhabit a fairyland of color.

There is always a plus to any collection which can be amassed for itself as well as its practicality. Costume jewelry is just such. Rhinestones are now worn proudly to all the best places, they are more than socially acceptable, but if bought only to wear the owner's attitude is different from that of the collector. The jewelry in any collection can always be worn of course, but the casual buyer and the collector buy for different reasons and look for different attributes, but everybody can wear the jewelry almost anywhere although good taste should dictate the time of day and the quantity of stones. Trying to dazzle at the local supermarket or while typing a legal brief would merely distract, well worn and artfully chosen rhinestones should enhance. No one could ever deny the early pieces were made to attract attention in the most flamboyant way. In their heyday the jewelry followed fairly traditional designs, except for the abstract Art Deco pieces, and so today they can fit into any but the most unusual life style. After all, classic is classic no matter what the genre.

Collecting rhinestone jewelry is exciting, you are racing against heavy price rises, keen competition and a scarcity of the older, marked pieces. Fortunately there is still much that has not come out of the jewel boxes. This jewelry is not so old that we need haunt dusty attics, although in truth there may be some there, probably much of it still rests in dresser drawers. Much of it was worn in the lifetime of the most dedicated of collectors, people who liked it when it was new and as with so much jewelry felt it didn't take up large amounts of space, so they kept it. Two or three generations have come behind these original owners, they have come to appreciate it too, like its style and avidly seek it. There is hardly a person over 60 who did not own some of this 'junk' so you are sure to find bits and pieces in the family home. Relatives have gobs of it, but the danger is that now realizing its value, they are thinking in terms of selling it. Dealers are now regularly advertising for it for resale and rhinestone and colored stone jewelry is now finding its way into general antiques appraisals, a sure indicator that the market is really moving.

Any collector is fortunate to find this jewelry in its original box. Often this is not the box of the manufacturer but that of the retailer and the fact that there is the box at all puts that piece several steps above the kind that was put into bags. The retailer's name and address is an important information source. It can tell you immediately the price range of the piece for only fine jewelry stores and better department stores, such as Saks Fifth Avenue, New York, carried higher priced lines. So as with all collectibles the box original to the contents is a fine thing to have, in this case it also indicates the type of jewelry and its price range. This not only lends credibility to your collection, but is intensely interesting in a social way.

If you are lucky enough to buy from the original owner try for all pertinent information, where it was bought and when, and how much did it cost. Did it come in a box, did it have a paper label? Memories can be faulty especially when it comes to price, but a surprising number of women do recall exactly when and where and why they bought a certain piece and even where they wore it. It brings back memories of big bands and proms on hotel roof gardens. It was the stuff of dreams and those who wore it may have mislaid it but they never forgot it.

And now many of them collect it.

Garage sales and house sales are still the best route. You can still find this jewelry in boxes of trinkets for 50¢ or less, while flea markets, the well-attended, larger flea markets, are no longer such a good source. Many of the regular sellers are semi-professionals who keep aware of trends and price accordingly. When an item such as rhinestone jewelry begins to evoke substantial interest, the professional flea market seller begins to scale prices upward. But then one never knows what may turn up at a flea market.

The thrift shops often have beautiful examples and they are still way underpriced. The personnel are not professional, and although they too are aware of great interest in rhinestones, the merchandise is donated so prices will still be less than in shops. A few years ago I paid $6.95 for a set of Coro 1940s moonstone and rhinestone jewelry which should have been priced at a minimum of $35. So the values are there, it just takes time.

Shops and dealers at shows whose business it is to keep abreast of what is happening in the market place already know the value of some of this jewelry and their prices reflect that. Again a recent purchase at a show for $85 brought a magnificent early Hobé piece. It was a bargain at the price, but much of this jewelry is still underpriced no matter where you find it.

Competition besets the collector on other fronts. Other collectors, museums which now often feature fashion displays which include this jewelry, theatre groups and individual actors and actresses who appreciate the glamour rhinestones project from a stage, and the specialized collector of buttons, or shoe buckles, or hatpins who can fit the rhinestone examples into their collections.

One of the great threats to the collector, especially of the colored stone jewelry is the artisan, home or professional, who prises these stones out of their settings for use in crafts. The jeweled Christmas tree creator has for many years now sought out this jewelry and used the stones to fashion the rather large two dimensional trees which are mounted and used during the holiday season. Some of these are displayed all year long because they are so attractive, but millions of lovely jewelry pieces must have been lost in this way. Stones have been used on handbags, on glass, in many ways that would not occur to a lover of jewelry as it is.

If specialization is your aim there is a very inexpensive way to begin. Dress clips of the 1930's and early 40's were possibly one of the largest categories made. Usually they came in pairs and were often of the finest quality. They come in every conceivable size and with rhinestones as well as colored stones of every shade. Shoe clips and shoe buckles can be truly beautiful and they too, come in pairs. Very often today we find one dress clip or one buckle, sparkling as ever, but minus its mate. If you are a person who likes examples of types, if you are interested primarily in the stones and settings, this is for you. Obviously, when one of a pair is missing, the price is often minimal. At least several collections of this type have already been formed and one collector is intent on showing a comprehensive overview of the designs. The entire collection of 40 pieces has cost under $125 and it is quite magnificent. So while a pair of good rhinestone shoe buckles will have a beginning price of around $25 and may go anywhere on up, this inexpensive way to collect sounds enticing. When dealing with any collectible in a rising market, it is important to use your ingenuity. So when everyone is after large Victorian hatpins, seek out the short plastic and rhinestones from the 30's and 40's. When others are wildly searching for the outstanding, impressive jewelry, look for the enchanting little animal and bird pins made in such vast numbers. But having bought any of these, take care of them, display them. Rhinestones, like diamonds were made to refract light. Frame them if the items are small, have a plant window put into your bathroom or bedroom and use it for your jewelry, hang them with hidden pins on strips of black velvet. Wear them. Enjoy the dazzle and put it all where it will catch the light.

Remember that even the least expensive pieces can be set by hand in prongs, although more likely the stones would be pasted in. Kresge's and Woolworths were the key to the widespread popularity of the cheaper lines. How many adults can now recall standing at the jewelry counter before Christmas trying to make the momentous decision about which of those glittering baubles would best please Mom. Was Mother ready for that great rhinestone butterfly? Definitely yes!

Americans have always felt at home in the 5 and 10. Woolworth's is a household word, it used to be our second home, anything anyone ever needed could be found there and lots of it really did cost nickel or a dime. Much of the jewelry which sold there by the millions of pieces is now high style and if you bought some there all those years ago and kept it, take a look at it and be amazed at the value we used to get for our money. After heavy use, this jewelry with its stones pasted in, is still intact and twinkling

Because so much of the jewelry was unmarked and most of the larger manufacturers do not have extensive records of their output, it is difficult today to make proper attributions. Some of the jewelry does have the characteristic look of the company which made it. Trifari has its own style for example, and after trial and error the collector should begin to recognize it. Trifari pieces, for the most part, are marked but the output of the factory is interesting for its quality and the fact that the recognition factor exists. To help build a valuable collection, the collector should try to add a marked piece by every company for comparison with the unmarked pieces. This may not even be possible given the fact that the largest makers churned it out in order to keep up with demand. Marks didn't seem to matter. In 1946 and 1947 many of the big companies had to turn away orders, they could not fill the ones on hand and reputedly lost hundreds of millions of dollars in orders due to the fact their production was not able to take on extra work. It is difficult to understand the passion this jewelry excited in the female breast. Not that it isn't lovely, it certainly can be, but the buying atmosphere was like a 40 year obsession. Not only women liked it, men bought it regularly for gifts and many of the sets still in original boxes testify to the way the recipients treasured it.

Still there were writers in those days who maintained that those in the trade called the whole output 'junk' regardless of quality and that only the very finest quality was referred to as 'costume gems'. Nevertheless the whole rhinestone industry was a marvel of American know-how, of very shrewd business acumen and at the same time a public ready, more than that, eager, for something to cheer them and make them sparkle. Only in those days, at that time could the rhinestone have surfaced, captivated, and succeeded to such a degree. It was a sociological phenomenon based on all the human wants and needs, and its history is as fascinating as its future.

HISTORY OF RHINESTONES

World War I left its mark on the jewelry trade. Business was bad, after all it's an item we can survive without, and the large manufacturers were still dealing in hairpins and hatpins and childrens bar pins. Lingerie pins too, all those charming little trinkets collectors now vie for. In those days 'imitation diamonds' were tacky, definitely déclassé. Déclassé then is ultra chic now. The trick is finding those early pieces.

Into the breach, into the semi-depressed jewelry industry stepped Coco Chanel, that talented and wily French Fashion Designer. Something new, an unusual touch was what her new dresses needed, a little something, she decided that would brighten up the scene. She began to show long chains with rhinestones on some of the clothes, they glittered and they emphasized the waistline. Soon American buyers for the larger stores were startled to see artificial fruits, crystals, other inexpensive stones, even wood whimsies attached to her garments. It certainly was an idea whose time had come although there seems some doubt as to the exact date, either 1925 or 1927. Soon all Paris was aping that idea of Chanel's jewelry for her 'costumes'.

Costume jewelry had been born and it was a healthy baby indeed. Eventually these beads and baubles decorated hats and dresses and shoes and gloves in all price ranges. Chanel had a winner, she stimulated a whole new industry to keep pace with the fashion and it was American industry which benefited the most.

Soon the manufacturers could discard much of the trinket line or at least overlay it with much more productive jewelry. In the early 20's these pins and barrettes and combs and fancy hairpins were a lucrative line but even before Chanel could change her world, fashion itself took a hand.

'Bobbed Hair' said Fashion. Soon the glamour girls of Hollywood were sporting the short, sleek hairdos. Now where to put the combs and pins? The trinket business floundered and almost expired.

The bobbed hairstyle demanded long, dangling earrings which swayed with the body to give it a sensual look, the dropped waistline required long beads or chains, and the cocktail party literally cried out for the glittering, glaring, overdone cocktail ring. The jewelry was an integral part of fashion and because of fashion the jewelry industry changed direction and revived. Then enter Mlle. Chanel and her jewelry for costumes and the industry never looked back.

Amazingly the costume jewelry industry was not crushed by the depression of the 30's. It is a fact of life that craving for beauty in some form will survive all odds and nowhere could this have been more true than the United States in the thirties. Women have always coveted jewelry, so when they found that major clothing purchases, or perhaps, any new clothing at all, could not be made, they found a way to refurbish the existing wardrobe. So where a new dress might be out of the question due to the economy, a cheap rhinestone clip or brooch was not. It was attractive and well-made, it scintillated, it looked smart, it was a cheerer-upper. Where else for 47¢ on the main floor of a major department store could you buy hope and humor and beauty and an inch or two of happiness?

Rhinestone jewelry was considered expendable. It was mass-produced inexpensively, sold for very little and fashion decreed and its makers expected that it would be worn for only a short period of time then discarded. Its fashion life was deliberately intended to be brief. There had been nothing quite like it ever before. It was strictly an outgrowth of its time and the circumstances which made life so difficult in the 30's are responsible for the incredible success of the rhinestone.

This jewelry craze was somewhat of a surprise even to the manufacturers. During the Victorian years there had been inexpensive jewelry, rolled gold or gold-filled and intricately worked sterling silver, and even the wealthier classes wore this type on occasion. But in a general way the attitude in those days was that there was little sense in buying jewelry that would survive only a season or two. And in the years before the depression women tended to think in terms of precious gems, jewelry that was expensive when bought and would last a lifetime, indeed become an heirloom. An investment as well as a decoration. The whole concept of rhinestone jewelry was new and revolutionary. Throw away baubles, easy come, easy go.

Never until the rhinestone period was the feeling about jewelry such an insouciant one, a here today and gone tomorrow philosophy. Jewelry had always been considered portable wealth to be worn and cherished, but there was certainly no intrinsic value in the jewelry of the 20s, 30s, and 40s. Its owners did not even think of it in those terms. They would tire of one piece, put it aside and buy another. The public was so enamoured of this 'junk' the biggest makers did not actually do any significant amount of advertising. Retailers often included it in their full page ads obviously happy to proclaim the lure of their marvelous imitations. Rhinestone jewelry, was and is again, a happening.

Although there was no reason to treasure these fripperies, fortunately for us, although the general attitude was one of 'it's not important', most women did not discard them. For whatever reason much of it was preserved. Drawers are still full of it, pure razzle dazzle; and in the 1930's it was so pervasive it could have been bought at the most elegant of 5th Avenue jewelers as well as at the corner drugstore.

The whole business erupted into one of the great success stories of all time. The pieces from those very early days are rare and expensive. People who remember those bad 'good old days' recall prices of up to $200 in some of the better shops. To justify these prices in those days the jewelry must have been superior. It was.

The jewelers who were accustomed to work with precious metals and the finest stones were laid low by the economy during those early depression years. They had no alternative if they were to survive but to accomodate to this new jewelry form, the cheap brass and base metal of the big manufacturers. They did not surrender, they compromised. If we can work with better pieces which will sell for higher prices at better outlets, we will do it. And they did. It may have bruised the ego at first to be associated with this 'junk' but production figures and profits must have been very comforting.

To the fine jewelers' demand for quality we owe some of the greatest vintage pieces. But this in no way demeans the cheaper examples turned out by the millions. They are really charming and almost always interesting and some are of remarkable quality. The differences in the nature of 'junk' and 'junque' can often be pronounced but all of the early production is intriguing. Sometimes it has a primitive look as if someone made it in a hurry with cheap materials. Precisely right. But today, the descendants of those jewelry pioneers are carrying on the rhinestone tradition but the high prices reflect the times, they are immensely proud of what their fathers and grandfathers accomplished.

As the fine jewelers rebelled at first, so did the fine jewelry shops. They carried it with misgivings, after all it was mass-produced, inexpensive by their standards, and bought, for the most part, by people who could not afford to think in terms of carats. It offended the dignity of many of the jewelry houses in the affluent city locations. But a distressed economy is a great leveler and the trade had a severe need for items to take up the slack since the time was not right for selling luxuries. Since the jewelers wanted better quality the jewelry stores benefitted and that is why so much of the jewelry is so truly grand, the jewelers were reluctant to carry it at all and when they did they demanded better quality.

Quality though is not always the aim of the collector although having some outstanding examples is always desirable. It is the jewelry itself which should spark interest and excitement. It is really a collectible which should stand on its own merits as an individual thing responding to individual taste. In the 1930's there was a most distinctive look to the rhinestone.

Much of it was made specifically to complement the styles of the clothing. Hats were worn everywhere, small hats often featuring one of the rhinestone jeweled clips or small pin, usually worn to the side. These clips are easy to find because hats were the style and for each hat it seems, there must have been a pin or a clip. The dresses with the classic V neck called for a large clip at the deep end of the V. The square neckline which was fashionable demanded a clip at each corner. The clips in the shapes of inverted triangles and often with rhinestones or colored stones are typical of the 30's. The sizes vary considerably as do the colors of the stones, they are still wearable and eminently collectible. The whole look of the 30's was rather streamlined and simplified and could carry this jewelry very well. While the strands of long beads from the 20's are legendary, the 'chunky' look in necklaces began to surface in the 30's and many of the rhinestone pieces adapted beautifully to the Art Deco influence. Again, the period of Art Deco reflects the aura of hope, a reaching upward that was rife in the 30's in spite of the hardships the economy fostered. Art Deco is an easily recognizable style, strong, geometric with all its angles, related to cubism and at its most effective when it is kept simple. In the thirties it was referred to as 'Art Moderne' and now it is the province of expensive dealers in this specialty or private collectors who admire the design and period and are willing to pay dearly for it. Much of the Deco was done in magnificent gems and costly settings, but some rhinestone jewelry can be found in Deco and it's so sought after that if you find a piece do not even turn your back to think about it, it will be gone. Still Art Deco is a small part of the jewelry of the period and does not attract all collectors.

The 30's were an innovative period. It saw the development of the flexible bracelet which became a large segment of the jewelry trade. Flexible bracelets were easy to wear. In themselves they were a new thing and their popularity was surely magnified by the colored stones or rhinestones which gave them flash and glitter. This bracelet moved easily with the wrist and had a large impact in the marketplace.

Gold was expensive in the 30's but this was of little consequence to those who dealt in rhinestones. Gilt continued to be the primary covering for the base metal. This gave the effect of gold and wore very well because a good alloy was usually used. A thin layer of gilt was applied over the base metal to give the piece a shining brilliance. Gilding has survived and prospered but some of the early pieces show signs of wear. As in anything older that was useful signs of wear are bound to occur. While this can lend credibility it makes for less than a perfect piece; not for wearing perhaps but as a sample for a collection, why not?

Pewter, in this case a leaded alloy, was sometimes used in backing the early 30's jewelry. This heavy lead type material is what makes the early jewelry so heavy, handle a few pieces and feel the weight. Often with this kind of metal setting the edges seem blurred and not so sharp. Rhinestone pieces set this way are usually higher priced as a testimony to their age rather than their craftsmanship.

The individual jewelry craftsman was somewhat passe in the 30's. Only the wealthy could afford him and the masses really didn't want him. They were happy with their fakes.

The whole emphasis was on color and price. "One Dollar costume jewelry sale," reads one 1930's advertisement, "the new bubble effects, metals, rhinestones, clips, bracelets, necklaces, pins, all with stones." Another proclaimed, "necklaces, clips, big brooches, bracelets, earrings, $1 value, 69¢ on the main floor." The bigger the better.

These early ads indicate that the jewelry, in spite of low prices, was considered important enough in terms of sales to be positioned in a prominent place on the main selling floor. People who bought it in its heyday tell me that regardless of the economy, or perhaps because of it, the jewelry counters were always crowded. Today it gives the same pleasure at 30 to 40 times the original price.

Some of the higher priced lines utilized coral or turquoise in the very early days, and these were set in sterling silver. Examples of these types are rare and will cost as much as $500, but those are for the definitive collector. There is too much less expensive ware around if your purse is thin, to dwell on the unattainable, gaze your fill, drool, then buy that Coro rhinestone pin for $20.

In the 1930's people were looking for inexpensive diversion, anything amusing that could rouse them from the doldrums, something different. Life was dark and rhinestones were bright. And then came 1939.

In the early 1940's most of the jewelry factories had already converted to war work. The smaller manufacturers of rings, pins and brooches continued making jewelry, but part of their work force, the metal tool makers for instance, were switched to war production. The government began to restrict certain metals such as tin and copper and also rhodium which had been used to prevent tarnish in silver products and which was also used as a plating by some of the better manufacturers. Some silver allotments were cut, but by and large the jewelry industry continued to produce its usual lines.

In 1941 magazines were featuring layouts with models wearing rhinestones, "clips, bracelet and earrings with simulated gems to form a matching set", and "a sparkling jewelry ensemble with imitation rubies". Throughout this period the factories kept churning out jewelry and people kept buying, but postwar enthusiasm sent production to a new high, the craze for rhinestones was reignited and almost every woman's fantasy was to glitter and glow as much as possible. It was a post war high.

In the mid-forties female morale could be gauged by the number of rhinestones a woman owned. By this time too, enough years had passed so that costume jewelry was firmly entrenched as a fact of American life.

Mark-up was high in this industry, at retail about 40 to 50% over wholesale and the bulk of sales was seasonal.

It was the custom in the business for factories to create enough merchandise so that spring samples could be shown early in the year, January and February, and the sale of these lines depended on salesmen successfully showing these samples to the various wholesalers and retailers. While this push was going on, production was low, the business rested for the most part on the orders coming in. Many of the large outlets though, such as the department stores, did keep a supply of costume jewelry always on hand. The peaks and valleys in sales were simply the way the business operated, after the spring rush, things would taper off, then in summer Christmas orders would build up and by the end of August production would reach a high.

In 1952 a new concept in selling this jewelry to the wholesalers surfaced. The manufacturers commandeered two floors of the Sheraton-Biltmore Hotel and showed all their wares at one time to all the visitors. So many large orders were taken at this show the factories could work at much fuller production for longer periods. It also convinced one writer at the time "that anybody can sell anything right now to a jewelry buying public." Such was the state of the rhinestone business in the early 1950's.

As in 1947 when Dior staggered the fashion scene with his 'New Look' which required a whole new jewelry aspect, it was once again proved that all jewelry is rooted in the best fashion traditions, but after World War II elation led women to buy almost any rhinestone piece, quality or not. As more exposure to these baubles led to more sophistication, the buying public became more selective and factories making bottom-of-the-line, cheap jewelry began to fail. This is one of the reasons the poorly made, heavy wares are difficult to find. Many were badly designed and to today's eye look decidedly old fashioned, bulky and often with dull looking stones. Nevertheless these can be whimsical and endearing in a primitive way and are certainly of much importance to the collector since they represent a phase of this jewelry which passed and was never revived in the same way with the exact materials.

Although rhinestone jewelry continued to sell well it began to move out of the compulsive stage, women were turning to the plastics and other pop types, and though it never really died you might say the rhinestone continued in poor health.

7

Through it all, the long beads and the rhinestones, through expensive and cheap, through good times and bad, the pearl, the ubiquitous pearl wended its way. Given to some restraint in our use of jewelry in the 1980's it's difficult for us to imagine how the world was dominated by rhinestones and pearls. Where the pearls were, there were usually rhinestones.

The rhinestone collector can combine the two very different materials with great success. In fact some of the most extravagant designs and beautiful stones went into the clasps on the pearl necklaces and bracelets. A new phase of rhinestone collecting is a result of the earlier passion for fake pearls. So many were sold so cheaply that once broken they were not repaired, but again for mysterious reasons, were kept. Even when the pearls were discarded often the clasp was saved. These survivors make a really beautiful collection if carefully chosen. They are still inexpensive, not even sold in more expensive shops, there is no great demand for them and they represent every possible style and size and shape of rhinestone. In the mid 1930's these clasps were actually featured above the quality of the pearls themselves — such descriptions as "dainty, attractive, crystal color clasp, baguette, crystal clasp," a pearl necklace with a pendant of "dazzling imitation diamonds about 2" long", another with a "real stone clasp", and yet another with "genuine imitation diamonds". So clasps have had their moment in the sun. And now they represent a tremendous opportunity to the rhinestone collector.

The pearl chokers are abundant, the style lasted a long time in every material, and the pearl and rhinestone combination was a happy one. Trying to gather a collection of rhinestone chokers or rhinestones with pearls in choker style would be an amusing challenge and a profitable one. Any specialized collection is always of great interest.

There were many familiar names in pearls during the 40's and 50's Richelieu, LaTausca, Marvella among them. There were others. They all add lustre, you might say to the costume jewelry craze.

THE MANUFACTURERS

In the 1940's there were 929 costume jewelry manufacturers concentrated in New York and Providence, Rhode Island. New York had long been a center of the jewelry trade but Providence and neighboring Attleboro, Massachusetts fell into the great costume jewelry bonanza by virtue of their backgrounds. Since the early days of America, the days of metal shoe buckles and hat buckles, big and square and impressive, these cities had been involved in the manufacture of silver items as well as unimportant gee-gaws for personal wear. It was natural that after a meager start, a few cheap trinkets in the jewelry manner which were surprisingly successful, Providence with its historic affinity for metal work, should ultimately prove to be the major producer of non-precious jewelry. At one time, figures as high as 85 to 90% of the total jewelry output were quoted as being Providence's contribution to all production.

There are now no accurate figures to indicate the strength of this industry at its peak but guesses fluctuate around the $250,000,000 range in annual gross, retail. We, today, would have to restructure our whole thinking about jewelry buying and wearing to appreciate what those figures mean to individual purchases. The whole concept was to sell a piece of jewelry at a minimal price geared to the average woman. Something which could be admired for its visual appeal and good workmanship and could fit into a low budget. The watchword was "Made well and sold cheap".

The whole business was guided by astute businessmen who were willing to take a chance. They saw the need to produce an appealing object at low cost with no long term validity. Probably never in history had there been such a reading of the public mind as these entrepreneurs practiced. They were wizards.

Many of them became millionaires and left behind successful enterprises which their heirs still guide. Others did not upgrade with the increased sophistication of their customers and the poorly made jewelry they sold became a drug on the market. Some of these factories began to close. By the time rhinestones had settled into their comfortable fashion niche and the intensity of the original love affair with sparkle faded, the companies which survived had updated, produced what the contemporary market called for and continued to give the public what it craved.

"Give the lady what she wants," recommended a famous merchant. It was foolproof advice. Nobody, anywhere, at any time did that better than the jewelry manufacturers of the first half of the 20th century. In their way they were manipulators of public taste as well as servants of it they were clever; they understood merchandising; they learned to anticipate trends; they were willing to work, they deserved their success. They were in the grand American tradition.

They were first and foremost, at least in size and production figures, CORO. The name is a contraction of an earlier trade name COHN & ROSENBERGER and the company has been around a very long time, since 1902. Coro was considered within the industry itself as the leader in sales and profits. This happy circumstance could be directly traced to the fact that when the passion for jewelry flowered, Coro was ready, it had the room to make enough of it to assure profits. During the Depression Coro built itself a huge plant in Providence which some scorned as a waste of money, but after WWII it found itself in the unique position of being 'the mostest with the bestest'. Given the size of its physical plant, its equipment, experience and shrewd business heads, Coro surged ahead of competition.

The factory produced thousands of different designs each month and based on the number of design patents submitted on behalf of the company in any twelve month period this does not seem unreasonable. The work ethic was never more pronounced than in the number of potential jewelry pieces based on these hundreds of designs created month after month, year after year.

Because of this really enormous output CORO jewelry is relatively easy to find today. Its quality varies, the company made something for everybody regardless of purse or taste. In the 1940's, its highest price line was COROCRAFT, but it also made jewelry so inexpensive it sold through 5 and 10 cents stores. Certainly all, or most of it, was marked with the company trademark, which varied with quality and type.

CORO's success is also the success of Royal Marcher, dynamic sales manager who masterminded the progress of Coro in those years, reputedly a whirlwind of energy who made instant decisions which almost always worked well for the company. Marcher was Horatio Alger in modern dress, he began as an office boy at 13, became a salesman and at 22 was on his way with COHN & ROSENBERGER. If ever an industry had a fairy godfather it was Marcher with his RUSSIAN ANTIQUE jewelry inspired by a swinging chandelier which had a gold finish and gleamed as it caught the light. This line with its colored stones sold phenomenally and the giant costume jewelry business was born. Regardless of inspiration these colored stones did indeed take the world by storm and kept 2,000 or more employees busy.

For collectors, CORO is a fairly easy way to start. The early jewelry can be inexpensive and the various company marks lend interest. The products of this company sold originally for prices ranging from under $1 to $100, and made much that is intriguing and some that is beautiful. CORO has twice in its history made stock offerings to the public. Wouldn't it be wonderful to own a few shares that could be displayed with the collection?

While the bulk of the colored stone and rhinestone jewelry was crafted for women, men were not entirely forgotten. Cuff links, shirt tacs, tie pins, rings, tie clasps were all set with rhinestones or colored stones and were quite popular. The biggest name in men's costume jewelry was SWANK, almost a household word in the 1940's and 50's. Time was when the bridegroom's gift to the best man and ushers at any wedding was a nicely boxed set of SWANK jewelry. Large numbers of these sets are still intact and in the original boxes. Collectors should not overlook this segment of the rhinestone era. SWANK had a characteristic look, it was fairly simple in design and nicely executed.

The colored stone jewelry of SWANK CO., has a long tradition. The company was founded in 1897 in Attleboro, Massachusetts as a small operation with a few machines to manufacture ladies jewelry. When the biggest fire in Attleboro's history destroyed the original plant, the employees not only helped fight the fire but rescued the machinery and started immediately to finish the projects they had begun. They must have known then that some day we would want to collect it.

The very next day the company was back in business and from that day on, no one ever looked back. Expansion was so rapid that in 1908 an associate organization was formed to manufacture men's jewelry and the company now claims to be "the world's leader" in this field.

It was good old Yankee ingenuity, a small design improvement, which proved so significant to the company. By 1918 the company's KUM-A-PART cuff button made such an impact it sparked the success which followed. Although, not embedded with stones, almost every American male has been influenced by SWANK for they were the makers of dog tags, those all important metal tags worn by every G.I.

Success with the male line was so great, the company discontinued its original line of ladies jewelry. Although this firm first organized in 1897, the name SWANK did not appear until 1927 with ads for a new collar holder. Another war, another change of pace, war work, Bronze Stars, and Purple Hearts, Korean war work. Today the company again manufactures ladies' as well as men's jewelry, it is 80 years old and the history of SWANK reads like the recent history of America. Of course you should include it in your collection.

Some older pieces of rhinestone and colored stone jewelry bear the name RICHTER'S. This was the product of RICHTER'S JEWELERS, INC. Located now at 680 Fifth Avenue, New York, not such a far cry from their original place in a small brownstone on that same famous street. Then newest RICHTER'S catalogue shows only precious jewelry — diamonds and rubies set in 14K gold. It is absolutely gorgeous, prices reflect the quality, it is extravagant but unfortunately it is the real thing. The company did produce costume jewelry however, and it seems to bear the company mark in most cases. The style of its manufacture would indicate an early period and since quite a number of pieces still survive and are already in collections we can assume it was made in quantity. Although no mention is made of costume jewelry in this current literature, Charles Richter assures me that "costume jewelry was very much a part of their early production". Rhinestones and colored stones appear in all the pieces I have seen marked with this name and a 1949 advertisement displays a "designer's showpiece copy of a fabulous diamond wrist-watch the entire bracelet band hand-set with flashing rhinestones, matching the brilliance of hand-set diamonds". With this truly magnificent rhinestone bracelet the watch was included, as was the tax. Total price $27.50 with a money back guarantee.

In pursuing any catalogue of fine jewelry such as that issued by Richter's be aware of close adaptations rhinestone designers made to the more expensive models. This is nowhere more evident than in the workmanship of KREMENTZ.

There may have been more expensive jewelry made but any collector should be willing to pay more to acquire the beautiful objects crafted by KREMENTZ & CO. Even to the untutored eye the designs and sheer quality of the pieces are apparent. Krementz has had long practice.

Its history began in 1866 when five men formed a company to manufacture jewelry, but it was in 1922 that George Krementz and Julius Lebkeucher joined their families into Krementz & Co., and used the humble collar botton as the ladder to great prosperity. By 1900, says the company most of the collar buttons produced in the world came from their New Jersey plant. When the partnership was divided in 1936, KREMENTZ & CO. continued with their specialty, the clad-metal line and some 10K and 14K gold manufacturing.

The English Sheffield silver process is probably the best way to define Krementz' overlay which is basically a clad-metal process. Sandwiching you might call it, a base metal coated with thin strips of precious metal and bonded together under intense heat and pressure. In the case of KREMENTZ the bar which results is "then rolled down to mirror-like strips from which the jewelry is made". Their overlay is 14K gold.

Krementz calls this jewelry 'unique' and since the materials and the process itself is expensive this is probably true. KREMENTZ is also famous for its 'rose'. The company says that over the decades the rose has remained a steady and reliable seller. It has also 'maintained its original design concept since before the turn of the century' which proves once more that a thing of beauty really is a joy forever.

Unlike SWANK which began with ladies' jewelry and switched to that for men, KREMENTZ started with jewelry for men and not until the 1930's when the collar button went the way of the dodo bird did it develop a major line for women. Richard Krementz Jr. says that by 1950 this was 50% of their business.

The KREMENTZ CO. has always been a leader in the use of machines and early developed techniques for welding which replaced the old hand-soldering methods. This made it possible to manufacture a very high quality bangle bracelet without annealing the frames. This was a major advance since it eliminated the need for heating and slow cooling which toughened and reduced the brittleness of the metal. The overlay line continued to expand and in 1950 KREMENTZ purchased a company which made colored stone jewelry and this became an important adjunct to KREMENTZ production.

All collectors of this period jewelry should include as many KREMENTZ pieces as they can afford. It is chic and elegant, beautifully made with the finest materials and is really in a class by itself. It is one of the types which has a characteristic look and can often be recognized on sight without checking for the signature. This is indeed fortunate since the original boxes carry the company name, and the little standing paper trademark, but the jewelry itself is often not marked in any way.

TRIFARI as most collectors and dealers call it is really TRIFARI, KRUSSMAN & FISHEL and while it could not compete in numbers with the largest CORO, it left most of the others standing while it raced off with all the high style accolades. Its design work was so superb that others in the trade referred to it as the 'Trifari look'. It was a refined approach, subtle and quite beautiful especially in some of the earlier pieces, in the 1950's some of the output did resemble much of whatever else was coming out of Providence.

TRIFARI used for its trademark a crown with the word TRIFARI, as all good collectors should know. Of all the spectacular rhinestone jewelry made, TRIFARI probably best approaches the real thing. It too has a definite characteristic look that you can easily train yourself to watch for wherever it is, well lighted display case or neglected box of old, broken jewelry. Here is one manufacturer which used only the finest designs and materials, and this is so evident that recently I purchased a lovely rhinestone spray pin for $5 made by Trifari. The shopkeeper had no knowledge and no feeling for this pin but she did recognize quality when she saw it so it was saved from the broken jewelry bin. And after all what is it worth? It is truly beautiful, set with tiny stones and bearing the company mark. It has a look of high elegance and almost defies detection as a fake and workmanship such as this goes beyond price.

Trifari made jewelry in the classically traditional designs in the early years and between 1941 and 1946 most of the stones were set in sterling silver. Leo Krussman of Trifari once said "you wouldn't take a bargain basement copy for an original Molyneux" in talking about using the best material and craftsmanship. The company always felt that 'class will tell' and that is why today TRIFARI is considered every collectors goal, even though prices are high.

Today TRIFARI is owned by Hallmark Cards, Inc., but still producing magnificent 'gems' after 50 years.

While TRIFARI was never the largest it produced in quantity and probably most of it still exists. Indeed some people have worn it consistently since it was first made, it is that worthwhile and I know of two cases where it has appeared in wills. A genuine heirloom, that's TRIFARI.

When we collectors talk of old EISENBERG or HOBE we lower our voices and use hushed tones. It is that awe-inspiring.

Even in the old days of the depression, EISENBERG did everything in a big way. The older jewelry is monumental not only in design but in size. It is large without being clumsy and always impressive. The stones are, and have always been, of the finest quality Austrian crystal. EISENBERG ICE is one of the most coveted names to any collector although it is not the first mark the company used.

The EISENBERG company too has a long history which began in 1914. Karl Eisenberg says today "the original Eisenberg pieces were set in sterling, but during World War II white metal was used due to scarcity of sterling and since then rhodium plating. The rhodium is impervious to most elements and maintains a wonderful finish". Rhodium is a corrosion resisting element which gives a bright silvery finish to jewelry. It is tarnish resistant so all the Eisenberg pieces are found in excellent almost new condition.

Karl Eisenberg tells the story of the evolution of the family rhinestone business. "Eisenberg Ice evolved when a major department store suggested to my grandfather that he maintain a store facility to satisfy the demand for the rhinestone pins which were being stolen off the EISENBERG ORIGINAL dresses." The theft of these glittering decorations became so commonplace, Eisenberg took the advice, and the perfect name, EISENBERG ICE, was conjured up by Mr. Karl Eisenberg's father.

The firm has always used top grade Austrian stones from the firm of SWAROVSKI in the Tyrol region of Austria. Swarovski has been producing jewelry stones since 1889 and the company says the flawless clarity of their 32% full lead crystal combined with the remarkable precision of the facets enable each piece to refract sunlight perfectly. Swarovski describes its wares as "Strass Austrian crystal" and while Mr. Eisenberg says "the stones we use are magnificently cut and have foil backs to give them greater light refraction" some of the earlier jewelry with the same Austrian crystal did not have any backing of any kind. But the stones are definitely a major factor in the grace and symmetry, the general aspect of elegance and splendor in all Eisenberg.

This quality, which has never been compromised, is the reason the EISENBERG ICE name is so respected and why any definitive collection must include their work. To be able to wear an early Eisenberg jewel is tantamount to proclaiming your excellent taste and affluence. They do not come cheap and they are not diamonds, but close enough.

Glancing at Eisenberg catalogues of the early 70's makes one long to turn back the clock. Some truly outstanding jewelry was listed as costing $25 or less. In 1976 a gorgeous rhinestone rope necklace in floral design was selling for $50 and emerald cut studs, "pierced, or clip for $3.50." In 1990 a shop near famed Yosemite Valley was offering an Eisenberg for $1,000, and now, in 1993, this is not even considered high for a good old original.

Eisenberg continues to amaze. The rise in prices of the annual Christmas tree pins is an example of a very old company keeping current. A good lesson for successful collectors. I receive countless inquiries about these little holiday delights - the Eisenberg company tells me that for a long time they were unmarked but since the publication of the first edition of this book all Christmas trees have been marked with the Eisenberg name. I have found Nordstroms in Seattle and Houston an excellent mail order source. The people are efficient and pleasant. The Christmas tree pins are issued in various sizes and come in a range of prices. There is something for everyone. It is important to order early. Start thinking Christmas tree pins at the first sniff of evergreen. Be sure to add annually.

In its later advertising the firm used such descriptives as "terrific twinklers, divine dazzlers, and personally precious". Ads talk of "unmitigated luxury and instant charisma". Eisenberg is all of these, still after all of this is said it's not like holding an older Eisenberg in your hand, 'the fairest of the fair'.

Another company produced exquisite jewelry with an unusual touch. Hobé.

A friend tells the story of her original quest for early rhinestone jewelry. One shop had many pieces, one a beautiful wide bracelet. When the dealer was asked about it, she replied in an awestruck voice, "Oh, that's an Hobe."

And that is the way the collecting world reacts to the superior product that was the end result of the imaginative designs of William Hobé. Past advertising by the company points out "that finely crafted rhinestone jewelry was made from specially tempered glass with particular qualities of refraction and brilliance." It is not only the stones however beautiful they may be that makes Hobe what it is. Essentially it is the design work. Collectors who yearn for a valuable collection of rhinestone and colored jewelry should certainly try for the best — among them Hobe.

The principal factory of the firm is in Mount Vernon, New York, with showrooms in six major cities including Los Angeles.

'And it is to Los Angeles that the company owes some of its well deserved fame. Anyone interested in the times and chronicles of rhinestone jewelry must surely remember the dozens of actresses who lent their faces and forms to promote various products or to the fashion layouts of the 1940's, all of them wearing a full complement of rhinestones.

Some of these celebrities were so impressed they commissioned individual pieces made to their special order from William Hobé. Celebrity patronage is always a booster and Hobé became a well known name among those who sought the unique in rhinestone jewelry.

Strangely enough, the few writings available dealing with the rhinestone era do not list Hobe among the many producers, possibly because of the individuality he brought to the field. The production must have been less, since there seem to be fewer older pieces about, but what there is is marvelous.

The company still claims "handskilled craftsmanship, art and originality in design at affordable prices have remained a Hobé family standard", and uses the designation "JEWELS BY HOBÉ" with the Aladdin Cave touch "JEWELS OF LEGENDARY SPLENDOR". Many of the older Hobé examples are truly lovely beyond description and the family carries on the tradition so that in 2050 A.D. collectors will have something to look for.

In the mid 1940's the rhinestone craze was at its zenith. Companies of every size were producing vast amounts of this jewelry and could still not fill orders fast enough. Interest was world-wide, such unlikely places as India and South America clamored for it. Some of the noteworthy firms whose older jewelry is often found with trademarks and can still be found in good condition cover a wide range of price and quality.

CASTLECLIFF of New York was considered a style leader and its prices hovered around $5 for a bangle bracelet. At the rate of inflation in this country what a bargain such a bracelet would be today at $20 or $25 in some shops. Castlecliff was sold through such outlets as Bloomingdale's in New York, and Joseph Magnin's in San Francisco. Castlecliff's WILLIAM MARKLE is considered to have been a "top notch designer."

MAZER is a mark frequently encountered in this search for older jewelry. MAZER BROS. NEW YORK made quantities of jewelry which sold for somewhat lower prices.

De Rosa of New York was also a big producer, but so far is a more difficult mark to find. Other names during this period which should be sought out by collectors are ACCESSOCRAFT whose jewelry sold for $1, $2 and $3 in the 40's; priced a bit above much of CORO which was being advertised for $1 a piece; SANDOR, JERRY DeNICOLA, VENDOME in the slightly higher bracket; KRAMER whose jewelry is almost always marked and of excellent quality; HOUSE OF SCHRAGER which made some spectacular pieces; BENEDIKT which sold through fine stores; R.M. Jordan, a New York firm, was also a prolific manufacturer of jewelry which sold well. Their prices were in the middle range.

THE BRIER MANUFACTURING CO., of Providence, Rhode Island, manufactured and sold jewelry under the trade name LITTLE NEMO. Unfortunately their pieces often bore paper labels or were carded rather than marks appearing on the jewelry itself so often it is difficult to identify accurately. Much of it is lower line and it does not have the distinctive look of an Eisenberg or Trifari.

SILVERMAN BROS. of RHODE ISLAND was owned by Archibald Silverman who emigrated from Russia as a boy and started work in the jewelry business. The story goes that he eventually invested less than $10 in his first venture which was such a success it led to his fortune.

Both Brier and Silverman produced cheaper jewelry which caught the public's fancy because it was timely. A piece to commemorate some event, it would sell well, and the companies moved on to something else.

HATTIE CARNEGIE was firmly entrenched at Saks Fifth Avenue and Filene's in Boston and was considered very high fashion jewelry. Although today much of Hattie Carnegie does not seem to tower over some of its competitors either design-wise or in its materials, in those days it was more expensive and considered more select than much of the jewelry available. As Vintage Clothing dealers say of designer labeled clothing, "snob appeal".

EMMONS was the forerunner of Sarah Coventry. The jewelry was sold only at home jewelry parties through representatives. It is good quality if somewhat unimaginative. One owner says her Emmons crown pin survived being run over by her car, which certainly testifies to the excellence of its manufacture. In the later 1950s the jewelry began carrying the Sarah Coventry name even though the home parties were being booked under the name of EMMONS. The mark is not easily found.

SARAH COVENTRY, not yet widely collected in the context of the rhinestone period, is abundant and much of it is tailored in style. Their advertising budget was large and the jewelry, for its time, was considered fairly expensive. William J. Slattery of Sarah Coventry, Inc. says that "in the fall of 1984 the Home Party Plan operation of Sarah Coventry was discontinued and all the facilities, inventory and equipment has been sold. A licensed manufacturer in Canada is producing and distributing the jewelry in the U.S." Thus the early Sarah Coventry becomes immediately collectible.

HASKELL JEWELS, LTD. is still functioning, still making "high fashion costume jewelry" and still located in New York. The early Haskells are among the most sought after of the period jewelry.

MONET has long been active in the costume jewelry field but in the 1940s in New York it produced tailored jewelry with no stones. Their later production including rhinestones is beautifully crafted and has great potential. Many of the Monet pieces have great elegance and the company advertises them as "hand crafted."

MARCEL BOUCHER, operating in NY in the 1940s, was considered on a par with the great manufacturers, Trifari, Coro, Mazer, Castlecliff and DeRosa. In retrospect though, Boucher has the elegance and restrained touch more in keeping with the memorable classic jewelry than with much of the 1940s mundane output. Boucher is becoming a prize for collectors.

One of the great names of rhinestone jewelry is BOUCHER. Beauty, excellence of design and materials and classical good taste are all factors in the rise of this jewelry. It is not such an easy mark to find that we can be complacent but persistence will eventually bring a few Boucher pieces into your collection. Before beginning his own business in the 1930s Boucher worked for Joseph Mazer. The daughter of a plater who worked for Boucher has many carded Mazer pieces which her Father acquired from Boucher himself. Boucher jewelry is different from Mazer in both feeling and execution although much Mazer is also lovely. Boucher imported his stones from Austria and early on used two different marks - Boucher and M.B. The latter mark employees remember as being used on a less expensive line. Also there is jewelry made by Boucher but not bearing his name since at one point he worked for a store on Madison Ave. in New York and the jewelry he designed was sold under their name, not his.

Although his was the creative mind at Marcel Boucher (he was the Chief Designer) the well respected Raymonde Semersohn also did some design work for the company. Boucher was not only an artist, he also understood all the technical aspects of manufacturing jewelry. Apparently when Boucher died, his wife took over for a time before the firm closed.

RICHELIEU considers itself a company with "A Pearl Point of View" a wonderful summation of 100 years of producing America's favorite every day jewel.

The company was founded in 1885 and was acquired in 1979 by Victoria Creations. Victoria was formed in 1962 by Robert Andreoli, and today the company has five divisions, of which ENCORE, BIJOUX, GIVENCHY and KARL LAGERFELD are part.

The company says "Our jewelry styles today are comparable to the 1950s styling with strict quality control over product".

Since the beauty of Richelieu pearls coupled with rhinestones is often breathtaking it can probably be traced to the care the company takes with the jewelry..."Our pearls assume the appearance of natural pearls. Alabaster glass pearls are handmade of high quality lampen beads. These beads are covered with sealer and then coated with a pearl essence. After the 'pearl' is coated a dulling process is applied in order to achieve the look of a cultured pearl. A sealer coat is the last application to ensure lasting quality." No wonder my prom 'pearls' with the rhinestone spacers and gorgeous rhinestone clasp still look marvelous.

While Richelieu has never 'adapted' the old pieces it says many of the styles have been reorderable for over 100 years. No wonder Mamie Eisenhower's pearls never seemed to wear out.

LISNER is now under the umbrella of VICTORIA CREATIONS. Another old American company, founded around the early 1900s, it was acquired by Victoria in 1979. Lisner still uses the LISNER mark and is considered by the parent company to be "the second oldest company in the jewelry business." Certainly the company has made quantities of jewelry, the mark is not difficult to find. For some reason collectors do not go into ecstasy over Lisner jewelry although many of the early pieces are striking and lovely. There is much too that is interesting, and given so much manufactured over so long a time there is some that is inferior. Collectors should buy all early LISNER even the lesser pieces. Remember the golden age of rhinestone jewelry, with its attendant well-known makers marks is receding further into history every day. Lisner's older pieces carry the designation of a fine old American company and some of the 1940s, 30s and earlier pieces are well worth the low prices.

NAPIER company located in New York uses as its current slogan NAPIER IS JEWELRY. Since so many companies today are conglomerates making diverse products the fact that Napier, an old manufacturing jewelry company makes only jewelry indicates a commitment to excellence. A cursory examination of current production indicates the truth of the company's claim. Napier is a signature collectors respect and prices on older pieces are fairly high.

CINER can be considered venerable, having been founded in 1892 as a manufacturer of precious jewelry. The company calls itself "a quiet giant" and is still family owned and operated, a rarity indeed in today's corporate-dominated jewelry world. Pat Ciner Hill and her husband, David Hill, own CINER FASHION JEWELRY and are enormously proud of the workmanship and quality of the product - "highest quality components, lustrous pearls, heavy gold plating, translucent crystals, multi-faceted stones and high gloss enamels". Ciner continues to strive for excellence in "basic good design" and "finest materials". This company produces high fashion without being trendy. While older Ciner is available in the marketplace it is undervalued and underpriced. Any company which has existed for 100 years has been doing something right, and its 1940s jewelry owes its appeal to the "revolutionary manufacturing process invented by Irwin and Charles Ciner in the 1940s, an "Innovative jewelry mold, the first ever in this country to produce costume jewelry that looked real." So says Ciner history.

The company, which keeps a low profile, has been growing at a steady rate, but elects to keep its image as a low-key, albeit very fashion conscious energetic producer of "exquisite costume jewelry pieces." Pat Hill notes "the Ciner name and copyright sign are the same, as are the materials, techniques, etc. that have been used ever since Ciner changed from working in silver to working in white metal. We may use different sizes and colors of stones now but all are glass and made to our specifications." An entire collection of Ciner would be accomplishment for any collector.

LOUIS HIRSCH of Jeray was convinced that successful costume jewelry manufacturers needed "A Sixth Sense" about trends. He was absolutely right and the philosophy still holds. Jeray, which is still a relatively unknown quantity, did anticipate trends and its jewelry endures and is becoming quite collectible. Another mark which is not abundant but which is worth searching for.

In the hierarchy of costume jewelry the substantial manufacturers were the biggest producers and money makers, they were thoroughly dependable and solid. Reputable, if not quite so solid, were the people who wholesaled jewelry made to their specifications and were called jobbers. They stood one rung down the ladder from the leaders, and did not have their own factories. There were also 'syndicates' whose sole task was to sell to the lower priced outlets such as the 5 and 10 cent stores.

Although so many companies produced so much, it was a relatively small world. Insular in that the manufacturers knew each other or of each other and what everyone else was doing. It was a big world in that the sheer numbers of people trying to make it could probably never be documented. Some rose and fell, some limped along and some prospered and are still thriving.

The fact that so many makers did not mark their jewelry makes positive attribution difficult in most cases and is a great loss to the researcher and collector.

When the rhinestones were set in silver which was fairly common in the 1940's the jewelry tends to have a realistic look especially if the design is subtle and engaging. In the matter of the stones themselves you can argue the case for Czechoslovakian or Austrian or American but like arguing politics, you'll probably not find a consensus.

In the matter of colored stones, America excelled but most of the good quality rhinestones were imported from Czechoslovakia and Austria. Research indicates that many important pieces of French rhinestone jewelry also used stones from those countries, but did manufacture rhinestones on a smaller scale.

Before World War II Czechoslovakia had been exporting synthetic gems and jewelry up to the value of $8,000,000 each year. That was a tremendous amount of money in those days and is a wonderful indication of the popularity of rhinestone jewelry.

The Czechs had the largest segment of the rhinestone market and the glass they shipped with foil backing coated with gold colored lacquer was almost too beautiful. There is a difference between the older rhinestones and the new, there is a difference even between the Austrian stones and the Czech but it takes a great deal of experience to detect these variations.

Making rhinestone jewelry was a laborious business, the manufacturers made a jewelry that was truly populist, of the people, all the people. A piece from Kresge or Woolworth's might cost 10¢ or a quarter but is no less a piece for all that, the women who wore it were just as proud as the deb sporting her baubles at Club Zanzibar. That is the great achievement of those entrepreneurs, they saw us through depression and war, they were shrewd, they had a good thing and they knew it, they never tried to change public taste, they catered to it and they moved with the times.

If ever there was a case for American know-how these men made it.

THE DESIGNERS

Design is all. Unless you are including pieces of jewelry for their rarity or some extraordinary qualities, remember that design is the important factor. A well designed piece can rise above the fact that it includes rhinestones and not diamonds, that it's not truly a ruby but a red glass stone. It can rise above the metal, base though it be.

Jewelry is a visual art, it must be pleasing to the eye, its totality must be beautiful to be accepted. That this rhinestone jewelry was such a success was due primarily to the designers who created it.

Since the heavy use of large, glittering stones could well be offensive, the people who created the style of the setting, who chose the arrangement of the stones, the overall look, were of necessity people of taste and humor. They had to understand the way the design could be transferred to metal, many of them were superb craftsmen.

Even the lesser pieces turned out by the thousands bear the mark of their skill. The stones may not be as lovely in these, although sometimes they were, the metal may lose some of its luster from wear but basically even in the cheap jewelry the design was good. This is the primary reason we have begun to appreciate rhinestone jewelry for its own sake.

It is a marvel that some of the flamboyant and really outrageous designs of the early jewelry now appeal for those very reasons; it has become chic again because it is different and rather daring, and although the designer may have been having fun with it, we seem now to have matured enough to appreciate it.

The overall designs were fairly constant in that most of them were taken from examples of traditional precious jewelry. The designers were interpreting a time farther back with these classic designs, but much costume jewelry spoke for and interpreted its own time.

Although the design was of major importance, the designers have had little recognition. Probably the premier designer of this kind of jewelry was Alfred Philippe of TRIFARI. Although he worked originally with precious gems he adapted more than well to his new artistic environment. Reputedly his ideas were all classically inspired and it is true that many of his designs are in the grand manner, but he was a master of whimsy. In his later designs Philippe included the animals and other appealing trifles which kept this jewelry selling.

Design patent applications show his having moved from Providence to Scarsdale, New York, which doesn't seem to have affected either the quality or quantity of his work.

His output was prodigious and was surpassed only by Adolph Katz of Coro. These men seemed to have had unlimited imaginative powers, month after month, year after year, hundreds of designs spewed forth. Such was Philippe's ability to dream up new creations one wonders at such creativity. His standards were high as were those of the company and his various baubles had elegance and style. It was Philippe who gave Trifari its distinctive look, and forever marked it as a producer of some of the best costume jewelry ever made.

It is impossible to scan records of the time without realizing the cooperation which must have existed between Philippe and Adolph Katz of CORO. The flavor of the jewelry was not the same but both men were prolific to the point of genius.

Katz was the master of the movable jewelry which still abounds and still amuses. It can be picked up rather inexpensively even though it is signed CORO and it is as delightful now as it was then. Recently a friend took her door knocker by Katz and wore it to a party. The little knocker actually moves and before long she, a shy person, was the center of the evening. She never heard of Katz, didn't realize it was Coro or who Coro was, but she now treasures that pin. That was the way with Katz, his jewelry moved, it quivered on springs, the arms of windmills went round, monkeys swung on chains, the whole array was a boon to the spirit. It was also well made and lasted forever. Some of Katz's pieces are lovely in the traditional way and many are beautiful.

Both Katz and Philippe designed crowns with multi-colored stones in honor of the wedding of Princess Elizabeth of England. Many other companies followed suit and today one of the most beautiful collections possible would be a complete set of crowns, they came in a great variety of sizes and varying colored stones and metals, but the crown by Philippe is exquisite.

Katz was also a fine businessman and had a hand running the Coro factory, his was a different approach to jewelry. Even now if you look at enough of his jewelry, you can feel the vitality the man must have had, the sense of fun.

In studying the designs of William Hobé a feeling comes through of infinite care and wonderful craftsmanship. This is not to be wondered at since the Hobé family has been making quality jewelry since the 1880's.

William Hobé, the son of a Parisian jeweler made his mark in America as the company puts it "as an innovative master craftsman, in great demand by Hollywood stars and producers for his creativity in both jewelry and costume design". The family carries on the tradition today in New York where rhinestones by Hobé are still master works of art.

Sylvia Hobé was a designer of utmost originality. Many of her pieces feature the human form in small size and the jeweled head, for instance, itself adorned with jewels. No one else in the design field executed this kind of work with such care and fine detail. Her work was exotic and unique.

Hobé lay claim to "handskilled craftsmanship, art and originality in design at affordable prices, attention to detail not readily discernible to the untrained eye."

The claim does not do justice to the reality. If you find an older piece by Hobé all the beauty and fine workmanship come through, even to the novice.

One of the great female designers was Natacha Brooks who owned her own costume jewelry factory in New York, she was another prolific producer of ideas and at the same time a clever businesswoman.

Natacha Brooks was "a glamorous redhead" who was also an insomniac. Her best designs were concocted during her wakeful nights, especially her famous Chinese lantern on a smiling elephant pin. Working and designing in New York during the golden period of rhinestone jewelry Brooks made detailed sketches of her ideas. If you should find any of these or any made by the other noted designers, you will have done us all a service and will have added appreciably to your estate. These sketches are now coveted by collectors. Brooks wore quantities of her own jewelry "all at once" and was reputedly her own best model. People remember seeing her wearing brooches, several on one shoulder, bracelets, necklaces, hat ornament and rings. One older jewelry person told me "she was really something". Of course memory often plays us false, but the right costume jewelry does make one memorable.

Miriam Haskell created what many collectors refer to as "different" jewelry. Haskell combined seemingly disparate materials in unorthodox ways for unusual effect especially in the early innovative years. She started the company in 1924, after working with another maker, Robert de Mario, and it has been making "high fashion, manipulated costume jewelry since the beginning. Ms. Haskell sold the company in 1953 and died in 1983," according to Sanford Moss, President of Haskell Jewels, Ltd. of N.Y. Haskell had a highly developed sense of color and many collectors are drawn to her jewelry. Since she established her company so early she was certainly in the forefront of the new wave. Her life spanned years of the greatest achievements in the history of the world and if her name has become widely recognized only in recent years for her jewelry designs, she joins illustrious company.

Hakell's use of beads, wood, leather, metal, rhinestones and the trademark pearls for rather esoteric combinations often makes recognition less than instantaneous since Mr. Robert or "Originals By Robert" used similar materials and concepts during the same period. Some of the advertising work done for Robert is magnificent in itself.

Haskell and another clever woman, Alice Cavines, fit into the same category — females who met the challenge of this male dominated industry and were successful. Cavines' jewelry sometimes exhibits a strong sense of whimsy, especially in some of the smaller pieces such as her insect pins.

Even the name sounds flamboyant — SCHIAPARELLI — Elsa, that is. A woman of exotic background whose shop was located on 5th Avenue in New York and whose clientele spanned the illustrious celebrity world. The use of the one name signature is reflective of the personality of the designer herself. Her approach to design mirrored the woman. Her career began in 1927 with a black sweater of "chic melancholy" and by 1935 she had graduated to a sumptuous establishment on the Rue Vendome in Paris. She became a "style refugee" to this country after the fall of France in 1940 but always felt Paris was the hub of fashion and returned there. Schiaparelli was always considered an "exotic" and her jewelry is often large and commanding although not always "pretty". Costume jewelry with her signature, underpriced today, is investment jewelry.

Fortunately for collectors of costume jewelry Hattie Carnegie's father changed the family name when they entered the United States from Vienna. Henrietta Kanegeiser certainly does not have the same rhythm. Designing was always her passion and by 1933 she was hugely successful. Her gospel of fashion was to keep it "simple and beautiful." This theme dominates her jewelry too - much of it is tailored and many of the pieces with rhinestones and colored stones are executed in a tailored way. She preferred quiet, classic lines.

The highly collectible early jewelry with Hattie Carnegie's signature is available but expensive and difficult to find in any great quantity. It was costly in its heyday and it should be coveted for its future.

Lily Daché, is known primarily for her hats, which she invariably called "ots". This volatile Frenchwoman who never quite lost her accent, came to the United States in 1924. Almost all her other design work was done to enhance her hats and dresses. She claimed she was a collector of dresses, some of which she never wore. Her jewelry is scarce and expensive and should always be bought when found. It represents a designer and an era of such individuality as to be in itself rare.

How could one not react to any creation of a man who changed his name legally from John Pico Harberger to John Pico John? Among the most scarce of all the jewelry made by big name designers is that of Mr. John. Many people today remember Mr. John, they remember him at fashion shows, at appearances in the fine department stores at displays of his hats, they recall his mannerisms and his personality. Anyone who ever met him seems to remember him vividly. His jewelry has the same impact - the quality simply imprints itself on the consciousness in the way of early Eisenberg. It is almost never signed so unless the label is attached attribution is impossible. If a Mr. John presents itself - buy it.

McClelland Barclay should be a cherished name in American art with a widely respected reputation. Instead he is a well kept secret. Jewelry was only a minor part of his artistic production which included paintings, posters, exquisite bronzes and popular magazine covers. Barclay's accomplishments are too many to be documented in a short biography but his jewelry reflects his involvement with sculpture. It is rare, although collections do exist and anyone who has some of his work made during the 1930s should be doubly happy. In Barclay's case owning a piece of his costume jewelry rates you as a genuine American art collector. He was killed while serving as a Naval Commander in the South Pacific in the early 1940's.

Often the owners of the factories would do the designing or at least a part of it. Louis Kramer of Kramer Jewelry Creations, N.Y., for example, was actively creating and establishing Kramer as a premier maker with his eye for beauty and form in jewelry. During the 1950s much of the production of Kramer was his design. It was that kind of business, highly competitive, a constant striving to keep costs down to increase profits and keep prices low, a business which the people involved seemed to enjoy passionately and which they seemed to consider a part of their lives rather than just a job.

In the late 1940s and early 1950s, André Fleuridas of Connecticut was designing for Mazer Bros., Inc., Raymonde Semensohn of New York was creating for Marcel Boucher et Cie, of New York. Marcel Boucher himself did much of the designing for the firm. Many of the really delightful pins of the 1950s were his work - the ballerinas, the clowns, harlequin, ornamental brooch watches.

Many collectors are concerned about the jewelry of Eugene Joseff. Joseff is considered a "Hollywood Jewelsmith". Fabulous Fakes has certainly become an overworked designation but in the case of JOSEFF whose jewelry was worn in films by the superstars of yesteryear, it was certainly fake and it was certainly fabulous. As diverse personalities as Bette Davis and Marilyn Monroe wore his creations and in many cases his jewelry is more memorable than the films which featured it. So complete was his hold on the spectacular jewelry required by so many important stars it may be possible to see a JOSEFF jewel a night if you are addicted to old films on late night TV.

Frequently my mail has reflected the excitement of collectors who felt they had found original JOSEFF pieces from the early period. Most of it was made later from jewelry which had been copied and reissued. The original jewelry bears the signature JOSEFF-HOLLYWOOD or JOSEFF in block letters. The pieces made in the 1960s and later are marked in script 'Joseff'. Joseff's jewelry is usually larger than life as befits its original purpose, but these reissues are worth collecting and are not inexpensive. It is interesting that in 1945 Eugene Joseff assigned some of his designs to a partnership in Los Angeles bearing the name "Breakfast in Hollywood".

CHANEL and DUC DeVERDURA — some Chanel jewelry is actually turning up at auctions so be alert. This legendary figure was partial to costume jewelry not only for her 'costumes' but for personal wear. Her favorite piece of jewelry in fact was reputed to be a brooch made with green and red stones and rhinestones set in filagree. She wore this pin so often it became a recognized trademark. In the late 1970s it sold at auction for nearly $2,000. Look for the bar pins and other small pieces with the Chanel name. Anything is possible. The equally legendary Duc DeVerdura whose heyday was the late 1930s-1940s and whose custom-made fine jewels were crafted for the Hollywood elite, also designed some costume jewelry, some of it specifically for Chanel. De Verdura was a jewelry genius and if ever an opportunity arises to view his gem creations seize the moment.

MOSELL as a signature on jewelry is really climbing to the top of the charts. Frederick Mosell, who was born in France, came to the United States from Paris and started designing at his own kitchen table. From his beginning novelties, which he supposedly sold for very little, he graduated to more sophisticated jewelry which he placed in the elegant stores. Mosell jewelry is quite beautiful and the mark is fairly scarce. It is well worth looking for.

KENNETH JAY LANE (KJL) was not part of the great period of rhinestone jewelry which existed before the early 1950s. Although his signature jewelry is widely collected, he came late to the field. Lane began designing on his own after a stint in 1963 with Christian Dior where he "decorated shoes".

When he crafted earrings on his own which "sold out immediately" in Bonwit Teller's, New York, he expanded his horizons to Europe where he opened a boutique. When he later established his U.S. boutique the success continued as he attracted "all the right people". Many celebrities wear and collect his jewelry. Lane sold his business to CIRO's in 1988. Some of Lane's earliest inspiration came from the designs of Jeanne Touissant of Cartier's and from David Webb of England, but his designs are far-ranging.

Eugene E. Bertolli (a forgotten name) of Connecticut did some elegant design work for NAPIER. He designed a particularly beautiful fan brooch for the Napier Co. of Meriden. Some of the most tasteful design work was done for the powder compact market and one of the most attractive in rhinestones was designed by Alfred Reilly of Massachusetts for the Evans Case Co., Paul Flato conceived many outstanding designs for the compact market. These unrecognized heroes and heroines did magnificent work of heirloom quality. Names we never hear: inventive, ingenious minds which with others, have received little recognition for their achievements.

They looked on the making of this jewelry as a special assignment, their particular thing, it brought vast monetary rewards and lots of happiness, the successful felt they were a bit different, they were the ones who had the instinctive feel for it.

No one person in any large factory can claim sole responsibility for the success of the entire output, but if anyone steered the costume jewelry business to prosperity and popularity, it was the designers, the unsung heroes and heroines.

THE PROCESS

All costume jewelry, regardless of price, was designed and manufactured to resemble genuine jewelry in a larger-than-life, overstated way. It was mass-produced, a term which in this case belies the complexity of the process.

The overall cost of production was low in relation to selling price but the merest trifle went through a series of complicated operations which began at the designing board.

There were basically two general categories of manufacture: stamping and casting, and the method used depended on the type of jewelry being made — stamping for the cheaper line, casting for the more expensive items.

The mass-production techniques developed and utilized by the manufacturers were most efficient, by the time demand reached the heights they had everything down to a science. It was these methods which made the lower lines so inexpensive, stamping out the jewelry in quantity was possible because of the way the factories operated.

Much as in silver manufacture, a sketch was made by a designer then passed on to a model or sample maker. Although these first steps sound simple, consider what was involved. Designers first need inspiration, that inspiration must be translated into an easily understood sketch, the sketch must then be interpreted and molded into a sample or model done by hand. An arduous, exacting task which could take up to two weeks.

With the completion of the model, the toolmakers cut dies in steel. This too is a highly skilled craft and upon the detail in these dies the ultimate effectiveness of the piece depended. In these first steps rested the fate of the jewelry.

In some factories when the stamping process was used, the making of a model was bypassed and the designer's sketch went directly to the die cutter.

The dies were part of gigantic presses which dropped to literally stamp out thousands of pieces in the original design. The stamping was usually done on thin brass, with unskilled labor setting up the metal to be stamped out.

Most older employees refer to "thousands" of pieces being stamped out in a day, but in truth probably nobody knows an exact count, for as one long-ago employee says "there were too many coming too fast to count".

When the piece had been stamped out the assembly line technique took over, and except for certain refinements by different factories, the process was more or less the same.

The jewelry was electroplated, then assemblers did separate tasks such as soldering. In later years and in the cheapest jewelry making, soldering furnaces were used.

After various coatings had been applied, the jewelry was assembled.

Casting used many of the same steps: design, sketch and then model, except that in casting the model was made in hard rubber in two sections. In some cases a bronze model was created. Liquid metal was poured into the molds then formed models of the original. Sometimes liquid wax was used with a ceramic plaster, when the wax was heated and poured off, the design appeared in reverse. Silver jewelry was made this way.

The companies constantly sought ways to make the manufacture of the jewelry more efficient. The fact that the expensive first steps could be made cost effective in terms of the latter mass production techniques, shows how well they succeeded. They used the most inexpensive materials available to them and overcame this deficiency with the blazing stones.

The disciplined order of long lines of women feeding the machines and doing the setting and assembling worked to such a degree that the jewelry itself rarely broke and even the stones which were pasted in are for the most part, intact and held fast. And all this before crazy glue.

The jewelry made by either method, stamping or casting, depended finally on the imagination of the design. In most cases the designs caught the female fancy but even if they didn't, materials were so cheap and production so high a few mistakes didn't make much difference in the long run. There was room for error, that's why so much of it endured, the failures could be discarded without regret.

Today, a great deal of emphasis is put on 'hand-set' rhinestones and it is true that the higher priced jewelry was made this way, but this must not be the first consideration of the collector. The stones were set in the prongs by hand, adding to the original cost, but in some cases lower line jewelry which had the stones pasted in is equally attractive and desirable and often more interesting.

THE CARE AND KEEPING OF RHINESTONES

Since rhinestones are foiled jewelry they require some care. Many of the stones are pasted in and as the glue dries it sometimes becomes brittle and stones are easily dislodged.

Never, under any circumstances, put more than one piece of rhinestone or other stone jewelry in a box or container, not only may you loosen the stones, you may scratch them.

Some of the older jewelry is strung on chains which have aged badly, rust can weaken the chain and since the chains may be quite thin be sure those never have to be untangled because of having been tossed together with other necklaces or bracelets. This is a difficult repair should part of the chain be lost or ruined so you want to avoid having it done.

Be sure all necklaces are laid flat if they are heavy, stones upward and not touching anything else. The dangling earrings should be suspended from holders or wires, or if stored away, each in a separate box. The care of rhinestones demands common sense.

Because of the foil backing, the greatest threat to rhinestone jewelry is water. If water seeps behind the stone it tarnishes the foil and the stone becomes dull and lifeless and has to be replaced. Never wash your jewelry by immersion. Do not hold it under a faucet to clean it.

There are now electronic cleaning devices which work well, but the simplest way is to take a Q-tip or very soft small brush and use one of the preparations for cleaning glass. Coat the brush or tip with it, make sure you are touching only the surface of the stone and carefully brush each stone lightly. Some stones are so small as to require a sweeping motion over the entire piece, but care must be exercised. In pronged jewelry be sensitive to the cotton possibly catching the prongs. A very small amount of dishwashing liquid can be substituted for the glass cleaner.

Then polish dry with a soft linen cloth, rubbing only as hard as you can without exercising undue pressure on the stones.

Water is the natural enemy of your rhinestone jewelry and must not be allowed to come between the stone and the foil which is what gives the stone its luster. The grey, colorless stone which results can ruin the jewelry.

Some collectors who buy only for collecting and not to wear, frame their choice pieces because dust, too, is a problem with jewelry. Many of the early 30's pins and clips are coated with grime, have a few stones missing and are otherwise derelict because of lack of proper care. With a little attention these can be restored and since scarcity is becoming a factor in collecting earlier jewelry, and price a factor in perfect pieces, these broken examples are a bargain.

Do not wear pieces which knock together. Two bracelets which move with the arm and into each other endanger the stones, do not clip or screw earrings together when storing or displaying. The jewelry should be considered fragile.

Always look for well designed pieces with the manufacturer's mark, do not let a few missing stones deter you. If the price is right for condition think in terms of repair.

Missing stones can be replaced but bear in mind any rhinestone replacement may not do. Make sure the stone has the same quality as the one it will match. There is an amazing difference in quality of rhinestones, particularly in the older jewelry. Before you buy any rhinestone piece make sure the stones are all original, or the replacements are an exact match.

Replacing rhinestones is not yet a costly exercise. You can, in fact, do it yourself. Toward this end buy any boxes or bags of broken jewelry you find which include rhinestones and colored stones. Many long-established jewelers have older rhinestones on hand and will replace your stones for a small fee. If you choose to do it yourself, your local lapidary shop is a great source of these stones. Many of the owners will spend an inordinate amount of time looking for the precise stone, and set it for you for a minimal charge. Or they will sell you the stones so you can do it yourself.

If you choose to do the replacements yourself and have found broken pieces from which you can transplant stones, or if you have bought exactly matching stones, go to a local hobby shop and buy EPOXY 330 which is a water-clear bonding agent. Directions on the box are easy to follow and this type glue is made especially for bonding materials to metal findings which is what your settings are called. The contents of the two tubes of 330 will be mixed together and applied. A simpler method is contained in a single tube of Industrial Cement 1333 made specifically for the repair of rhinestone and costume jewelry by Prince Laquer & Chemical Corp., Brooklyn, NY

11211. This no-fuss cement is easy to use and has proved remarkably effective. Products are now being sold exclusively for the repair of rhinestone jewelry. Most are inexpensive and readily available.

If you find jewelry which is broken in other ways, the edge torn or bits of it missing, or the back clips on buckles or dress clips imperfect, the pin to fasten the piece off, the choice must be yours. If the price is very small buy any piece with stones so they can be used for replacement, if a piece needs repair you must consider whether the cost will be worth it in terms of time and money, and whether you like the piece enough to bother, or if it is unique enough to justify the effort.

People who are collecting rhinestone jewelry, or any jewelry should take a local adult education class in jewelry making or repair. The low cost and time expended will repay you in that you will have a new sense of how jewelry is made, how the materials differ, how to appreciate and involve yourself in design and understanding the how and why of repair.

If you deplore complications of any kind and want and can afford to build a collection of perfect rhinestone jewelry the cost will be higher and you may not have as much fun. Life will be easier though.

At the very least consult a manual on jewelry making which can be found in any public library, the illustrations alone should give you insights into the craft, knowledge of the metals and stones you are dealing with.

Display is a matter of taste; specimen cases such as those used for insects allow the jewelry to be seen and can be placed in an area to catch light — these are quite popular and have the added property of inexpensive protection. The jewelry cases can be shifted easily and can be exhibited without handling the jewelry itself. Your best pieces can be set into a glass-topped coffee table; you can frame your favorites; you can line drawers with mirrors and set the pieces in; one of the most spectacular displays is a bathroom plant window, the same could be done in a bedroom depending on lighting. Display is limited only by your imagination and preference, but displaying your rhinestones is a must.

The rhinestone era was unique in many ways. It encompassed the dizzy days of the 1920's, the deep depression of the 1930's, the tragedy and heroism of the 1940's and the radically changing culture of the 1950's. Rhinestones blended with the beads on the dresses of the flapper, on the classic styles of the 30's matron, on the lapels of those who waited during the 40's with their little eagle or rhinestone flag, and on the extravagant costumes of the entertainers of the 50's. You might say they were there, those shiny baubles, they were in fact everywhere, they've seen it all.

Not only the jewelry itself is unique, this uniqueness extends to its collectors, many of whom lived through the times in which this jewelry was worn. They have turned to it again in a wave of nostalgia and in appreciation for its memories and magnificence.

There will probably never be anything like it again, something so enormously popular over so long a span of time.

Enjoy those glittering, glamorous rhinestones, wear them, display them, collect them. By all means, collect them.

TRADEMARK SECTION

Much of the jewelry of the period with which this book deals was not marked in any way. When trademarks do appear they can be found on the jewelry itself, or in the form of a paper label, or on cards to which smaller pieces, such as ornamental pins, were attached.

The trademarks are listed alphabetically and include manufacturers who did not necessarily deal in rhinestones exclusively, e.g., many of the producers of pearl jewelry incorporated rhinestones and colored stones in their pieces.

The dates noted as "since" or "first use" indicate the first use of the mark as claimed by the manufacturer.

Mark of AURORA JEWELRY CO., Providence, RI for men's and women's and children's jewelry. First used September, 1954.

Mark of NAPIER COMPANY, Meriden, CT for bracelets, brooches, pins, rings, ornamental metal mounted combs, ornamental hairpins, necklaces, lockets and earrings. This mark was also used on cases of all kinds. First used December, 1923.

Jewelry mark JUERGENS & ANDERSON CO., Chicago, IL. First used 1907.

Mark of A.B. MANUFACTURING CO., Providence, RI for jewelry. First used 1919

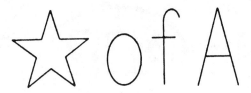

Jewelry mark of STUCKEY & SPEER INC., Houston, TX. First used Dec. 1952

ARTHUR P. BEAR of ARTHUR P. BEAR CO., New York, NY mark for jewelry. First used 1959

AXEL BROS. INC., New York, NY for finger rings, bracelets, watch bracelets and attachments. First used 1941

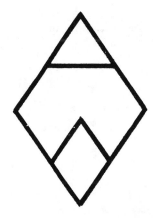

Mark of AISENSTEIN—WORONOCK & SONS, INC., New York, NY for rings and ring mountings and other jewelry. First used Jan. 1934

ANCHOR CASTING CO., INC., New York, NY for necklaces, bracelets, earrings, etc, and jewelry with pearls. First used March, 1951.

ABRAHAM BROUNSTEIN, New York, NY used this mark for rings, pendants, bracelets, pins and earrings. First used 1962

ADAMS WATCH, INC., New York, NY mark for jewelry. Since 1949

AVON JEWELRY MFG. CO., INC., Providence, RI mark for costume jewelry. First used June 1962

JOSEPH ZELLER d.b.a. ASTORIA JEWELRY MFG. CO., New York, NY mark for brooch pins, charms, cuff links, bracelets, earrings, rings and pendants. First used 1952

MORRIS ADWAR d.b.a. CASTING CO., New York, NY. Mark for jewelry of all the usual types including scatter pins, cuff links and clasps. Used since January, 1959.

ARTISTIC NOVELTY CO., INC., New York, NY for necklaces, brooches, bracelets, etc. with rhinestones. This mark was also used for precious stones and jewelry. First used 1920.

DUPUIS PROCESS, INC., New York, NY mark for necklaces, bracelets, rings, earrings, beads, clips, brooches, lockets, pins, ornamental hat pins, pins for dress ornaments, name pins, hair ornaments, compacts, comb cases etc. First used 1941

Mark of AARON PERKIS, New York, NY for finger rings, charms, charm bracelets, pendants, brooches, pins, cuff links, necklaces, and snaps and catches for jewelry. First used about January, 1947.

ANNETTE CREATIONS, INC., Providence, RI used this mark for costume jewelry. First used October 1964

A.R.

ROSE RATHOUS of R & Y JEWELRY MANUFACTURING, New York, NY mark for jewelry since April 1962

ABON MANUFACTURING CO., INC., New York, NY for gold plated holders and cases for articles of personal wear, e.g., lipstick holders, perfume puff cases, lingerie clips, handbag ash trays, etc. Since October, 1949.

Acacia

THE TAILORED WOMAN, INC., New York, NY used this mark for simulated pearls, finger rings, bracelets, brooches, pins, necklaces, clips, earrings, tiaras, buttons and buckles. All made in whole or in part or plated with precious metals. Since March 1953.

ACADEMY AWARD

ACADEMY AWARD PRODUCTS, INC., New York, NY used this mark for novelty jewelry, beginning February, 1946.

Accessocraft

ACCESSOCRAFT PRODUCTS CORP., New York, NY mark for rings, bracelets, brooches, pins, necklaces, clips, earrings, tiaras, buttons and buckles. First used June 1935

A. MICALLEF & COMPANY, Providence, RI, mark for jewelry since April, 1935.

ADAM AND EVE

RICHTON INTERNATIONAL CORP., New York, NY used this mark for jewelry since about July 1971

CHARLES ROTHMAN COMPANY, INC. Providence, R.I. mark for ladies' costume jewelry. First used May, 1954.

Adelcia

Mark of ADELICIA, St. Petersburg, FL for earrings. Used since 1950

Admark

Mark of ALBERT ADLER, Philidelphia, PA. In use since May, 1945.

ADMIRA

Jewelry mark of WALTER ARONHEIM, New York, NY. Since January, 1947.

ADMOR

STEIN & ELLBOGEN COMPANY, Chicago, IL for cultured pearl jewelry. Since September, 1956.

KANTOR BROTHERS, New York, NY used this mark for pearl necklaces. First used November, 1923.

ADORA

C.F. MUELLER CO., Jersey City, NJ mark for earrings and pendants. First used Dec. 1960

Aduration

WALTER LAMPL of LAMPL, New York, NY mark for rings, brooches, bar pins, bracelets, necklaces, garment clips and earrings. Since Sept. 1942

AERONAUT

PROVIDENCE STOCK COMPANY, Providence RI, mark for jewelry. Used since February, 1930.

AIRFLOW

L.G. BALFOUR CO., Attleboro, MA mark for jewelry. First used Sept. 1941

CORO, INC., New York, NY mark for pearl necklaces and strings of pearls. Often these had elaborate rhinestone clasps. Since July, 1948.

A. L. L. CO.

A.L. LINDROTH COMPANY, Attleboro, MA. Mark for costume jewelry, brooches, bracelets, necklaces, earrings, pendants and lockets.

Alberta

ALBERT WEINER, d.b.a. ALBERT MANUFACTURING COMPANY, Providence, RI, for synthetic pearls and jewelry novelties, namely, dress clips which are ornamental and worn as jewelry. First used about 1935.

ALEX

PRISCILLA A. SLADE, Springdale, Conn. Mark for handmade jewelry. Earrings, bracelets, pins, clips, necklaces, hair ornaments, coronets and charms. Since December, 1949.

Alice

ALICE JEWELRY COMPANY, Providence, RI, used this mark for earrings, brooches, pins, anklets, pendants, bracelets and necklaces. Since about May, 1950.

ALICE-IN-WONDERLAND

COHN & ROSENBERGER, INC., New York, NY mark for all the usual types of jewelry plus hair ornaments, pins for dress ornaments, buckles for hats, ornamental shoe buckles. First used Dec. 1933

"Allegro"

Mark of STANDISH—WEBER INC., New York, NY for costume jewelry. First used June 1961

ALBERT ADLER, Philadelphia, PA. Mark for chokers and bracelets. Since April, 1947.

ALLURE

JOSEPH H. MEYER BROS., Brooklyn, NY for necklaces, bracelets, finger rings, jewelry clips, bracelets and earrings. First use January, 1945.

Almanac of Life

CORO, INC., New York, NY used this mark for charm bracelets. Since December, 1954.

ALOHA

Mark of PAKULA AND COMPANY, Chicago, IL, for pearls and pearl necklaces. Since May 6, 1962.

ALPINE CRYSTAL

LOUIS FLEISCHMANN CORP., New York used this mark for jewelry with crystals, namely pendants earrings, bracelets, brooches, rings and necklaces. First used Feb. 1957

ALU-MINN

LUDWIG J. WEBER, New Kensington, PA mark for costume jewelry since Nov. 1945

WYNNE PRECISION COMPANY, Griffin, GA, for jewelry of base and precious metals. September, 1945.

LAY & BORGES, NEW YORK, NY mark for imitation pearl necklaces, earrings and bracelets. This mark in use since October 1, 1944.

Mark of A. MICALLEF & CO. INC., Providence, RI for jewelry. First used 1935

AM LEE JEWELRY COMPANY, INC. Providence, RI mark for broochs, pins, earrings, bracelets, necklaces and pendants. First used January, 1946.

AMERICAN SHOE SPECIALTIES CO., INC., New York, NY for rhinestone settings, pearls and rhinestones. First used 1944

American Beauty

Trademark used by New England Glass Works of Providence, Rhode Island for imitation pearls. In use since October 1921.

American Queen

PITMAN & KEELER, Attleboro, MA mark for bracelets, vanity cases and compacts. First used March, 1917.

AMERICANA

CORO, INC., New York, NY used this mark for ornamental pins, jewelry clips, hair ornaments, comb cases, belt buckles, charms, key chains, tie holders, buttons, scarf holders, hat ornaments, dress ornaments and beads, tiaras, pearls, necklaces, etc. Since 1936.

EXHIBIT SALES CO., Philadelphia, PA for men's and women's costume jewelry, gold-filled plated and rhodium finished. Rhinestone bracelets, earrings, brooches, scatter pins packaged separately and in matched sets, necklaces. Since June, 1949.

AMnA

Mark of EMANUEL DEUTSCH d.b.a. AMERICANA JEWELRY MFG. CO., New York, NY for charms, bracelets, brooch pins, necklaces, finger rings, earrings, clips, tie clasps and pendants. First used June, 1962.

Amoret

NOVEL PRODUCTS CO., INC. Long Island, NY, for necklaces, ornamental pins, earrings, rings, pendants, brooches, bracelets and charms. First used May, 1950.

AMORITA

ROBERT C. BARNSTONE, New York, N.Y. began using this mark in August, 1930, for a variety of articles including fine jewelry. Also scarf pins, mesh bags, belt buckles hand bags, match boxes, fraternity emblems, dresser accessories, lingerie clasps, cigarette holders, combs, shoe buckles, ear studs, coin holders and hand mirrors.

Amourelle

KRAMER JEWELRY CREATIONS INC., New York, NY used this mark for all the usual types of jewelry as well as for beads, jewelry initials, hair ornaments. Since 1963

ANCESTRAL

COHN & ROSENBERGER INC. New York, NY mark for pearls, necklaces, rings, brooches, shoe buckles, etc. Since 1930.

ANCESTRAL

CORO INCORP. of RHODE ISLAND, Providence, RI used this mark for jewelry since June 1964

ANCHOR

TAUNTON PEARL WORKS, Taunton, MA mark for scarf pins, bar pins, lingerie pins and brooches. First used January, 1912.

ANCHOR BRAND

Still active in 1949, NORTH & JUDD MANUFACTURING COMPANY, NEW BRITAIN, CONN., used this mark for buckles for footwear, belt buckles, and among many other items, shoe ornaments. The mark first appeared in 1890.

André hair fashions

CORO, INC., New York, NY mark for tiaras, combs, hair ornaments, ponytail barrettes, barrettes, hair bands, clip combs, chignon pins, bobby pins. First used March 1937.

Andrée

COHN & ROSENBERGER, INC., New York, NY for finger rings, earrings, jewelry clips, brooches, lockets and the following goods made in whole or in part of precious metal or plated with same - beads, pins, hat ornaments, hair ornaments, powder compacts, comb cases, cigarette cases, fancy cigarette boxes, fancy buckles, jewelry initials. First used March, 1937.

"THE ANGEL OF LOVE"

CORO mark for all the usual types of jewelry and beads, pins, hat ornaments and jewelry initials made in whole or in part of precious metal or plated with such metal. Since September, 1952.

ANGEL PINS

FORSTNER INC., Irvington, NJ for novelty pins with dangling charms. First used about March, 1959.

ANGELA

ANGELA, INC., Providence, RI used this mark for pins, brooches, earrings, necklaces and bracelets. First used 1963

ANGELITE

PRINCESS PRIDE CREATIONS, INC., Chicago, IL mark for finger rings, earrings and pendants. First used 1960

ANK

ANTONETTE PEARLS, INC., Newark, NJ mark for rings, bracelets, charms, necklaces, earrings pendants, brooches and findings. Since June 1962

ANN BARTON

Mark used by B. HAIG, Boston, Mass., for jewelry for personal wear and compacts, vanity cases and cigarette cases. Used since 1938.

ANNIE OAKLEY

Mark of ANNIE OAKLEY ENTERPRISES, Los Angeles, CA for bracelets and lapel pins. Since March 1951.

Anniversary

MAYBAUM BROS., INC. New York, NY used this mark for pearl jewelry. First used August, 1921.

This familiar mark was used by ANDERSON TOOL & DIE WORKS, Providence, RI, for men's jewelry, including tie pins, cuff links and bill clips. July, 1945.

ANSON

ANSON, INCORPORATED, Providence, RI used this mark for men's jewelry. First used July, 1945.

ANTHONY NOVELTY CO., INC. Providence, RI used this mark for costume jewelry made with plated metal. First used Nov., 1948 on earrings, necklaces, bracelets, brooches and pendants.

Mark of FERDINAND L. BAUM, PROVIDENCE, R.I., for jewelry since December, 1947.

ELIZABETH ARDEN SALES CORP., New York, NY used this mark for hair pins, hat pins, garment buckles. Clips and clasps for hair. Since March 1939

AQUADROP

Mark of AVON PRODUCTS INC., New York, NY for costume jewelry. First used Nov. 1971

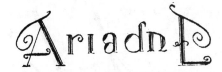

ARNOLD CONSTABLE & CO., New York, NY mark for artificial pearls, necklaces, chokers, rings, bracelets, bandeaux, buckles. First used Dec. 1924

JOSEPH H. MEYER BROS., Brooklyn, NY for necklaces, bracelets, finger rings, jewelry clips, brooches and earrings. Since January, 1941.

Arista

Another CORO INC. mark for all the usual types of jewelry used since March, 1954.

Aristocraft

MELVIN WHITNEY & CO., Los Angeles, CA, mark for costume jewelry namely gold filled, gold plated, silver plated, glass necklaces simulated pearls and ornamental pins. First used Feb. 1946

CORO mark for simulated pearl jewelry. Since August, 1950.

ARISTO-GRAM

SWANK INC., Attleboro, MA mark for jewelry for personal wear. Since March 1941

ARJÉ ORIGINAL

Mark of RENE JEWELRY CO., INC. Philadelphia, PA. For costume jewelry including bracelets, earrings, necklaces, cuff links, pendants, anklets, pins and brooches, chatelaines, hair ornaments and dress clips, but excluding rings. First used September, 1956.

Mark of ARLE JEWEL, INC., Atlanta GA, since June, 1946.

IZ-BEL PRODUCTS INC., New York, NY mark for men's jewelry. Since 1958.

ARNO WRAZLOWSKY, New York, NY used this mark for novelty and women's costume jewelry - earrings, finger rings, bracelets, lapel pins, ornamental dress clips, lockets, brooches and tiaras. First used December, 1952.

Aro-Sac

Mark of ALPCO, INC. of Providence, RI, since August, 1946.

ARROW

S AND S MANUFACTURING CO., Providence RI used this mark for all types of jewelry including watch bracelets, rings, hair ornaments, scarf pins, bracelets, necklaces, etc. Since January, 1928.

ART-LOVE

ART'S INC., CANTON, OH used this mark for jewelry. Since 1970

WALTER CERVENY, Portland, Oregon used this mark for earrings, ornamental pins, necklaces, bracelets, lockets, barrettes, tie pins, cuff links, studs and buckles. First used September, 1954.

ARTEL

Mark of ARTEL JEWELRY MFG. CO., INC. Providence RI for finger rings, pins, earrings, necklaces, tie clips, bracelets and cuff links. First used January, 1931.

ARTS OF THE WORLD

SWANK, INC., Attleboro,, MA for men's jewelry. First used May, 1960.

"AS YOU LIKE IT"

Mark of JACOB SCHORSCH, New York, NY in 1931, for necklaces and clasps.

"AS YOU LIKE IT"

COHN & ROSENBERGER, INC., New York, NY for all the usual types of jewelry including compacts, boxes, etc. First used May 1939

ASTA

JOSEPH TITTMAN d.b.a. ASTA-TITTMAN JEWELRY MFG. CO., New York, NY mark for brooch pins, charms, clips, bracelets, earrings, and pendants. First used Aug. 1955.

CHESLEY L. BENJAMIN, San Francisco, CA used this mark on jewelry — bracelets, pins, pendants, medallions, etc. August, 1945.

ASTRO-CLAD

Jewelry Mark of SALVATORE P. IORIO, Jr. of AERO JEWELRY CO., Providence, RI since Jan. 1965

AT - A - TIME

MAYBAUM BROTHERS, INC. New York, NY. Mark for pearls and precious stones (real or imitation) set and/or unset; and articles or jewelry such as necklaces, bracelets, earrings, pins and finger rings. Used since April 17, 1925.

ATOMIC

CORO, INC., New York, NY. Mark for finger rings, earrings, jewelry clips, brooches and the following made wholly or partly of precious metal — beads, pins, hat ornaments, hair ornaments, compacts, etc. Used since October 1, 1945.

attaché

Mark of WEINGEROFF—LARAMI—PRESIDENT CORP. Providence, RI for men's jewelry. Since April 1971

attaché

RAY CURRAN & CO., Providence, RI for men's jewelry. First used July 1962

AUTOCRAT

VARGAS MANUFACTURING CO., Providence, RI used this mark for jewelry since April 1971

AUTOMADE

AUTOMATIC CHAIN CO., Providence, RI mark for jewelry. First used 1934

COHN & ROSENBERGER, INC., New York, NY. Mark for bracelets, bar pins, brooches, earrings, necklaces and mesh bags, powder compact cases and vanity cases made of or plated with precious metal. This mark was first used in January, 1925.

AVON MEMORY MAKERS

AVON PRODUCTS, INC., New York, NY mark for costume jewelry. First used June 1971

SPEIDEL CORP. of Providence, RI, mark for costume jewelry. Used since October, 1936.

GULF COAST JEWELRY & SPECIALTY CO., INC., Mobile, AL. Mark used both for costume jewelry and diamond jewelry - rings, bracelets, earrings, pendants and ornamental pins. Since December, 1949.

BASKIN BROTHERS, New York, NY mark for rings, bar pins, scarf pins, earrings. Used since January, 1907.

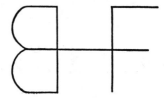

B.F. HIRSCH, INC., New York, NY for jewelry. Since Nov. 1935

Mark of JOSEPH BOBLEY JEWELRY, INC., New York, NY for brooches, pins, necklaces, bracelets and earrings. First used May, 1955.

L.G. BALFOUR COMPANY, Attleboro, MA for finger rings, ornamental pins, charms made of precious metal. First used February, 1936.

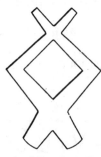

Jewelry mark of Joseph C. Brown d.b.a. BROWN'S JEWELRY, Stockton, CA. First used November, 1944.

B.A. BALLOU & CO., INC., Providence, RI used this mark for anklets, ascot pins, baby bar pins, bracelets, necklaces, brooches and charms. Since 1947

H.F. BARROWS CO., North Attleboro, MA for lockets, crosses, bracelets and pendants. Since December, 1901.

Mark of BEAUCRAFT, INC., Providence, RI for rings, charms, earrings, bracelets, pins, necklaces and pendants. First used Dec. 1961

MARK of BROOKS & CO. JEWELRY, INC., New York, NY, for jewelry. Since June 1962

FEDERATED DEPARTMENT STORES, INC., New York, NY mark for rings, bracelets, pins, brooches, earrings, clips, belt buckles, shoe buckles some of which are plated with precious metals. First used 1939

Jewelry mark used by M. FABRIKANT & SONS INC., New York, NY since May 1962

B.A. BALLOU & CO., INCORPORATED, Providence, RI. Jewelry mark first used in 1908, still active 1949.

Mark of BAR-TAN MANUFACTURING CO., Providence, RI for jewelry. Since about June, 1965.

BERMAN BROTHERS, Pittsburgh, PA mark for jewelry. First used 1962

BLISS BROTHER COMPANY, Attleboro, MA used this mark for compacts, cigarette, lipsticks, pill boxes, lockets and all costume jewelry. Since 1918 on cases and on jewelry since 1908.

Mark of BARNABUS BARNA, Beverly Hills, CA for rings, earrings, charms, bracelets, pins, cuff links, necklaces, tie clips and clasps. First used June 1962

BINDER BROS. INC. New York, NY mark for jewelry cases, lipstick holders, etc. Since May, 1920.

BERNARD BLUM CORPORATION, New York, NY mark for rings, brooches, pendants, bracelets, necklaces, cuff links and earrings. First used 1963

B & C

This is the mark found on clamps and clasps of jewelry made by B & C Mfg. Co., New York, NY. First used 1962

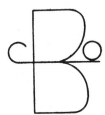

BENJAMIN & CO., New York, NY jewelry mark since 1962

BARONET CREATIONS, New York, NY mark for rings, brooches, necklaces, bracelets, earrings, charms, clasps cuff links and pendants. First used 1962

BEVERLY CREATIVE JEWELERS, Los Angeles, CA used this mark for bracelets, earrings, finger rings, lockets, ornamental pins. First used March 1962

FRED M. BIRCH d.b.a. FRED M. BIRCH CO., Providence, RI mark for costume jewelry and men's jewelry. First used 1962

B & H JEWELRY CO., INC., New York, NY for jewelry, specifically pins, pill boxes, cuff links, bracelets and rings. Since June 1962

Costume jewelry mark of BEATRIX JEWELRY CO., Providence, RI first used 1962

BAUMAN—MASSA JEWELRY CO., St. Louis, MO. Mark for rings, pins, bracelets, chains, necklaces, pearls, emblems. First used 1889.

Jewelry mark of BERNARD ROSS INC., ISLAND PARK, NY since Nov. 1954

BAYARDI BROTHERS, INC., New York, NY used this mark for jewelry. First used 1962

FEDERATED DEPARTMENT STORES, INC., Miami, FL used this mark for pins, rings, clasps, earrings, combs and other costume jewelry. First used 1962

BOUCHER

MARCEL BOUCHER ET CIE of New York, NY marks in use in the 1940s and 50s.

MARCEL BOUCHER ET CIE, New York, NY mark for brooches, bracelets, necklaces, lavalieres, pendants, buckles and finger rings. First used Aug. 1944

Bab's
Kiddie and Doll Jewelry

Mark of GLADYS LESLIE MOORE, New Rochelle, NY for doll jewelry and children's costume jewelry. Since October, 1954.

BABETTE LINE

W & R JEWELRY CO., Attleboro, MA mark for necklaces, rings, earrings, bracelets and other jewelry. Since 1944

Jewelry mark of LIPPMAN, SPIER & HAHN, New York, NY. First used Jan. 1925

BABYFAIR

E.M. ROSENTHAL JEWELRY CO., Washington, D.C. used this mark for jewelry for children particularly rings, lockets, bracelets, crosses, pendants, necklaces, and combs. First used June 1940

Bachelor Button Products

Stuart A. Thompkins d.b.a. BACHELOR BUTTON PRODUCTS, San Francisco, CA for men's jewelry. Since May, 1952.

BAKELAND

ARSENE J. VAN EXEM, New York, NY mark for jewelry made with pearls and artificial stones. First used about July, 1922.

MORRIS BALICER, New York, NY mark for men's jewelry. First used 1922

BALFOUR

L.G. BALFOUR COMPANY, Attleboro, MA for finger rings, emblems, badges, etc. First used December, 1947. The mark has been used for jewelry since 1913.

BALL

Mark of MILDRED L. BALL, Winston-Salem, NC for jewelry. Since February, 1959.

Mark used by UNITED PEARL CORP., New York, NY since June, 1954 for pearl necklaces, chokers, earrings, pins and 'lounge' pearls.

B. A. B.
BALLOU

BETTER RHINESTONE JEWELRY CO.,
Mark, New York, NY, 1940s and 50s.

BALLOU

B. A. BALLOU & CO. INCORPORATED,
Providence, RI, used this mark on bracelets,
brooches, charms, earrings, fob pins and tie
clasps. Also barrettes, belt buckles, bib
holders, lingerie clasps and money clips. This
mark has been in use since 1919, still active
in 1949.

BAMBOO MAGIC

AVON PRODUCTS, INC., New York, NY
mark for jewelry. First used May 1970

BARBARA

GEMEX COMPANY marks for the usual
types of jewelry plus buckles, fobs and
charms. Since March, 1930.

Barbara Lee

THE ASSOCIATED MERCHANDISING
CORP., New York, NY used this mark for
necklaces made with artificial pearls. First
used 1939.

BARBIE

MATTEL INC., HAWTHORNE, CA mark
for combination sets of costume jewelry for
young girls and dolls. First used February
1962

Barclay — ART IN JEWELRY

BARCLAY JEWELRY, INC., Providence,
Rhode Island, mark for earrings, bracelets,
necklaces, chokers, etc. Since May, 1948.

BARJON

M. EDWARD POPE d.b.a. EDDIE POPE &
CO., Altadena, CA mark for necklaces, earrings, tie pins, pendants, bracelets, etc. Since
1961

BARODA

THE R.L. GRIFFITH & SON CO., Providence, RI used this mark both for imitation stones for jewelers' use sold either alone
or mounted in jewelry of the usual types.
First used 1912

BERTHA J. HAIG of B. HAIG, BOSTON
MA used this mark for costume jewelry since
1938

BARTON - NEW YORK

This mark was used by B. HAIG BOSTON,
MASS. for jewelry for personal wear and for
compacts, vanity cases and cigarette cases.
Used since 1938.

BEADS O' PARIDISE

Lee H. Pelzman, d.b.a. LEE PELZMAN
CO., New York, NY Mark for costume
jewelry. Since about December, 1958.

BEAU

BEAUCRAFT, INC., Providence, RI used
this mark for rings, charms, clips, earrings,
bracelets, pins, necklaces and pendants. First
used 1947

BEAU BAIT

HABERMAN, INC., Cincinnati, OH mark
for costume jewelry. First used July 1961

Beau Brummell

S AND S MANUFACTURING Co., Providence, RI mark for all the usual types of
jewelry for men including fobs, belt buckles
and cuff links. Beau Brummell was an arbiter
of English fashion in the early 19th century.
This mark in use since January, 1928.

BEAUCRAFT

BEAUCRAFT, INC., Providence, RI mark for rings, charms, clips, earrings, bracelets, pins, necklaces and pendants. First used 1947

BEAUCRAFT, INC., Providence, RI, for costume jewelry since 1947.

BEAUTIFUL BEGUILERS

Mark of AVON PRODUCTS INC., New York, NY for costume jewelry. First used Oct. 1971

Beautycrest

Mark of J.J. SCHMUKLER & SONS, New York, NY for jewelry. Since June 1930

BEAUZAL

ZAYRE CORP., Natick, Mass., for rings, earrings, necklaces, pins and bracelets. First used April, 1963.

A.C. BECKEN CO., Chicago, IL mark for finger rings, bracelets, pendants, and other jewelry. First used 1934

BEGUILING

Mark of AVON PRODUCTS INC., New York, NY for costume jewelry. First used Jan. 1972

BEJEWELED
by Gaylin

Gaylin Jewelry, New York, NY mark in use since March, 1946 for finger rings, bracelets, brooches, earrings, necklaces and pin clips.

BEL-AIR

BEL—AIR INC., New York, NY used this mark for men's jewelry. Since 1962

bel-cor

BEL-COR, INC., Chicago, Ill, for costume jewelry. Since June 30, 1947.

BELNORD

Costume jewelry mark of SWISS RADIUM & DIAL PAINTING CO., New York, NY. Since May, 1949.

bennard

VARGAS MANUFACTURING CO., Providence, RI mark for jewelry. First used 1969

BENTLEE

Mark used by Ben Felsenthal & Co., New York, NY, for costume jewelry of every type including pendants, necklaces, bracelets, brooches, pins, earrings and rings. First used in July, 1917.

bergère

L. ERBERT & POHS, INC. New York, NY mark for clips, pins, necklaces, bracelets and earrings. First used July, 1947.

JACK J. FELSENFELD, New York, NY mark for natural, cultured and synthetic pearls. In use since September, 1922.

Betsy Ross

Mark of L. HARVEY CLAP & COMPANY, Attleboro, MA for jewelry. Since November, 1931.

Betta

HENRY DURLACHER of LS & L SET-TING CO., New York, NY used this mark for jewelry. Since March 1970

BETTER RHINESTONE JEWELRY CO. Mark. New York, NY. 1940s and 1950s.

BIBETTE

JOSEPH H. MEYER BROS., Brooklyn, NY mark for necklaces. Since June, 1958.

BICKSON

HARRY S. BICK & SON, New York, NY. Mark used for ladies' jewelry, specifically bracelets, brooches, earrings, necklaces and chatelaine pins. First used January, 1948.

BIG NAME BANDS

TRIFARI, KRUSSMAN & FISHEL, INC., New York, NY mark for jewelry. First used 1971

BINNIE CREATIONS, Dearborn, Michigan began to use this mark in May of 1946 for jewelry.

BLACK BEAUTY

CORO, INC. New York, NY mark for all the usual jewelry plus buckles, cigarette cases, compacts, etc. First used July, 1946.

BLACK MAGIC

ELZAC CALIFORNIA JEWELRY CREA-TIONS, Los Angeles, CA mark for jewelry clips, brooches, earrings, lockets and bracelets made of ceramics, lucite and plexiglass. First used July 1943

BLAKRAFT

BLACHER BROTHERS, Providence, RI for earrings, bracelets, bar pins, hat ornaments, brooches. This mark was also used on hand bag frames. First used August, 1924.

Blithe Blossom

CORO, INC. New York, NY for all the usual types of jewelry made by the company. First used March, 1956.

STEIN & ELLBOGAN CO., Chicago, IL for artificial pearls, rings, scarf pins, bar pins, bracelets, brooches, earrings, and necklace clasps. First used 1920

STEIN & ELLBOGEN COMPANY, Chicago, IL for jewelry made with artificial pearls. Since March, 1920.

THE HENSHEL CO., INC, New York, NY mark for finger rings, scarf pins, bar pins, bracelets, brooches, earrings. First used April, 1924.

Blue Danube

CORO INC., New York, NY for the usual types of jewelry. First used January, 1929.

BLUEDROP

Mark of AVON PRODUCTS INC., New York, NY for costume jewelry. First used Nov. 1971

Blue Nocturne

KAUFMAN AND RUDERMAN CO. INC., New York, NY mark for costume jewelry. Used first August, 1946.

WELLS MANUFACTURING CO., Attleboro, MA mark for jewelry. First used 1936

Blue Ribbon

SIG DAWER & CO. INC., New York, NY used this trademark on jewelry beginning May 21, 1929.

BO-PEEP

BAUMAN-MASSA JEWELRY CO., St. Louis, MO. Mark for children's jewelry — namely finger rings, bracelets, brooches, lingerie and beauty pins and necklaces. First used February, 1923.

BOBBLESTONES

PHILIP MORRIS INCORPORATED, New York, NY used this mark for jewelry. First used 1970

Bob O Link

EISENSTADT MANUFACTURING COMPANY, St. Louis, MO for bracelets and parts thereof, made of or plated with precious metal. Since April, 1915.

JEWELS BY BOGOFF

Mark of SPEAR NOVELTY CO., of Chicago, 1940s and 50s.

jewels by
BOGOFF

Mark of JEWELS BY BOGOFF, Chicago, IL for costume jewelry, namely bracelets, necklaces and brooches. Since November, 1946.

BOLITA

FORSTNER CHAIN CORPORATION, Irvington, NY, used this mark for bracelets, scarf pins, ear ornaments, shirt studs, cuff links and watch chains. Since January, 1950.

BONA-FIDE

EISENSTADT MANUFACTURING CO., St. Louis, MO mark for costume rings but also used on fine jewelry. Used since before 1908

BONANZA

WM. R. KATZ CO., Dallas, TX, used this mark for jewelry since July 1965

BONA-FIT

SPEIDEL, d.b.a. SPEIDEL CHAIN CO., Providence, RI for pendants, bracelets, brooches, scarf pins, cuff links, earrings. First used 1913.

Mark used by Morton E. Millis d.b.a. THE BOOKER T. WASHINGTON JEWELRY CO., Brooklyn, NY for costume jewelry. First used July, 1947.

KITTY KELLY SHOE CORPORATION, New York, NY mark for bracelets, necklaces and medallions. First used 1967

BOTAY

PAUL FLATO SALES CORPORATION, New York, NY mark for rings, trinkets, necklaces, bracelets, earrings, brooches and ornamental clips. First used June, 1953.

LINMARK INTERNATIONAL CORP. New York, NY for jewelry incorporating pearls. Since December, 1952.

BRAMSON, INC., Oak Park, IL used this mark for ladies' jewelry namely, rings, bracelets, earrings, brooches, necklaces, hair ornaments, cuff links. First used December, 1932.

BRASON

J. BRAUNSTEIN INC., Philadelphia, PA mark for finger rings, bracelets, ornamental pins, brooches, necklaces, anklets, earrings, pendants and clasps. Since August, 1949.

BRAZILIA FIRE

VARGAS MANUFACTURING COMPANY, Providence, RI, used this mark for jewelry since 1971

THE LAWS I LIVE BY

BRIGGS, BATES & BACON CO., Attleboro, MA used this mark for charms for jewelry items such as necklaces and bracelets. First used about December, 1955.

BRIDALOK

COLONIAL MFG. CO., New York, NY mark for rings, earrings, brooches, bracelets, necklaces, jewelry clips and lockets. First used 1948

Bright-A-Cut

JEWEL-SMITHS, INC., Boston, Mass., mark for rings, ornamental clips, necklaces, ornamental pins, earrings, bracelets, ring mountings and semi-precious and imitation stones. Since June, 1946.

BRILLION

D. SWAROVSKI & CO., of Austria used this mark for jewelry. Since 1962

Mark of BRITE MANUFACTURING CO., Providence, RI for men's and women's costume jewelry. Mark first used about March, 1941.

Brocade

THE WEIDLICH BROS. M'F'G Co., Bridgeport, Conn., used this mark on their silver plated novelties such as cigarette boxes. First used December, 1923.

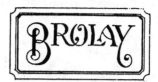

The Costume Jewelry Mark of BROWN, BARZILAY, INC., New York, NY. Used for novelty bead necklaces, bracelets, earrings, pendants and rings. Used since October, 1930.

BRS

MORRIS BRESSMAN d.b.a. MORRIS BRESSMAN JEWELRY MFG. New York, NY mark for brooch pins, charms, bracelets, necklaces, rings, earrings, clips, cuff links, tie clasps. First used June 1962

ROBERT J. CORCORAN, d.b.a. BUBBLE-O-BILL COMPANY, Beverly Hills, CA for medallions, rings, necklaces and bracelets. Since January, 1951.

BUBBLEITE

GALL NOVELTY COMPANY, INC. Dallas, TX for costume jewelry earrings. First used November, 1955.

BUNNY

UNCAS MANUFACTURING CO., Providence, RI mark for finger rings. Since Jan. 1960

THE BURNING BUSH

CAROLE ACCESSORIES, Los Angeles, CA mark for use on both men's and women's jewelry. First used April 1963

Harold Goldkrantz, d.b.a. BURNTWOOD PRODUCTS CO., New York, NY. Mark used for costume jewelry of all the usual types plus cultured and artificial pearls. First used February, 1958.

PHYICHRIS CORP., Providence, RI used this mark for jewelry. First used 1962

RICHTON INTERNATIONAL CORP. New York, NY mark for jewelry since Dec. 1970

HAROLD WEISS d.b.a. CREST JEWELRY CO., New York, NY mark for rings, pendants and other jewelry. First used Sept. 1945

CRAFT RING & FINDING CO., Los Angeles, CA mark for rings and pendants. Since 1962

CARL-ART INC., Providence, Rhode Island mark for all the usual types of jewelry plus cigarette cases, buckles, tie pins, cuff links, crosses, charms. Mark in use since January, 1937.

COLLISION BROS. Philadelphia, PA mark for rings, bracelets, pendants, pins and brooches. First used May 1962

Mark of ALLAN L. SELTZER of CHATHAM CREATIONS, Providence, RI for jewelry. First used about Jan. 1962

JAMES J. BURKE CO., St. Louis, MO, for rings and ring mountings. Since 1952

THE CURTMAN CO., INC., Providence RI used this mark for costume jewelry. First used April, 1950.

CATHAY CRAFTS CORP. New York, NY mark for earrings, bracelets, pins, charms, rings, pendants, and other jewelry. Since June 1962

Costume jewelry mark of CHARLES MFG. CO., INC. Providence, RI used since May 1962

C.T.

CHEEVER, TWEEDY & CO., INC., North Attleboro, Mass. used this mark for jewelry and claimed use since 1880.

CINER MANUFACTURING CO., New York, NY mark for gold ring mountings, stone rings, scarf pins, necklaces, bracelets and earrings, lavalieres. Also for diamond rings and platinum rings. Since Jan. 1914

CABALLEROS De DIMAS-ALANG, INC., San Francisco, Calif. mark for ornamental pins, fobs, finger rings, brooches, lavaliers, watch fobs and watch charms. Since January, 1921.

CADILLAC

This mark was used by PARKWAY MANUFACTURING COMPANY, Providence, RI for costume jewelry. Since March, 1960.

CADORO

CADORO, New York, NY used this mark for jewelry since 1955

CALF-LINKS

JOSEPH J. MCDERMOTT, New York, NY mark for beads, chains, bracelets. First used February, 1956.

Mark of NATHANIAL M. KIRSCHNER, Los Angeles, California for its rings, buckles, clasps, pendants, brooches, charms, etc. which were plated with gold or silver. Mark in use since March, 1931.

CALLING CARD

FUTURE HOUSE, INC. Omaha, NE used this mark for decorative articles of jewelry. First used July, 1955.

CORO, INC., New York, NY, mark for necklaces, bracelets, lockets, chatelaines, fobs, hair barettes, rings, brooches, charms and jewelry clips. Since 1957.

CAMBRIDGE

Another mark of SIMON GOLUB & SONS, INC., for men's costume jewelry including money clips and cuff links and dress sets. Since May 1963

This CANASTA mark was used by SPERRY MFG. CO., Providence, RI for bracelets, charm bracelets, watch bracelets, rings, scatter pins, breast pins, lapel pins, brooches, pendants, necklaces and earrings. Since March, 1948.

CANASTA

CASTLEMARK, New York, NY, used this mark for brooches, earrings, bracelets, and necklaces since September, 1949.

CANDIDA

Another WILLIAM RAND OF NEW YORK mark, also used on synthetic pearls and costume jewelry dating from November, 1946.

CANDLELIGHT

WEINREICH BROTHERS COMPANY, New York, NY, mark for pearl jewelry for personal wear. Since December, 1947.

HICKOK MANUFACTURING CO., INC. Rochester, NY. Buckles, cuff links, etc. Since May, 1954.

BAUMAN-MASSA JEWELRY COMPANY, St. Louis, MO mark for all the usual kinds of jewelry and compacts. Since January, 1935.

CARESS

WEINREICH BROTHERS COMPANY, New York, NY for pearl jewelry. Since March, 1949.

CARIBBEAN SUMMER

AVON PRODUCTS, INC., New York, NY mark for jewelry since May 1970

Car-Mates

JOSEPH M. RUBIN & SONS, Gloversville, NY for cuff links, tie pins and earrings since May 1955

Samuel Rosen d.b.a. CRESCENT JEWELRY COMPANY, Richmond, VA. Mark for costume jewelry including necklaces and bracelets. Since December, 1952.

BRIGGS, BATES & BACON CO., Attleboro, MA for expansion bracelets, ornamental pins, pendants, earrings and watch bracelets. First used 1950

CARMEN

ASSOCIATED ATTLEBORO MANUFACTURERS, INC., Attleboro, MA for bracelets. First used December, 1900.

Carnegie

HATTIE CARNEGIE, INC., New York, NY used this mark for bracelets, brooches, pins, earrings, pendants, finger and scarf rings, lockets, lavallieres, breast pins, necklaces, jeweled hair ornaments, jeweled shoe buckles, jeweled cases and holders. First used January, 1919.

Carol Antell

CAROL ANTELL, New York, NY used this mark for Costume Jewelry, namely brooches, pins, earrings, rings, anklets, bracelets and charms. Mark first used January, 1943.

CAROL BRENT

MONTGOMERY WARD & CO., INCORP., Chicago, IL used this mark for simulated pearl jewelry. Since April 1, 1961

Mark of MACK HENFIELD & SONS, INC., Cleveland, OH for costume jewelry - necklaces, bracelets, pins, brooches and finger rings. First used March, 1953.

CAROL-DEB COMPANY, Pawtucket, RI for hair ornaments, necklaces, pendants, chokers, earrings, brooches, lapel pins, ornamental pins and clips, bracelets and rings. First used April, 1949.

CAROL—DEB CO., Pawtucket, RI mark for hair ornaments, necklaces, pendants, chokers, earrings, brooches, pins, clips, bracelets and rings. Since April 1949

CAROL-DEB

CAROL-DEB CO.

CAROL—DEB CO., of East Providence, RI, used these marks in the 1940s and 50s.

CAROL WESTLAKE

Carol Westlake Molitor d.b.a. CAROL WESTLAKE ORIGINALS, Cincinnati, OH used this mark for jewelry since February, 1954.

CAROLE ACCESSORIES, Los Angeles, CA used this mark for costume jewelry, namely rings, necklaces, bracelets, pins, earrings, pendants, sweater guards and tiaras. First used July 1962

CAROUSEL

GEMEX CORPORATION, Union NJ for watch bracelets. Since October, 1955.

GARRACA

COHN & ROSENBERGER, INC., New York, NY. Mark used for necklaces and bracelets, finger rings, earrings, jewelry clips, brooches, lockets and the following made wholly or partly of precious metal or plated with the same — beads, pins, hat ornaments, hair ornaments, holders for face powder compacts, comb cases, cigarette cases, fancy cigarette boxes, fancy buckles and jewelry initials. First used January, 1940.

CARSTA

CARSTA JEWELRY COMPANY, Providence, RI for brooches, earrings, pins, bracelets, lockets, pendants and necklaces, all made of precious and semi-precious metal. Since January, 1946.

Casino

JOSEPH H. MEYER BROS., Brooklyn, NY mark first used January, 1945 for necklaces, bracelets, finger rings, jewelry clips, brooches and earrings.

CASSANDRA

CASTLECLIFF, INC., New York, NY mark for jewelry using simulated pearls, including necklaces, bracelets, pins, earrings, etc. First used October, 1957.

BURT CASSELL

BURT CASSELL, INC., Providence, RI used this mark for costume jewelry beginning 1953

CASTLE

J. R. WOOD & SONS, INC., New York, NY for jewelry since April, 1931.

CATHE JEWELS INC., Torrence, CA for costume jewelry. First used January, 1961.

DOLAN & BULLOCK., Providence, RI, for men's jewelry since October, 1954.

CAVU

CAVU CO., DOWNEY, CALIFORNIA, used this mark for bracelets and chokers since October, 1945.

STEIN & ELLBOGEN CO., Chicago, IL for jewelry and novelties. The usual jewelry as well as fans, jewel cases, vanity cases, canes, powder boxes, perfume atomizers and bottles, shoe buckles and combs. First used July, 1925.

CHEEVER, TWEEDY & CO. INC., No. Attleboro, MA mark for jewelry for personal wear or adornment. Used since August, 1945.

CHINA OVERSEAS, NEW YORK, NY for jewelry of personal wear, since October, 1945.

Cellini

CORO, INC., New York, NY for all the usual jewelry plus jewelry made with pearls. First used January, 1942.

CELLINI

Mark of AUTOMATIC GOLD CHAIN COMPANY, Providence, RI for jewelry. First used February, 1930.

KATZ & OGUSH, INC., New York, NY mark for all the usual jewelry types as well as vanity cases, shoe buckles and cigarette cases. First used April, 1923.

WILLIAM B. OGUSH, INC., New York, NY for all the usual types of jewelry as well as shoe buckles, snaps and veil pins. First used December, 1950.

Cézanne

JOSEPH H. MEYER BROS., Brooklyn, NY mark for beads, necklaces, earrings and ear clips. Since April, 1957.

CHA-CHA

This mark was used by Joseph O. Morrissey, d.b.a. DAMBALA CO., St. Louis, MO for costume jewelry. Since March, 1959.

CHALET

Mark of Max Petschek d.b.a. PETSCHEK, New York, NY for jewelry for personal wear. First used April, 1929.

Chamberlain's Necklace

JOHN RUBEL of JOHN RUBEL, CO., New York, NY mark for brooches, bracelets, necklaces, lavalieres, pendants and buckles. First used 1943

CHAMPION

TAUNTON PEARL WORKS INC., Taunton, MA for tie clasps, pins, etc. Since January, 1921.

CHANEL

Mark of CHANEL INC., New York, NY for necklaces. First used 1914.

CHAMPS-ELYSEES

AMERICAN & CONTINENTAL PATENTED PRODUCTS, INC., New York, NY mark for necklaces, bracelets, rings, earrings, jewelry clips, brooches, lockets pins and hair ornaments, compacts comb cases and frames, fancy cigarette boxes, fancy buckles and jewelry initials. Used since Jan. 1941

CHAREL

Mark of CHAREL JEWELRY CO., INC., Brooklyn, NY for costume jewelry including necklaces, bracelets, earrings, pins and clasps. First used July, 1945.

CHARLES OF THE RITZ

LANVIN—CHARLES of THE RITZ, INC., New York, NY mark for jewelry. First used at least as early as March 1958

CHARLOTTE

One of many marks of GEMEX COMPANY, Newark, NJ for watch bracelets and straps. This mark was also used for bracelets, scarf pins, finger rings, belt buckles and ear and hair ornaments. First used October, 1929.

Charm Girl

ORIGINALITIES OF NEW YORK, INC., Long Island City, NY, for children's bracelets and necklaces. First used August, 1953.

CHARMBELS

ASSOCIATED MANUFACTURERS, Providence, RI. Mark for brooches, earrings, pins, bracelets, lockets, pendants, and necklaces all made of precious or semi-precious metal. Mark first used December 1, 1945.

CHARMERS

CORO, INC, New York, NY mark for all their usual jewelry. First used April, 1959.

CHATTER PINS

CORO INC., New York, NY mark for all the usual types of jewelry as well as beads, pins, hat ornaments, comb cases and jewelry initials. Also pearl necklaces, pearl bracelets and pearl earrings. Used since 1948

Cherubin

CORO, INC. used this mark for all its usual types of jewelry since May, 1956.

Chez Lindelle

LOUIS KIPNIS & SONS INC., New York, NY. Mark for costume jewelry - pins, clips and brooches. First used February, 1949.

Chi-Chi

DAVETTE PRODUCTS, INC., Clayton, MO. Mark for jewelry - namely pins and clips. First used June, 1955.

CHIFFON

MARVELLA, INC., New York, NY mark for jewelry. First used January, 1941.

RICHARD E. WEINREICH of WEINREICH BROTHERS CO., New York, NY for jewelry and jewelry made with pearls. First used Jan. 1941

CHINA OVERSEAS, New York, NY mark for all the usual types of jewelry for personal wear. Since Feb. 1944

"America's Jewels of Tomorrow-Today"

CHRISTY M. DELMAS, New York, NY mark for jewelry - finger rings, bracelets necklaces, brooches, lockets, lavalieres, scarf pins, and jewel boxes. First used Sept. 1946

Churchill Downs

CORO, INC. mark for charms and charm bracelets. Since February, 1960.

BLANCARD & COMPANY INC., New York, NY, for rings, earrings, lockets, etc. First used August, 1928.

CINDERELLA

BLANCARD & COMPANY, INC., New York, NY for rings, earrings, lockets, bracelets, brooches, charms, necklaces, buckles and mountings. First used August, 1928.

CINER

CINER MANUFACTURING COMPANY, New York, NY, mark for rings, earrings, necklaces, bracelets, and ornamental pins and clips. Since 1892.

ANSON, INCORPORATED, Providence RI used this mark for men's jewelry. Since December, 1952.

DICKSON MFG. CO., Providence, RI mark for ornamental pins, brooches, necklaces, pendants, finger rings, hair ornaments, bracelets, lockets, earrings, neck chains, arm bands, fobs, buckles, cigarette cases, and ornamental trimmings. First used Aug. 1946

CIRO

CIRO PEARLS LIMITED, London, England (Ciro of Bond Street, Inc., New York, NY) mark for rings jeweled pins, earrings, necklaces, tie-pins, brooches, bracelets, decorative studs and cuff links (all being articles of imitation jewelry) and imitation pearls. First used May 1917

CIRO PEARLS LTD., London, England. Mark for imitation pearls, and reconstructed gems. Since Sept. 1916

Ciro

CIRO OF BOND STREET INC., New York, NY used this mark for all kinds of jewelry. First used 1938

Ciro

CIRO of BOND STREET, INC., New York, NY mark for watches. Since 1921

CIROLITE

CIRO OF BOND STREET, INC., New York, NY mark for jewelry containing both synthetic and semi-precious stones. First used 1970

CLAIROL

Mark of CLAIROL INC. New York, NY for jewelry. First used January, 1962.

Clasper

EISENSTADT MANUFACTURING COMPANY, St. Louis, MO, mark for bracelet and wristlets. Used since March, 1923.

Claudette

PREMIER JEWELRY CO., INC. New York, NY mark for costume jewelry. First used December, 1945.

CleO

CLARENCE E. EDSON, Cleveland, OH mark for jewelry with artificial pearls. Since January, 1921.

CLEO

KLEIN & MULLER INC, New York, NY for ladies jewelry - bracelets, necklaces, earrings, rings, charm bracelets, anklettes, tiaras, etc. First used January, 1959.

Cleopatra

CORO, INC., New York, NY mark for all the usual types of jewelry plus pearls, beads, pins and jewelry initials. Since 1959

CLICK-O

WM. FISHER, New York, NY mark for clasp fasteners. First used June, 1922.

Click OF THE MONTH

DAVID GRAD COMPANY, New York, NY for COSTUME JEWELRY since October, 1945.

Clip-Ease

CORO, INC., New York, NY mark for necklaces, bracelets, rings, earrings, jewelry clips, brooches, lockets, etc. Since January, 1941.

CLIP-EASE

COHN & ROSENBERGER, INC., New York, NY used this mark for all the usual types of jewelry plus beads, pins, hat ornaments, hair ornaments, compacts, fancy buckles and jewelry initials. Since January 1941

HARRY MORRIS ASSOCIATES, Chicago, IL mark for necklaces, bracelets, brooches, lavalieres, earrings, pendants, used since Dec. 1944

Cloudrift

CORO, INC., New York, NY mark for necklaces, bracelets, rings, earrings, clips, lockets, beads, pins, ornaments for hats and hair and jewelry initials. First used Jan. 1950

CLIP-MATES

TRIFARI, KURSSMAN AND FISHEL INC., New York, NY used this mark for jewelry - dress clips. First used July, 1936.

CLIPPER

TAUNTON PEARL WORKS, Taunton, Mass., for men's jewelry. Since May, 1944.

CLIMATEST

FORSTNER CHAIN CORPORATION, Irvington, NJ for usual types of jewelry including bracelets, scarf pins, etc. Since December, 1949.

W & H JEWELRY CO., INC., Providence, RI, for the usual jewelry types as well as compacts, cigarette cases and hair ornaments. First used 1940.

COBB

W.R. COBB CO., Providence, RI for clasps, mountings, swivels, safety catches. First used August, 1957.

COCKTAIL SET

CORO, INC., New York, NY mark in use since December, 1947 for necklaces, bracelets, earrings, jewelry clips, brooches, lockets and the following articles made in whole or in part of precious metals or plated with precious metals: beads, ornamental hat pins, hat ornaments; holders for face powder such as compacts, comb cases and jewelry initials.

Coeur de Feu

ILLINOIS WATCH CASE CO., operating under the name ELGIN AMERICAN DIVISION OF ILLINOIS WATCH CASE CO., Elgin, IL used this mark for simulated pearl bracelets, necklaces, earrings and brooches since Aug. 1950

COHN & ROSENBERGER, INC., New York, NY mark for all the usual types of jewelry plus beads, pins, hat ornaments, hair ornaments, holders for face powder, compacts, comb cases, cigarette cases, fancy buckles and jewelry initials. First used July 1939. This mark re-published by Coro.

COLETT'S

Mark of VINCENT COLETTA of COLLET'S Jewelry, Johnston, RI, for jewelry. First used 1963

COLLECTABLES

Mark of Ronald H. Taub d.b.a. COLLECTABLES, Chicago, IL for jewelry. First used Oct. 1964

COLLEGIATE

Another CORO mark used on their jewelry line which included compacts and cigarette boxes and comb cases. Since about 1940.

COLONIAL BEAD CO., INC., New York, NY used this mark for necklaces, earrings, brooches, bracelets and jewelry pins trimmed with beads. This mark used since 1937

COLONIAL

COLONIAL BEAD CO., INC., New York, NY mark for necklaces, earrings, brooches, bracelets and other jewelry trimmed with beads. Mark used since 1920

COLONIAL

COLONIAL BEAD CO., INC., New York, NY mark for jewelry. First used 1920

COLOR à la CARTE

CORO, INC., New York, NY for necklaces, bracelets and the usual jewelry including pearls. Also beads, pins and jewelry initials made in whole or in part of plated precious metals or plated with same. Since May, 1959.

COLORAMA

CORO, INC., New York, NY mark for all the usual types of jewelry. This mark was first used November, 1954.

THE STYLIST SPRAYERS CO., New York, NY mark for articles of jewelry - pins, necklaces, watches, earrings. First used August, 1955.

COLOSSA

Mark of MARVELLA PEARLS, INC., New York, NY for costume jewelry, pearl jewelry and bead jewelry. First used June, 1958.

COLUMBIA

WALTER B. DORRER d.b.a. Higbee & Dorrer, Los Angeles, CA mark for pearls. First used May, 1954.

COLTURA

ARKE, INC., New York, NY used this mark for costume jewelry such as necklaces, bracelets, earrings, clips, pins, cuff links, hair ornaments. First used June 1960

COME SUMMER

Mark of AVON PRODUCTS INC., New York, NY for costume jewelry. First used Dec. 1971

COMET

D. SWAROWSKI & CO., Austria. Mark for imitation jewelry - artificial precious stones and beads made of glass or plastics. First used October, 1957.

MARVEL JEWELRY MFG. CO., Providence, RI, used this mark for jewelry since 1942, especially expansion bracelets.

[OMMERCIAL

KATZ & OGUSH INC., New York, NY for rings, bar pins, scarf pins, bracelets, sautoirs, earrings, necklaces, etc. First used July, 1923.

COMPELLING

Mark of AVON PRODUCTS INC., New York, NY for costume jewelry. First used Oct. 1971

COMPLEXION - TONE

SOL E. WEINREICH of WEINREICH BROS., New York, NY mark for pearls. Since Jan. 1940

COMTESSE

ERNEST K. HIRSCH, Greensboro, NC mark for costume jewelry, namely bracelets, necklaces, earrings, brooches, rings, and compacts. First used 1959

CONCORD MANUFACTURING CORP. Providence, RI used this mark for jewelry findings. Since 1950

CONCORD

CONCORD MANUFACTURING CORP. Providence, RI jewelry mark. First used 1945

CONCRAFT

CONCORD CRAFTSMAN, INC., Brighton, MA used this mark for jewelry beginning April 1962

CONSTELLATION

CORO, INC., New York, NY. Mark for necklaces, bracelets, finger rings, etc. Used since March, 1946.

CONSUELO

GEMEX COMPANY marks for the usual types of jewelry plus buckles, fobs and charms.. First used March, 1930.

ALBION JEWELERS, Chicago IL used this mark for costume jewelry - pins, necklaces, earrings and bracelets made of base metal and plated with precious metal. Mark used since May, 1955.

CONTESSA

CORO, INC., New York, NY mark for the usual types of jewelry. In use since 1952.

CONVERTIPEARL

ELMER ELLSWORTH AND SON, Tulsa, OK for pearl jewelry. First used October, 1955.

Mark of SAMUEL PLATZER of SAMUEL PLATZER CO., New York, NY for all types of jewelry. First used July 1939

COPLEY CREATIONS

SAMUEL PLATZER CO., INC., New York, NY mark for jewelry used since 1939

COPPERWOOD

RENOIR OF CALIFORNIA, INC., Los Angeles, CA for costume jewelry. Since June, 1959.

COQUETTE

CORO mark for all the usual jewelry as well as cases for cigarettes, combs and powder compacts. Also fancy buckles. First used October, 1945.

COQUILLE DE MER

Another JOSEPH H. MEYER BROS., Brooklyn, NY mark for simulated pearl necklaces and earrings. Since January, 1958.

CORNELIA'S JEWELS

SHIMAN MANUFACTURING CO., Newark, NJ used this mark for rings, pins, brooches, earrings and clips since Dec. 1961

CORELLE

RICHTON INTERNATIONAL CORP. New York, NY mark for jewelry since about April 1971

CORELLE

RICHTON INTERNATIONAL CORP., New York, NY mark for jewelry beginning 1963

for that priceless look

CORO, INC., New York, NY. Mark for pearl necklaces, pearl earrings, pearl bracelets, pearl brooches, pearl rings, pearls and jewelry for personal wear such as necklaces, bracelets, earrings, jewelry clips, brooches, lockets and the following made wholly or partly of precious metals or plated with same — beads, pins, hat ornaments, holders for face powder compacts, comb cases, fancy cigarette boxes, fancy buckles and jewelry initials. Mark used since January, 1944.

CORO, INC., New York, NY mark for watches. First used in 1940

CORO, INC., New York, NY, and Providence, RI, mark for brooches, necklaces, bracelets, finger rings, earrings, lockets and the following goods made in whole or part of precious metals or plated with the same; beads, pins, hat ornaments, comb cases, jewelry initials; and strings of pearls. Mark used first in July, 1919.

CORO, INC., New York, NY mark for bracelets, jewelry clips, brooches, lockets and the following made in whole or in part or plated with precious metal – beads, ornamental pins, hat ornaments, compacts, comb cases and jewelry initials, pearl necklaces, pearl bracelets and pearl earrings and brooches. First used June, 1945.

CORO INC., NEW YORK, NY for necklaces, bracelets, finger rings, earrings, jewelry clips, brooches, lockets, imitation pearls and pearl necklaces and the following goods made in whole or in part of precious metals or plated with the same: beads, pins, hat ornaments, holders for powder compacts, comb cases and jewelry initials. Since June, 1945.

CORO, INC., New York, NY for necklaces, bracelets, rings, earrings, jewelry clips, brooches, lockets, etc. First used March, 1938.

Coro

COHN & ROSENBERGER, INC., New York, NY mark for chain and bead necklaces, imitation pearls, slipper and belt buckles, shirt studs, bar pins, brooches, hat pins, watch chains, watch charms, finger rings, bracelets, hair ornaments, vanity cases, lavallieres, these are made of, or plated with, or mounted in, precious metals, i.e. Sheffield silver, sterling silver and gold plate on brass foundation. First used July, 1919.

CORO-CLAD
CORO-KLAD

CORO INC., New York, NY mark for jewelry since June, 1965

CORO, INC., New York, NY used this mark for 'fashion' watches. First used October 1958

CORO, INC., New York, NY mark for necklaces, finger rings, earrings, jewelry clips, brooches, lockets, charms, charm bracelets, fobs, jewelry initials, pearls and other jewelry for personal use. First used March, 1938.

Corocraft

This CORO, INC., New York, NY mark has been used since March, 1938 for the usual jewelry types as well as jewelry with pearls.

Coro Craft

COHN & ROSENBERGER, INC., New York, NY mark for all the usual Coro jewelry plus compacts, comb and cigarette cases, fancy cigarette boxes, fancy buckles and jewelry initials. First used about 1935.

COHN & ROSENBERGER, INC., New York, NY mark for all the usual types of jewelry as well as beads, hat ornaments, hair ornaments, compacts, comb cases, cigarette cases, fancy cigarette boxes and jewelry initials. First used Jan. 1937

Coro Elegante

CORO INC., New York, NY for pearl necklaces, pearl earrings, pearl bracelets, pearl brooches, pearl rings, pearls and other jewelry for personal wear. Used since January, 1944.

Coro Magic

This mark was used by CORO, INC., New York, NY for all the usual types of jewelry including pearls. First used February, 1960.

Coro Originals

CORO, INC., New York, NY used this mark for necklaces, bracelets, earrings, jewelry clips, brooches, lockets and the following made in whole or in part or plated with precious metal - beads, ornamental pins, hat ornaments, powder compacts, comb cases and jewelry initials. Since August, 1947.

A Coro Original

CORO, INC., New York, NY mark for ornamental pins, jewelry clips, hair ornaments, charms, dress ornaments, beads, as well as all the usual type jewelry and tiaras, pearls and lockets. First used June 1947

COHN & ROSENBERGER, INC., New
York, NY. Mark for necklaces and bracelets,
earrings, jewelry clips, brooches, lockets and
other jewelry made wholly or partly plated
with precious metal. Mark used since 1932,
still in use in 1944.

Coro Supreme

CORO, INC., New York, NY for pearl
necklaces, pearls and jewelry of all types for
personal wear. Mark used since June, 1943.

CORO-TEENS

CORO, INC., New York, NY for necklaces,
bracelets, earrings, jewelry clips, brooches,
and lockets. Mark also used for other jewelry
made wholly or partly of or plated with
precious metal. Since 1940.

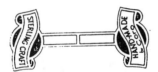

CORO, INC., New York, NY mark for
necklaces, bracelets and other jewelry as well
as for pearls, beads, pins and initials. First
used September, 1941.

CORO, INCORPORATED of New York,
NY mark for jewelry. First used May 1965

Corochrome

CORO, INC., New York, NY mark for
necklaces, bracelets, earrings, jewelry clips,
brooches, charms and the following which
were plated with precious metal; beads, pins
and jewelry initials. First used May, 1957.

COROGRAMS

CORO, INC., New York, NY, mark for
jewelry initials. Since April, 1922.

COHN & ROSENBERGER, INC., New
York, NY for all the usual CORO jewelry
as well as vanity cases, puff boxes and
jewelry sets. First used about 1923.

CORONADO

UNCAS MANUFACTURING COM-
PANY, Providence RI for men's and
women's jewelry. First used August, 1955.

CORONATION

MERCHANDISER'S ASSOCIATION,
INC., Chicago, IL used this mark for
bracelets, earrings, scatter pins, and also on
clasps and Shriner and Masonic pins. First
used February 1965

Coroteens

Mark of CORO, INC., New York, NY for
all types of jewelry and finger rings and ring
mountings. Jewelry of all types made with
pearls, cultured and simulated. Since March,
1951.

Corotots

CORO, INC., New York, NY mark for all
the usual jewelry types as well as charms and
charm bracelets, and pearls. Also beads, pins
and jewelry initials. First used March 1941

CORSAIR

AUTOMATIC GOLD CHAIN COM-
PANY, Providence, RI changed to
SPEIDEL CORPORATION and used this
mark for jewelry. July, 1931.

COSMORAMA

Mark of AVON PRODUCTS INC., New
York, NY for costume jewelry. First used
Oct. 1971

COSTUMAKERS

LIDZ BROTHERS, INC., New York, NY
for costume jewelry. Since January, 1958.

LIDZ BROTHERS, INC., New York, NY. Mark for buttons buckles and articles of jewelry such as pins, brooches, clips, apparel slides, slide fasteners and necklaces. June, 1945.

COTILLION

Mark of COTILLION, INC., New York, NY for costume jewelry of plastic and non-precious metals: bracelets, pins, necklaces, earrings and clips. First used January, 1943.

E. COPLAN SONS., Baltimore, MD for ornamental cuff links and tie clasps. First used March, 1955.

COURT JESTER

CORO mark for all its usual jewelry in addition to tiaras, hat ornaments and pearl jewelry. First used January, 1955.

LEO GLASS & COMPANY, INC., New York, NY. First used in March, 1946 for costume jewelry including necklaces, bracelets, earrings, brooches, clips, lockets, rings and chatelaines.

"COVER GIRL"

LEFCOURTE COSMETICS CO., NEW YORK, NY used this mark for costume jewelry including brooches, bracelets, earrings, necklaces, rings, jewelry clips, jewelry initials, beads, belt buckles, and plated hair ornaments, hair ornaments, holders for cosmetics, compacts, combs and comb cases, cigarette boxes and match boxes. May, 1944.

Used since July 1945, by REVOC, INC., NEW YORK, NY, for jewelry such as bar pins, lapel pins, brooches, finger rings, earrings, ankle bracelets, charms, chokers, necklaces and hair ornaments.

VARGAS MANUFACTURING COMPANY, Providence, RI. Mark used for children's jewelry including pendants, necklaces, pins, bracelets and finger rings. Since September 5, 1946.

THE CRAFT COMPANY, Indianapolis, IN for finger rings, ornamental buttons, charms, fobs and earrings. First used August, 1904.

CRAFTMAID MANUFACTURING CO., INC. Brooklyn, NY. This mark was used for costume jewelry and novelty pins, earrings, and bracelets and imitation semi-precious and non-precious stones. Used since April, 1945.

CREA

CREA-D'OR Jewelry Inc., New York, NY mark for brooch pins, charms, bracelets, rings, necklaces, earrings, clips and cuff links. Since 1962

CROCODILE GRIP

HICKOK MANUFACTURING COMPANY, INC. Rochester, NY used this mark for necktie holders, belt buckles, money holders and key holders beginning July, 1946.

Crosby

A. COHEN & SONS CORP., New York. NY mark for bracelets, lockets, rings, brooches, crosses and men's jewelry. First used 1931

CROSBY

A. COHEN & SONS CORP. New York, NY mark for the usual jewelry as well as pearls, jewel boxes and religious emblems. Since April 1937

CROWN PRINCE

WEINREICH BROTHERS, CO., New York, NY mark for pearl jewelry. Since June, 1949.

CORO, INC., of New York, NY used this mark for jewelry. First in 1965

The Crusader

J.J. WHITE MFG. CO., Providence, RI used this mark on base metal or base metal plated with precious metal. First used June, 1923.

CRYSTALETTE

JOSEPH H. MEYER BROS., Brooklyn, NY used this mark for necklaces and earrings. Since December, 1957.

CRYSTALIA

D. LISNER & CO., New York, NY mark for jewelry. First used 1926

CRYSTYLE

Jewelry mark of DAVID J. DAWSON, New York, NY. First used June 1965

CUFF-PACT

S. PACKALES & CO., New York, NY mark for costume jewelry - bracelets equipped with lipstick and other make-up compartments. Since July, 1947.

CULTIQUE

HELLER-SPERRY INC., New York, NY used this mark for simulated and cultured pearls. Since May, 1957.

CULTURESQUE

Mark of HASKELL FABER d.b.a. CHATANI PEARL CO., Los Angeles, CA for jewelry made with simulated pearls as well as cultured pearls. First used 1965

HASKELL FABER d.b.a. CHATANI PEARL CO., Los Angeles, CA mark for earrings, necklaces, and other types of jewelry made with simulated pearls as well as cultured pearls. First used Feb. 1965.

CULTURETTE

MANON PEARLS, New York, NY mark for earrings and necklaces made of simulated pearls and stones. First used Oct. 1959

Cupid

BARODA PEARL CO., INC., New York, NY for jewelry made with artificial pearls. First used October, 1923.

Ā
Curtis
Creation

THE CURTMAN COMPANY, INC. Providence, Rhode Island mark used on bracelets, chains, brooches, lockets, necklaces and pins. First used March, 1941.

Mark of CURTIS JEWELRY MANUFAC-
TURING COMPANY INC., Providence,
RI for jewelry clasps, bracelets, lockets,
necklaces, pendants, brooches, jewelry pins
and earrings. First used May, 1951.

ANDERSON TOOL & DIE WORKS, INC.
Providence, RI. Mark for ornamental
jewelry, buckles, collar holders, cuff links.
First used February, 1947.

CZARINA

CORO INC., New York, NY mark for
necklaces, bracelets, rings, earrings jewelry
clips and lockets. First used Jan. 1950

DIAMOND—ITE INTERNATIONAL,
INC., New York, NY mark for necklaces,
earrings, jewelry clips, pendants, brooches,
lockets, rings, charm bracelets, and charms,
etc. First used May 1960

CORLETTO, INC., New York, NY mark
for all types of jewelry including brooch pins,
charms, bracelets, rings, necklaces, earrings,
clips, cuff links, tie bars and pendants. First
used June 1962

CURTIS JEWELRY MANUFACTUR-
ING COMPANY, INC., Providence, RI
mark for jewelry clasps, bracelets, lockets,
necklaces, pendants, brooches, jewelry pins
and earrings. First used 1950

DONLEY MANUFACTURING CO.,
INC., North Attleboro, MA mark for pendants, pins, lockets, rings, bracelets and earrings. First used 1962

DAVID FRIEDMAN & SONS, New York,
NY used on jewelry for personal wear. First
used September, 1955.

DGS

DAVID G. STEVEN, INC., New York, NY
mark for necklaces, bracelets, earrings, clips,
pendants, charms and rings. First used 1958

DAVID FELBERBAUM d.b.a. D.F.
JEWELRY SPRING VALLEY, New York,
NY mark for jewelry. Since June 1962

D M C

Daniel Malachuk d.b.a. DANMAL CREA-
TIONS, Plainfield, NJ for costume jewelry.
First used April, 1956.

DPL

DIPLOMAT JEWELRY MANUFAC-
TURING CORP., New York, NY mark for
rings, charms, earrings, pendants, brooches
and bracelets. First used 1964

DS

DAVE SCHNEIDER WHOLESALE
MANUFACTURING JEWELERS, Long
Beach, CA for jewelry. First used 1946

DAVE SCHNEIDER wholesale mfg.
jewelers, Long Beach, CA used this mark for
rings, pins, and other jewelry. Since June
1946

ERNEST LOWENSTEIN, INC., New York, NY for imitation gems and cut glass bodies adapted for use in the manufacture of costume jewelry and accessories, novelty items and general ornamental purposes. First used February, 1949.

D. SWAROVSKI & CO., of AUSTRIA in 1960 claimed priority on this mark for both genuine and imitation stones.

Mark of D. SWAROVSKI & CO., Tyrol, Austria for both genuine and imitation gems. 1961

DAVID P. BARRY, CORP., New York, NY for jewelry - buckles, cuff links, collar holders, etc. First used about February, 1947.

D'eri

JEWELS BY D'ERI, INC., Providence, RI for hat ornaments, hair ornaments and the usual jewelry. First used September, 1951.

This mark was used by DAVE L. RUBIN, Houston, Texas from March, 1943, for rings, pins, earrings, etc.

Danté

SHIELDS INC., of Attleboro, MA used this mark for men's jewelry. First used July 1960

DAILY DOUBLE

CORO mark for necklaces, bracelets, earrings, etc. as well as jewelry with pearls and hair and hat ornaments. Since April, 1951.

H. WEINREICH CO., Philadelphia, PA for bracelets, earrings, rings, lockets, necklaces, ornamental pins, anklets and barrettes. First used March, 1952.

Daintymode

B. A. BALLOU & CO., INC. Providence, Rhode Island, used this mark for its garment supporting shoulder straps made wholly or partly of precious metal. First used September, 1923.

DAISIES WON'T TELL

Mark of AVON PRODUCTS INC., New York, NY for costume jewelry. First used Oct. 1971

Dancing Birds

JOHN RUBEL CO., New York, NY mark for brooches, bracelets, necklaces, lavalieres, pendants and buckles. First used August, 1943.

DANECRAFT

Mark of FELCH & CO., Providence, RI for jewelry. First used June, 1938.

DANIELLE

DANVIN, INC., New York, NY mark for costume jewelry. First used June, 1953.

Ernest Albert Buck d.b.a. DARIUS, New York, NY for costume jewelry - necklaces, bracelets, brooches, ornamental pins, lockets, pendants, earrings. First used September, 1945.

DASON

DAVIDSON & SONS JEWELRY CO., INC., New York, NY used this mark for finger rings, pendants, brooches, bracelets, etc. all made in whole or in part, or plated with, precious metal. First used March, 1936.

DateTimer

MARVELLA PEARLS, INC., New York, NY for necklaces, bracelets, earrings, brooches and charms. First used June, 1956.

DATING REGULAR

David Karp Company d.b.a. HAND KRAFT, New York, NY for all the usual types of jewelry including belt buckles. First used September, 1958.

Mark of O.S. DAVIGNON CO., North Attleboro, MA for jewelry. Used since Jan. 1947

Dawn-Glo

MARK DOTTENHEIM, New York, NY, mark for pearl jewelry. Since October, 1919.

DAY and NIGHT

COHN & ROSENBERGER, INC., New York, NY for all the usual type jewelry as well as compacts and cigarette cases and fancy buckles. First used about January 1938

DAYFLOWER

Mark of AVON PRODUCTS INC., New York, NY for costume jewelry. First used Oct. 1971

DeMARIO

Mark of ROBERT DeMARIO of New York, NY

DE NICOLA

Costume jewelry mark of JERRY DeNICOLA, INC., New York, NY. First used 1956

DE ROCHEMONT

Mark of PIONEER INDUSTRIES, INC., Darby, PA for cuff links, tie fobs, and other men's jewelry, since Sept. 1956

William S. Orkin, d.b.a. W.S. ORKIN & COMPANY, Boston, MA mark for pearls. Since May, 1923.

Debutante

COHN & ROSENBERGER, INC., New York, NY mark for comb cases, cigarette cases, compacts, initials, lockets, pendants, clips, containers, hat ornaments, buckles and other jewelry for personal wear. First used 1935.

DEBUTANTE

COHN & ROSENBERGER, INC., New York, NY. This Coro mark dates from 1926 and was used for brooches, bar pins, pins for dress ornaments, ornamental hat pins, ornamental pins and buckles used on hats, ornamental shoe buckles, necklaces, bead necklaces, bracelets, earrings, hair ornaments and finger rings.

"Debutante"

CORO, INC., New York, NY for pearl necklaces, pearl earrings, pearl bracelets, pearl brooches, and pearl rings. Since November, 1935.

DECLOTÉ

Mark of OS-DA COMPANY, New York, NY for imitation pearl necklaces. Since May, 1923.

In spite of the manufacturer's name and trademark DEE'S FOR DIAMONDS, Olean, NY, made a full range of novelty and costume jewelry including pearls, brooches, lockets, bracelets, pins, pendants, chokers, watch bracelets, charms, bangles, religious crosses and stars, combs and barrettes made of metal, etc. Mark first used January, 1935.

DEEP WOODS

Mark of AVON PRODUCTS INC., New York, NY for costume jewelry. First used Jan. 1972

DEFENDER

SPEIDEL CORPORATION, Providence, RI mark for jewelry - ornamental hearts, Stars of David, necklaces, anklets, and ornamental charms. First used May, 1930.

J. A. DEKNATEL & SONS, INC., Queens Village, NY, mark for simulated pearl necklaces. Used since November, 1948.

CHARMCO CO., INC. Matawan, NJ (older name — Charmo Mfg. Co., Inc.) mark for costume jewelry and cosmetic compacts. First used February, 1945.

DELGAR

DELGAR, INC., New York, NY. Mark for jewelry clasps since February, 1947.

B. D'ELIA & SON, New York, NY for pearl jewelry. First used 1941.

DELMA MANUFACTURING CO., INC., Providence, RI. Mark for all the usual types of jewelry, made in whole or in part, or plated with, precious metal. Since May, 1949.

DELROY

ROYAL BEAD NOVELTY CO., INC., New York, NY mark for necklaces, bracelets, and earrings incorporating simulated pearl beads. First used May 1962

DELMA, MFG. CO., OF R.I., Providence, RI mark for necklaces, bracelets, finger rings, jewelry clips, brooches, earrings, cuff links and tie slides. First used January, 1954.

Déjà

DEJA, INC., New York, NY used this mark for jewelry since 1929

J.A. DEKNATEL & SONS, Queens
Village mark for necklaces. First used 1938

Mark of J.A. DEKNATEL & SONS, Queens
Village, NY for jewelry including pearls and
jewelry made with semi-precious stones and
beads. First used Feb. 1940

DELTAH

HELLER-SPERRY INC., New York, NY
mark for jewelry incorporating pearls -
necklaces, bracelets, brooches, rings, earrings
and cuff links. First used this mark in 1934.

DeNATALE

DeNatale Jewelry Company d.b.a.
DeNATALE BROS., New York, NY used
this mark for bracelets, necklaces, brooches,
finger rings, anklets, compacts, cigarette
cases, buckles, charms, fobs, scarf pins,
ornamental clips and all costume jewelry.
Mark first used 1923.

DENISE FIFTH AVE.

DENISE JEWELRY CO., INC. used this
mark for costume jewelry. First used 1964

RALPH DE ROSA COMPANY, New
York, NY for pins, clips, earrings, bracelets
and necklaces. Since January, 1946.

DESERT FASHIONS

SANFORD & CO., Los Angeles, CA. Mark
for costume jewelry - earrings, necklaces,
rings, bracelets and pins. Since July, 1955.

DESIGN-LINE CO., Lincoln, NE for
necklaces, earrings and pins. Since August,
1955.

DESSY

Mark for DESSY JEWELERS, INC., New
York, NY for jewelry. First used 1942

F. WHITAKER CO., Providence, RI mark
for religious jewelry for personal wear. Since
1946

DEVOTION

Mark of AVON PRODUCTS, INC., New
York, NY for costume jewelry. First used
Feb. 1971

DEW DROP

C.F. MUELLER CO., Jersey City, NJ mark
for pendants, earrings, and pins. First used
1970

Dew Drops

WEINREICH BROTHERS COMPANY,
New York, NY. Mark for jewelry clips. First
used November, 1949.

DI-GOR

DI—GOR EARRING & JEWELRY MFG.
CO., INC., New York, NY mark for earrings,
brooch pins, charms, bracelets, finger rings,
necklaces and clips. First used 1962

Dı Roma

MARK OF MAURICE J. KARPELES, INC., Providence, RI for jewelry and religious jewelry. First used May 1940

Diagem

DIAMOND-ITE INTERNATIONAL, INC., New York, NY used this mark for imitation gems sold as part of finished articles of jewelry - rings, necklaces, bracelets and pins, jewelry clips, charms and pendants. Since 1959

DIAMODA

GERALD SEARS CO., INC. New York, NY for costume jewelry. Since February, 1960.

DIAMON-GOL

HICKOK MANUFACTURING CO., INC., Rochester, NY for men's jewelry since May, 1954.

THE VICTOR COMPANY, New York, NY for necklaces. First used October, 1920.

DIAMOND CUT

THE VICTOR CO., New York, NY used this mark for glass bead necklaces, other imitation stone necklaces. First used Oct. 1920

Du BARRY FIFTH AVENUE, INC., Brooklyn, NY used mark for precious metal jewelry as well as jewelry made of base metal. First used Nov. 1969.

DIAMOND FIRE

ALEX & LEO WOLF, New York, NY mark for rings and pendants with synthetic stones. First used April 1960

"Diamond Jim" Brady

D. LISNER & CO., New York, NY mark for necklaces, bar pins, pins, clips, bracelets, rings, earrings, buckles, combs. First used Jan. 1935

KRAMER JEWELRY CREATIONS, INC., New York, NY. Mark for costume jewelry, namely chokers, rings, bracelets, earrings, brooches. Since July, 1948.

JOSEPH H. MEYER BROS. Brooklyn, NY used this mark since January, 1945 for necklaces, bracelets, finger rings, jewelry clips, brooches and earrings.

DINA

Mark of DINA JEWELRY CORPORATION, New York, NY for jewelry. Since April, 1957.

444

WALLACE L. DIXON, d.b.a. PACIFIC GEM—STONES, Granada Hill, CA mark for bracelets, necklaces, pins, earrings, brooches and pendants. Since April 1971

DOBBS & CO., New York, NY mark for necklaces, chokers, pendants, earrings, bracelets, brooches and men's jewelry. First used July, 1908.

DOLLUP

NAT LEVY, New York, NY used this mark for costume jewelry. First used Jan. 1943

Donna

DAVID GRAD COMPANY, New York, NY. Mark for costume jewelry since January, 1946.

Donna

Mark of HERMAN S. KEYS d.b.a. JEWELS BY DONNA, Berkley, MI, for cuff links, necklaces, pins, etc. First used September 1969

COSTUME jewelry by Donna

DAVID GRAD CO., New York, NY mark for costume jewelry. First used Jan. 1946

DOODLE

Mark of NAT LEVY New York, NY for costume jewelry. First used Jan. 1943

Dorette

VENTURA-ASSAEL & CO., New York, NY mark for pearls. First used January, 1956.

Double Exposure

HATTIE CARNEGIE, INC., New York, NY mark for earrings. Since January, 1948.

Drapette

HELEN D'OR INC., New York, NY for costume and novelty jewelry and ornaments - amulets, bracelets, brooches, chokers, lavaliers, lockets, necklaces, pendants, jewelry pins and lapel pins. Since April, 1954.

Dreamboat

CORO, INC., New York, NY for lockets. Since April, 1959.

DRÉGA

HATTIE CARNEGIE, INC., New York, NY mark for costume jewelry, including buckles, buttons, bracelets, brooches and pins, earrings, pendants, finger and scarf rings, lavalieres, jeweled hair ornaments and jeweled shoe buckles, etc. First used Feb. 1965.

In February, 1931, Harry Drespel of Brooklyn, NY began using this mark for jewelry.

Drouvé

HENRY W. FISHEL & SONS INC., New York, NY used this mark for the usual jewelry as well as bandeaux, scarf, hat and bar pins and shoe buckles. First used September, 1920.

Drouvé

HENRY W. FISHEL & SONS, INC., New York, NY used this mark for bandeaux, earrings, scarf, hat and bar pins, lavallieres, ornaments and clasps for clothing, bracelets, necklaces, brooches, pendants and shoe buckles. First used September, 1920.

DuAmour

Mark of OSTBY & BARTON CO., Providence, RI for rings, earrings, pendants, brooches, bracelets, and charms. First used May 1950

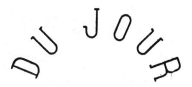

NOVELTY JEWELRY CORP. New York, NY mark for necklaces, bracelets, rings, clips, brooches and earrings since 1931

PARAMOUNT NOVELTY CO., INC., New York, NY mark for costume jewelry particularly necklaces, earrings, pins and bracelets. First used 1961

DUBL PLAY

MARVELLA INC., New York, NY mark for pearls, necklaces, bracelets, earrings, jewelry clips, brooches, lockets, finger rings, charm bracelets, and charms and bead necklaces. Marvella first used this mark Sept. 1960

DUCHESS

WERNER FINK, Long Branch, NJ, used this mark for pearls and other jewelry since August, 1945.

Duchess

H & S ORIGINALS, New York, NY used this mark for simulated pearls. January, 1945.

Duchess

JOSEPH H. MEYER BROS., Brooklyn, NY with co-partners George Herzig and Fred Stone d.b.a. H & S ORIGINALS, New York, NY, for necklaces, bracelets, finger rings, jewelry clips, brooches and earrings. Mark first used January, 1937.

DUETTE

COHN & ROSENBERGER, INC., New York, NY mark for finger rings, necklaces, bracelets, earrings and brooches, hat pins, hat ornaments, necklace clasps, vanity cases, cigarette cases, mesh bag frames. First used October, 1929.

DUR-A-LUX

Edward N. Smith d.b.a. GEODE INDUSTRIES, New London, IA. This mark is found on blanks and components for jewelry. Since January, 1960.

DYNASTY

MARVELLA, INC., New York, NY mark for jewelry. First used about June 1959

Mark of Celia Maskit d.b.a. EMPRESS NOVELTY JEWELRY CO., New York, NY for costume jewelry. First used January, 1958.

E.B.

ED BENJAMIN & SONS, San Diego, CA used this mark for jewelry beginning 1955

EMR

LITTON SYSTEMS, INC., Morris Plains, NJ mark for jewelry including rings mounting simulated stones. First used Oct. 1970

ER

ERNEST RUBINSTEIN, New York, NY mark for bracelets, earrings, chokers and necklaces. First used Dec. 1957

ESR

EMPIRE SMELTING & REFINING CO., Philadelphia, PA for jewelry such as rings, charms, bracelets, etc. First used June 1962

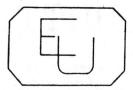

EUGENE UNGER & CO., INC., New York, NY mark for jewelry. First used 1962

BLOCK RINGS CORPORATION, Buffalo, NY mark for finger rings and other jewelry for personal wear. First used Jan. 1910

E·W·R·

E.W. REYNOLDS CO., Los Angeles, CA mark for jewelry. Since 1920

EX

MIGLIO JEWELRY MANUFACTUR-ING CO., New York, NY mark for jewelry namely bracelets, charms, necklaces, and religious jewelry. First used 1963

Ear Brette

BEN-HUR PRODUCTS INC., New York, NY combined ear clamp and pin in the form of a spray. Since January, 1952.

Ear Charmers

CORO, INC., New York, NY used this mark for earrings. First used July, 1956.

Ear Fashions

LON L. WALLACE, Shoreham, Long Island, NY used this mark for novelty earrings. Since January, 1954.

Ear-Mates

Mark of Ralph R. Daddio, Newington, CT to TRIFARI, KRUSSMAN & FISHEL, New York, NY for earrings. Since July, 1953.

EAR-RESISTIBLES

MERCURY RING CORPORATION, New York, NY for jewelry consisting of rings, pendants, brooches, tie tacs, festoons and mountings. Since April, 1943.

Ear Ribbon

JOHN RUBEL of John Rubel Co., New York, NY mark for brooches, bracelets, necklaces, lavaliers, pendants and buckles. First used 1943.

Earjoys

Anna G. Lenz d.b.a. THE PERFECTION MANUFACTURING CO., Jamaica, NY for clip type earrings. Since May, 1954.

Earline

HARRY MAILAND, New York, NY used this mark for earrings. Since May, 1951.

EARRITE

MARCEL BOUCHER, New York, NY mark for earrings. Since January, 1950.

earthbeads

Mark of ROBERT W. NICKLE of EARTHWORKS, Chicago, IL, for beads and beadwork, necklaces, earrings and bracelets since June 1970

Ebonex

JACOBY-BENDER INC., New York, NY mark for colored gem simulating inserts used in links for watch bracelets. Since November, 1952.

ECKFELDT & ACKLEY, INC., Newark, NJ mark for anklets, brooches, pins, bracelets, bangles, chokers, lip stick cases, vanity boxes, hat ornaments, lockets, necklaces, and clasps of all kinds. First used 1898.

EISENBERG ICE

EISENBERG JEWELRY, INC., Chicago, Ill., for clips, rings, pins, bracelets, and earrings. Since February, 1942.

Current Mark

EISENSTADT MANUFACTURING COMPANY, St. Louis, MO. Mark for lockets, scarf pins, buckles, bracelets, key rings, key chains and various types men's jewelry. First used in February, 1944.

EISENSTADT MANUFACTURING COMPANY, St. Louis, MO. Mark used for brooches, stick-pins, scarf-pins, and other ornamental pins, earrings, lockets, charms, charm bracelets, etc. Mark in use since January, 1893.

LIPPMAN, SPIER & HAHN, New York, NY for all the usual jewelry types as well as girdles, bandeaux, combs, barrettes, fancy pendants, hat ornaments, watch bracelet holders, perfume holders and containers, folding comb cases, cigarette holders. First used October, 1923.

ELBE

MORRIS LACKOW d.b.a. LACKOW BROS., New York, NY mark for finger rings, pins, brooches, earrings, bracelets and charms. Since June 1962

ELECTRA TRISEMBLE

COHN & ROSENBERGER, INC., New York, NY for strings of pearls, necklaces, bracelets, earrings, finger rings, brooches, barpins and ornamental hatpins. Also used for jewelry made wholly or in part or plated with precious metal. Used since October, 1931.

ELECTROCLAD

CELLINI CHARM CO., INC., Providence, RI mark for costume jewelry since 1962

CORO, INC., New York, NY mark for jewelry with pearls and beads, pins and jewelry initials. First used April 1948

Elgin American

ELGIN AMERICAN DIVISION OF IL-LINOIS WATCH CASE CO., Elgin, Ill. Mark for costume jewelry and compacts, combs, brushes, mirrors, jewel boxes, etc. as well as synthetic stones. Company claims usage since 1893.

Elgin American

ILLINOIS WATCH CASE CO., of ELGIN AMERICAN DIVISION OF ILLINOIS WATCH CASE CO., Elgin, IL used this mark for a wide variety of accessories such as dresser sets, powder sifters and compacts and vanity cases. First used on combs and cases 1932; on combs since 1928; on dresser sets since 1930 and powder sifters since 1936

Elgin American

ELGIN AMERICAN MANUFACTUR-ING CO., Elgin, Illinois made jewelry but is probably most noted for its powder compacts and cases which often incorporated rhinestones and colored stones. The company claims it has used this mark since 1893. On powder boxes since 1936, on combs since 1928 and men's dresser sets since 1930.

Elgin Craft

Mark of ELGIN AMERICAN MANUFACTURING CO., Elgin, IL for vanities, combined vanities, compacts, powder containers, cigarette holders, etc. First used April, 1930.

ELIZABETH ARDEN

ELIZABETH ARDEN SALES COR-PORATION, New York, NY used this mark for finger rings, wrist and ankle bracelets, brooch pins, and all costume jewelry. First used May, 1939.

Mark of ELIZABETH COWAN, Washington, D.C., for earrings, clips, pins, brooches and other jewelry. Since Sept. 1943

ELIZABETH POST

The Lander Co., Inc. d.b.a. ELIZABETH POST, New York, NY mark for costume jewelry. First used February, 1958.

Elite

Another CORO mark for jewelry with pearls. Since April, 1948.

Embassy

ROSENBERT & CO., INC., New York, NY used this mark for pearl Jewelry. First used September, 1923.

Embracelet

URUS SALES CORPORATION, New York, NY for bracelets. First used February, 1943.

EMMOLITE

EMMONS JEWELERS, INC., Newark, NY used this mark for base metal composition made into costume jewelry. First used January, 1955.

EMMONS

Mark of EMMONS JEWELERS, INC., Newark, NY for costume jewelry. First used March, 1949.

EMPRESS

EMPRESS PEARL SYNDICATE, Los Angeles, Calif., mark for pearl jewelry such as rings, earrings, pins, tie pins and necklaces. Since January, 1946.

Mark of NORTHWESTERN JEWELRY CO., INC., St. Paul, MN for necklaces, bracelets, finger rings, earrings, brooches, lockets, crosses, lavaliers, ornamental pins, jewelry for men and all their costume jewelry. Since June, 1942.

EMPRESS
EUGENIE

COHN & ROSENBERGER, INC., New York, NY. Mark for strings of pearls, necklaces, bracelets, earrings, finger rings, brooches, bar pins and ornamental hatpins. This mark also used for jewelry made wholly or partly of precious metal or plated therewith. Used since September, 1930.

Empress of India

STIX, BAER & FULLER COMPANY, St. Louis, MO for necklaces. Since June, 1919.

PAKULA AND COMPANY, Chicago, IL used this mark for all the usual types of jewelry, earrings, necklaces, etc., as well as for pearls. First used July, 1946.

ENCHANTRESS

PAKULA & CO. Chicago, IL mark for pearls and costume jewelry such as bracelets, necklaces, initial pins, rings, earrings, lockets, brooches and charms. First used July 1946

Encore

A.H. POND CO., INC., Syracuse, NY mark for costume jewelry including scatter pins and spray pins. First used Sept. 1949

Entwined Love

FEATURE RINGS CO., INC. of New York used this mark on rings, bracelets, earrings, brooches, and necklaces as well as on jewelry mountngs. Used since February, 1947.

ENVOY

ANSON INCORPORATED, Providence, RI used this mark for men's jewelry since Oct. 1957

EREV

HAROLD FREEMAN JEWELRY MFG. CO., INC., New York, NY mark for rings, earrings, pendants, pins and brooches. First used June 1962

ERINIDE

Mark for synthetic stones for jewelers used by L. HELLER & SON, INC., New York, NY since 1930.

ESCAPADE

GEMEX COMPANY, Union, NJ mark for bracelets and watch bracelets. First used October, 1954.

ESEMCO

SHIMAN MFG. CO., INC., Newark, NJ used this mark for all jewelry, gold, silver and platinum but also for jewelry made of white metal, copper and silver plated. First used October, 1921.

ESPO

ESPO—FLEX MFG. INC., Providence, RI (Esposito Jewelry, Inc.) used this mark for rings. First used 1951

ESPO-FLEX

ESPO—FLEX MFG., INC., Providence, RI mark for costume jewelry. First used 1951

M & M MFG. CO., Providence, RI used this mark for pendants, necklaces, bracelets, pins, earrings, brooches, chokers, buckles, rings, and ladies' cuff links. First used about Dec. 1954.

ESTHER REECE

ESTHER REECE, INC., New York, NY for costume jewelry, earrings, dress clips, hair ornaments. Since February, 1957.

OBER MANUFACTURING CO., Pawtucket, RI for earrings, brooches, bracelets, necklaces, pins, pendants and cuff links. Since September, 1950.

TRIFARI, KRUSSMAN & FISHEL, INC., New York, NY mark for costume jewelry. First used October 1961

ETHEREAL

Mark of AVON PRODUCTS INC., New York, NY for costume jewelry. First used Nov. 1971

EVANS CASE CO., North Attleboro, MA for compacts for powder. Since January, 1948.
Since 1930 this mark has been used for cigarette cases, lighters and vanity cases as well as compacts.

EVANS CASE CO., Attleboro, MA used this mark for cigarette lighters, cigarette cases, compacts, vanity cases, since 1930.

EVE

EVE NATHANSON EAST GREENWICH, RI for all the usual types of jewelry plus compacts, ladies' dress ornaments, etc. Since Sept. 1939

EVENING GLORY

AVON PRODUCTS, INC., New York, NY mark for jewelry since Sept. 1970

EVENING IN STYLE

AVON PRODUCTS, INC., New York, NY used this mark for costume jewelry. First used Feb. 1971

EVENING STAR

WEINREICH BROTHERS COMPANY, New York, NY. Mark used for pearl necklaces, pearl earrings, pearl bracelets and other jewelry containing pearls. Used since January, 1939.

Mark of EVERFINE JEWELRY MFG. CO., Providence, RI for lockets, novelty jewelry and all types of bracelets. Since September, 1945.

Every Day of The Week

MORTON MARKS d.b.a. DIVISION SALES, Chicago, IL for cuff links, other men's jewelry, rings, pendants, charm bracelets, necklaces, charms, jewelry clips, brooches, and lockets. First used February 1962

EXCELL MANUFACTURING COMPANY, Providence, RI, for lockets, crosses, pendants, circle pins and jewelry findings. Since February, 1936.

Excelsior

EXCELSIOR JEWELERS FINDINGS, New York, NY used this mark for the usual types of jewelry as well as fasteners and clasps, and castings. Since 1941

EXETER

Mark of SIMON GOLUB & SONS, INC., Seattle, WA for men's costume jewelry, namely cuff links, tie tacks, tie bars and dress sets. Used since 1963

Lesilie Claymont d.b.a. CLAYMONT COMPANY, Jackson Heights, NY for pearls and jewelry - necklaces, earrings, bracelets, pins, brooches, clips and pendants. Since 1937.

Mark of FORSTNER INC., IRVINGTON, NJ for jewelry. First used 1962

MAURICE GOLDSTEIN d.b.a. FRANCO AMERICAN JEWELRY CO., Philadelphia, PA for jewelry. First used June 1926

FISHER AND COMPANY, Newark, NJ for ladies' brooches, earrings, bracelets, necklaces and men's jewelry. First used 1948.

FAJ

FACET JEWELRY CO., INC., New York, NY mark for earrings, pins, brooches, necklaces, pendants, rings and bracelets. First used 1962

Jewelry mark of JACK FISHER, New York, NY. Since 1962

LOSSAU & KRAMER, INC., Chicago, IL mark for rings, charm bracelets, charms, pendants, and crosses. First used 1934

FORSTNER CHAIN CORPORATION, Irvington, NJ jewelry mark. First used December, 1920.

WALTHAM WATCH CO., Chicago, IL used this mark for jewelry including costume jewelry. First used May 1962

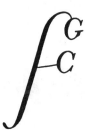

George Colbert d.b.a. FASCINATION JEWELRY MANUFACTURING CO., Beverly Hills, CA used this mark for costume jewelry and other jewelry for men and women. First used April 1962

FRENCH JEWELRY CO., Philadelphia, PA, for ornamental jewelry, namely pins, brooches, necklaces, pendants, rings, bracelets, lockets, earrings. Used since January, 1933.

Jewelry mark of FRANK L. WILMARTH CO., Chicago, IL. Since Feb. 1964

F.M.CO.

FINBERG MANUFACTURING CO., Attleboro, Mass. for jewelry for personal wear since March, 1944.

FERRO NOVELTY CO., INC., Johnston, RI mark for earrings. Since June 1962

FRL

FEDERATED DEPARTMENT STORES INC., d.b.a. THE F & R LAZARUS & CO., Columbus, OH mark for jewelry. First used 1962

SAMUEL RUBIN, New York, NY. Mark for simulated pearls, cultured pearls and other jewelry including brooches, bracelets, hair ornaments, necklaces, lavalieres, lingerie clips, lockets, ornamental pins, pendants, hatpins, rings, scarf pins, watch bracelets. Mark used since March, 1940.

FABIL, MFG. CORP., New York, NY mark for boys' and girls' jewelry consisting of cuff links, tie clasps, barrettes, charm bracelets, scatter pins and necklaces. First used 1945.

Mark of the FELCH-ANDERSON CO., Providence, RI since March, 1946.

ORIGINALITIES OF NEW YORK, INC., Long Island City, NY for children's bracelets and necklaces. Since August, 1953.

FAIRYLAND

B.B. GREENBERG CO., Providence, RI used this mark for boys' and girls' jewelry since 1962

F A L A PRODUCTS

AURELIA BACHMAN, New York, NY. Mark for charms, bracelets, rings, earrings, pins and watchfobs. Used since January, 1945.

FANCY NOTIONS

Mark of AVON PRODUCTS INC., New York, NY for costume jewelry. First used Oct. 1971

ATLAS CREATIONS, INC., New York, NY used this mark for plastic jewelry. First used July 1942

FARA

BEN BERCHMAN & CO., INC. New York, NY used this mark for bracelets, necklaces, hair ornaments, pins, finger rings, cuff links. Since July, 1952.

FASHION ART

Mark of MAYER BROS., Seattle, WA for earrings, necklaces, individually or in sets. Since June 1957

Fashion Craft

LOSSAU & KRAMER, INC., Chicago, IL mark for rings, charm bracelets, charms, pendants and crosses. First used 1934

Fashion Flair

CORO, INC., New York, NY used this mark for necklaces, bracelets, etc. as well as hair barrettes, chatelaines, beads and pearl jewelry since February, 1957.

fashion fun

INTERNATIONAL ASSEMBLIX CORPORATION, Toledo, OH used this mark for hobby craft kits for the making of costume jewelry. First used September 1971

Mark of BERGER JEWELRY, MFG., CO., St. Louis, MO for jewelry. First used July 1941

FASHION STATEMENTS

Mark of AVON PRODUCTS INC., New York, NY for costume jewelry. First used Nov. 1971

"FASHION SQUARE"

COHN & ROSENBERGER, INC., New York, NY. Mark used for pearls, necklaces, bracelets, earrings, finger rings, brooches, bar pins, and ornamental hatpins; pins for dress ornaments, ornamental pins and buckles for decorating hats, ornamental shoe buckles, and hair ornaments made wholly or in part of or plated with precious metal. Used since February, 1931.

Fashionata

CORO, INC., New York, NY mark for jewelry. Since February, 1960.

FASHIONATIONS

FEDERATED DEPARTMENT STORES, INC., d.b.a. FILENE'S & SONS Co., Inc., Cincinnati, OH mark for girls' and ladies' jewelry. First used 1953.

FASHIONLANE

Mark of Arno Wrazlowsky, d.b.a. FASHIONLANE JEWELRY CO., Providence, RI for finger rings, earrings, bracelets, brooches, necklaces, shoulder pins, clasps, belt and shoe buckles and hat ornaments. First used January, 1920.

Mark of KEN ORIGINALS LTD., New York, NY for kits for making costume jewelry. First used Nov. 1970

FEATHAGOLD

ACCESSOCRAFT PRODUCTS CO., New York, NY for plastic plated jewelry such as necklaces, bracelets, finger rings, earrings, jewelry clips, brooches, lockets, beads, ornamental pins, hat ornaments, hair ornaments, holders for face powder, comb cases, cigarette cases, all made of precious or semiprecious metal, fancy buckles and jewelry initials. Since August, 1945.

FEATHER TOUCH

RA-CE TOOL & METAL STAMPING CO., INC., New York, NY for jewelry findings. Since February 11, 1946.

Feather Touch

ALICE JEWELRY COMPANY, Providence, RI mark for earrings. First used about February, 1955.

CLAIR C. THOMAS, Ault, CO, mark for earrings, brooches and pins incorporating feathers. Since December, 1953.

GREENBAUM NOVELTY CORP., New York, NY mark for earrings. Since January, 1947.

FEATURE-FLASH

FEATURE RING CO., New York, NY mark for ornamental jewelry. In use since January, 1940.

FEATURE LOCK

FEATURE RING CO., INC. New York, NY. This mark was used not only for bracelets, earrings, brooches, lapel pins and necklaces but also for jewelry findings. First used October, 1946.

Fedway

FEDERATED DEPARTMENT STORES, INC., Cincinnati, OH used this mark for bracelets, earrings, necklaces, lapel and breast pins. Since January, 1952.

JACK FERRIS, Springfield Gardens, NY. Mark for jewelry since 1961

fi

FITHIAN, Sun Valley, CA used this mark for bracelets, earrings, charms, sets consisting of matching belt buckle and cuff links. Since June, 1954.

Fiance

GOLDSTEIN-GERSON, CO., INC., New York, NY for clips, pins, rings, and watch bracelets. First used November, 1954.

Fidget

GEORGE J. HECHT, New York, NY for strings of beads of various materials and with semi precious stones. Since April 1941

HARRY H. FIELD, San Francicso, CA, for costume jewelry - bracelets, necklaces, brooches, pins and pendants. Since May, 1950.

FIELD FLOWERS

Mark of AVON PRODUCTS INC., New York, NY for costume jewelry. First used Oct. 1971

Filcraft Imports

STERN & FRIEDMAN, New York, NY. Used for costume jewelry beginning April 30, 1946.

WM. FILENE'S SONS COMPANY, Boston, MA used this mark on scarf pins, breast pins, bar pins, earrings, bracelets, brooches and on a great variety of useful personal ornamental objects as well as jewelry. First used October, 1912.

FILENE'S

FEDERATED DEPARTMENT STORES INC., d.b.a. WM. FILENE'S SONS & CO., Boston, MA mark for both fine and costume jewelry. Of all the usual types. First used sometime prior to 1940 on costume jewelry.

FIRE BIRD

CORO, INC., New York, NY for all the usual types of jewelry including pearls. Since May, 1963.

FIREFLY

Mark of ARTHUR E. NEUMANN, Chicago, IL for earrings, bracelets, brooches, necklaces, ornamental pins, rings, chatelaines, jeweled belt and shoe buckles, jeweled hair combs, jeweled barrettes and jeweled hat pins. First used August, 1947.

Fireglow

ILLINOIS WATCH CASE CO., operating under the name ELGIN AMERICAN DIVISION OF ILLINOIS WATCH CASE CO., Elgin, IL used this mark for simulated pearl bracelets, necklaces, earrings and brooches. First used Aug. 1950

RALPH H. BODMAN, Hyannis, MA mark for pearl necklaces. First used September, 1923.

Fleur de France

MARK DOTTENHEIM, New York, NY mark for pearl jewelry. Since January, 1920.

FLEUR DE MER

JOSEPH H. MEYER BROS., Brooklyn, NY used this mark for bracelets, necklaces and earrings. First used 1948

FLEX-LET

F & V MANUFACTURING CO., Providence, then FLEX-LET CORPORATION, East Providence, RI, mark for ornamental bracelets and bracelets for watches. Since February, 1944.

FLIRTEEN

S. NATHAN & COMPANY, INC. New York, NY mark for necklaces. First used May, 1947.

JOSEPH H. MEYER BROS., Brooklyn, NY. Mark used for bracelets, necklaces, rings, clips and earrings since 1938.

Mark of PETER L. SHEA, Union City, NJ for plastic novelty jewelry and all types of costume jewelry. Mark first used June, 1946.

Florentine Lace

FELCH & CO., INC., Providence, RI mark for all the usual types of jewelry. Since March, 1952.

Mark of DAN KASOFF, INC., New York, NY for decorative desk accessories. First used 1956

Florenza

DAN KASOFF INC., New York, NY used this mark for costume jewelry - necklaces, bracelets, earrings, charms, brooches and lockets. First used February, 1956.

FLOWER FANCY

Mark of AVON PRODUCTS INC., New York, NY for costume jewelry. First used Jan. 1972

FLOWER FINERY

Mark of AVON PRODUCTS INC., New York, NY for costume jewelry. First used Dec. 1971

FLUID LOOK

CORO, INC., New York, NY mark for necklaces, bracelets, earrings, etc. First used Sept. 1959

FLUTTERBYS

RICHTON INTERNATIONAL CORP., New York, NY mark for jewelry. First used 1963

FLUTTERBYS

CORO, INC., New York, NY mark for necklaces, bracelets, earrings, jewelry clips, brooches, lockets, rings, charm bracelets, charms, pendants, pearls, beads, pins and jewelry initials. First used Jan. 1963

FLYING TIGERS

 FLYING TIGERS

MARKS OF THE FLYING TIGERS (American Volunteer Group — Chinese Air Force, Incorporated, NY, NY) for jewelry of precious and base metals, lapel pins, charms, bracelets, etc. Second mark listed duplicate of first, but larger. First use of these marks was November, 1945.

for that priceless look

CORO, INC., New York, NY, for all the usual types of jewelry as well as jewelry made with pearls. First used January, 1944.

FORBIDDEN FRUIT

Mark of RICHTON INTERNATIONAL CORP. New York, NY for jewelry. Used since Feb. 1963

foreign TEEN

HAROLD GOLDKRANTZ, New York, NY mark for costume jewelry - necklaces, bracelets, brooches, jewelry clips, lockets, hair ornaments, jewelry initials, artificial pearls, etc. Since February, 1956.

Forstar

FORSTNER CHAIN CORPORATION, Irvington, NJ used this mark for watch bracelets, bracelets, scarf pins, ear ornaments, cuff links and studs. Since June, 1950.

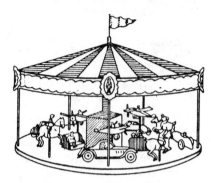

FORSTNER CHAIN CORP., Irvington, NJ mark for necklaces, bracelets, rings, buckles, pins, brooches, earrings, pendants. First used June 1935

Forstner

FORSTNER CHAIN CORPORATION, Irvington, NJ for all the usual types of jewelry. First used January, 1937.

 FORTRESS

FORTRESS WATCH & JEWELRY CO., INC., New York, NY used this mark for bracelets, ornamental pins, earrings and rings. First used January, 28, 1946.

The Four Hundred collection by La Tausca

HELLER-SPERRY, INC., New York, NY mark for breast pins, lapel pins, earrings, necklaces, buckles, scatterpins, hair ornaments and for imitation pearl scatterpins, hair ornaments, breast pins, bracelets, pendants, brooches, etc. Used since May, 1952.

François

This CORO Mark has been used since January, 1937.

CORO, INC., New York, NY mark for all the usual types of jewelry. First used January, 1937.

JOHN FREDERICS

JOHN—FREDERICS, INC., New York, NY mark for earrings, bracelets, necklaces and rings. First used 1929

JOHN RUBEL CO., New York, NY. Mark for brooches, bracelets, necklaces, lavaliers, pendants, and buckles. First used 1943.

FREEMAN-DAUGHADAY COMPANY, Providence, RI, mark for jewelry used since June, 1946.

FRENCH PLUME

C.F. MUELLER CO., Jersey City, NJ mark for earrings, pins. Since Dec. 1960

THE FRENCH TOUCH

PARFUMS CHARBERT, INC., New York, NY mark for bracelets and necklaces. In use since November, 1945.

FRESHURA

Mark of MARVELLA PEARLS, INC., New York, NY for costume jewelry. Since December, 1958.

LEADING JEWELRY MANUFACTURING COMPANY, Mamoroneck, NY used this mark for costume jewelry. Since September, 1951.

FUTURA

CORO, INC., New York, NY for brooches, earrings, necklaces, lockets, bracelets, pin clips. Since August, 1953.

CORO mark for all the usual types of jewelry. First used October, 1953.

Jewelry mark of THE R.L. GRIFFITH AND SON COMPANY, Providence, RI. First used 1894.

E. GUBELIN, New York, NY for necklaces, pendants, finger rings, cuff links, bracelets, clips, brooches, earrings and watch bracelets. This company also made compacts and cigarette cases which were made of or plated with precious metal. First used about 1927.

WILLIAM C. GREENE COMPANY, Providence, RI used this mark for buckles, clasps, buttons, brooches, ear attachments, rings and lavallieres. First used June, 1913.

GEMSTONE, INC., New York, NY mark for jewelry. First used 1964

THE GREEN CO. INC., Kansas City, MO., mark for jewelry. First used Jan. 1935

Mark used by E. & V. GREENFIELD JEWELRY MANUFACTURERS, New York, NY since June 25, 1946.

J.M.G. MANUFACTURERS & POLISHERS, INC., New York, NY used this mark for jewelry since December 1962

G

MARK OF RUDOLF FRIEDMAN, New York, NY for jewelry. First used May 1962

This mark was used by EDWARD C. GRASSMAN, INC., Newark, NJ for necklace clasps. Since June 1949

THE GREEN CO., INC., Kansas City, MO used this mark for brooches, lapel pins, rings, bracelets and necklaces since 1947

ARTHUR W. HEIN of GOLD CROWN SPECIALTIES, New York, NY used this mark for rings, charms and brooches. Since Dec. 1946

GENERAL FINDINGS & SUPPLY CO., Attleboro, MA mark for jewelry. First used Jan. 1934

GK

GUS KROESEN, INC., Oakland, CA mark for articles of jewelry. First used 1956

This mark of GRAND PRODUCTS CO., Chicago, IL was used for purse sized perfume containers and dispensers. Since Feb. 1943.

PAUL P. GREENE of WICK & GREEN JEWELERS, Ashville, NC mark for rings, bracelets, brooches and other jewelry items. First used 1960

CODE WEISBROT, New York, NY used this mark for earrings, brooch pins, charms, bracelets, rings, necklaces, clips, tie clasps, cuff links, tie tacks and pendants. First used June 1962

GEMEX COMPANY, Newark, NJ mark for bracelets, scarf pins, belt buckles and hair ornaments. First used May, 1921.

KAUFMAN & RUDERMAN, INC., New York, NY first used this mark for children's costume jewelry in September, 1943.

This is the mark used by TRIFARI, KRUSSMAN & FISHEL, INC., New York, NY for pearls. First used September, 1932.

Gainsborough by
TRIFARI

Mark of TRIFARI, KRUSSMAN & FISHEL, INC., New York, NY for simulated pearls in the form of necklaces. This mark was first used April, 1959; the "Gainsborough" was first used by Trifari on pearl jewelry in September, 1932; and the "Trifari" on costume jewelry was first used December, 1937.

GᴀLA

GAY TOOL COMPANY, INC., Providence, Ri for both men's and women's jewelry. First used June, 1955.

GALAXY

CORO, INC., New York, NY mark for the usual jewelry as well as lockets and strings of pearls. First used 1949.

GALE CREATIONS, INC., New York, NY mark for costume jewelry. Since July, 1955.

GARDEN OF EDEN

C.F. MUELLER CO., Jersey City, NJ used this mark for costume jewelry pins. First used 1965

Garden OF *Gold*

THE NAPIER COMPANY, Meriden, CT used this mark for necklaces, brooches, earrings, bracelets, clips, finger rings and hair ornaments made wholly or partly of, or plated with, precious metal. Since August, 1951.

Garland

THE BALL COMPANY, Chicago, IL mark for rings, earrings, brooches, bracelets, clasps, necklaces, pendants and other jewelry. First used Feb. 1924

Garné

GARNE JEWELRY, New York, NY used this mark for necklaces, brooches, bracelets, earrings, chatelaines, and fobs. Since June 1945

GĀWOOD

David E. Garre, d.b.a. THE DAVID COMPANY, St. Paul, MN for costume jewelry particularly earrings, hair clips, ornamental pins and cuff links. First used December, 1955.

Gay Lady

Mark of DAVID JACOBS, Lincoln, NE for costume jewelry – bracelets, necklaces, brooch and lapel pins, earrings, pin and earring sets, chatelaines. Since December, 1951.

JACQUES KREISLER MANUFACTURING CORP., North Bergen, NJ mark for men's jewelry. First used Oct. 1949

"GEISHA"

INTERATLANTIC TRADING CORP., New York, NY used this mark for costume jewelry - necklaces, brooches, finger rings, bracelets and earrings with, and of, cultured pearls. Since July, 1949.

GEMEX COMPANY, Union, NJ. Mark for jewelry including scarf pins, bracelets, belt buckles, ear ornaments, hair ornaments, made of or plated with precious metals. Used since June, 1944.

GOODMAN & COMPANY, Indianapolis, Indiana, mark for rings, necklaces, bracelets, earrings, jewelry clips, brooches and lockets. First used November, 1941.

Gem Galleries

MARCUS & CO., INC., New York, NY used this mark for rings, clips, necklaces, pins, earrings, bracelets, mountings and imitation stones as well as precious and semi-precious stones. Used since 1945

Gem O'My Heart

CHAS. SCHWARTZ & SON, Washington, DC used this mark for a variety of things jewelry, jewel boxes, mesh bags, buckles, cigarette holders and puff boxes. Since October, 1930.

Gem-Art

Mark of THE VICTOR CORPORATION, Cincinnati, Ohio, for rings, bracelets, pendants, earrings, ornamental pins, lapel pins, and emblem pins. Since April, 1948.

Gemcraft

PHILIP E. STETSON, Boston, MA jewelry mark used since 1935

GEMETTES

JOSEPH H. MEYER BROS., Brooklyn, NY mark for necklaces, and earrings. First used December, 1954.

GEMEX JEWEL

GEMEX COMPANY, Union, NJ mark for bracelets. Since June, 1951.

FREDERIC J. ESSIG & CO., Chicago, IL for pearls. First used February, 1957.

JEROME RICHHEIMER, New York, NY used this mark for all the usual types of costume jewelry. Since 1929

THE MARK JEWELRY CO., New York, NY for rings, bracelets and brooches. First used February, 1930.

GEMS OF PARIS MFG. CO., INC. New York, NY used this mark for rhinestone necklaces, earrings and bracelets as well as simulated pearl jewelry with rhinestones. Since June, 1952.

GEM-TONE

C.L. STUEMPGES, Seattle, WA for hand carved costume jewelry. First used Dec. 1946

GEM-TONES

Mark of JOSEPH H. MEYER BROS., Brooklyn, NY for costume jewelry necklaces, bracelets, earrings and brooches. First used July, 1957.

Mark of GENTLY JEWELRY MANUFACTURING CO., NY for jewelry including bracelets and charms. Since Feb. 1962

GENCO

GENCO is the mark of GENERAL CHAIN COMPANY, Providence, RI, for jewelry, used since August, 1925.

Genie de Paris

D. RODITI & SONS, New York, NY used this mark for imitation pearls, bracelets, finger rings, neck chains, earrings, jewelry clips. In use since October, 1945.

GEO — METS

GEOMETS INCORPORATED, New York, NY mark for necklaces, bracelets and earrings. First used June, 1954.

GEVERTS & CO., INCORP., New York, NY for rings, bracelets and brooches. First used 1962

GIFTIME

THE SEA GEM COMPANY, INC., New York, NY mark for necklaces, rings, breast pins, earrings, bracelets, made with pearls. First used April, 1948.

GIFTPAK

CORO mark for all the usual types of jewelry including pearl brooches, pearl necklaces, pearl earrings and pearl clips. Also hat ornaments, beads, pins, hair ornaments and jewelry initials. Since August, 1953.

GILDA

WILLIAM RAND, INC., New York, NY used this mark for costume jewelry earrings, brooches, necklaces, bracelets and ornamental pins. First used Dec. 1949

GIOVANNI

Costume jewelry mark of GIOVANNI, INC., Providence, RI. First used April 1959

GLAMOR

CORO, INC., New York, NY mark for pin clips, brooches, bracelets, necklaces, pendants, lockets, charms, earrings, buckles, rings, anklets, hair ornaments, tiaras and fobs. All of these being made of or plated with precious metal. First used January 5, 1940.

CORO mark first used January, 1941 for charm bracelets, charms, necklaces, bracelets, earrings, jewelry clips, brooches, lockets and jewelry made with pearls.

CORO, INC., New York, NY mark for all the usual types of jewelry - necklaces, bracelets, earrings, etc., as well as jewelry with pearls. First used August, 1958.

ALFRED H. GLASSER CORP., New York, NY for bracelets, rings, pins, charms. First used on or before the summer of 1953

Glitter Bobs

CORO, INC., New York, NY mark for heavily ornamented and decorated bobby pins. First used February, 1956.

Glö Charm

HY FRACKMAN d.b.a. ALAN MANUFACTURING CO., NY, mark for charms. First used March 1961

GLO-RAY

RITE GRADE CORPORATION, New York, NY used this mark for costume jewelry. Since October, 1957.

G. FOX & CO,. INC., Hartford, CT used this mark for necklaces, rings and bracelets. Since January, 1930.

UNCAS MANUFACTURING CO., Providence, RI for finger rings, bracelets, brooches, necklaces, and earrings. First used Jan. 1942

RONALD F. SILVER, St. Paul, MN mark for finger rings, earrings, bracelets. First used June, 1955.

GOLD-BOND

Costume jewelry mark of A. MICALLEF & CO., Providence, RI. First used 1968

GOLD-KLAD

Mark of JACQUES KREISLER & CO., New York, NY for vanity cases, brooches plated with precious metal. First used April 1921

Gold-M-Brace

Mark used by BELLAVANCE, INC., Attleboro, MA for articles of jewelry. Since April, 1953.

GOLD TONE

Daniel Silverman, d.b.a. JAMECO METAL PRODUCTS CO., New York, NY used this mark for music boxes and other decorative wares. First used May 1957.

GOLDEN ART

GOLDEN ART IMPORTING COMPANY, San Jose, CA for jewelry - pins, earrings, bracelets, necklaces and men's jewelry. Since January, 1955.

GOLDEN FLEECE

This is the mark of AMERICAN & CONTINENTAL PATENTED PRODUCTS, INC., of New York for necklaces, bracelets, earrings, clips, rings, lockets, hat and hair ornaments, compacts comb cases cigarette cases, jewelry initials and cuff links. Used since May 1941

PAKULA AND COMPANY, Chicago, Ill. used the mark for expansion, charm and identification bracelets, charms, pins, earrings, lockets, pearls, rings and compacts, made wholly or partly of precious metals. Used first January, 1947.

Golden Knight

One of the marks of the SPEIDEL CORPORATION, Providence, Rhode Island and used on bracelets (not including watch bracelets). Used since August, 1946.

THE "Golden Look"

Mark of KRAMER JEWELRY CREATIONS, New York, NY for necklaces, bracelets, brooches, earrings, finger rings, pin clips. First used December, 1954.

GOLDEN WEST

THOMAS & CO., INC., Seattle, Wash. Mark for rings, earrings, necklaces and brooches. Since June, 1953.

Goldette

Mark of Ben Gartner d.b.a. CIRCLE JEWELRY PRODUCTS, New York, NY for costume jewelry. Used since October, 1958.

Golden Rod

COHN & ROSENBERGER, INC., New York, NY used this mark for rings, earrings, necklaces, brooches, bracelets, bar pins and vanity cases. Since 1926

"Golden Threads"

Mark of WALTER LAMPL of LAMPL, New York, NY brooches, clips, earrings, rings, necklaces, bracelets, charms, vanity cases, ornamental hat pins, pins for dress ornaments. First used 1940

GOLDKIST

AMERICAN & CONTINENTAL PATENTED PRODUCTS INC., New York, NY mark for all the usual jewelry plus fancy cigarette boxes, compacts, comb cases, buckles, jewelry initials, etc. Since Jan. 1941

GONE WITH THE WIND

LEVER BROTHERS CO., Cambridge, MA used this mark for brooches since May 1940

GOOD NEIGHBOR

AMERICAN RENAISSANCE ASSOC. INC., White Plains, NY mark for jewelry. First used Dec. 1937

THE GRACEFUL THREE

JOHN RUBEL of JOHN RUBEL CO., New York used this mark for brooches, bracelets, necklaces, lavalieres, pendants, and buckles. First used 1943

Ernest F. Gray d.b.a. GRAYS JEWELERS, Los Angeles, CA for earrings findings, a mark sometimes mistaken for that of a jewelry manufacturer. Since December, 1953.

GRAND PRIX

SWANK, INC., Attleboro, MA for men's jewelry. Since 1955

GRANDEE

VARGAS MANUFACTURING CO., Providence, RI used this mark for jewelry since April 1971

CORO, INC., New York, NY, Used this mark for pearl jewelry, namely, necklaces, bracelets, finger rings, earrings, brooches and lockets. First used January 1950

CATAMORE, INC. d.b.a. CATAMORE ENTERPRISES PROVIDENCE, RI used this mark for costume jewelry. First used June 1970

THE GREEN CO., INC., Kansas City, MO for jewelry - brooches, lapel pins, finger rings, bracelets and necklaces. First used April, 1947.

GREMLIN

D. LISNER & CO., New York, NY used this mark for pins, brooches, necklace, clips, earrings, bracelets and rings. First used Oct. 1942

GROTTO BLUE

COHN & ROSENBERGER, INC., New York, NY mark for all the usual types of jewelry plus jewelry with pearls, dress ornaments, ornamental hatpins and hairpins, shoe buckles. First used 1926

AXEL BROS., INC. Long Island City, NY. For adjustable costume finger rings and components. First used August, 1954.

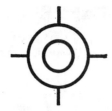

HERFF-JONES COMPANY, Indianapolis,
Ind. Mark for emblem jewelry, mainly rings
and pins. First used in May, 1946.

HERMANN BRANDES, New York, NY
mark for rings, pins, necklaces, and bracelets.
First used 1962

HAMILTON WATCH CO., Lancaster, PA
for jewelry namely pins. First used March
1957

HUTZLER BROTHERS CO., Baltimore,
MD for rings, bracelets, charms, earrings etc.
First used Nov. 12, 1934 or before.

Mark of THE HOUSE OF CLASPS New
York, NY for clasps, pins, rings, bracelets,
charms and earrings. Since March 1962

Mark of B.F. HIRSCH, INC., New York,
NY for jewelry for personal wear. First used
May, 1934.

ALVIN H. HANKIN, Seattle, WA used this
mark for rings, charms, bracelets and buckles
and for emblematic jewelry. First used
Aug. 1920

Jewelry mark of HOPKINS & CARLISH,
INC., New York, NY. First used March
1934.

H.G.E.

UNCAS MANUFACTURING CO., Providence, RI mark for jewelry since 1965

THE H.A. WILSON CO., Newark, NJ mark
for finger rings and other articles of jewelry.
First used June 1935

HELLER & HELLER, Newark, NJ mark
for necklaces, pendants, bracelets, and clasps
and shorteners. First used Jan. 1945

HENRY LANDIS, New York, NY mark for jewelry. First used 1961

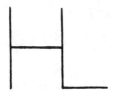

H. LEWKOWITZ, INC., New York, NY mark for jewelry. First used Jan. 1939

H. L. P.
HANDCRAFTED

Niash Refining Company, d.b.a. HIS LORDSHIP PRODUCTS COMPANY, New York, NY for cuff links, cuff link sets, earrings, pins, bracelets, etc. Since December, 1953.

THE H. M. H. CO., Pawtucket, Rhode Island, trademark for religious articles of jewelry as well as bracelets, belt buckles, lockets, pendants, finger rings, dress clips and chains. First used in August, 1944.

HOWARD M. TAFT of H.M. TAFT, Plymouth, NH used this mark for jewelry beginning 1950

Mark of HARVEY & OTIS, Providence, RI used this mark for jewelry. Since June 1904

HARVEY & OTIS, INC., Providence, RI used this mark for finger rings, brooches, charms, jewel badges, tie chains and tie clasps. Used since November, 1947.

HERBERT ROSENTHAL JEWELRY CORP., New York, NY used this mark for rings, bracelets, earrings and necklaces beginning Dec. 1962

HRH

MARTIN HERSH, New York, NY mark for brooch pins, charms, bracelets, rings, necklaces, earrings and clips. First used 1961

HADLEYITE

THE HADLEY COMPANY, INC., Providence, RI mark for bracelets. Since April, 1931.

THE RAYELL CO., New York, NY. Costume jewelry of all kinds including belt buckles, ornamental shoe buckles, ornamental buttons, hat pins, hairpins, hair ornaments and tiaras. Mark first used February, 1946.

Mark for jewelry used by HALGREEN, INC., New York, NY since May 1945

Hallmark

HALLMARK RING CORP. Chicago, IL mark for rings, mountings, cultured and simulated pearls and pearl rings and all types of jewelry made with pearls. Since March, 1951.

HALPERN JEWELERS INCORP. New York, NY mark for jewelry since Aug. 1962

HAMPDEN

SABIN MANUFACTURING CO., Providence, RI - watch chains, tie chains, key chains, link bracelets, scarf pins, collar holders, brooches, finger rings and other jewelry. First used April 1928.

Hand of Friendship

RHINECRAFT COMPANY INCORPORATED, Brooklyn, NY used this mark for costume jewelry - necklaces, cultured pearls, bracelets, earrings, cuff links and scarf pins. First used May, 1958.

hanD Kraft

DAVID KARP COMPANY, INC., New York, NY for finger rings, necklaces, bracelets, brooches and watch bracelets. First used about June, 1950.

HANOVER

Mark of C.H. STUART & CO., Newark, NY for costume jewelry. First used 1961

LEHOM NOVELTY MFG. CO., Newark, NJ mark for genuine and imitation pearls and jewelry. Since October, 1949.

HARLEQUIN

CORO, INC., New York, NY mark for the usual jewelry as well as lockets and strings of pearls. First used 1928.

HARMAN

HARMAN WATCH COMPANY, INC., New York, NY used this for jewelry other than watches since 1936.

HARMONY

MEYER JEWELRY COMPANY, Kansas City, MO. Mark used on rings and compacts of semiprecious metal, since November, 1942.

Harmor

HARRY MORRIS ASSOCIATES, Chicago, IL used this mark for necklaces, rings, bracelets, lavaliers, earrings and pendants all plated with precious metal. Since November, 1947.

HARPER

PERRY NOVELTY COMPANY, Providence, Rhode Island, mark for ornamental jewelry and cigarette cases, lipstick holders and compact holders. Mark in use since April, 1944.

Hartley's

HARTLEY'S INC., Miami, FL used this mark for charms, rings, and all the usual types of costume jewelry. Since Sept. 1938

Harwood

W & H JEWELRY COMPANY, Providence, RI for all the usual types of jewelry made wholly or partially of precious metal. First used April, 1937.

Hattie Carnegie

HATTIE CARNEGIE, INC., New York, NY mark for buckles and buttons made or plated with precious metal and bracelets, brooches, pins, earrings, pendants, finger and scarf rings, lockets, lavallieres, breast pins, necklaces, jeweled hair ornaments and shoe buckles, jeweled cases and holders. First used January, 1919.

Hattie Carnegie

HATTIE CARNEGIE, INC., New York, NY mark for cigarette boxes and containers, lighters and other accessories to do with smoking. First used Nov. 1938

Miss Hattie

HATTIE CARNEGIE, INC., New York, NY mark for buckles and buttons, bracelets, brooches, earrings, pendants, finger and scarf rings, lockets, breast pins, lavalieres, necklaces, jeweled hair ornaments, jeweled shoe buckles, and jeweled cases and holders. First used April 1958

HAYMAKER

HAYMAKER SPORTS, INC., New York, NY for women's jewelry namely cuff links, collar pins, tie pins and studs. Since 1953.

Hayward

AMTEL ARTS INC., Attleboro, MA for both men's and ladies' jewelry. First used Sept. 1968

Heavenly Creations

HEAVENLY CREATIONS, INC., Norfolk, VA mark for ornaments for the hair - braid rings, clasps, decorated combs, and tiaras. Since April 1964

Heiress

JOSEPH H. MEYER BROS., Brooklyn, NY for pearl necklaces. First used January, 1937.

Heirloom Pearls

MORTON B. FARRELL COMPANY, Detroit, Mich., for pearls, pearl necklaces, and pearl mounted jewelry, since March 1944.

"HEIRLOOM PEARLS"

Esther C. Shapiro, d.b.a. AMERICAN DIAMOND & JEWELRY CO., Chicago, IL for jewelry with pearls. Since June, 1921.

HELCO

Mark of HELFER & CO., Chicago, Illinois for earrings, brooches, bracelets. In use since 1937.

Mark of HUGO HERZBERG CO., St. Louis, MO for costume jewelry. First used June 1955

L. HELLER & SONS, New York, NY used this mark for pearls, imitation pearls and reproductions of pearls. Since September, 1922.

KREMENTZ & COMPANY, Newark, NJ for collar buttons, cuff buttons, links, buttons, tie holders, bar pins, handy pins, bracelets, belt buckles, necklaces, pendants, finger rings, vanity boxes, tie clasps, snaps and catches, scarf pins, all made of precious metal or plated therewith. Since July, 1930.

HERE'S MY HEART

Mark of AVON PRODUCTS INC., New York, NY for costume jewelry. First used Oct. 1971

Hi-Art

HICKOK MANUFACTURING CO., INC. Rochester, NY mark for men's jewelry and ladies' necklaces, brooches, ornamental pins, bracelets and earrings. First used January, 1953.

81

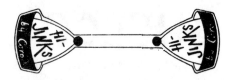

COHN & ROSENBERGER, INC., New York, NY for necklaces, bracelets, finger rings, earrings, jewelry clips, brooches, lockets, beads, pins, hat ornaments, hair ornaments, powder compacts, comb cases, cigarette cases, cigarette boxes, fancy buckles and jewelry initials. First used about 1940.

HI-RISE

MARVELLA PEARLS, INC., New York, NY for necklaces. Since October, 1958.

HICKOK

HICKOK MANUFACTURING CO. INC., Rochester, NY mark for all the early jewelry (collar buttons, collar holders, lingerie and suspender clasps, etc.) The mark has been used on collar buttons since March, 1934; since December 1932 on clasps; since December, 1934 on ornamental chains; since 1909 on ornamental initial, monogram, emblem or insignia articles and since March, 1934 on cravat ornaments.

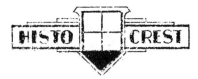

ALBERT NALICK, Los Angeles, Calif. mark for rings, pins, and emblems, used since November, 1941.

THE HITCHING POST

SWANK, INC., Attleboro, MA mark for costume jewelry and dress accessories for men first used 1964 on necktie clips, and 1965 more generally on jewelry.

Hobé

Another mark of HOBÉ CIE LTD., New York, NY for bracelets, brooch pins, lapel pins, earrings, necklaces, finger rings, charms and lockets. First used January, 1926.

Hobé

Mark of HOBÉ CIE, New York, NY for bracelets, brooch pins, lapel pins, earrings, necklaces and finger rings. First used Jan. 1926

1918-1932   1903-1917

1933-1957   1958-1983

Thousands of different guide styles are originated every year by the Hobés. The conscientious attention to style and taste, to quality and detail, are hallmarks of —"Jewels by Hobé."

HOBCO

HOUSE OF BORVANI INC., Providence, RI mark for jewelry. First used 1965

HOBSON

Jewelry mark of J.H. HOBSON CO., North Attleboro, MA since 1939

HOCUS-POCUS

Mark of WILLIAM REISS, INC., New York, NY for jewelry. First used January, 1933.

HOJA

NON-RETAILING CO., INC., Lancaster, PA mark for brooches, bracelets, necklaces, earrings, finger rings, pendants and men's jewelry. First used October, 1952.

Mark of HOLLYWOOD JEWELRY MFG. CO., INC., New York, NY for costume jewelry, namely - metal pins, necklaces, pendants, bracelets, earrings, fob pins, finger rings. First used April, 1948.

HOLIDAY

INTERATLANTIC TRADING CORP. New York, NY used this mark for costume jewelry - necklaces, bracelets, rings and earrings all of which contain simulated pearls. Since Oct. 1949

HOOPON

WINGBACK, INC., New York, NY mark for earrings. First used 1959

HOPE CHEST

THE HOPE CHEST COMPANY, Minneapolis, MN used this mark for costume jewelry beginning Oct. 1960

HOPPEROO

WILLIAM McLEOD CREIGHTON, Charleston, SC. Mark used for costume jewelry since April, 1946.

HOT-CHA

Mark of ERNEST STEINER & CO., New York, NY for bracelets, earrings, pins, clips and finger rings. Since February, 1932.

Jewelry mark of HOUSE of BORVANI, INC., Providence, RI. Since April 1965

House of Stones

WILLIAM V. SCHMIDT CO., INC., New York, NY mark for jewelry. First used 1925

HUG-BUG

ELISABETH NOVELTIES, Fort Wayne, Indiana, mark for fanciful creatures, such as insect jewelry for personal wear. Mark used since October, 1945.

IRONS AND RUSSELL COMPANY, Providence, RI jewelry mark. First used 1870.

IZI FISCHZANG, New York, NY used this mark for rings, charms, bracelets and earrings since Nov. 1962

INTERNATIONAL HARVESTER CO., Chicago, IL mark for earrings, tie clasps and cuff links. Since 1946

I·MILLER

I. MILLER & SONS INC., Long Island City, NY, used this mark for ornamental buckles. First used 1915

Illusion

ALLIED STORES CORPORATION, New York, NY (doing business as THE BON MARCH, Seattle, Wash., and DEY BROTHER & COMPANY, Syracuse, NY, and QUACKENBUSH COMPANY, Paterson, NJ) used this mark for simulated pearls and ornamental jewelry containing simulated pearls namely necklaces, earrings and bracelets, rings, brooches, stick-pins and cuff links. First used June, 1947.

Imperial

IMPERIAL PEARL SYNDICATE, INC., mark for pearl jewelry and gold and gold filled earrings, scarf pins, cuff buttons, bracelets, studs. Since 1933.

IMPERIAL BOUQUET

COHN & ROSENBERGER, INC., New York, NY. Mark for strings of pearls, necklaces, bracelets, earrings, finger rings, brooches, barpins, ornamental hat pins and pins for dress ornaments, ornamental pins and buckles for decorating hats, ornamental shoe buckles and hair ornaments made wholly or in part of or plated with precious metal. Used since July, 1931.

Inde-Pendant!

WEINREICH BROS. CO., New York, NY used this mark for pearl earrings. First used Nov. 1949

Indra

Mark of CORONA MFG. CO., New York, NY for simulated pearls and costume jewelry. First used July, 1946.

INKY DINKY

ICE FOLLIES NOVELTY COMPANY, Los Angeles, CA for novelty pins. Since September, 1950.

INTERAMERICAN IMPORTING CO., Peoria, IL for bracelets, necklaces, cuff links, pins, brooches and pendants. First used July, 1954.

INTRIGUE

ARKO INC., New York, NY for costume jewelry consisting of necklaces, bracelets, earrings, clips, pins, cuff links, hair ornaments, pearls. First used August, 1959.

IRIDELLE

JOSEPH H. MEYER BROS., Brooklyn, NY mark for necklaces, bracelets, rings, clips, brooches and earrings since 1931

JOSEPH H. MEYER BROS., Brooklyn, NY mark for men's and women's costume jewelry - necklaces, bracelets, finger rings, ornamental clips, brooches and earrings. First used 1931.

IRILITE

Mark of THE RICHELIEU CORPORATION, New York, NY for costume jewelry - necklaces, bracelets, finger rings and pendants. Since June, 1948.

IRIS

Anther mark used by JOSEPH H. MEYER BROS. Brooklyn, NY for necklaces, bracelets, clips, etc. This mark was first used in 1938.

ISIS, INC. Providence, RI for jewelry and semi-precious and precious gems. First used October, 1942.

ISLAND FLOWER

Mark of AVON PRODUCTS INC., New York, NY for costume jewelry. First used Dec. 1971

ISLAND LIFE

Mark of AVON PRODUCTS INC., New York, NY for costume jewelry. First used Nov. 1971

IT'S RINGTIME

UNCAS MANUFACTURING CO., Providence, RI mark for Ladies' finger rings. First used 1960

TURCHIN BEAD & PEARLIZING CO., Brooklyn, NY for jewelry with synthetic pearls and beads carrying a synthetic pearlized finish. First used January, 1948.

JO—DI JEWELRY MANUFACTURING, INC., New York, NY for charms, bracelets, pins, cuff links, crosses and other jewelry. First used June 1962

JOSTEN MANUFACTURING CO., Owatonna, MN, mark for rings, ornamental pins, and medals. First used Jan. 1913

R. M. JORDAN AND COMPANY, Providence, RI, mark for jewelry. Used since December, 1944.

Mark of JABLOW MANUFACTURING CO., INC. New York, NY for lockets, crosses, bracelets and baby bracelets. First used January, 1904.

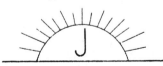

Henry Paulson, d.b.a. HENRY PAULSON & CO., Chicago, IL used this mark for finger rings and bracelets. First used September, 1931.

JOCOBY—BENDER, INC. Woodside, NY mark for bracelets and watch bracelets. First used 1946

J.D.

NAT YOUNG, New York, NY mark for earrings, and pendants. First used July 1962

J.H.H.

JAMES H. HALL of JAMES H. HALL CO., Providence, RI, mark for costume jewelry. Since May 1962

JLC

Mark of JOHN L. COLE, New York, NY for pearl clasps, bracelets, rings, pendants, earrings and necklaces. First used July, 1962.

Mark of JEWEL MASTERS, INC., Beverly Hills, CA for jewelry. First used 1955

JAECKEL MFG. CO., INC., Providence. RI used this mark for necklaces, pendants, bracelets, rings, earrings and brooches. First used September, 1929.

J.M.F. CO.

J. M. FISHER COMPANY, Attleboro, Mass. used this mark for watch attachments and pendants, bracelets and lockets, as well as for vanity cases, card cases, buckles, lorgnettes, which were plated or made of precious metal. The company claimed use of this mark since 1893. Still active in 1949.

JMF CO.

J.M. FISHER COMPANY, Attleboro, MA for swivels and clasps, pendants and precious metal plated bracelets, lockets, charms and ornamental pins. First used July, 1914.

JOBE-ROSE JEWELRY COMPANY, Birmingham, AL used this mark for jewelry. First used July, 1951.

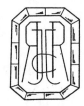

JOHN RUBEL CO., New York, NY mark for brooches, bracelets, necklaces, lavalieres, pendants, and buckles. Used since August, 1943.

J & R KOCH CO., INC. New York, NY for rings, pendants, brooches, earrings, cuff links. First used 1932

JOHN ULLENBERG, INC., Chattanooga, TN mark for jewelry. Since 1940.

JABEL

JABEL RING MANUFACTURING CO., Newark, NJ for finger rings and settings, brooches, jeweled clips, pendants, earrings, bracelets, necklaces. Since December, 1916.

Mark of NEWARK JEWELRY MANUFACTURING CO., Newark, NJ for "fancy" jewelry including the usual types and cameos. Since May, 1946.

Jacques Kreisler

Mark of JACQUES KREISLER MANUFACTURING CORP., North Bergen, NJ for all the usual types of jewelry made for both men and women. Since August, 1941.

JAG

MIGLIO JEWELRY MANUFACTURING CO., New York, NY mark for jewelry including religious jewelry. First used February 1963

JAGUAR

BRUNER-RITTER INC., New York, NY for bracelets, wrist watch bracelets and cuff links. Since April, 1954.

JAIS SCARABÉ

This is the mark of D. SWAROVSKI of Austria for ornamental stones and beads of glass or of plastics having a vapor coating, imitation ornamental stones or beads provided with a cut facet surface. First used January, 1956.

Mark used by Hank J. Owen d.b.a. THE OWEN COMPANY, Miami, FL for costume jewelry made of metal, of imitation stones, simulated pearls, etc. Since February, 1954.

JANTZEN, INC., Portland, Ore., for costume jewelry. Mark first used July, 1950.

JANTZEN, INC., Portland, Ore., for costume jewelry. Mark first used July, 1950.

HEIFERMAN & BERGER, INC., New York, NY used this mark on its costume jewelry. First used August 23, 1946.

J. POSNER & SONS, INC., New York, NY mark for rings, charms, pendants, brooches, etc. This company made jewelry with precious metal as well as jewelry which was plated with precious metal. Mark first used December, 1948.

JEANNE

MARK DOTTENHEIM, New York, NY, mark for pearl jewelry. First used October, 1919.

JMS JEWELRY MFG. CO., Bloomfield, NJ for earrings, bracelets, pendants, pins. Since 1945.

JERAY

RICE-AWEINER & CO., Providence, RI, mark for costume jewelry.

Mark of NEW ENGLAND GLASS WORKS, INC., Providence, RI for ornamental jewelry, namely pins, brooches, lockets, earrings, bracelets, necklaces, compacts, rings, pendants and cigarette cases. First used Feb. 1946

THE JEWEL BOX

GEORGE R. KENNEY d.b.a. THE JEWEL BOX, Sioux Falls, SD used this mark for costume jewelry. First used Dec. 1958

Jewel-Galleries

MARCUS & CO., INC. New York, NY mark for all the usual types of jewelry as well as mountings. First used February, 1943.

The mark of S.H. CLAUSIN & CO., Minneapolis, MN for jewelry. Used since May, 1955.

JEWELART

JEWELART CO., East Providence, RI mark for costume jewelry. First used Nov. 1946

JEWELCRAFT

CORO, INC., New York, NY. Mark for necklaces, bracelets, finger rings, earrings, jewelry clips, brooches, lockets and the following made wholly or partly of precious metal or plated with the same: beads, pins, hat ornaments, holders for face powder compacts, comb cases and jewelry initials. First used 1920.

Jewelcraft

CORO, INC., New York, NY mark for chains and pendants, lockets, bracelets, rings, neck chains and brooches. Made wholly or partly of sterling silver, silverplate, gold or goldplate. First used 1920.

JEWELERS DESIGN, INC., New York, NY mark for rings, necklaces, pins, charms cuff links. Since 1961

JEWELER'S QUALITY PEARLS

SOL E. WEINREICH of WEINREICH BROTHERS CO., New York, NY used this mark for jewelry and jewelry with pearls since March 1929

Jewelette

Celia Maskit d.b.a. EMPRESS NOVELTY JEWELRY CO., New York, NY used this mark for costume jewelry. First used December, 1957.

JEWELFULLY YOURS

CORO, INC., New York, NY mark for necklaces, rings, bracelets, earrings, jewelry clips, brooches, lockets. First used August, 1947.

KANTOR NOVELTY INC., New York, NY used this mark for jewelry made of plastic and ornamented with precious metal including pins, hat ornaments, hair ornaments, compacts, comb cases, cigarette cases, fancy buckles and jewelry initials. First used 1942

BEN FELSENTHAL & CO., INC., New York, NY mark for costume jewelry - novelty sets, pendants, pins, necklaces, bracelets, brooches, compacts and cigarette cases. First used January, 1933.

Herman S. Kessler d.b.a. GOLD SEAL ENTERPRISES and also as JEWELRY COMPANY OF AMERICA, Baltimore, MD used this mark for costume jewelry. Since September, 1958.

JEWELS BY BAZAAR

Mark of LEE H. PELZMAN d.b.a. LEE PELZMAN CO., New York, NY for costume jewelry. Used since May, 1959.

JEWELS BY BERNADETTE

J.B. BERNSTEIN CO., Pittsburgh, PA mark for jewelry, particularly pins and earrings. First used 1970

Mark for jewelry of JEWELS BY EDWAR, Beverly Hills, CA first used Jan. 1956

MARNER JEWELRY CO., Providence, RI mark for brooches, earrings, necklaces and clasps. First used about May 1953.

BENJAMIN R. LEVY & IRVING LANDSMAN, Brooklyn, NY mark for costume jewelry as well as semi-precious jewelry. First used 1937

JEWELS OF JOSANNA

JOSANNA, INC., New York, NY mark first used October 8, 1945.

Jewels of the Seven Seas

John H. Standen d.b.a. J.H. STANDEN, Glen Arbor, MI for jewelry made from seashells. First used August, 1953.

JEWELS ROYALE

F—K COMPANY, Tulsa, OK, mark for jewelry since August 1971

JINGLE JANGLE

CORO, INC., New York, NY mark for necklaces, bracelets, earrings, jewelry clips, brooches, lockets, finger rings, charm bracelets and charms. First used December, 1958.

JINGLE RINGS

CORO mark for finger rings, necklaces, bracelets, earrings, jewelry clips, brooches, lockets, charm bracelets and charms. First used December, 1958.

JOAN BARI

EDISON BROTHERS STORES, INC., St. Louis, MO used this mark for jewelry. The name JOAN BARI is fictitious. First used, 1958.

Jo Mar

BARKER & BARKER, Providence, RI, for finger rings, brooches, pendants, necklaces, clips, earrings and tie clasps. Since 1946.

MARGARET J. COOK, Bethesda, MD used this mark for bracelets, earrings, pins, necklaces and rings. First used Sept. 1946

John Alden

EISENSTADT MANUFACTURING COMPANY, St. Louis, MO, mark for tie clasps, emblem charms, buttons, lockets, badges, cluff links, scarf pins, buckles, fobs, shirt studs, key chains, key rings and money clips. First used May, 1942.

Jolly Jewels

Jewelry mark of JOLLY JEWELS, Baltimore, MD. First used Feb. 1946

Mark used by JOSEPH J. MAZER & CO., INC., of New York in the 1940s and 50s.

by Jordan

R.M. JORDAN & CO., Providence, RI mark for jewelry. Used since 1942

Joseff

JOSEFF—HOLLYWOOD, Burbank and Beverly Hills, CA mark for necklaces, rings, ornamental pins, various items of custom made and costume jewelry, made in whole or in part of, or plated with precious metals. First used Sept. 1938

JUDY-LEE

Costume jewelry mark of BLANCH—ETTE, Chicago, IL first used 1958

Costume jewelry mark of BLANCH—ETTE INC., Chicago, IL. First used July 1958

Jule Thads

Mark of JULES-THAD CREATIONS, San Francisco, CA for earrings, brooches, lapel pins, pendants, hat ornaments, and ring mountings. Since November, 1945.

JULIA SCHWARTING, Hollywood Fla., for articles of jewelry made of fancy shellwork, namely pins, brooches, earrings and the like. Since December, 1945.

JULONS

JULONS, INC., New York, NY for self-attaching costume ornaments - pins, earrings, brooches, necklaces, ankle bracelets, rings, chatelaines. Since April, 1951.

JUNGLE

CRAFT PRECISION COMPANY, Los Angeles, CA, mark for costume jewelry. Used since January, 1946.

" Junior Miss "

ZELL BROS., Portland, OR used this mark for jewelry "suitable for young women of the boarding and finishing school age." First used Jan. 1944

JUNIOR PROM

Mark of D. LISNER & CO., New York, NY for necklaces, bracelets, earrings and brooches. First used June, 1956.

JUNO LITE

Eric Weinberger d.b.a. JUNO PRODUCTS CO., Cleveland, OH for necklaces, bracelets, pins and earrings. First used May, 1957.

KNIGHT MANUFACTURING CO., INC., Providence, RI mark for jewelry. First used Aug. 1965

The mark used by J.P. KNIGHT, Cincinnati, OH both for jewelry and mounts and blanks used in jewelry. Since February, 1952.

KESTENMAN BROS. MFG. CO., Providence RI for jewelry including bracelets, clasps and buckles made wholly or partly of precious metal. Mark first used March, 1920.

KOSTAN BROTHERS, Beverly Hills, CA mark for rings, earrings, bracelets, brooches, clasps, pendants, necklaces, since October 1962

K-C

Jewelry mark of K.C. JEWELRY MANUFACTURING CO., INC., Tenafly, NJ, since March 1955

THE KINNEY COMPANY, Providence, RI mark for rings, pins, bracelets, lockets, buckles, tie clips and cuff links. First used January, 1908.

KRESGE DEPARTMENT STORE CORPORATIONS, Newark, New Jersey, began using this mark in February of 1927 for beads, including beads of coral, turquoise, base metal, amber and celluloid; hair pins and combs, and buttons and other jewelry.

KI

Jewelry mark of JULIUS KATZ of JULIUS KATZ & SON, New York, NY since May 1962

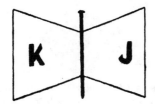

JOSEPH KAHAN of KAHAN JEWELRY CO., New York, NY mark for jewelry. First used 1962

CLASSIC JEWELRY MFGRS., New York, NY used this mark for jewelry beginning July 1962.

ERNEST LOWENSTEIN INC., New York, NY mark for imitation gems and cut glass bodies adapted for use in the manufacture of costume jewelry and accessories, novelty items and general ornamental purposes. First used February, 1949.

KSK

Mark of K.S.K. JEWELRY CO., New York, NY used this mark for rings, brooches and pins. First used Jan. 1946.

WM. R. KATZ COMPANY, Dallas, TX for rings and necklaces. Since July, 1953.

Karen Kraft

SHERRY CRAFT, INC. Philadelpnia, PA mark for novelty and costume jewelry - anklets, bracelets, barrettes, brooches, rings, earrings, lockets, necklaces and ornamental pins. First used June 1, 1953.

Mandel Bead Company, New York, NY mark for novelty and costume jewelry since June 1941

KAUFMAN & RUDERMAN, INC., New York, NY used this mark for costume jewelry. First used June 1940

KASHMIR

PEARLS BY DELTAH, INC., Pawtucket, RI for simulated pearls and other jewelry incorporating simulated pearls such as necklaces, bracelets, earrings, etc. and necklace clasps and shorteners, lavalieres, sautoirs, tie pins, cuff links and studs. First used January, 1950.

KAYANO

KATZ & OGUSH, INC., New York, NY mark for all the usual jewelry including bar pins, scarf pins, sautoirs, vanity cases, buckles, shoe buckles, lockets and necklace clasps. First used September, 1924.

KAYEN

Nathan Kusnitz d.b.a. KAYEN JEWELRY CO., New York, NY mark for jewelry. First used November, 1964.

KENCO

WILLIAM E. KENNISON of W.E. KENNISON CO., Providence, RI mark for bracelets, necklaces, earrings and jewelry snaps and clasps. Since Jan. 1925

KESTENMADE

KESTENMAN BROS. MFG. CO., of Providence, RI began using this mark in April, 1924 for its wrist-watch bracelets.

KESTENMADE

KESTENMAN BROS., MFG. CO., Providence, RI, mark for bracelets, clasps and buckles since 1924. This is a smaller version of the mark used for watch bracelets.

KEY

ANSON INCORPORATED, Providence, RI used this mark on men's jewelry. Since July, 1959.

Keynote of Fashion

Another UNCAS MANUFACTURING COMPANY, Providence, RI, mark for jewelry including brooches, bracelets, necklaces, pins and earrings. First used February, 1947.

KIDDIEGEM

UNCAS MANUFACTURING CO., Providence, RI mark for jewelry. Since 1934

KIDDLEY LINX

Mark of MAX SILVERMAN d.b.a. MAX-IMILLIAN JEWELRY, New York, NY for bracelets, necklaces charms and brooch pins. Since June 1954

KI-GU

CHARLES KIASCHEK, New York, NY mark for pins, pendants, brooches, lockets, clasps, earrings, bracelets, necklaces and rings. First used 1938

KIK-A-POO

HOLLYWOOD JEWELRY MANUFAC-TURING CO., INC., Hollywood, CA used this mark for rings, earrings and bracelets of sterling silver. First used April, 1946.

Kimberley Gems

Mark of ISAAC J. ADELSON d.b.a. ROBERTS JEWELRY CO., Kansas City, MO for "Imitation white diamonds." First used Oct. 1921

KINDKRAFT

S. KIND & SONS, Philadelphia, PA for fashion jewelry made on base metal — namely earrings, brooches, bracelets, necklaces, scatter pins and simulated pearls. Mark used since April, 1952.

KING

AROPAX CORPORATION, New York, NY for costume jewelry such as earrings, necklaces, brooches, bracelets and the like. First used May, 1955.

King Craft

H. WEINREICH COMPANY, INC., Philadelphia, PA for bracelets, brooches, finger rings, earrings, lockets, necklaces, ornamental pins, anklets and barrettes. First used about March, 1950.

KING SOLOMON

PORTER & BUFFINGTON CO., Providence, RI mark for jewelry since April, 1921.

KliK-EtteS

KLIK PROMOTIONS, INC., New York, NY for decorative pins and clips. First used March, 1952.

HARRY KLITZNER CO., INC., Providence, RI, used this mark for jewelry. First used 1962

KNIGHT'S COLLAR

WEINREICH BROTHERS COMPANY, New York, NY, mark for pearl necklaces, pearl earrings, bracelets, and all pearl jewelry. Since June, 1949.

Mark of GEORGE J. HECHT, New York, NY for strings of beads made of plastic, glass and semi precious stones. First used 1941

KONDA
Prince of Pearls

SAMSTAG & HILDER BROS., New York, NY for imitation pearl jewelry. Since April, 1923.

"KOO-KEY"

Costume jewelry mark of CAROLE ACCESSORIES, INC., Los Angeles, CA. First used Feb. 1961

KOPY KAT

Rankin & Hambro, Inc., d.b.a. KOPY KAT, Boston, MA mark for costume jewelry. Since March, 1959.

KRAMER

Mark of KRAMER JEWELRY CREATIONS, INC., New York, NY for necklaces, bracelets, finger rings, earrings, jewelry clips, brooches, lockets, charms, charm bracelets, fobs. First used 1943.

Kreature-Kraft

Mark of BROWN & MILLS INC., Providence, RI, for brooches, clips, pins, necklaces, earrings. First used 1941

JK

STYLED BY

Jacques Kreisler

JACQUES KREISLER MFG., CORP., of North Bergen, NJ used these marks on their jewelry. Additional marks used were GAY NINETIES, KREISLER QUALITY, AMERICAN MODERN, SLIDE-IT and FOREVER YOURS.

Kreisler

JACQUES KREISLER MANUFACTURING CORP. North Bergen, NJ used this mark for jewelry since the fall of 1951

Kreisler

JACQUES KREISLER MANUFACTURING CORPORATION, North Bergen, NJ mark for jewelry. First used Sept. 1955

Kreisler

JACQUES KREISLER MANUFACTURING CORP. used this mark for men's jewelry as well as bracelets, charm bracelets and neck chains for women. First used in 1951

JACQUES KREISLER MANUFACTURING CORP., North Bergen, NY, used this mark for men's jewelry as well as bracelets, charm bracelets and neck chains for women. First used in May 1939.

Kreisler Craft

JACQUES KREISLER MANUFACTURING COMPANY, North Bergern, NJ used this mark for men's jewelry. Since March 1948 although the word KREISLER was first used in 1941.

7K

Mark of FRANK KREMENTZ CO. of Newark, NJ

KREMENTZ

KREMENTZ & COMPANY, Newark, NJ used this mark for its studs and buttons of all kinds as well as scarf pins, brooches, bar pins, necklace clasps, bracelets and lingerie clasps all made of rolled gold plate. First used in 1884.

KREMENTZ & COMPANY, Newark, NJ mark for jewelry made of precious metal, including child's sets, clasps and finger rings. First used March, 1896.

CURRENT MARK OF KREMENTZ & CO. of Newark, N.J.

KREMENTZ & CO., Newark, NJ used this mark for men's jewelry as well as crosses, medals, brooches, earrings, necklaces, bracelets, and charms some of the silver, and gold overlay. First used 1884.

S.H. KRESS & CO., New York, NY used this mark on dresser accessories. First used April 1945

E.L. LOGEE CO., Providence, RI for brooches, stickpins, cuff links, finger rings, tie clasps. Since 1899.

Mark of PETER LINDEMAN, New York, NY for jewelry since March 1962

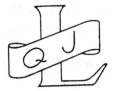

LEAVENS MANUFACTURING COMPANY, INC., Attleboro, Mass., mark for finger rings, brooches, cravat holders, since March, 1948.

L.A.

LEVY-ANDERSON CO., INC. Providence, RI mark for bracelets, earrings, necklaces, brooches, lockets and watch bracelets. First used 1936.

L & B

Mark of L. & B. JEWELRY MANUFAC-TURING COMPANY, Providence, RI, since 1945.

Mark of LEIF BROTHERS, New York, NY for jewelry such as clips, pendants, chokers, tie clasps, rings, pins, bracelets, earrings and brooches and buckles, lapel buttons, clasps. Used since July, 1945.

LC

Mark of SARAH COVENTRY, INC., Newark, NY for costume jewelry. First used March 1965

LG

LIND-GAL INC., New York, NY mark for costume jewelry - decor for eye glass frames. First used July, 1952.

GEORGE LEDERMAN, INC., New York, NY mark for jewelry. First used 1962

LGB

Mark of L.G. BALFOUR COMPANY, Attleboro, MA for jewelry. First used 1919.

LITTON INDUSTRIES INC., Beverly Hills, CA, used this mark for jewelry with simulated gem stones. First used 1970

LOEWI'S JEWELRY, New York, NY mark for rings, charms, necklaces and other articles of jewelry. Since July 1962

LAZARUS JEWELERS, INC., New York, NY mark for charms, rings, brooches and earrings. First used 1959

LOUIS MILLER, New York, NY mark for costume jewelry. First used 1962

L&M

L & M JEWELRY CREATIONS, New York, NY mark for brooch pins, charms, bracelets, finger rings, necklaces, earrings, clips and pendants. First used about May 1962

Jewelry mark of PETER CARRAO of LAFAYETTE MFG. CO., of New York. First used 1963

Jewelry mark of LEVART ORIGINALS, INC., New York, NY. First used June 1961

L-S

LEVINE—SIMSON CO., INC., New York, NY mark for jewelry. First used Dec. 1947

L'Aiglon

BERNARD RICE'S SONS, New York, NY mark for buckles, etc. First used April, 1921.

L' Aiglon

L. & B. JEWELRY MANUFACTURING COMPANY, Providence, RI began using this mark in 1940 for its jewelry.

WEINREICH BROTHERS CO., New York, NY for necklaces, bracelets, earrings, pin clips and brooches. First used October, 1952.

CHARLES A. KEENE, New York, NY mark for artificial pearls, necklaces, bracelets, brooches, lavallieres and stickpins. Used since March, 1921.

LA BELLE

CORO, INC., New York, NY for all the usual types of jewelry including pearls. Since May, 1963.

Les Ballet Des Oiseau
THE BALLET of The BIRDS

JOHN RUBEL CO., New York, NY mark for brooches, bracelets, necklaces, lavaliers, pendants, and buckles. First used August, 1943

Les Ballet Des Fleurs
THE BALLET of The FLOWERS

JOHN RUBEL CO., New York, NY mark for brooches, bracelets, necklaces, lavaliers, pendants, and buckles. First used August, 1943.

La Bohême PERLES

CZECHOSLOVAK BEAD CO., INC. New York, NY used this mark for pearls and stones. Since January, 1920.

La Bohême

HENRY GORDY, New York, NY mark for costume jewelry containing pearls - necklaces, rings, pins and earrings. First used 1945

La Conga

Mark of ALFRED POHL, New York, NY for simulated pearls and costume jewelry. Used since April, 1946.

La Danse Des Fleurs
DANCING FLOWERS

JOHN RUBEL CO., New York, NY mark for brooches, bracelets, necklaces, lavaliers, pendants, and buckles. First used August, 1943.

EULENE PEARLCRAFTERS New York, NY. Mark used for synthetic pearls, often in combination with rhinestones. November 1, 1946.

LA FAVOR

KAUFMAN DEPARTMENT STORES, INC., Pittsburgh, PA for pearl jewelry. First used June, 1920.

La Fouragere

JOHN RUBEL CO., New York, NY mark for brooches, bracelets, necklaces, lavaliers, pendants, and buckles. First used August, 1943.

La Helene

SIGSBIE GUTTER, New York, NY for pearls. First used July, 1920.

La Louise

MANHATTAN BEAD CHAIN CO., New York, NY mark for pearls and pearl jewelry since Dec. 1919

La Madelaine

THEIL-SCHOEN CO., New York, NY. Mark for non-precious and semi-precious brooch pins, earrings, clip pins and imitation pearl necklaces, used since July, 1946.

LaMar

Mark of MARLA PEARL NOVELTY CO., Providence, RI. Used on pearl necklaces, and brooches, earrings, bracelets, lockets and pendants. In use since July, 1930.

CHARLES A. KEENE, New York, NY for artificial pearls, bracelets, necklaces, brooches, lavallieres and stickpins. Used since March, 1921.

ROBERT FLEISCHER, New York, NY mark for artificial pearl necklaces and pearl beads, since October, 1944.
Also used for bracelets and brooches.

RIPLEY AND GOWEN CO., INC., Attleboro, MA for bracelets, necklets, brooches, lockets, bar pins, finger rings and other jewelry for ladies and for men's jewelry. First used January, 1924.

La Monna Vanna

Mark used by BERNARD COHEN, New York, NY for pearl jewelry. First used October, 1923.

FAIR TRADING CO., INC. New York, NY for pearls. First used December, 1923.

LA REINE

PEARLS BY DELTAH INC., Pawtucket, RI. Mark not only for pearl necklaces, but for clasps, rings, earrings, bracelets, brooches, cuff links and studs. First used April, 1939.

L. HELLER & SON, INC., New York, NY mark for its pearl jewelry and for other jewelry plated in whole or in part with precious metal. Since April, 1939.

LA REL ORIGINALS, New York, NY for costume jewelry - rings, earrings, bracelets, lockets, pendants, pins and brooches. First used June, 1955 and without the words "rhinestone magic" on April, 1953.

COLONIAL BEAD CO., INC., New York, NY mark for pearl jewelry. First used January, 1923.

LAYKO, ROSS & CO., INC. Seattle, Wash., for rings, lockets, crosses, necklaces, pendants, brooches, bar pins, earrings, watch bracelets, tie clasps. First used 1918.

LA ROYAL

ROYAL BEAD NOVELTY CO., INC., New York, NY mark for necklaces, bracelets and earrings with simulated pearl beads. First used March 1926

LA REPLICA

SOL E. WEINREICH of WEINREICH BROS. CO., New York, NY mark for pearl necklaces, pearl earrings, bracelets and other jewelry. First used August 1938

LA TAMBA

ARAM D. MANCHESTER, Providence, RI for artificial and imitation pearls. First used August, 1920.

La Touraine

REGAL PEARL AND JEWELRY CO., New York, NY Began using this mark in April, 1945 for its pearl, artificial pearl and other jewelry.

LA TAUSCA

HELLER & SONS, INC., New York, NY for imitation pearl bracelets, brooches, earrings, rings, hair ornaments, lavallieres, necklaces, sautoirs and tie pins. First used July, 1939.

La Traviata

TRAVIATA JEWELRY CO., New York, NY for non-precious costume jewelry and simulated pearls. Used since May, 1946.

CARLA'
LA VANITA

NATIONAL COSTUME JEWELRY CO., of Buffalo, NY mark for jewelry.

H. WOLFF & CO. New York, NY for jewelry with imitation pearls. First used November, 1920.

La Vie

LaVIE JEWELRY CORP., New York, NY mark for costume jewelry. First used 1960

La Vie Pearls

LA VIE PEARL COMPANY, New York, NY for pearl jewelry. First used August, 1922.

LACHAISE

HENRI L. LIBMAN d.b.a. LA CHAISE JEWELRY CO., Chicago, IL for costume jewelry. In use since September, 1955.

ISIDORE JAFFE, New York, NY used this mark for costume jewelry. First used April 1944

PARMOR PRODUCTS COMPANY, Atlanta, GA. Mark for lockets, bracelets, rings, earrings, compacts, necklaces, lavalieres and brooches. Used since October 30, 1945.

Lady Claire

SCHEIN BROTHERS, INC., New York, NY used this mark for costume jewelry made of base metals. First used February, 1940.

LADY COVENTRY

SARAH COVENTRY, INC., Newark, NY mark for costume jewelry. This mark first used March 1965

LEDERER BROTHERS, New York, NY used this mark for simulated pearl necklaces, pins and earrings. First used June 1948

Lady Esther

SCHEIN BROTHERS, INC., New York, NY for jewelry. First used December, 1932.

LADY FAIR

LADY FAIR PEARLS, Brooklyn, NY mark used for simulated pearls used in connection with ladies' necklaces, earrings, bracelets and pins. Since February, 1948.

LADY JOAN

J.J. NEWBERRY, CO., New York, NY mark for earrings, bracelets, necklaces, rings, charms and brooches. First used June 1949

"Lady Lenore"

J. GLADSTONE COMPANY, New York, NY mark for pearls, and jewelry, since November 1945.

RICHCRAFT, INC., Southhampton, PA for bracelets, earrings, necklaces, pin and earring sets and matching sets consisting of necklace and earrings. First used about March, 1956.

Lady Monaco

RICHCRAFT, INC. Southhampton, PA for bracelets, earrings, necklaces, pins, pin and earring sets, and matching sets consisting of necklace and earrings. First used about March, 1956.

Lady Pam

PAMEL IMPORT CORPORATION, New York, NY for cultured pearls and cultured pearl necklaces, finger rings, bracelets and brooch pins. June, 1953.

Lady Ro-Ann

ARTLAC INC., New York, NY for simulated pearls and necklaces, earrings, bracelets, amulets and pin and dress ornaments incorporating simulated pearls. Since June, 1942.

LADY SWANK

SWANK, INC., Attleboro, MA mark for costume jewelry. First used March 1965

LADYETTE

MARATHON CO., Attleboro, MA mark for finger rings, bracelets, lockets, pendants, brooches, compact cases, lavalieres and neck chains with pendant drops, bead necklaces and earrings. First used March 1931

LAG

JOSEPH N. WINEROTH INC., d.b.a. L.A. GIABOBBI & CO., San Francisco, CA, used this mark for jewelry beginning in 1962

LAGUNA

ROYAL BEAD NOVELTY CO., New York, NY used this mark for jewelry made with simulated pearls. Since 1944

Laguna

ROYAL CRAFTSMEN, INC., New York, NY used this mark for simulated pearls made of plastic and ornaments (jewelry) for 'personal adornment.' First used February, 1944.

"THE UNITED FRONT ★★★ ★★★ BEHIND THE FRONT"

LAMPL, New York, NY. Mark for rings, bar pins, bracelets, necklaces, charms, dress clips, key chains, earrings and brooches. Since July, 1942.

by Lampl

Mark of WALTER LAMPL, New York, NY for rings, earrings lapel pins, necklaces, lavalieres, lockets, charms, dress clips decorative combs, hair ornaments and barrettes. First used June 1921

"LAN"

LANCOR MANUFACTURING COMPANY, Providence, RI, for hair clasps, lingerie clasps, bow holders, necklaces, bracelets, ear ornaments, brooches, and rings. Used since 1925.

LANCETTE

SILSON, INC., New York, NY used this mark for jewelry clips, brooches, lockets, pins, hat ornaments and hair ornaments. First used March 1941

IRVING LANG of LANG MANUFACTURING CO., New York, NY mark for brooch pins, charms, bracelets, necklaces, rings, earrings, clips, and cuff links. First used 1961

LANG JEWELRY COMPANY, Providence, RI, mark used on sterling silver costume jewelry since April, 1946.

Langley

WOLF & KLAR WHOLESALE SUPPLY CO., Fort Worth, Texas for jewelry, namely artificial pearls, finger rings, bracelets, brooches and earrings. Mark in use since December, 1945.

Lawré

LAWRENCE MFG. INC., Providence, Rhode Island, used this mark for jewelry beginning May 8, 1946.

THE LAWS I LIVE BY

BRIGGS, BATES & BACON CO., Attleboro, MA mark for charms for bracelets and necklaces. First used Dec. 1955

Lazy Louie

ALPHA-CRAFT COMPANY, New York, NY started using this mark October, 1945 for its costume jewelry.

Le Beau

ROYAL BEAD NOVELTY CO., INC., New York, NY mark for necklaces and bracelets of simulated pearls. Used since May 1940.

Le' Cultra

JOSEPH H. MEYER BROS., Brooklyn, NY for pearl jewelry — namely necklaces, bracelets, finger rings, jewelry clips and earrings with pearls since March, 1949.

Le Grand

The jewelry mark of LE GRAND S. ELEBASH, Selma and Montgomery, AL, Jackson, MS, Roanoke, VA and Atlanta, GA. First used November, 1928.

Le PARADIS

WEINREICH BROS. COMPANY, New York, NY mark for pearl necklaces, pearl earrings, pearl bracelets, pearl brooches and strings of pearls. First used July, 1935.

LE ROY'S

LE ROY'S JEWELERS, Los Angeles Calif., used this mark for all types of costume jewelry since December, 1929.

Le Touquet

TRIFARI, KRUSSMAN & FISHEL, INC., New York, NY mark for sport jewelry, namely necklaces, bracelets, and earrings. First used 1929.

LEADING BAND

W & H JEWELRY COMPANY, Providence, RI for bracelets, watch bracelets, rings, earrings, brooches, necklaces, pendants, lockets, pins, hair ornaments. First used August, 1940.

W. & H. JEWELRY COMPANY, INC., Providence, RI mark for necklaces, bracelets, earrings, jewelry clips, brooches, lockets, pendants, rings, scatter pins, breast pins, all made in whole or part of precious or plated metal. Since June, 1940.

Ledo

LEADING JEWELRY MANUFACTURING COMPANY, Mamaroneck, NY mark for costume jewelry - earrings, necklaces, bracelets, pins and brooches. First used July, 1949.

RIST-LETTE
By
Ledo

LEADING JEWELRY MANUFACTURING COMPANY, Mamaroneck, NY for costume jewelry - earrings, necklaces, bracelets, pins and brooches. First used July, 1953.

LEGACY

MAX KOHNER INC., Baltimore, MD used this mark on costume jewelry - necklaces, pendants, bracelets, rings earrings and brooches. First used 1964

LEONARDO

DaVINCI CREATIONS, INC., Providence, RI mark for jewelry. First used May 1945

LERU

PELTAN & LERU CORP. New York, NY, used this mark for bracelets, necklaces and earrings. First used November 1956

LESTER & CO., Newark, NJ mark for brooches, rings, pendants, bracelets, ear clips, tiaras, necklaces, hair ornaments, jeweled hat ornaments and lockets. First used Nov. 1934

LEYS, CHRISTIES & CO., INC., New York, NY jewelry mark. First used June, 1899.

LICHT

LICHTMAN JEWELRY MFG. CO., INC., New York, NY mark for charms, discs, charm bracelets and bangle bracelets. Since June 1962

LIGHTS AND SHADOWS

Mark of AVON PRODUCTS INC., New York, NY for costume jewelry. First used Oct. 1971

Accents by LILIBET, INC., of New York, NY used this mark on costume jewelry since 1956

Mark of LILY DACHE INC., New York, NY for costume jewelry. First used March, 1923.

Lind-Gal

LIND-GAL INC., New York, NY for costume jewelry, namely, decor for eye glass frames, ladies' pins, men's cuff links and tie bars. First used June, 1951.

Link-it

ROYAL BEAD NOVELTY CO., INC. New York, NY used this mark for costume jewelry necklaces, bracelets, etc. and jewelry with pearls. Since September, 1955.

LINMARK INTERNATIONAL COR-
PORATION, New York, NY used this
mark for jewelry with cultured pearls, namely earrings, bracelets, brooches and rings.
First used December, 1952.

VOLUPTÉ, INC., Elizabeth, NJ used this
mark for vanity cases beginning in 1949

LIPPMAN'S, Altoona, PA mark for artificial
pearls. First used August, 1920.

SOL E. WEINREICH of WEINREICH
BROTHERS CO., New York, NY mark for
jewelry since 1940

D. LISNER & CO., New York, NY used this mark for costume jewelry for
children. First used May, 1935.

∟isner

D. LISNER & CO., INC. New York, NY
mark for necklaces, bracelets, earrings and
brooches for personal wear. First used exactly as pictured since May, 1959. The
Lisner mark was used initially in 1938.

Mark of D. LISNER & CO., INC., New
York, NY for necklaces, bracelets, earrings,
brooches. Entire mark as pictured first used
June, 1956. The mark 'Lisner' was first used
in 1938.

Mark of LITWIN & SONS, Cincinnati,
Ohio, for rings, bar pins, bracelets, brooches
and necklaces. Used since September, 1930.

LIT

LITWIN & SONS, Cincinnati, OH, for finger
rings, bracelets, brooches, and necklaces. First
used Sept. 1930

Little Folks

TROOB-GORDON CO., Providence, RI.
Mark for all the usual types of jewelry,
necklaces, earrings, brooches, etc. Since
January 1, 1935.

Little Lady

BATES & KLINKE, INC., Attleboro,
Mass., used this mark for jewelry beginning
May 10, 1946.

"Little Miss"

THE CHARMORE COMPANY, Paterson, New Jersey and New York, NY used
this mark for jewelry beginning in July,
1946.

LITTLE MISS

COSTUME JEWELRY mark of DONLEY
MANUFACTURING CO., INC. First used
January 1956

LITTLE PRINCESS

McGRATH — HAMIN INC., Providence,
RI used this mark on costume jewelry for
children. First used Nov. 1958

Little Sweetheart

Mark used on babies' bracelets since 1945 by BATES AND KLINKE, INC., Attleboro, Mass.

"LITTLE TEX"

MRS. JAY D. PIGG, Garland TX used this mark for pendants, bracelets, earrings and novelty costume jewelry since October, 1952.

Mark of LEONARD KROWER & SON, INC., New Orleans, LA for pearl necklaces and costume jewelry "made of any kind of stone copied from an old fashioned style." Since June, 1929.

LONGCRAFT

THOMAS LONG CO., Boston, MA used this mark for imitation pearls (and other type pearls) and the usual types of jewelry. First used 1946

SOL E. WEINREICH of WEINREICH BROTHERS CO., New York, NY used this mark for pearls. First used Oct. 1928

LORD COVENTRY

SARAH COVENTRY, INC., Newark, NY mark for costume jewelry. This mark first used March 1965

SCHULSTER & GOLDBERG, New York, NY for both ladies' and men's jewelry including cuff links, tie pins, brooches, necklaces, chokers, bracelets, combs, earrings, perfume containers, ankle bracelets and charms. First used May, 1952.

LORELEI

RICHTON INTERNATIONAL CORP., New York, NY mark for jewelry. First used 1947

LORELEI

One of the many CORO marks. For necklaces, jewelry clips, brooches, lockets, beads, pins, hat ornaments, compacts for face powder, comb cases and jewelry initials. Since June, 1947.

LORRAINE MARSEL

COSTUME JEWELRY mark of JEWELS BY MARSEL, INC., Detroit, MI since April 1962

LASSNER & BAMBURGER, INC., New York, NY mark for artificial pearls and imitation jewelry. Since about November, 1919.

CORO, INC. mark for bracelets. Since August, 1957.

LOVE BOW

Jewelry mark of C.R. MUELLER CO., Jersey City, NJ for pins, pendants, and earrings. Since 1970

CORO, INC., New York, NY mark for lockets. First used June, 1953.

HARRY E. KRISMAN, St. Louis, MO used this mark for jewelry since Aug. 1934

MICHAEL P. PATTERSON, Wayzata, MN mark for ornamental jewelry for both men and women. Since Nov. 1970

"LOVE STORY"

WEINREICH BROS. CO. New York, NY used this mark for jewelry with pearls. Since Aug. 1948

LOVING CARE

CLAIROL INCORPORATED, New York, NY for earrings. First used October 1964

JOE LOWE CORPORATION, New York, NY mark for novelty pins, bracelets and finger rings. First used February, 1949.

Lu Benay

B. HECKER CO., New York, NY used this mark for compacts, lockets, necklaces, cuff links, pendants, rings, pins, pin and earring sets, charm bracelets, brooches and imitation pearl jewelry. Since March 1945

LU-KO

L.H. LEWIS CO., Dallas, TX mark for brooches, tie clasps, etc. Used since September, 1920.

A. BLUMSTEING, INC., New York, NY mark for jewelry including costume jewelry. Cuff links, buckles, pins, earrings, rings, pendants, bracelets, clasps. First used January, 1947.

LUCILLE

JOSEPH H. MEYER, BROS., Brooklyn, NY, mark for pearl jewelry, namely necklaces, bracelets, rings, jewelry clips, brooches and earrings. Since February, 1945.

Lucky Buck

CORO mark for necklaces, charms, charm bracelets, brooches and lockets, key rings. Since November, 1959.

LUCKY DEVIL

ASSOCIATED PRODUCTS, INC., Chicago, Illinois. Mark for ornamental pins, brooches, earrings, finger rings, costume jewelry and necklaces. Used since March, 1946.

LUCKY ELEPHANT

UNCAS MANUFACTURING CO., Providence, RI mark for finger rings. First used 1960

LUCKY SPIKE

LINDSEY L. VANCE of LANE ENTERPRISES, Denver, CO mark for earrings, pendants, cuff links. First used 1959

Lucky-Star

HAROLD G. ESSAYAN, Providence, RI mark for all the usual types of jewelry. Since April, 1921.

LUCKY STAR

Stella J. Reed, d.b.a. STELLA, New York, NY for jewelry in the shape of a star of displaying a star. Since January, 1956.

NATIONAL STEEL FABRIC COMPANY, Pittsburgh, PA mark for bracelets since June, 1946.

NANCY J. PAYNE, Deale, MD used this mark for earrings. Since March 1954

LUSTIGEM

Mark of FLORENCE LUSTIG CROSSMAN, d.b.a. FLORENCE LUSTIG, BAY HARBOR ISLANDS, Miami Beach, FL for costly synthetic gems set in precious metal and sold in the form of finished jewelry. First used March 1961

LUSTRA-GEMS

ALBERT KOEHLER, Foley, AL mark for baroque type jewelry. First used 1960

Lustralite

CORO, INC., New York, NY. Mark for pearl necklaces, pearl earrings, pearl brooches, pearl bracelets, strings of pearls and lucite beads. Since January, 1950.

Lustre - Bright

EMPCO METAL PRODUCTS COMPANY, New York, NY mark for gold, silver or copper costume jewelry - namely earringsly, pins, necklaces, scatterpins, cuff bracelets, link bracelets. Since June, 1954.

LUXOR

DANIEL SMILO, New York, NY used this mark for pearls, necklaces, bracelets and earrings. First used February, 1923.

L. & C. MAYERS CO., INC., New York, NY have used this mark since 1928 for jewelry.

Lyra

Mark of LLOYD MANUFACTURING COMPANY, Brooklyn, NY for simulated pearls and costume jewelry. Since September, 1946.

JOSEPH H. MAYER BROS. Brooklyn, NY. Mark used on necklaces, bracelets, finger rings, jewelry clips, brooches and earrings since 1938.

FRAY JEWELRY CO., Providence, RI mark for rings, brooches, pendants, bracelets and other articles of jewelry. First used 1914

B.B. GREENBERG CO. Providence, RI mark for jewelry. First used 1962

This mark of MIENHARDT & CO., INC., New York, NY. First used May 1962

SOLOMON MANTZOWITZ MFG. CO. New York, NY for novelty charms, bracelets, discs and lockets as well as religious jewelry. First used June, 1953.

MERCURY RING CORPORATION, New York, NY mark for rings, pendants, brooches, earrings, tie tacs, festoons and lovers' knots. Since April, 1943.

FRANK MORROW COMPANY, INC., Providence RI used this mark for jewelry findings, stampings and castings for jewelry parts, also on jewelry and compacts and cigarette cases. Used first September, 1946.

Mark of J. MILHENING INC., Chicago, Illinois, for finger rings, scarf pins, scarf rings, necklaces, dress studs, necklace snaps, bracelets, earrings, brooches, bar pins, and other jewelry. First used February, 1909.

MARCHAL, INC., New York, NY for charms, rings, brooches, pins, earrings, cuff links and other jewelry. First used January, 1944.

Mark of MARVEL JEWELRY MFG. COMPANY, Providence, RI for ladies jewelry - pins, necklaces, earrings, bracelets and crosses and men's jewelry. First used August, 1942 on bracelets.

Mark of MARIA V. VOGT. New York, NY for brooch pins, charms, clips, bracelets and cuff links. First used 1958

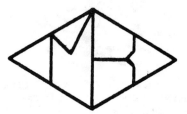

MURRAY M. BRAUNSTEIN, INC., New York, NY for jewelry since 1962

MC

Mark of MURRAY CHUVEN, Newark, NJ for jewelry. First used June, 1950.

MOLDING CORPORATION OF AMERICA, INC., Providence, RI used this mark for jewelry and ornamental novelties consisting of bracelets, brooches, earrings and vanity cases, rouge containers, bag ornaments and frames, cigarette holders and cases. First used June, 1932.

MCP

MAURICE C. PEYSTER INC., New York, NY mark for rings, bracelets, and other items of jewelry. First used 1962.

AARON PERKIS, New York, NY used this mark for jewelry including rings and snaps made for necklaces and bracelets. Since January, 1947.

M F C

METAL FINDINGS CORP. New York, NY mark used for metal jewelers' findings such as metal clips, metal pins, metal bars, hooks and eyes safety catches etc. It is not a manufacturer of finished jewelry. First used 1941

McGRATH-HAMIN INC., Providence, RI mark for rings, bracelets, pendants, pins, earrings and cuff links. First used December, 1951.

MGS

Jewelry mark of MARTIN GLUCK & SONS, Pittsburgh, PA since 1965

M. BLAU, New York, NY mark for bracelets, charms, earrings, brooch pins, necklaces, pendants and clips. First used 1961

MERIT JEWELRY CASTING CO., New York, NY mark for jewelry since April 1962

MJI

MONTREAUX JEWELRY INC., New York, NY mark for necklaces, bracelets, pins, earring and rings. First used 1962

MJK

MERMOD—JACCARD—KING jewelry company, St. Louis MO, used this mark for jewelry beginning in 1945

M & L

MANDELBAUM & LAUFER, New York, NY mark for jewelry. First used 1962

M' & M

M & M JEWELRY CREATIONS, INC., New York, NY mark for its base metal jewelry such as earrings, necklaces, etc. The company also made jewelry of precious metals. First used Nov. 1960

M & N

M & N SILVERS, New York, NY used this mark for jewelry. First used May 1962

MPC

JEWELSMITHS INTERNATIONAL, INC., New York, NY mark for finger rings, clips, pins, necklaces, earrings, bracelets and mountings. Since April, 1967

S. MASTROYANNI & BROS. INC., New York, NY used this mark for earrings, cameos, crosses, pendants, pins and bracelets. First used 1962

Mark of M.S. COMPANY, Attleboro, MA, bracelets and jewelry made with chains. First used January, 1915.

MIDWEST JEWELERS, Oklahoma City, OK for rings, pins, charms and other jewelry. First used Nov. 1935

MWCO

MANOR WHOLESALE CO., Detroit, MI mark for jewelry. First used Jan. 1962

CHARLIE McCARTHY INC., New York, NY for ornamental pins worn as jewelry. Since 1937

SCHNEIDER LEATHER NOVELTY CO., New York, NY mark for jewelry, cuff links, tie clasps, necklaces, chokers, earrings, brooch pins, bar pins, bracelets, and dress clips. Used since November, 1944.

MACALADY

ELSIE J. BOUCHER, COLVILLE, WA used this mark for necklaces and bracelets. First used 1960

Mark of MACE'S, Kansas City, MO for all types of jewelry for personal use. First used 1937

MAD MONEY

Costume jewelry mark of ALPHA-CRAFT INC., New York, NY, first used October 21, 1946.

MADAM QUEEN

Mark used by KAUFMANN DEPART-MENT STORES, INC., Pittsburgh, PA for bracelets, finger rings, necklaces, brooches and pins ornamented with imitation stones. First used April, 1930.

Madame DuBarry

WALTER M. MYERS, New York, NY first used this mark for costume jewelry, especially simulated pearls, in October, 1945.

MADEMOISELLE DE PARIS

Costume jewelry mark of HENRY JONAS, New York, NY since 1954

Madonna

THOMAS B. WILSON, Minneapolis, Minnesota. Mark for lockets. Used since September, 1945.

Madora Pearls

Mark used for pearls by SYNDICATE TRADING CO., New York, NY. First used May, 1928.

MAESTRO

AUTOMATIC GOLD CHAIN CO., Providence, RI for jewelry. First used November, 1929.

Magic Eye

CORO INC., New York, NY mark for all the usual types of jewelry. First used July, 1938.

MAGIC GARDEN

Mark of AVON PRODUCTS INC., New York, NY for costume jewelry. First used Jan. 1972

MAGICLIP

CORO, INC., New York, NY mark for necklaces, bracelets, rings, earrings, jewelry clips, brooches, lockets and jewelry initials. First used March 1950

CORO INC., New York, NY mark for earrings. First used Aug. 1960

Another mark used at the same time by
JOSEPH H. MEYER BROS., Brooklyn,
NY for its jewelry.

MAGNIFIED

COLONIAL MFG. CO., INC., New York,
NY, mark for jewelry including earrings,
brooches, necklaces, jewelry clips and
lockets. Since January, 1942.

MAGNI-TOP

GOODMAN & COMPANY, Indianapolis,
IA mark for rings, brooches, scarf pins and
earrings. Since September, 1954.

Magnolia White

BYCK BROS. & CO., INCORPORATED,
Louisville, KY for costume jewelry. Since
April, 1945.

Mab-Jongg

COHN & ROSENBERGER, INC., New
York, NY for jewelry and vanity cases, puff
boxes, coin purses, mesh bags, all of or plated
with precious metal. First used June, 1923.

Maharani

COHN & ROSENBERGER, INC., New
York, NY mark for earrings, rings, brooches,
clips, necklace, buckles, vanity cases, cigarette
cases and boxes, compacts, ash trays,
bracelets, trinket boxes, etc. First used 1937

Maharani

CORO, INC., New York, NY mark for all
their usual types of jewelry. First used April,
1935.

Jewelry mark of LITWIN & SONS, INC.,
Cininnati, OH. Since about January, 1958.

BOURJOIS, INC., New York, NY used this
mark for jewelry clips, earrings, and jeweled
hair ornaments since Sept. 1940

LUSTRE Maja

SOBEL BROTHERS, INC., PERTH AM-
BOY, NY used this mark for jewelry. First
used 1965.

MAJORICA

DANIEL BENNETT, d.b.a. DANIEL
BENNETT CO., Los Angeles, CA used this
mark for necklaces, bracelets and earrings
made with artificial pearls. First used about
December, 1957.

MAKE-BELIEVABLES

Mark of AVON PRODUCTS INC., New
York, NY for costume jewelry. First used
Nov. 1971

CORO mark for all the usual types of
jewelry and jewelry with pearls as well as
beads, pins, hat ornaments and jewelry initials plated with precious metal. Since
December, 1952.

MAMSELLE

Mark of B.B. GREENBERG CO., Providence, RI for women's jewelry. First used
June 1962

"Man About Town"

BRITE MANUFACTURING CO., Providence, RI mark for men's jewelry. Since
about April, 1953.

MANHATTAN

MANHATTAN JEWELRY CENTER, New York, NY began using this mark in April, 1944 for its jewelry.

MANUFACTURING JEWELERS EXPORT COMPANY, INC., New York, NY finger rings, bracelets, necklaces, ornamental pins, pencils and all jewelry for personal wear. Since February, 1921.

MANLEIGH INC., Providence, RI mark for men's costume jewelry. First used about May 1962

DESIGNED BY
Arthur Mann

UNIVERSAL JEWELRY CORP. New York, NY mark for costume jewelry. First used Jan. 1971

Manrey

Mark of ASSOCIATED MANUFACTURERS, Providence, RI, for brooches, earrings, pins, bracelets, lockets, pendants and necklaces. Used since September, 1944.

CORO INC., New York, NY mark for necklaces, bracelets, rings, earrings, clips, brooches, lockets, pearl earrings, pearl brooches, pearl bracelets, strings of pearls. First used 1949

MAR-KAY

MARVIN PRANGER of MAR—KAY JEWELRY MANUFACTURERS, Orlando, FL used this mark for bracelets, necklaces, earrings, rings, and ankle bracelets since Sept. 1954

Mar-Rina

RHODE ISLAND PEARL COMPANY, Edgewood, RI, for jewelry since March, 1944.

MARATHON CO., Attleboro, MA mark for jewelry for personal wear. Since August 1937

MARATHON

MARATHON COMPANY, Attleboro, Mass., mark for all types of jewelry for personal adornment since January, 1914.

ATTLEBORO CHAIN COMPANY, Attleboro, Mass. Mark for lockets and bracelets. First used August, 1909. Still active in 1949.

MARATHON COMPANY, Attleboro, Mass., (mark first registered in 1921 by SAMUEL M. EINSTEIN) Ornamental clasp pins, finger rings, chain-fastening rings, snap-fasteners, pendants, card cases, jewel cases and other type chain jewelry. Still active in 1949 but mark first used in January, 1914.

MARBOUX

MARCEL BOUCHER ET CIE, New York, NY used this mark for brooches, bracelets, necklaces, pendants, ornamental pins, earrings, finger rings and compacts. First used March, 1937.

MARCEL BOUCHER

Mark of MARCEL BOUCHER ET CIE, New York, NY for costume jewelry. First used about 1938.

JULIO J. MARSELLA, Providence, RI mark for costume jewelry including necklaces, bracelets, brooches and earrings. First used November, 1955.

MARCHAL INC., New York, NY mark for charm rings, brooches, pins, earrings, cuff links and all costume jewelry. First used Jan. 1944

MARCHAL JEWELERS

MARCHAL, INC., New York, NY costume jewelry mark. This mark was also used for jewelry of precious metal. First used January, 1944.

JOSEPH H. MEYER BROS., Brooklyn, NY for necklaces, bracelets, rings, clips, brooches and earrings. First used in 1938.

MARGARITA

D. SWAROVSKI & CO., Austria, used this mark for both genuine and imitation stones. First used 1964

Mark of MARINO JEWELRY CO., INC., Pawtucket, RI, for earrings, bracelets, pendants, brooches, necklaces and ornamental pins. Since Jan. 1945

Mark of ELLIOT, GREENE & CO. New York, NY for jewelry including pearls. First used May 1925

WILLIAM RAND, INC., New York, NY Mark for necklaces and bracelets made with simulated pearls and earrings "consisting of supports mounted in the same." First used about Nov., 1953.

MARQUETTE Creations

Mark of MORRIS KAPLAN & SONS, New York, NY for jewelry made of or designed to simulate precious or semi-precious stones and metal. Since January, 1926.

MARTELLI

MARTELLI JEWELRY COMPANY, Providence, RI. Mark used for bracelets, rings, pendants, earrings, brooches. In use since March, 1947.

MARTHA WEATHERED SHOPS, Chicago, IL for ladies jewelry - rings, bracelets, earrings, brooches, necklaces, hair ornaments and cuff links. First used March, 1921.

MARVA-STAR

Marvella Inc., New NY for all the usual kinds of jewelry as well as pearls and beads, pins and jewelry initials made of or plated with precious metal. Since June, 1963.

MARVANIUM

WEINREICH BROTHERS COMPANY, New York, NY for jewelry clasps and jewelry clips for all jewelry such as necklaces, bracelets, earrings, brooches, lockets. First used September, 1950.

Mark of MARVELLA, INC., New York, NY for pearls, necklaces, bracelets, earrings, jewelry clips, broches, lockets, finger rings, bracelets with charms, and bead necklaces. First used 1961

ELLIOT GREENE & CO., New York, NY used this mark for imitation stones, simulated pearls and costume jewelry necklaces. Since May 1, 1926

MARVELLA

SOL E. WEINREICH d.b.a. WEINREICH BROTHERS, New York, NY mark for jewelry and pearls. First used Jan. 1911

Marvella

WEINRICH BROTHERS COMPANY, New York, NY mark for pearl necklaces, pearl earrings, pearl bracelets. Used since January, 1911.

Marvella

MARVELLA PEARLS, INC., New York, NY for jewelry of all types incorporating pearls. First used January, 1911.

MARVELLA Coutura

MARVELLA, INC., New York, NY mark for pearls, necklaces, bracelets, earrings, jewelry clips, brooches, lockets, rings, charm bracelets, charms, and bead necklaces. First used June 1961

Marvella Fabulous

WEINRICH BROTHERS COMPANY, New York, NY, mark for pearl jewelry. Since January, 1949.

Marvella MINERVA QUALITY

WEINRICH BROTHERS COMPANY, New York, NY. Mark for pearl necklaces, pearl earrings, pearl bracelets and pearl brooches and other pearl jewelry sometimes with stones. Used since January 1939.

MARVELLA PEARLESCENT

MARVELLA, INC., New York, NY mark for pearls, rings, necklaces, bracelets, earrings, jewelry clips, brooches, lockets, charm bracelets, charms and bead necklaces. First used June 1961

Marvella Pearl Nuggets

WEINREICH BROTHERS CO., New York, NY mark for jewelry with pearls. Since 1948.

WEINREICH BROTHERS CO., New York, NY began using this mark January, 1941 for pearl necklaces, pearls and jewelry containing pearls for personal wear.

WEINREICH BROTHERS CO., New York, NY, for pearl necklaces, pearls, and jewelry containing pearls since January, 1941.

WEINREICH BROS. COMPANY, New York, NY used this mark for its jewelry findings. Since April, 1950.

Marvella

the loveliest pearls made by man

WEINREICH BROTHERS CO., New York, NY. This mark was used for pearl necklaces, pearls for personal wear and other jewelry. Since September, 1945.

ZENITH
QUALITY

WEINREICH BROTHERS CO., New York, NY for pearl necklaces, pearl earrings, pearl bracelets and pearl brooches, strings of pearls. Since Jan. 1939

MARVELLA "95"

MARVELLA, New York. Mark for pearls, necklaces, bracelets, earrings, jewelry clips, brooches, lockets, rings, charm bracelets, and charms. First used July 1, 1960

MARVELLESCENCE

MARVELLA, INC., New York, NY for all the usual types of jewelry, necklaces, brooches, earrings, etc., as well as beads, pins and jewelry initials made of or plated with precious metal. Since June, 1963.

MARVELLESQUE

MARVELLA PEARLS, INC., New York, NY for costume jewelry and pearl jewelry. First used June, 1958.

MARVELLETTE

Mark of MARVELLA PEARLS, INC., New York, NY for simulated pearl necklaces. First used September, 1958.

MARVELLIER

MARVELLA PEARLS, INC., New York, NY for costume jewelry - necklaces, bracelets, pins, earrings, charm pearl jewelry and beads. Since January, 1958.

MARVELLISSIMO!

Mark of MARVELLA PEARLS INC., New York, NY for pearl and costume jewelry, including necklaces, bracelets, earrings, jewelry clips, brooches, lockets, finger rings, charm bracelets and charms. Since January, 1948.

WEINREICH BROTHERS CO., New York, NY mark used on jewelry findings and closures. Since April, 1950.

MARVEL JEWELRY MANUFACTURING CO., Providence, RI, used this mark for watch bracelets beginning June, 1946.

MARVELUSTRE

Mark of MARVELLA, INC., New York, NY for costume jewelry. First used 1960

MASCOTS

CHARLES DU B. ARCULARIUS, New Canaan, CT, used this mark for sterling silver jewelry - cuff links, collar pins, necktie clips, bracelets and earrings. First used September, 1941.

MASTERFOLD

THE HADLEY COMPANY, INC., Providence, RI mark for bracelets. First used June, 1928.

A MASTERPIECE OF FASHION JEWELRY

CORO, INC., New York, NY mark for all the usual types of jewelry plus beads, pins, hat ornaments, hair ornaments, compacts, comb cases, cigarette cases, cigarette boxes, buckles and jewelry initials. Since Jan. 1943

Mata Blue Eyes

H.C. MUSSELLS COMPANY, Oakland, CA, Berkeley, CA mark for rings, earrings, pendants, bracelets and chokers. First used Aug. 1945

MATISSE, LTD., Los Angeles, CA mark for lavallieres, charms, pendants, bracelets, watch bands. Since July, 1952.

Mark of MATISSE, LTD., Los Angeles, CA for costume jewelry consisting of necklaces, lavallieres, charms, pins, pendants, bracelets, etc. Since December, 1956.

MATISSE

MATISSE LIMITED, Los Angeles, CA mark for costume jewelry consisting of pins and copper belts and for cuff links and tie slides. First used July, 1952.

MATSU

MATSU PEARL IMPORTING CO., of New York, NY mark for costume jewelry - earrings, pendants, and bracelets. First used Jan. 1960

MATURELLE

Mark of MARVELLA PEARLS, INC., New York, NY for simulated pearl jewelry. Since June, 1957.

Mark of MAXANN MFG. CO., Providence, RI for earrings, bracelets, ornamental pins, necklaces and brooches. First used March, 1944.

MAXINE

JOSEPH H. MEYER BROS., Brooklyn, NY. Mark for necklaces, bracelets, rings, jewelry clips, brooches and earrings, all made of or containing as an essential element, pearls or simulated pearls. First used 1938.

Maya de México

MAYA DE MEXICO, Los Angeles, CA used this mark for men's and women's costume jewelry - rings, earrings, tiaras, bracelets, necklaces, ornamental dress clips and belt buckles and cuff links. Since July, 1949.

GLAMOUR JEWELRY, INC., Providence, RI for pendants, necklaces, brooches, lockets, rings, charms, charm bracelets, and jewelry made with pearls. First used Jan. 1957

MARTIN—COPELAND CO., Providence, RI used this mark for lavalieres, pendants, necklaces, bracelets and earrings. First used 1929.

COSTUME JEWELRY mark of MAYTREE PRODUCTS CO., New York, NY. First used Feb. 1944

MARK OF JAMES McCUTCHEON & CO., New York, NY for novelty jewelry. First used 1866.

MEDITERRANEAN

Mark of Daniel Bennett, d.b.a. DANIEL BENNETT CO., Los Angeles, CA for artificial pearls. Since September, 1958.

Memories of Life

CORO INC., mark for charm bracelets. First used December, 1954.

Memory Hearts

OLIVE SELLE, St. Louis, MO mark for necklaces, bracelets and pendants. First used August, 1930.

MEMORY HEARTS

EISENSTADT MANUFACTURING CO., St. Louis, MO mark for charms, either separately or when connected to other jewelry. First used 1959

Men from Mars

D. LISNER & CO., INC., New York, NY mark for all types of jewelry. First used December 1940

GEMEX COMPANY marks for the usual types of jewelry plus buckles, fobs and charms. Since March, 1930.

MERINGUE

COHN & ROSENBERGER, INC., New York, NY mark for all the usual jewelry types and jeweled accessories such as compacts, boxes, etc. First used 1942

Metalite

CORO, INC., New York, NY mark for pendants, necklaces, bracelets, lockets, finger rings, charms and pearls. First used October, 1929.

MIDGETS

Mark used by SCHEIN BROTHERS, New York, NY for jewelry. First used February, 1915.

MILADY

WILLIAM RAND, INC., New York, NY mark for the usual types of costume jewelry. Since Dec. 1949

Mark of MIGLIO JEWELRY MFG. CO., New York, NY. Since January, 1946.

Millionears

CORO INC., of New York mark for earrings. First used Sept. 1949

Milly and Tilly

ALPHA-CRAFT COMPANY, New York, NY first used this mark in August, 1945 for costume jewelry.

Milvern

MILVERN COMPANY, INC., Beverly Hills, CA for earrings and men's and women's cuff links. First used September, 1954.

Mark of ERNEST R. NEYHARD, Pottstown, PA for costume jewelry. First used February, 1950.

Minetta

GUGLEILMINA ANNIBALI, East Rockaway, NY, mark for jewelry used since July, 1943.

MING TAI

SPEIDEL CORPORATION, Providence, RI, mark for bracelets, since April, 1947.

MINI-RING

KUSHNER & PINES, INC., New York, NY for necklaces and pendants. Since August, 1959.

MIRANDA

WILLIAM RAND, New York, NY used this mark for synthetic pearls and costume jewelry. First used November 22, 1946.

MISS FERNBROOK

FEDERATED DEPARTMENT STORES, INC. Cincinnati, Ohio mark for girls' and ladies' jewelry. First used 1971.

MISS INTERNATIONAL

EMPRESS PEARL SYNDICATE, Los Angeles, Calif., mark for tiaras and crowns, earrings, brooches, necklaces, jewelry mountings, natural, cultured and artificial pearls. Since April, 1956.

MISS RICHELIEU

JOSEPH H. MEYER BROS., Brooklyn, NY for necklaces and earrings. Since September, 1958.

Miss Universe

Mark of James J. Boutross, d.b.a. EMPRESS PEARL SYNDICATE, Los Angeles, CA for crowns and tiaras, rings, pins, necklaces, brooches, pendants, bracelets and other kinds of jewelry. Used since March, 1954.

Mark of the D. JACOBS SONS CO., Cincinatti, Ohio. Used first in May, 1931.

MISTER PICKWICK

MISTER PICKWICK, INC., Chicago, IL for jewelry - lapel buttons, stickpins, charms, bracelets, lockets, rings and earrings. First used March, 1958.

Jewelry mark of MOBA JEWELRY CORPORATION, New York, NY since 1957 for charms, bracelets, earrings, rings, necklaces, and ornamental pins.

Paul Roth d.b.a. P. ROTH & CO., New York, NY for pearls. Since May, 1923.

MONET

Mark of MONOCRAFT PRODUCTS CO., INC., New York, NY for pins, clips, bracelets, earrings, brooches, hair ornaments, necklaces, fobs and rings. First used Sept. 1937

Mark for BDA, INC., Providence, RI for jewelry. First used Feb. 1971

MONOCRAFT

MONOCRAFT PRODUCTS, CO., New York, NY for necklaces, bracelets, brooches, earrings and ornamental clips. First used May, 1927.

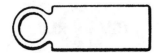

MONOCRAFT PRODUCTS CO., New York, NY mark for jewelry such as necklaces, bracelets, earrings clips and pins either plated with or made of precious metal. Used since 1937

MONOLINX

SAMUEL B. KAHN, Chicago, IL mark for cuff buttons and cuff links. Since May, 1920.

Monopearl

Trademark of MONOPEARL, INC., Providence, RI, used on jewelry and simulated pearls. In use since October, 1944.

Monte Carlo

Mark of HICKOK MANUFACTURING CO., INC., Rochester, NY for men's jewelry. Since May, 1953.

MONTE CARLO

C. RANDALL & CO., North Attleboro, MA used this mark for its jewelry which was made with or plated with precious metal. First used January, 1931.

Moon-Lite

MARK DOTTENHEIM, New York, NY mark for pearl jewelry. Since October, 1919.

Moonbeam

CORO, INC., mark used for all the usual types of jewelry and jewelry made with pearls. First used March, 1956.

COHN & ROSENBERGER, INC., New York, NY mark for all the usual types of jewelry and beads, pins, hat ornaments, hair ornaments, compacts, comb cases, cigarette cases, cigarette boxes, fancy buckles and jewelry initials. First used Jan. 1941

MOONGLO

SCHEIN BROTHERS, INC. New York, NY mark for jewelry. Used since September, 1933.

Moonrays

Another CORO, INC., mark for all the usual types of jewelry and jewelry made with pearls. Mark first used March, 1956.

MOONWIND

Mark of AVON PRODUCTS INC., New York, NY for costume jewelry. First used Oct. 1971

Mopey and Dopey

ALPHA-CRAFT COMPANY, New York, NY for costume jewelry since March, 1946.

BENJAMIN R. BRODY, New York, NY mark for costume jewelry of all the usual types. First used Nov. 1940

FREDERIC MOSELL JEWELRY, New York, NY used this mark for costume jewelry. First used December, 1940.

FREEMAN-DAUGHADAY CO., Chartley, MA, bar pins, scarf pins, cravat pins, children's dress pins, scarf clasps, all of gold, silver or enamel and baser or cheaper metals. First used July, 1930.

MOUNT ROYAL CORPORATION, New York, NY used this mark for brooches, hat pins, necklaces, pendants, lockets, cuff pins, cuff links, scarf pins, buckles, tie clasps, pin set, finger rings, etc. First used November, 1917.

Mark of MR. MOD SHOP INC., New Orleans, LA for jewelry. First used 1962

MURIEL

GEMEX COMPANY marks for the usual types of jewelry plus buckles, fobs and charms. Since March, 1930.

MUSIC BOX

Cohn & Rosenberger, Inc., New York, NY used this mark for vanity cases, powder compacts, other similar cases and necklace sets of precious metal or plated with precious metal, or of imitation composition, or of base metal. First used March, 1923.

My LiFE

Joseph Margolin, d.b.a. JOMAR, Los Angeles, CA for jewelry, namely pendants. Since December, 1953.

TRABERT AND HOEFFER, INC., New York, NY mark for costume jewelry - charms for bracelets and 'the like'. First used December, 1952.

MYRICA

FRANCET-PAISSEAU, INC., New York, NY for simulated pearl costume jewelry - necklaces, bracelets, earrings, pins, brooches, pendants and hair ornaments. Since April, 1955.

MYST

Mark of JOSEPH H. MEYER BROS., Brooklyn, NY for necklaces, bracelets, rings, clips, brooches and earrings. Mark first appeared in January, 1945.

Mystère

MAZER BROS., INC., New York, NY mark for earrings and brooches. Since July 1949.

The Mystery Emblem

Mark of EDGAR M. TOMLINSON, under the name MYSTERY EMBLEM NOVELTY COMPANY, Houston, Texas, for novelty jewelry. Mark first used December, 1, 1946.

Niash Refining Co., Inc. d.b.a. HIS LORDSHIP PRODUCTS COMPANY, New York, NY for earrings, pins, lapel pins and bracelets, men's jewelry. First used November, 1955.

THE NAPIER COMPANY, Meriden, CT used this mark for jewelry (necklaces, bracelets, etc.) and vanity cases, cigarette cases, compacts, rouge cases, etc. First used December, 1923.

NORLING & BLOOM COMPANY, Boston, Mass. used this mark first in August, 1913 on its jewelry for personal wear, including bar pins and jeweled accessories.

NE

NATHAN GOLDSTEIN of NATHAN JEWELRY, New York, NY mark for jewelry since July 1962

NEW—HOFF INC., St. Louis, MO mark for rings, pendants, earrings and cuff links. First used 1953

N ᴷᴼ EVER L ᴵᴺᴷ OSE

Mark of KOHL-PYE MANUFACTUR-ING CO., Rochester, NY for jewelry. Since September, 1921.

N-M

Mark of NEIMAN—MARCUS CO., Dallas, TX for men's, women's, and children's jewelry of all qualities. First used 1962

Mark of NOMO PRODUCTS, Johnston, RI, for costume jewelry. First used 1947.

$NS^ε_o$

Jewelry mark of H.L. MacLEOD d.b.a. N.S. CO., Atlanta, GA since 1960

NW

Hersh I. Druxman d.b.a. NORTHWEST JEWELERS, Seattle, WA mark for personal jewelry including rings. First used February, 1959.

Na-Nomah

FREDERICK ROBERT HEINICK, San Francisco, CA mark for jewelry with arti-ficial pearls. First used May, 1920.

NACO

THE NAPIER COMPANY, Meridian, CT mark for jewelry and cases, such as rouge containers, compacts, etc. First used December, 1923.

Nacrelon

JOSEPH H. MEYER BROS., Brooklyn, NY began in 1941 to use this mark for necklaces, bracelets, rings, clips, brooches and earrings.

NATIONAL DEPARTMENT STORES, INC., New York, NY used this mark for jewelry. First used April, 1924.

NAMELY YOURS

Mark of CORO INCORP. of RHODE ISLAND, Providence, RI for jewelry. Used since 1964

NANCY BARTON

Mark used by B. HAIG, Boston, Mass., for some jewelry since 1938.

NANCY LEE

PROVIDENCE STOCK CO., Providence, RI mark for necklaces, pins, bracelets, earrings, brooches and costume jewelry. First used Jan. 1929

THE NAPIER-BLISS COMPANY, Meriden, CT for all kinds of cases including powder and rouge compacts and combs and jewelry. First used October, 1920.

Mark of the NAPIER COMPANY, Meriden, CT. Scarf pins and slides, bracelets, brooches, dress clips, bar pins, rings, dress buckles, shoe buckles, ornamental mounted combs and other jewelry. Since July, 1942.

NAPIER-BLISS

NAPIER CO. OF MERIDEN, CT, used these marks in the 1940s and 50s.

THE NAPIER CO., Meriden, CT mark for necklaces, bracelets, brooches, dress clips, bar pins, rings, dress and shoe buckles, ornamental combs, hair ornaments and barrettes, lockets, tie clips, scarf pins, earrings, compacts, scarf slides and belt buckles all made wholly or in part of precious metal or plated with precious metal. This mark first used 1946.

NAPIER

THE NAPIER CO., Meriden, CT used this mark for all sorts of utilitarian household wares as well as toys, mesh bags, match and cigarette cases, vanity cases, powder and rouge cases, bracelets, brooches, dress clips, rings, shoe and dress buckles, ornamental combs, hair clips and barrettes, necklaces, lockets and earrings. First used June 1922

NAT LEVY, New York, NY. Mark for costume jewelry since January, 1943.

Natura "95"

Another mark of MARVELLA PEARLS, INC., New York, NY for necklaces, bracelets, earrings, jewelry clips, lockets, rings, charms. First used June, 1954.

Natura

MARVELLA PEARLS, INC., New York, NY for simulated pearls and jewelry containing simulated pearls. First used May, 1954.

NAUTIQUE

TRIFARI, KRUSSMAN & FISHEL, INC. New York, NY mark for costume jewelry and simulated pearls. First used 1965

Mark of NEIMAN-MARCUS COM-
PANY, Dallas, TX for rings, bracelets,
charms, pins, earrings, necklaces. First used
September, 1939.

Nemo

BRIER MANUFACTURING COM-
PANY, Providence, RI mark for brooches,
bracelets, dress clips, hair clips, tie clips,
chokers, hatpins, earrings, tiaras, pearl
necklaces, bracelets and earrings. First used
January, 1913.

NEMO

MILTON A. FISCHER, New York, NY.
This mark appears on scarf pin findings.
Since April, 1920.

NEPTUNA

ROYAL CRAFTSMEN, INC., New York,
NY for simulated pearls made of plastic or
like material and other jewelry. Since
February, 1944.

NEPTUNE

WEINREICH BROTHERS COMPANY,
New York, NY. Mark also in use since
January, 1939 for all kinds of pearl jewelry.

nettie post
ORIGINALS

NETTIE POST, New York, NY used this
mark for necklaces, bracelets, earrings and
hairpins, pins and combs. Since January,
1952.

NIGHT
OWLS

CORO, INC., New York, NY for necklaces,
earrings, jewelry clips, brooches, lockets.
Since May, 1944. Also used on jewelry made
of or plated with precious metal.

Mark of NIASH REFINING CO., INC.,
New York NY for jewelry findings. Not a
mark for jewelry itself. Since March 1938

NILO

FERRO NOVELTY COMPANY, INC.,
Johnston, RI for earrings. First used April,
1963.

NINA RICCI

NINI RICCI, Paris, France used this mark
for precious jewelry as well as costume
jewelry. First used Sept. 1960

NIRACOPIA

THE CORNUCOPIA MFG. CO., Chicago,
used this mark for rings and bracelets. First
used Nov. 1933

"NITELIFE"

Mark of RALSTON & GAGE, New York,
NY for brooches, pins, earrings, clips, charms,
bracelets and necklaces. Since 1942

◄NOREDNA'S►

The mark of ENAR S. ANDERSON, North
Attleboro, Mass., for jewelry. Used since
March, 1946.

Norma

Mark of JOSEPH H. MEYER BROS.,
Brooklyn, NY for use on necklaces,
bracelets, finger rings, clips, brooches and
earrings. Used since 1938.

NORTH STAR

WEINREICH BROTHERS COMPANY, New York, NY, mark for pearl necklaces, pearl earrings, pearl bracelets and jewelry containing pearls. January, 1939.

NU-KAY

KREMENTZ & COMPANY, Newark, NJ for jewelry made wholly or partly of precious metals. Since 1907.

NUMIUM

FORSTNER CHAIN CORPORATION, Irvington, NJ used this mark for bracelets, pendants, ornamental clasp pins, findings and various other types of personal articles. First used August, 1923.

NUTNIKS

COLORART CREATIONS CORP., New York, NY used this mark for costume jewelry. Used first in April, 1959.

OTSBY AND BARTON COMPANY, Providence, RI mark for jewelry. Since April, 1904.

Mark of WILLIAM B. OGUSH, New York, NY for jewelry. Since April, 1923.

OTSBY AND BARTON COMPANY, Providence, RI mark for jewelry. Since 1914.

OTSBY AND BARTON COMPANY, Providence, RI mark for jewelry. Since January, 1911

O-B

OTSBY AND BARTON COMPANY, Providence, RI mark for jewelry. Since July, 1907.

OTM

ORTEM PRODUCTS CO., INC., New York, NY mark for brooch pins, charms, bracelets, rings, necklaces, earrings and clips. First used 1961

WILLIAM B. OGUSH, INC., New York, NY mark for jewelry since 1944.

GOLDBERG-KIRSCHMAN COMPANY, New York, NY mark for jewelry since August, 1945.

Old World Jewels

SPEIDEL CORPORATION, Providence, RI, mark for bracelets (not including watches) pendants, brooches, lockets, earrings, jewelry clips, ornamental clips, breast pins and ornamental pins. Since 1949.

OLSEN & EBANN JEWELRY CO., Chicago, IL for rings, bracelets, bar pins, scarf pins, lavaliers, necklaces and fraternal jewelry. First used June, 1913.

OMAR

OMAR, INC., New York, made precious as well as non-precious jewelry and used this mark from July, 1946.

ONEIDA

PADRUSCH BROS., New York, NY, mark for watches - lapel watches, finger ring watches, and lavalier watches. First used January 1948.

OPULENTE COLLECTION

AVON PRODUCTS, INC., New York, NY mark for jewelry. First used May 1970

AGNINI AND SINCER, Chicago, IL used this mark for costume jewelry of all the usual types as well as dress buttons, belt buckles, shoe buckles all plated with precious metal and set with rhinestones. First used September, 1950.

JUNE C. JOHNSON, Medford, Oregon, for costume jewelry usually incorporating pine cones, acorns and other seeds. Mark used since November, 1948.

TRIFARI, KRUSSMAN & FISHEL, INC., Providence, RI mark for pearl jewelry - strings of pearls, pearl earrings, pearl brooches, pearl necklaces, pearl bracelets. First used January, 1950.

ORLEAN

Samuel E. Porter d.b.a. S.E. PORTER COMPANY, Providence, RI mark for pearl jewelry. Since February, 1920.

Orloff

THE ORLOFF CO., INC., Philadelphia, PA mark for watches and watch cases. First used 1947

Oscar de la Renta

Richton International Corporation, New York, NY mark for jewelry. First used July 2, 1970

OUR LITTLE DARLING

CORO, INC., New York, NY for necklaces, bracelets, rings, earrings, jewelry clips, brooches, lockets, also for plated jewelry, hat ornaments, pins, comb cases, holders for face powder compacts and jewelry initials. First used March, 1946.

OUT OF THIS WORLD

D. RODITI & SONS, INC., New York, NY for costume jewelry. Since February 2, 1946.

OUVRIER

OUVRIER FASHION ACCESSORIES, New York, NY for earrings, ornamental clips, bar pins, brooch pins, bracelets, rings of nonprecious materials. Since May, 1941.

OVELIES

JOSEPH H. MEYER BROS., Brooklyn, NY for necklaces, earrings, clips and brooches. Since January 1959.

PLAINVILLE STOCK CO., PLAIN-VILLE, MA mark for earrings, pendants, crosses, lockets pins and brooches. First used 1962

PAKULA AND COMPANY OF Chicago used this mark on all types of jewelry as well as on compacts. In use since January, 1941.

PLAINVILLE STOCK COMPANY, Plain-ville, MA mark for earrings, pendants, crosses, lockets, pins and brooches. First used Jan. 1962

ANDREW GATES of PARISIAN JEWELRY CREATORS, New York, NY used this mark for jewelry and jewelry findings. First used May, 1962

Bracelets by PRINCESS, INC., New York, NY used this mark for all its jewelry. First used Feb. 1962

Mark of PETER BLOS, Oakland, CA for bracelets, brooches, cuff links, earrings, necklaces, rings and tie pins. First used in 1947.

PALLISER JEWELRY CO., INC., New York, NY mark for charms, pins, earrings, bracelets, cuff links, rings, pendants, lockets and necklaces. First used April 1962

Isidor Gutgold d.b.a. PEER JEWELRY CO., New York, NY used this mark for charms, bracelets, pendants, pins, earrings and other items. First used August, 1958.

JAMES PERRY MFG., CO., Providence, RI mark for expansion bracelets and finger rings. Since October, 1946.

PHILLIPS MFG. CO., Brooklyn, NY mark for rings, pendants, bracelets, earrings, cuff links, crosses and tie slides. Since Jan. 1939

PHILIP REITER, New York, NY mark for
earrings. First used October, 1944.

MEDICATED PRODUCTS CO., d.b.a.
DONALD BRUCE CO., Chicago, IL used
this mark for costume jewelry consisting of
necklaces, earrings, bracelets and sets thereof.
First used June 1953

ALBERT B. KELEMEN d.b.a. PRETTY
JEWELRY CO., New York, NY used this
mark for bracelets, earrings, brooch pins and
pearl clasps beginning May 1962

PJP

PACIFIC JEWELRY & PEARL CORP.,
New York, NY used this mark for brooch
pins, charms, bracelets, rings, necklaces, earrings, clips, cuff links and pendants. Since
1962

P. O. M. G.

Mark of SAVITT, INC. Hartford, CT for
rings, bracelets, necklaces, brooches, and all
other jewelry since about November, 1947

PLAINVILLE STOCK COMPANY, Plain-
ville, MA mark for scarf pins, stick pins,
brooches, bracelets, chains, charms, sleeve
and shirt buttons. First used about 1884.

Mark of PHILLIP WOLMAN & CO., Los
Angeles, CA for costume jewelry. First used
1957

PALEY & THOMAS INC., New York, NY
for pearls. Since May, 1951.

Mark of PERE ORECK, San Francisco, CA
for brooches, earrings, finger rings, necklaces
and bracelets. Since June, 1948.

Mark of THE PROGRESSIVE RING
COMPANY, Providence, RI, for jewelry
and in use since July, 1931.

A. S. PERRY AND ASSOCIATES, Atlanta, GA used this mark from June, 1946, for
gold, gold-filled, sterling and plated jewelry
with or without settings of precious, semi-
precious, synthetic or imitation stones.

PACERETTE

PAKULA & CO., Chicago, IL used this mark for wrist watch bracelets. First used Jan. 1946

COHN & ROSENBERGER, INC., New York, NY mark for necklaces and bracelets, rings, earrings, jewelry clips, lockets, cigarette and powder boxes, comb cases, fancy buckles and jewelry initials. First used January 1941

PAINT-BOX

COHN & ROSENBERGER, INC., New York, NY mark for all the usual types of jewelry as well as compacts, cigarette boxes, fancy buckles and jewelry initials. Since 1937

PAKULA & CO., Chicago, IL mark for costume jewelry. First used 1932

Mark of Richard Polumbaum d.b.a. RICHARD POLUMBAUM CO., New York, NY used this mark for pins, earrings, pendants, rings, lockets and clips. Since November, 1942.

THE PALOMAR COMPANY, Los Angeles, CA for costume jewelry. Since September, 1946.

HYMIE SINGER of SINGER INDUSTRIES, Beverly Hills, CA for simulated pearl necklaces. Since Feb. 1965

paradis

COJEVA, INC., New York, NY used this mark for costume jewelry, simulated pearl and bead necklaces. First used Aug. 1961

Mark used by Abraham Rolnick d.b.a. ROLNICK JEWELRY CO., New York, NY for imitation pearl necklaces. First used January, 1924.

PARADISSIMO

COJEVA, INC., New York, NY mark for pearls, bracelets, necklaces, earrings, jewelry clips, brooches, lockets, rings, charm bracelets, charms and bead necklaces. First used 1962

Paragon

CORO mark for jewelry with pearls. Since April, 1946.

PARAGON

RICHTON INTERNATIONAL CORPORATION, New York, NY for jewelry. Used since April 1948

PARAMO

AUTOMATIC GOLD CHAIN CO., Providence, Ri for jewelry. First used September, 1929.

Parco

PARCO MFG. INC., Providence, RI used this mark for real jewelry and jewelry findings as well as on costume jewelry, necklaces, earrings, bracelets, and rings. First used June 1946

M. GUGGENHEIM, INC., New York, NY for imitation pearl jewelry. First used about November, 1920.

PARKLANE

OVAL MANUFACTURING CO., INC., New York, NY used this mark on men's jewelry. First used August 1929

Parquet

TRIFARI, KRUSSMAN & FISHEL INC., New York, NY mark for beach jewelry - necklaces, bracelets, earrings and also for jeweled shoe buckles. First used April 1929

PATCHWORK

Mark of AVON PRODUCTS INC., New York, NY for costume jewelry. First used Dec. 1971

PATTERNS

Mark of AVON PRODUCTS INC., New York, NY for costume jewelry. First used Oct. 1971

J.F. STURDY'S SONS COMPANY, Attleboro, MA for bracelets, earrings, charms, lockets, etc. First used April, 1954.

PAUL MORRIS FIFTH AVENUE

PAUL MORRIS, New York, NY mark for costume jewelry - necklaces, earrings and bracelets. Used since January, 1949.

Paulette

Mark of EARL WILSON, New York, NY for jewelry containing artificial pearls. Since Oct. 1945

Pearl Empire

JEWEL—SMITHS, INC., Boston, MA mark for jewelry made with pearls - earrings, rings, brooches, and bracelets. Since March 1956

PEARL - GLO

WHITE PEARL COMPANY, Pawtucket, RI mark for necklaces, pins, bracelets, and earrings. Used since March 1943

Pearlace

MARTIN A. KLEIN, New York, NY mark for artificial pearl necklaces. First used August, 1924.

PEBBLE-TONE

Mark of JOSEPH H. MEYER BROS., Brooklyn, NY for necklaces and earrings. Since January, 1958.

Pee-Wee

BRUNER-RITTER INC., New York, NY, mark for bracelets, lockets and neck chains in ornamental container for juveniles. Since August, 1948.

Peerless

KESTENMAN BROS., MFG. CO., Providence, RI used this mark for bracelets, clasps and jewelry buckles. Since January, 1933.

PEERLESS

Mark used by THE WOLFSON COM-
PANY, Chicago, IL then by PEERLESS,
WOLFSON, CO., Chicago. First used in
1912.

PELS-JONES
PERFECT JEWELRY

PELS-JONES, New York, NY used this
mark for jewelry. First used March, 1920.

PELTANIUM

BARCLAY COMPANY, Providence, RI
mark for costume jewelry. First used
January, 1953.

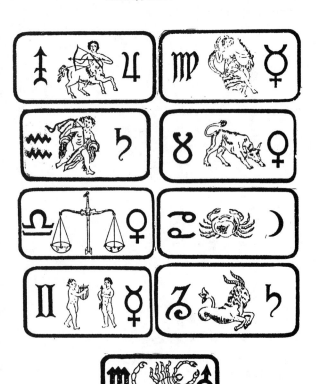

ORESTE PENNINO of PENNINO
BROTHERS, New York, NY used these
marks for rings, earrings, bracelets, pendants, necklaces, watch bracelets,
brooches, buckles, bar pins, lorgnettes,
scarf pins, hatpins, vest buttons, all made
of or plated with precious metal.
Marks first used Nov., 1926.

SPERRY MANUFACTURING CO., Providence, RI for watch bracelets, rings, scatter pins, pendants, necklaces, earrings and
other jewelry. First used Jan. 1949

PERLES DE LUNE

KRAMER JEWELRY CREATIONS INC.,
New York, NY used this mark for pearl
jewelry. First used Sept. 1962

Perltrix

L. HELLER & SON, INC., New York, NY
mark for necklaces, necklace shorteners,
necklace clasps and brooches. Since August,
1949.

PERMA CLAD

DAVINCI CREATIONS, INC., Providence,
RI used this mark for jewelry. Since April
1965

Permawear

KESTENMAN BROS., MFG. CO., Providence, RI for bracelets, clasps and buckles
in the nature of jewelry. First used January,
1933.

Personality

UNITED DISTRIBUTORS, Chicago, IL
mark for bracelets and rings since Dec. 1945

PERSIAN WOOD

Mark of AVON PRODUCTS INC., New York, NY for costume jewelry. First used Oct. 1971

PERSONALITY

UNCAS MANUFACTURING COMPANY, Providence, RI, mark for jewelry such as brooches, bracelets, necklaces, pins and earrings. First used September, 1941.

PERSONETTES

CORO INC., New York, NY mark for jewelry clips, necklaces, bracelets, rings, earrings, brooches and lockets. Since Jan. 1950

Pete 'n' Tweet

ALPHA-CRAFT COMPANY, New York, NY mark for costume jewelry. In use since October, 1945.

Philba

PHILADELPHIA BADGE COMPANY, INC of Philadelphia, PA used this mark for jewelry findings — ear screws, safety catches, stones and plastic findings. They did not manufacture the jewelry itself. Used first in February, 1947.

byPhilips

PHILLIPS MFG. CO., Brooklyn, NY mark for all the usual jewelry plus cuff links. First used Jan. 1939

Phoenix

Mark of JOSEPH H. MEYER BROS., Brooklyn NY for use on necklaces, bracelets, finger rings, jewelry clips, brooches and earrings. Used since 1938.

Phyllis

PHYLLIS ORIGINALS, INC., Providence, RI mark for chatelaines, ornamental pins, rings, bracelets and necklaces. First ued June, 1946.

ROYAL OF PITTSBURGH, INC., Pittsburgh, PA used this mark for jewelry. Since June 1962

PIK MANUFACTURING, New York, NY for costume jewelry including bracelets, earrings, and pins. Since November, 1948.

PIK-KWIK

ROBERT M. MANDLE CORP., New Rochelle, NY mark for costume 'imitation' jewelry including earrings, pins, cuff links, bracelets, necklaces and clips. Since September 1954.

PIN O GRAM

Mark of LORBER NOVELTY CO. Division of Button Center, NY used for costume initial pins, cuff links, etc. since March 1956

PIN TACS

VERITÉ JEWELS LTD., New York, NY for all the usual jewelry types plus charms, charm bracelets, bead necklaces and jewelry initials. First used 1962

WALTER LAMPL, New York, NY for ornamental dress and lapel pins, earrings and bracelets. Used since December, 1945.

PINAFORE

Mark used by COHN & ROSENBERGER, INC., New York, NY for necklaces and bracelets, rings, earrings, jewelry clips, brooches, lockets hat and hair ornaments, compacts, comb cases, cigarette cases, fancy buckles and jewelry initials. First used Aug. 1940

Pinch Pin

RÉJA, INC., New York, NY mark for costume jewelry necklaces, bracelets brooches, rings and earrings. First used Oct 1949

PINLESS PIN

FASHION CRAFT JEWELRY CO., INC., New York, NY mark for ornamental clip pins, used since January, 1945.

WALT DISNEY PRODUCTIONS, Los Angeles, CA used this mark for brooches, bangles, bracelets and lockets. First used 1939

PINTA PRODUCTS INC., Johnston, RI mark for jewelry. First used Oct. 1962

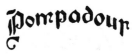

TAUNTON PEARL WORKS INC., Taunton, MA. Scarf pins, bar pins, cuff pins, lingerie pins, brooches and cuff buttons. First used November, 1921.

PIONEER

TAUNTON PEARL WORKS, TAUNTON, MA used this mark for cuff links, vest buttons and shirt studs and dress sets. First used Nov. 1921

PLACE VENDOME

AMERICAN & CONTINENTAL PATENTED PRODUCES INC., New York, NY used this mark for necklaces, bracelets, rings, earrings, jewelry clips, brooches, lockets and beads, pins, hat and hair ornament compacts, comb cases, fancy buckles, and jewelry initials. Since Jan. 1941

PLATINEX

THERESA GREENBERG, Brooklyn, NY used this mark for ornamental jewelry of all types. Since April 1943

PLASTIGOLD

ACCESSOCRAFT PRODUCTS CO., New York, NY mark for all the usual jewelry types plus fancy buckles, jewelry initials, hat ornaments, hair ornaments and compacts. First used Sept. 1940

REUBEN POMERANTZ JEWELRY CO., INC., New York, NY mark for jewelry. First use of this mark 1962

Pompadour

RAND BROTHERS, New York, NY mark for artificial pearl necklaces and beads. First used Oct. 1940

PONTIAC

Mark used by the PONTIAC COMPANY, Newark, NJ for jewelry - bracelets, scarf pins, belt buckles, ear and hair ornaments and charms. Since June, 1930.

POOPED PUSSY CAT

HATTIE CARNEGIE, New York, NY used this mark for all the usual types of jewelry including jeweled hair ornaments, jeweled shoe buckles and jeweled cases and holders. First used April, 1965.

POOPED POODLE

HATTIE CARNEGIE, New York, NY used this mark for all the usual types of jewelry including jeweled hair ornaments, jeweled shoe buckles and jeweled cases and holders. First used April, 1965.

powder·blend

D. LISNER & CO., New York, NY mark for artificial pearls. Since June 1940

Prairie

MUTUAL SUSPENDER AND BELT CO., d.b.a. PRAIRIE MANUFACTURING CO., Yonkers, NY for buckles, emblem jewelry, tie clips, etc. First used February, 1949.

PRECIOUS ALL
VAN DELL

Marks of VAN DELL CORP., Providence, RI

PRECIOUS-ALL

Mark of THE VAN DELL CO., Providence, RI for men's jewelry and ladies' jewelry, including bracelets, clips, lockets, pins and brooches and components made of gold and silver. First used Oct. 1941

PRECIOUS JEWELS
by Milano

Medicated Products, d.b.a. DONALD BRUCE CO., Chicago, IL mark for costume jewelry consisting of necklaces, earrings, bracelets and sets thereof. First used June, 1953.

PRECIOUS PRETENDERS

AVON PRODUCTS, INC., New York, NY used this mark for jewelry since 1970

Prestige

CORO mark for jewelry with pearls. First used April, 1948.

THE PRETENDER

WEINREICH BROTHERS COMPANY, New York, NY mark for pearl necklaces, earrings, bracelets, strings of pearls and all pearl jewelry and adornments, often with rhinestones. Since June, 1949.

PREVUE JEWELS

Mark of JEWEL-SMITHS, INC., Boston, Mass. for rings, clips, necklaces, pins, earrings, bracelets, mountings and semi-precious and imitation stones. April 22, 1946.

Prima Donna

MARK DOTTENHEIM, New York, NY mark for pearl jewelry. Since October, 1919.

PRINCESS ANNE

Mark of CLEINMAN & SONS, INC., Providence, RI, for costume jewelry pins and rings. First used 1954.

PRINCESS PRIDE CREATIONS

MEDICATED PRODUCTS CO., d.b.a. DONALD BRUCE COMPANY, Chicago, IL for costume jewelry consisting of necklaces, earrings, bracelets and sets thereof. First used June, 1953.

MEDICATED PRODUCTS CO., d.b.a. DONALD BRUCE CO., Chicago, IL mark for costume jewelry consisting of necklaces, earrings, bracelets and jewelry sets. First used June 1953

Priscilla

EISENSTADT MANUFACTURING CO., St. Louis, MO rings, necklaces, pins, brooches, service awards of precious metal, school and fraternal jewelry and artificial pearl jewelry. First used 1922.

"Priscilla"

EISENSTADT MANUFACTURING COMPANY, St. Louis, MO, mark for rings. The PRISCILLA mark was used by EISENSTADT for other jewelry but in a different form. This mark dates from 1914.

PRISCILLA

Mark of EISENSTADT MANUFACTURING COMPANY, St. Louis, MO for lavalieres, pin sets and other jewelry since January, 1916. Still active in the 1930's.

RALPH H. BODMAN, Hyannis, Mass. for artificial pearls made from fish scales and necklaces made from such pearls. Since July, 1921.

PUNCH 'n' JUDY

Costume Jewelry mark of ALPHA CRAFT, INC., New York, NY since March 1946

COHN & ROSENBERGER, INC., New York, NY used this label on all the usual types of jewelry as well as beads, hat ornaments, hair ornaments, compacts, comb cases, cigarette cases, fancy cigarette boxes, and jewelry initials. First used Sept. 1937

The PURPLE SAGE

Mark of OBER MANUFACTURING CO., Pawtucket, RI, for buckles, cuff links, money clips, cigarette cases, key chains, stick-pins, fobs, bandanna sliders or holders, pins, brooches, lockets, compacts, necklaces, bracelets, earrings and rings. February, 1946.

PYRALART

The FOSTER-GRANT CO., INC., of Leominster, Mass. used this mark for chokers, pendants, brooches, bracelets, fobs and rings, beginning in January, 1930.

PROVIDENCE STOCK COMPANY, Providence, RI, mark for necklaces, pins, bracelets, earrings, brooches and other costume jewelry. The company claimed use of this mark since March, 1890.

QUEEN ANN

THEODORE WALTER CO., New York, NY for genuine pearls, cultured pearls and simulated pearls since July, 1938.

QUEEN BEES

CORO, INC., New York, NY for necklaces, bracelets, jewelry clips, brooches and lockets. This mark also used for jewelry made in whole or in part of precious metal or plated with same. Used since January, 1943.

QUEEN QUALITY

WEINREICH BROTHERS COMPANY, New York, NY mark for pearl jewelry since 1916.

H. WEINREICH COMPANY, INC., Philadelphia, PA used this mark for jewelry which was partly or wholly plated with precious metal. Since about April, 1954.

ALPHA-CRAFT COMPANY, New York, NY mark for costume jewelry since August, 1945.

H. WEINREICH COMPANY, INC., Philadelphia, PA used this mark for jewelry which was partly or wholly plated with precious metal. Since about April, 1954.

REMBRANDT CHARMS, INC., New York, NY used this mark for charms and bracelets. Since 1959

QUEEN'S LACE

WEINREICH BROTHERS COMPANY, New York, NY, mark for pearl necklaces, earrings and other types of pearl jewelry. Since June, 1949.

Jewelry mark of WEMBLEY INDUSTRIES, INC., New Orleans, LA, since December 1970

"QUIK-TRIK"

CORO mark for earrings. First used May, 1956.

ROYALTY JEWELRY MFG. INC., New York, NY mark for brooch pins, charms, bracelets, rings, necklaces, earrings and clips. First used March 1955

PROGRESS JEWELRY MFG. CO., Providence, RI mark for ladies' costume jewelry consisting of necklaces, bracelets and brooches. Since June, 1948.

Quintette

CORO Mark for necklaces, bracelets pendants, jewelry clips, etc. First used May, 1938.

JOHN ROBERTS INCORPORATED, AUSTIN, TX mark for finger rings since April 1953

"Quivering Camellia"

COHN & ROSENBERGER INC., New York, NY mark for necklaces, bracelets, earrings, etc., also cigarette cases, hat pins, hat ornaments, hair ornaments, face powder compacts, comb cases, fancy buckles and jewelry initials. First used about 1939.

REEVES MFG. CORP. New York, NY used this mark for jewelry since 1961

JOHN ROBERTS INCORP., Austin, TX mark for rings. Since April 1953

Jewelry mark used by THE ROBBINS CO., Attleboro, Mass., since December 1945.

RACHMUTH BROS., New York, NY for jewelry - bracelets, charms, earrings, pendants and brooches. Since March, 1955.

Mark of CHARLES ROTHMAN COMPANY, Providence, RI for ladies costume jewelry. Since May, 1954.

CHARLES ROTHMAN COMPANY, INC., Providence, RI for ladies costume jewelry. First used May, 1954.

RICHARD P. RASEMAN & ELIZABETH B. RASEMAN, Ann Arbor, MI used this mark for costume jewelry. First used Nov. 1945

R & G CO., Attleboro, MA men's jewelry as well as lockets, buckles, bracelets, perfume balls, and accessories. Since 1880

Mark of ROLYN INC., Providence, RI for women's jewelry - brooches, pins, earrings, pendants and bracelets. First used 1961

JAMES MANECKE RANDALL, Wasau, WI, used this mark for handcrafted jewelry. First used June, 1968

RJCO

ROSE JEWELRY CO., DETROIT, MI mark for jewelry. First used 1962

FEDERATED DEPARTMENT STORES, INC., d.b.a. THE RIKE KUMLER CO., Dayton, OH mark for jewelry. First used May 1962

R.M.J.

MARY JOHNSON of R.M. JOHNSON, Chicago, IL mark for jewelry. Since June 1905

RNK

Jewelry mark of R.N. KOCH, INC., Pawtucket, RI, First used July 1971

ROBERT STOLL, New York, NY mark for stick-pins, brooches, cuff-buttons, finger rings. Since September, 1917.

R·T

KLEINMAN BROS., New York, NY mark for necklaces, bracelets, and other jewelry. Since 1953

wRe

W.E. RICHARDS, CO., Attleboro, MA jewelry mark. First used January, 1944.

RADIO

Mark of FORSTNER CHAIN CORPORATION, Irvington, NJ for jewelry with chains. First used October, 1920.

THE RALPH J. GILLETT IMPORTING CO., Cleveland, OH mark for jewelry. Since August, 1921.

RAINBOW

JOSEPH H. MEYER BROS., Brooklyn, NY jewelry mark since 1916.

CORO, INC., New York, NY for necklaces and bracelets, finger rings, earrings, jewelry clips, brooches, lockets. Since January, 1944.

RAY GANN & CO., Stockbridge, GA mark for jewelry. First used 1962

WILLIAM RAND, INC., New York, NY mark for synthetic pearls and costume jewelry - earrings, brooches, necklaces, bracelets, ornamental pins and finger rings. Since about December, 1952.

COHN & ROSENBERGER, INC., New York, NY mark for all the usual types of jewelry and accessories. First used Nov. 1942

RAVEN

CORO, INC., New York, NY for all the usual types of jewelry. Since May, 1963.

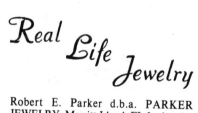

Robert E. Parker d.b.a. PARKER JEWELRY, Merritt Island, FL for jewelry made of seashells, etc. First used April, 1952.

THE REAL LOOK

JERRY De NICOLA, INC., New York, NY mark for necklaces, bracelets, earrings, brooches, rings and all costume jewelry. First used Feb. 1962

REBAJES INCORP., New York, NY mark for jewelry. First used Jan. 1932

RECORD

F. SPEIDEL COMPANY, Providence, RI used this mark for jewelry since September, 1913. The mark was later used by GENERAL CHAIN CO., INC., North Attleboro, MA.

The mark of BELL INDIAN TRADING POST, Albuquerque, NM for copper costume jewelry. First use December, 1947.

Regala

CORO mark for jewelry with pearls. First used April, 1948.

REGIMENTAL CRESTS

SANDOR GOLDBERGER, INC., New York, NY mark for all types of jewelry as well as beads, pins, hat ornaments, hair ornaments, comb cases, cigarette cases, fancy cigarette boxes, fancy buckles and jewelry initials. Since 1939

Reidún

UNITED POWDER PUFF CO., INC., used this mark on powder puffs and it is often mistaken for the manufacturer of the compact itself. First used July 1946

RÉJA

REJA, INC., New York, NY for costume jewelry. Used since May, 1940.

RÉJA
ROSE OPAL

REJA, INC., New York, NY mark for costume jewelry since May, 1940

REJA, INC., New York, NY mark for costume jewelry since May, 1940.

Artistry in Jewels by Réja

RÉJA, INC., New York, NY mark for costume jewelry - necklaces, bracelets, brooches, rings and earrings. First used May 1940

Relaxation

GEORGE J. HECHT, New York, NY used this mark for strings of beads made of plastic, glass and semi precious stones. First used March 1941

REMBRANDT

JEWELS BY REMBRANDT, INC., New York, NY mark for pendants and pins. First used 1965

Remembrance

FORSTNER INC., Irvington, NJ for bracelets. First used June, 1954.

RENARD

RENARD PRODUCTS, INC., of Long Island City, NY used this mark for its jewelry.

The necklace has seven single drops in graduated sizes.
The apple green centers are set in rhinestone frames. The necklace and bracelet marked Nettie Rosenstein but only one earring bears the designer name. *Value $1500 - $2000.*

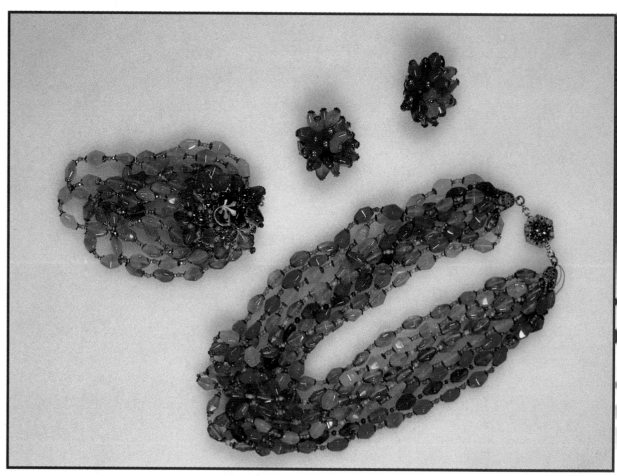

Miriam Haskell's Necklace, Bracelet and Earrings. Beads in shades of butterscotch, pink, green, red. Bracelet has a large center clasp designed in the shape of flowers with a gold metal leaf. The bracelet has a nice filagree back which carries the signature Miriam Haskell in an oval. The earrings are signed Haskell on the clip. 1950s.
Value of set $700 - $900.

Large green beads set in a gold filagree frame with colored spacers. A rust colored bead on the end of the necklace is a typical Haskell surprise touch. The gold filagree at the end of the necklace forms a bee. Signed M. Haskell (1940).
Value $600 - $750.

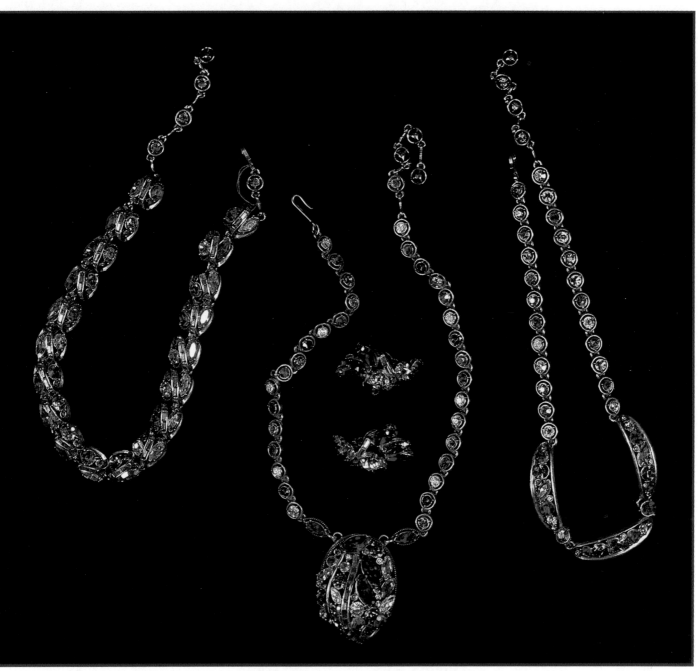

Left to Right: A selection of Hollycraft.
All are marked Hollycraft and dated. This is one of the few companies which
dated its jewelry, a real plus for collectors. 1950s.
Value of necklaces, left and right $145 - $175 each.
Value of necklace and earring set ,
center $275 - $375.

Top: This beautiful trifari
with its pinks and greens
and brilliant rhinestones is a Philippe design. Elegant as always. *Value $600 - $800.*
Right: A rare mark on this unusual bow-tied floral spray - Sterling Button Co. A different approach. 1930s. *Value $500 - $800.*
Bottom: The vibrant, unusual shades give this brooch life and the designer's departure from the ordinary garden daisy makes for a
piece of art. A Louis Mazer design. *Value $650 - $850.*
Left: The attractive topaz stone in this flower brooch gives it raison d'être. The open work leaves with their rhinestone edges are inter-
esting. Signed Nettie Rosenstein Sterling. *Value $600 - $800.*

Left: A highly original
bouquet in a con-
tainer theme by
R. DeRosa. The flower
pot is glass with
flowers. (1940s)
Value $400 - $500.
Center: This broach
shows a woven basket
with garden variety
flowers. Signed
Sandoe, a very scarce
mark and one well
worth collecting.
Value $350 - $450.
Right: This pin has
the "Victorian look"
with a lovely bouquet
of pinkish-red
globular flowers.
Value $300 - $400.

Left: A wonderful Boucher Brooch with delicious looking grape clusters surrounding a pearl center. Mid 1940s. Signed Boucher. *Value $400 - $500.*

Right: Boucher jewelry is always outstanding but his design work is often at its best in pieces which approach the esoteric. This jade green decorated with rhinestones is a tribute to that facet of Boucher. Signed Boucher. *Value $650 - $800.*

For a relatively short period many companies made 'face' pins. It is this daring design work which makes these pieces so desirable and valuable. They are scarce and owners treasure them above rubies. The overall look here is Mayan, the proportions of the face are cadaverous but the brilliance of the brightly colored stones rescue the face from the macabre. Both sensational. 1930s. Eisenberg Originals. *Value $2000 - $2500 each.*

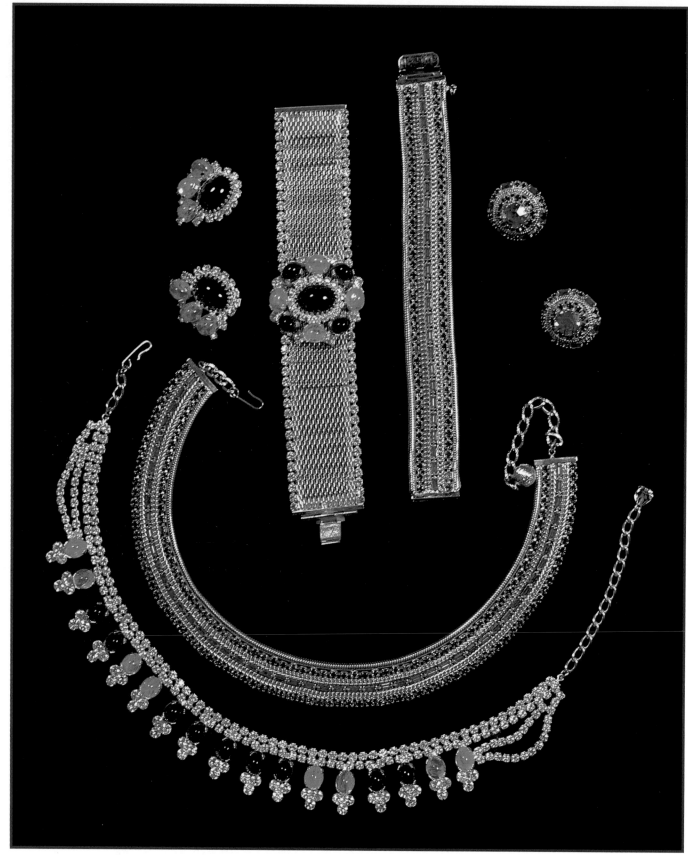

Two dramatic sets by Hobé set against gold tone mesh.

1st set: *Earrings, Bracelet on left, Necklace on bottom.* Bracelet has a 1½" center oval with pink stones surrounding a black center stone, encircled by rhinestones. The necklace has two rows of rhinestones with alternating pink and black drops. Bracelet and earrings are signed Hobé. Necklace has no signature. Late 1950s. *Value of set $500 - $600.*

2nd set; *Bracelet and Earrings on right, Necklace is 2nd from bottom.* Cranberry baguette shaped stones center the ½" bracelet with a choker length necklace. Smoke greystones add to the beauty. Bracelet and earrings signed Hobé, Necklace not signed. *Value $500 - $600.*

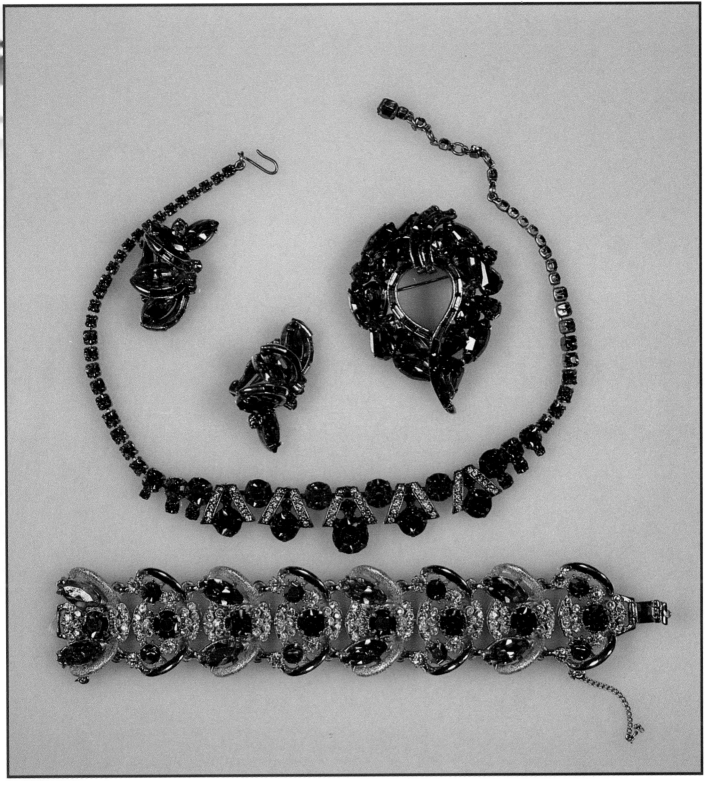

All pieces by Weiss.
The pin and earring set are gold tone metal with the beautiful quality Weiss stones in purple, cranberry and blue-green. Weiss has moved from collectible quality to collectible cult, justifiably so. Signed Weiss on a raised oval on all pieces.
Early 1950s. *Value of set $200 - $250.*
The bracelet is gold tone metal with purple, cranberry and glue green stones but is somewhat earlier than the earrings and pin set. The center stone is surrounded by rhinestones. Signed on an oval. *Value $250 - $300.*
The necklace is also gold tone metal with the same color stones-purple, cranberry and blue-green. The center drops are set in V-shaped channels of rhinestones. A lovely piece. Signed in oval on center stone. 1940s. *Value $250 - $350.*

Necklace 16" long, Bracelet 2" wide, Earrings are a substantial 1½", all by Schiaparelli..
Silver tone metal, clear blue and gray-green stones with iridescent leaves in purple tones. All pieces
signed. 1940s. *Value of set $1200 - $2000.*

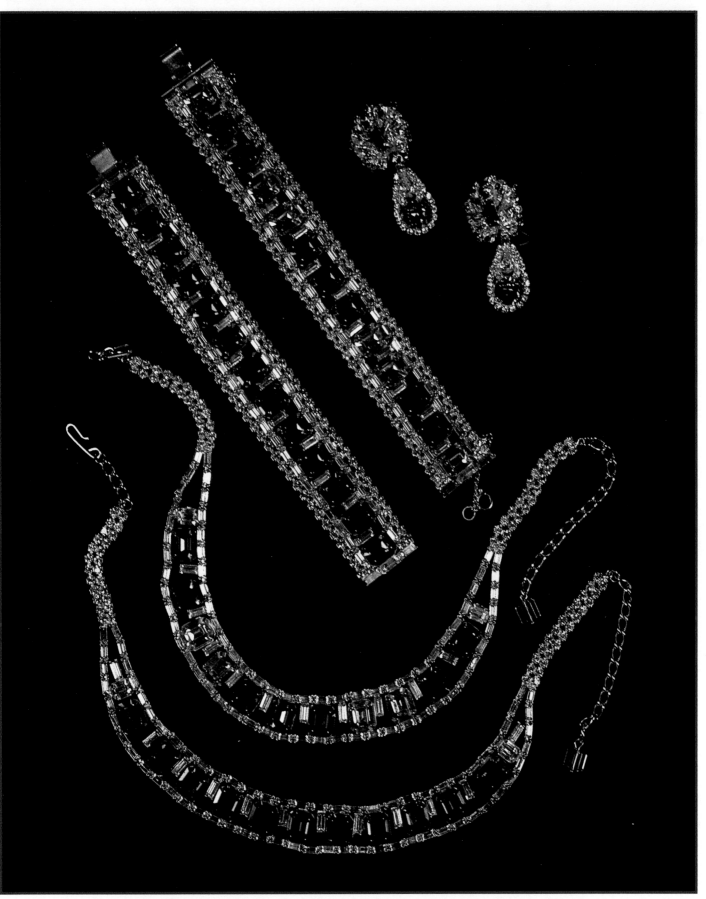

This photograph is a wonderful example of the way companies production by using
the same design with different color stones. These are two identical sets by Hobé. Both are gold colored metal,
one set has blue and purple stones, the other topaz and green stones. Both has emerald cut rhinestones and baguette shaped
rhinestones. As usual, very effective jewelry by Hobé. Signed on bracelets and earrings only.
Value of éach set $450 - $500.

Necklace 16" long, Bracelet 2" wide, Earrings are a substantial 1½", all by Schiaparelli.
Silver tone metal, clear blue and gray-green stones with iridescent leaves in purple tones. All pieces
signed. 1940s. *Value of set $1200 - $2000.*

Start at 9 o'clock: Flower spray brooch of base metal with large pink stones and rhinestones, tied with a rhinestone bow. Late 1930s or early '40s. 3" long, 1¼" wide. Signed on back Eisenberg Original in a circle. *Value $600 - $750.*

Center top: Dress clip, lead/pewter backing 2" x 1½". Rhinestones surrounded by turquoise colored stones. Not signed but Eisenberg Original. *Value $400 - $500.*

Right top: Fur clip, clear stones of topaz, blue, green, red, purple and rhinestones. Gold wash over sterling. Signed Eisenberg Sterling. 1940s. *Value $600 - $800.*

3 o'clock: Fur clip base metal. Pink stones of various sizes, bow is turquoise and rhinestones. Signed E and N is circle. 1930s. *Value $800 - $1000.*

Bottom: Rhinestone and bead dress clip. Green, blue and red beads of various sizes. Gold colored metal. Signed Eisenberg in script. Very early. distinctive piece of Eisenberg. Value $800 - $1200.

Left: Clip of purest Art deco and an unusually fine example of the genre. The pink stones and rhinestones highlight the green, tan and yellow shades of the insect body. Fabulous. 1930s. *Value $500 - $700.*

Center: A signed Blumenthal Pin, from the 1930s. If you owned this it would be a bit like possessing a 1909 Model T. You see one now and then but not an everyday sight. A rare mark on a multi stone, exceedingly colorful crown. The chunky look of some of the stones gives this a different look. *Value $600 - $850.*

Right: This target pierced by three arrows is almost unique among design work of the period although it seems an obvious theme. Rows of fine quality green stones give the pin life. This is as very wearable brooch because it is uncomplicated yet noticeable. A rare signature Lidz Bros., N.Y. *Value $700 - $1000.*

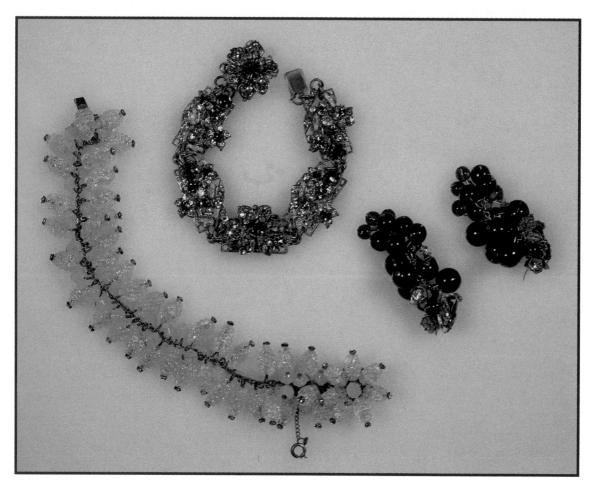

Right: Miriam Haskell earrings. 2½" drop with rose gold flowers with rhinestone centers which resemble a cluster of green grapes. Many of the Haskell designs were inspired by nature. Signed. *Value of the earrings $150 - $195.*

Center top: 8" bracelet in shades of green beads and green stones. The Bracelet is formed in 5 separate lines unusual when the dominant factor is beadwork. Signed. *Value $200 - $300.*

Left: Yellow glass bead bracelet all wired on a fine chain. 1940s. Signed Miriam Haskell. *Value $200 - $300.*

An unsigned beauty. The crescent shape of this gold metal collar can be traced to the Byzantine of the 17th century. Design is almost always influenced by what has gone before and never is that more obvious than here. This beautifully executed piece has multi-colored stones - amber, light green, yellow, brown, shades of blue, orange and purple. It is 16" long and 6" at its widest. 1940s. *Value $500 - $650.*

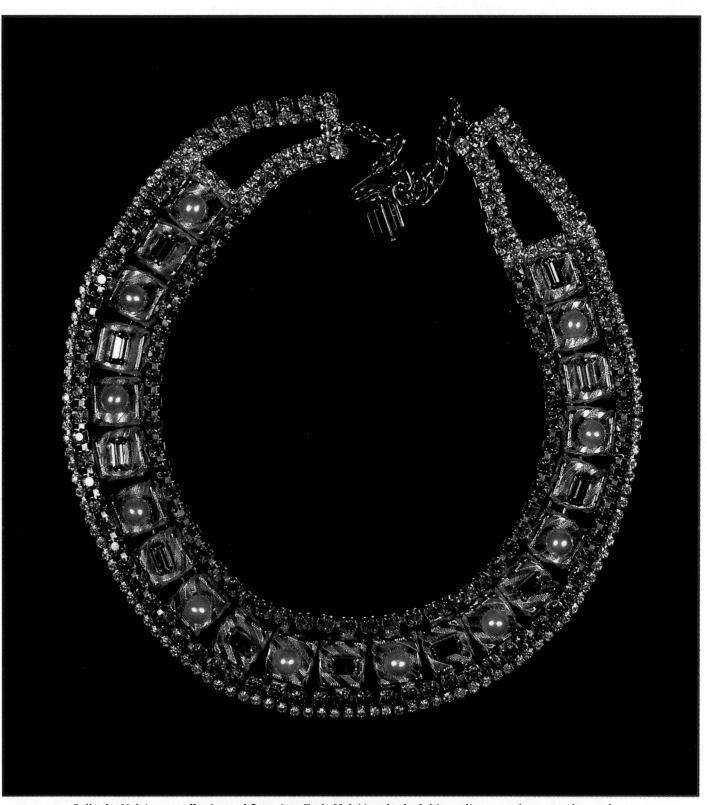

Collar by Hobé - very effective and flattering. Early Hobé jewelry had this quality more than any other maker.
Value $400 - $500.

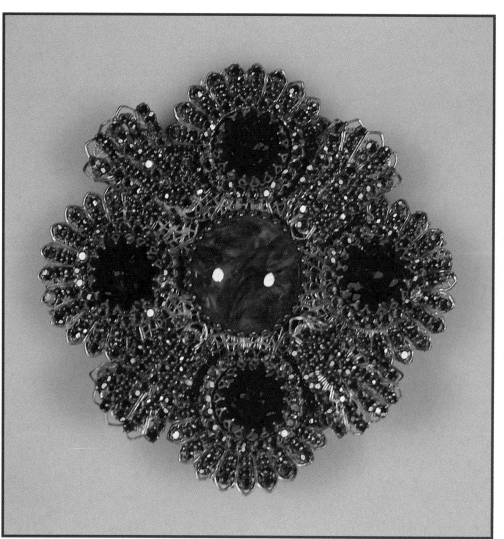

Miriam Haskell fans everywhere - this is for you. One of the most amazing of the Haskell pieces. This spectacular brooch/pin measures 4½" around but no photograph could ever do it justice. A filagree grass background incorporates so well with the many small pink and amber stones the pin seems to be 4½" of endless pleasing glitter. In Haskell fashion the purplish slag large center stone seems to have no relation to the whole but somehow it works very well. Four large (almost 1" each) hand set red stones set around the outside focus the eye. The filagree backing on this oversized piece is beautiful enough to stand alone. Overlapping layers of fine filagree are lace-like and indicate great attention to detail. Signed Miriam Haskell on applied disc. *Value $2000 - $2500.*

Left: Hinged bracelet, pearls and colored stones arranged in the usual way of Miriam Haskell, 1¼" wide. This bracelet has matching earrings, not shown. All the pieces are signed. *Value of set $650 - $850.*
Right: Pearl and chain bracelet, 1¼" wide. This bracelet with its bangle and soft cranberry colored beads and pearls is signed Miriam Haskell. *Value $400 - $450.*

Hobé bracelet and earrings. The bracelet which is unsigned is 2½" wide with black stones surrounded by aurora borealis and rhinestones. Ten small pearls on the bracelet. The matching earrings are signed Hobé. Gold Tone. *Value of set $600 - $850.*

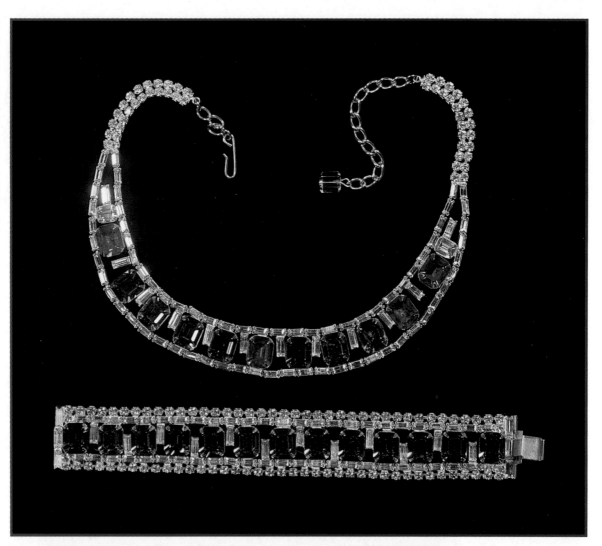

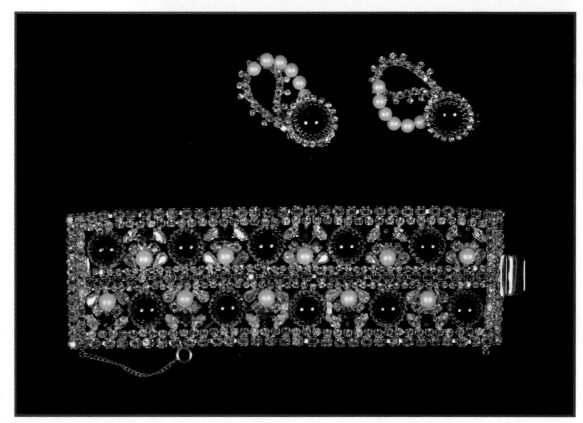

This bracelet and earring set is quite striking in its very size. Gold metal with aurora borealis stones frame the bracelet; rhinestones and domed black stones are held in place by crimped gold metal. Pearls and tear drop rhinestones add to the grandeur of this set. The bracelet is 2" wide, the earrings are 1½" long. Without the signature this would be an outstanding set, with the Hobé name on the earring clip (the bracelet is not signed) it becomes even more important. 1950s. *Value $400 - $500.*

This necklace and earring set by Hobé is a delight. It is pink and crystal and the fringe effect it a dressy, costume price. Signed Hobé. 1950s. *Value $400 - $500.*

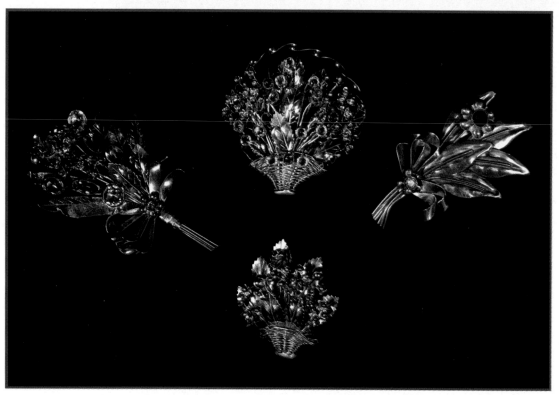

Start at 9 o' clock. Four pins by Hobé.
Left: Amethyst, green, pale green, pale pink amd cranberry stones are set in sterling silver with gold wash. This pretty floral spray is tied with a gold bow. Signed "Hobé 1/20 14K on sterling".
Value $300 - $400.
Center Top: Large 2 x2" flower basket. Round green pink and purple stones form the bouquet. The leaves are gilded with small gold flowers. The woven pattern of the basket is delineated in gold with a twisted gold handle. Signed "Hobé On Sterling, Design Pat'd". *Value $450 - $550.*
Right: Another sterling silver spray. 2½" long with 5 leaves, one large flower of purple stone tied with a sterling bow, one small flower with a light green stone. Signed "Hobé Sterling" on back of leaf. *Value $350 - $450.*
Right Center: 1½" sterling basket of gold overlay. Gold flowers, leaves, woven pattern basket. Signed "Hobé 1/20th 14K on sterling. Design Pat'd". *Value $300 - $400.* As a collection these baskets are gorgeous, as individual pieces of jewelry they reflect the genius of Alfred Philippe.

RENART JEWELRY CO., New York, NY claimed use of this mark since March 22, 1945 for its costume jewelry.

BARNARD HIRSCH COMPANY, San Francisco, CA for pearls. Since 1922.

Renée

Mark of RENEE NOVELTIES, INC., Woodmere, NY for costume jewelry - bracelets, earrings, pins, brooches and clips. First used December, 1934.

Renoir*

Mark of RENOIR OF CALIFORNIA, INC., Los Angeles, CA for brooches, lapel pins, scatter pins, earrings, necklaces and bracelets all made of copper. First used February, 1946.

Rénold

E.W. REYNOLDS CO., Los Angeles, CA for costume jewelry namely finger rings, earrings, bracelets and necklaces. This mark was also used on solid gold jewelry and gold filled jewelry. First used April, 1953.

REPLIQUE

REPLIQUE GEMS LTD., INC., Brookline, MA used this mark for rings, earrings, pendants, brooches. First used 1971

Jewelry mark of WEMBLEY INDUSTRIES, INC., New Orleans, LA, first used December 1970

REVERE

Mark of TAUNTON PEARL WORKS, Taunton, MA for all types of women's jewelry. They also used this mark on religious jewelry. First used October, 1957.

REVERE

TAUNTON PEARL WORKS, Taunton, MA used this mark for men's jewelry. First used May 1944

JULIUS FORSTER, New York, NY used this mark for pearls, genuine, cultured and simulated. First use August 27, 1946.

RHODIGEM

GOODMAN & COMPANY, Indianapolis, Indiana mark for finger rings, necklaces, bracelets, earrings, jewelry clips, brooches and lockets. First used January 1, 1941.

RHODO

Costume jewelry mark of PETER T. SCHLEISSNER, Los Angeles, CA since 1960

RIALTO

Gemex Company, Newark, NJ, for watch bracelets, bracelets, scarf pins, rings, belt buckles, and ear and hair ornaments. First used October, 1929.

Richelieu

JOSEPH H. MEYER BROS., Brooklyn, NY used this mark for men's and women's jewelry - necklaces, bracelets, finger rings, ornamental clips, brooches, earrings and all costume jewelry. Since April, 1911.

RICHGEMS

RICHTON JEWELERS, INC., New York, NY mark for rings, bracelets, earrings, necklaces, since Sept. 1966

RICHLINE

ULRICH ASSOCIATES, New York, NY mark for jewlery. First used June 1958

"RICHMAN POORMAN"

VERDURA, INC., New York, NY mark for bracelets. First used 1939

The Richter & Phillips Co.

THE RICHTER & PHILLIPS COMPANY, Cincinnati, OH made fine jewelry with diamonds, jewelry made wholly or partly of precious metal such as rings, brooches, bar pins, bracelets, necklaces and earrings. First used about January, 1896.

4 IN 1

RICHTON INTERNATIONAL CORP. New York, NY used this mark for jewelry beginning in 1971

Costume jewelry mark of J.H. MALCOLM & CO., INC., Boston MA. Since January, 1958.

RINALDO

RONNIE JEWELRY, INC., Providence, RI mark for jewelry. First used August 1964

RING-DANT

PALAIS JEWELERS, INC., New York, NY for items of jewelry convertible for use on the head and neck. First used July 1960

RING KING

MEDICATED PRODUCTS CO., Chicago, IL mark for necklaces, earrings, pendants and rings. First used March 1961

RIO DEL ORO

Costume jewelry mark of ALAN JEWELRY, INC., Providence, RI. First used Dec. 1963

RISTMASTER

KESTENMAN BROS. MFG. CO., Providence, RI for bracelets, ornamental clasps and buckles. Since June, 1948.

Mark of BEN BLUMENTHAL, New York, NY for artificial pearls, synthetic emeralds, rubies, sapphires and other synthetic stones for jewelers use. It was first used in July, 1930.

RIVAL

SOL E. WEINREICH of WEINREICH BROTHERS, New York, NY used this mark for jewelry and pearls. Since 1911

Mark of COURTLY JEWELS, INC., New York, NY for necklaces, bracelets, earrings, brooches and pin clips. First used December, 1952.

Mark of FASHION CRAFT JEWELRY CO., INC., New York, NY for imitation pearls, bracelets, brooches, chains, earrings, fasteners for necklaces, jewelry clips, lockets, lavalieres, novelty jewelry, ornamental pins, pendants, findings, jewelry stampings and castings. Mark in use since February, 1942.

ROBINWOOD

Mark of Campbell, Robinson, Batcheller, d.b.a. ROBINWOOD, New York, NY for earrings, cuff links, bracelets, necklaces and ornamental pins. First used September, 1941.

ROCK-N-ROLL

I. B. WEST & CO., New York, NY mark for jewelry - rings, bracelets, pins. Since March, 1956.

ROCHELLE

ROCHELLE JEWELRY INC., New York, NY mark for earrings and pins since June 1969

CHINA OVERSEAS, INC., New York, NY used this mark for 'imitation' jewelry. First used Jan. 1942

OSCAP MANUFACTURING CO., INC., mark for all the usual types of jewelry including jewelry for men. Used since May 1947

RODOX

RODOX, INC., New York, NY for costume and novelty jewelry - earrings, necklaces, bracelets, brooches and rings. Since April, 1947.

ROGER JEAN-PIERRE

ROGER JEAN-PIERRE, S.A. Paris, France, mark for costume jewelry, necklaces, earrings, bracelets, pins, clips and buttons. Since January, 1959.

ROMA

FAIRDEAL MANUFACTURING CO., Providence, RI mark for costume jewelry. First used Dec. 1963

ROMANTIC

COHN & ROSENBERGER, INC., New York, NY mark for necklaces, bracelets, earrings, finger rings, brooches, barpins and ornamental hatpins and other jewelry made wholly or in part of or plated with precious metal such as pins, buckles (shoe and hat), and hair ornaments. Used since July, 1931.

ROMANY

STERN & STERN, INC., New York, NY mark for rings, earrings and pins. First used January 1929

ROMOLO

JAR—DEAN, INC., New York, NY mark for jewelry since July 1962

RONCI

Mark of F. RONCI CO., INC., Centerdale, RI for shoe buckles and ornamental pins and pendants plated with precious metal. First used December, 1927.

ROSS

Mark of ROSS WATCH CASE COR-PORATION, Long Island City, NY. Mark for rings, earrings and bracelets. First used September, 1945.

ROUND THE CLOCK

CORO, INC. New York, NY mark for earrings. First used June, 1956.

ROUSSEAU

HOUSE OF ROUSSEAU, LTD., New York, NY for custome jewelry – earrings, bracelets and necklaces. First used October, 1951.

ROSS—BECK CO., Kansas City, MO used this mark for jewelry since July 1938

Royal Court

NEW ENGLAND GLASS WORKS, INC., Providence, RI used this mark for jewelry made of simulated pearls and costume jewelry - earrings, pendants, brooches, chokers, hair ornaments and bouquet holders. Since May 1949

ROYAL CRAFTSMEN

ROYAL CRAFTSMEN, New York, NY mark for jewelry incorporating simulated pearls. First used March 1944

ROYAL OF PITTSBURGH, INC., Pittsburgh, PA used this mark for custom jewelry consisting of metal necklaces, bracelets, earrings and imitation pearls. First used July, 1939.

ROYAL TREASURE

Mark of AVON PRODUCTS INC., New York, NY for costume jewelry. First used Feb. 1972

HELENA RUBINSTEIN

HELENA RUBINSTEIN (the name of the founder of the company) of New York, NY mark for bracelets, necklaces, earrings, finger rings, brooches and money clips. First used 1928.

LILLIAN RUSSELL, KEW GARDENS, Long Island, NY. Mark for costume jewelry. First used March 1934

GEORGE SASSEN, New York, NY mark for costume jewelry. Since October, 1945.

Jewelry mark of SWEET MANUFACTURING CO., Attleboro, MA since about May 1962

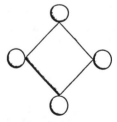

HARRIS STEINMEYER & CO., San Francisco, CA, for brooches, bar pins, pendants, rings bracelets and scarf pins. First used 1924

SEABORN CULTURED PEARLS, INC., New York, NY mark for all types of jewelry made with cultured pearls, earrings, pendants, bracelets, necklaces, rings, etc. Since June 1962

SHIELDS INC., Attleboro, MA mark for men's jewelry. First used Nov. 1962

Mark of CHARLES STONE JEWELRY CORP. New York, NY for jewelry. Since Dec. 1962

Mark used by SCHWARTZ BROS. JEWELRY, New York, NY for pins, charms and bracelets. Since June, 1961.

SAKS & CO., New York, NY mark for jewelry. First used July 1962

SHEFFIELD, INC., Attleboro, MA. Mark for costume jewelry. First used April, 1945.

SHB

Mark of SHOFEL BROS. MFG. CO., New York, NY for jewelry since 1962

HARRY CO. SCHICK, INC., Newark, NJ mark for necklace clasps and snaps and other articles of jewelry made of precious metals, filled gold and sterling silver. Since March, 1938.

SAVOY JEWELRY MFG. CO., New York, NY mark for brooch pins, charms, bracelets, necklaces, rings, earrings and clips. Since 1954

SC

SARAH COVENTRY, INC., Newark, NJ used this mark for costume jewelry. Since Oct. 1953

SIDNEY KRANDALL AND SONS, Detroit, MI mark for jewelry. First used 1959

S & C

Mark of SHVED & COHEN for jewelry. First used Dec. 1954

OSCAR SHERER, New York, NY mark for the usual types of jewelry. First used 1962

Mark of HARRY SOBEL d.b.a. SOBEL'S JEWELRY CO., New York, NY for jewelry. First used 1962

GENERAL CHAIN CO., Providence, RI, then of North Attleboro, MA for pendants, bracelets, brooches, scarves, pins, cuff links, lapel buttons and earrings. First used in 1894.

SS+

THE KINNEY CO., Providence, RI mark for jewelry. Since March 1965

MAURICE SPAIN & SONS, INC., New York, NY mark for bracelets, necklaces, brooches, pins, rings, charms, earrings and other items of jewelry. First used April 1962

Jewelry mark of S. WALDER CO., Hartford CT. First used Jan. 1962

SWL

Jewelry mark of S.W.L. INC., New York, NY since August 1961

SYL

SYLVANIA JEWELRY CO., New York, NY mark for all the usual types of jewelry. First used 1954

Saks-Fifth Avenue

SAKS & COMPANY, New York, NY mark for men's and women's jewelry and children's jewelry of all quality. First used September, 1924.

Mark of SAKS & COMPANY, New York, NY for opera glasses, sun glasses, lorgnettes, magnifying glasses, etc. First used September, 1924.

SALON D'OR

SHIRLEY MARKS, New York, NY mark for non-precious costume jewelry. Used since 1947.

SALON MICHELLE

BERG SELECTOR MERCHANDISING CO., INC. Washington, D.C. mark for costume jewelry. First used April 1960

SAN REMO

Mark of SAN REMO MARKETING CORP. New York, NY for jewelry. Since 1970

Mark of SANFORD AND COMPANY, INC., Los Angeles, CA for men's and women's costume jewelry plated with precious metal. First used January, 1951.

Jewelry mark of SAND AND SAGE MANUFACTURING CO., Denver, CO which also made compacts. First used August, 1956.

SANDRA POST OF FLORIDA, INC., Miami Beach, FL for costume jewelry finger rings, bracelets, necklaces, earrings, brooches. First used 1963

SANTA'S WORKSHOP

SANTA'S WORKSHOP, INC. North Pole, NY for earrings, bracelets, pendants and jewelry pins. First used July, 1949.

SAPPHIRITE

UNITED STATES QUARRY TILE COMPANY, Canton and East Sparta, Ohio and Parkersburg, W. Virginia. Mark used for jewels and formed ornamental jewel pieces for ring sets, brooches, pendants, earrings, tiaras, and necklaces. Since July, 1945.

SARAH COV.

SARAH COVENTRY INC., Newark, NY mark for costume jewelry. This mark dates from Jan. 1960

SARAH COVENTRY

SARAH COVENTRY, INC., Newark NY used this mark for men's and women's costume jewelry. First used May, 1949.

SARAHGLO

SARAH COVENTRY, INC., Newark, NY mark for costume jewelry. This mark dates from Jan. 1961

SARAHSHEEN

SARAH COVENTRY, INC., Newark, NY used this mark for costume jewelry since Jan. 1961

SARDE

Mark of SARDELLI & SONS, INC., Providence, RI for jewelry. First used Nov. 1966

SATINORE

JOS. H. MEYER BROS., Brooklyn, NY mark for necklaces, bracelets, rings, jewelry clips, brooches and earrings. First used May 1939

Satinore

Mark of JOSEPH H. MEYER BROS., Brooklyn, NY for men's and women's costume jewelry. Since 1939.

SAUTEUR

RENOIR OF CALIFORNIA, INC., Los Angeles, CA mark for costume jewelry. First used June, 1958.

HICKOK MANUFACTURING CO., INC., Rochester, NY for men's jewelry since December 1954.

SCARF BAIT

R. M. JORDAN & CO., INC., Providence, RI mark for scarf rings, scarf pins and scarf clips. Since January 1947.

SCATTER-TAKS

RHYTHM JEWELRY CO., New York, NY mark for costume jewelry, namely - ornaments for ladies' dresses. Since December, 1957.

SCEPTRON

REINAD NOVELTY CO., New York, NY and SCEPTRON JEWELRY CREATIONS (a partnership) used this mark for costume jewelry beginning June, 1944.

SCHEUER'S
"Wear Them With Pride"

C. SCHEUER COMPANY, New York, NY used this mark beginning in April, 1928. This company made every kind of jewelry as well as cigarette cases, mesh bags, dresser sets, etc.

HARRY C. SCHICK, INC., Newark, NJ mark for necklace clasps and fasteners. Since January, 1922.

HAVE - A - HEART

Mark of SOL M. SCHWARZSCHILD, Richmond, VA, for bracelets, necklaces and earrings. Used since 1945.

COHN & ROSENBERGER, INC., New York, NY mark for all the usual jewelry types and accessories. First used Jan. 1933

PHYLLIS ORIGINALS, INC., Providence, RI mark for chatelaines, ornamental pins, earrings, brooches, bracelets and necklaces. First used May 1950

MAZER BROS. New York, NY used this mark for strings and necklaces of artificial pearls. Since 1929

MARK OF THE SEA GEM COMPANY, New York, NY for jewelry containing pearls namely, necklaces, earrings, clips, crosses, brooches, studs, pendants, rings and stick pins. First used June 1945

SEA GIFT

A. MICALIEF & CO., Providence, RI mark for costume jewelry made with cultured pearls. First used Oct. 1955

A. C. BECKEN CO., Chicago, Illinois used this mark for pearl jewelry, cultured, simulated or artificial. Since October, 1946.

MAZER BROS. New York, NY mark for
strings of artificial pearls since 1929.

PAUL MORRIS, INC., New York, NY
used this mark for costume jewelry, namely
necklaces made with pearls, earrings and
bracelets. First used November, 1951.

Sea Nymph

This mark was used by LAY & BORGES,
New York, NY for imitation pearl necklaces,
bracelets and earrings. Since Jan. 1944

SEARAMA

PHILLIPS MFG. CO., Brooklyn, NY mark
for rings, pendants, earrings, pins, charms and
brooches. First used 1963

SECO

STEIN & ELLBOGEN COMPANY,
Chicago, IL for finger rings and necklaces.
Since January, 1908.

SELCO

SELECT JEWELRY MFG. CO., INC.,
Long Island City, NY mark in the 1940s and
50s.

SELECT

STEIN & ELLBOGEN COMPANY,
Chicago, Ill, mark for jewelry including baby
necklaces, necklaces, bracelets, dress clips
and also religious jewelry. Since July, 1951.

Senorita

SCHEIN BROTHERS, INC., New York,
NY for personal jewelry. First used
November, 1933.

SENSITIVITY

SENSITIVITY GAMES, Boston, MA mark
for jewelry since Feb. 1971

SENTINEL

KESTENMAN BROS., MFG. CO., Providence, RI Mark for wrist watch bracelets.
1926.

WEISBAUER'S SHA—SHA GEMS, Torrence, CA used this mark for costume
jewelry. Since Nov. 1964

SHADOWCRAFT

Mark of LATAMA, INCORPORATED,
New York, NY for earrings, ornamental
pins, tie bars and cuff links, etc. First used
March, 1956.

Shah

Mark of PRATT & WOLLMAN, INC., New York, NY for bracelets, chains, ornamental clasps, lockets, finger rings, brooches, bar pins, scarf pins, cigarette cases, vanity cases. First used January, 1948.

Shalimar

ABE. A. FRIEDMAN, Augusta, GA for simulated pearl jewelry. First used March, 1949.

SHALIMAR

Mark of SIMON GOLUB & SONS, INC., Seattle, WA for necklaces, brooches, finger rings, pins, earrings, arm bracelets, lockets, pendants and crosses. First used July, 1958.

SHERRY CRAFT, INC., Philadelphia, PA for novelty and costume jewelry - barrettes, bracelets, brooches, rings, earrings, lockets, necklaces and ornamental pins. First used January, 1953.

Shields FIFTH AVENUE

SHIELDS of Attleboro, MA used this mark for men's jewelry and compacts. First used March, 1950.

SHINING HOUR WING-DING

Mark of JACQUELINE COCHRAN, INC., Newark NY for a perfume pin. First used August, 1948.

THE SHOPPING CENTER

MILLER AND RHOADS, INC., Richmond, VA used this mark for costume jewelry-base metal pins, clips, brooches, bracelets and necklaces with simulated stones, as well as simulated pearl jewelry. This mark was also used for fine jewelry and silver-tableware. First used April, 1917.

SHOWPIECE

Mark of MASSOVER BROTHERS, INC., Chicago, IL for jewelry. First used August, 1955.

SICLE

JOE LOWE CORP., New York, NY mark for pearl sets, earrings and bracelets. Since January, 1957.

LOUIS SICKLES PHILADELPHIA, PA mark for brooches, bar pins, spray pins, bracelets, lavalieres, lockets, earrings, bracelets, anklets, rings and cuff links. First used July 1937

LOUIS SICKLES, Philadelphia, PA mark for brooches, hat pins, spray pins, lavalieres, and other types of jewelry since Aug. 1923

LOUIS SICKLES, Philadelphia, PA mark for lapel watches, chatelaine watches and other types of watches. Also used for other types of jewelry. Since July 1937

SIDEWALK SUPERINTENDENTS

FOSTER METAL PRODUCTS INC., Attleboro, MA for men's jewelry. Since January, 1956.

SILVER BROTHERS, Atlanta, GA used this mark for jewelry of the usual types as well as fraternal jewelry. Since June, 1950.

SILHOUETTE

COHN & ROSENBERGER, INC., New York, NY used this mark for all the usual types of jewelry, strings of pearls, ornamental pins and ornamental shoe buckles. Since 1929

SILMARC

GRABEN & BAUER, New York, NY mark for costume jewelry. First used June, 1946.

SIMMONS

Jewelry mark of R. F. SIMMONS COMPANY, Attleboro, Mass., for jewelry. The company claimed use of this mark since 1885 and was still active in 1949.

JUIL RILEY GOGGINS, Minneapolis, MN, used this mark for pins, rings, belt buckles, bracelets and necklaces. First used Jan. 1927

Siren

H.S. KRESS & CO. New York, NY used this mark for all the usual types of jewelry as well as sautoirs, compact cases, belt buckles and hair ornaments, all made or plated with precious metal. First used January, 1932.

Skin Pin

OSTIER, INC., New York, NY mark for brooches, pin clips, separable pins, earrings, lockets, necklaces and charms. Since September, 1950.

SKLIP

JOSEPH H. MEYER BROS. Brooklyn, NY mark for earrings. First used June 1940

SKYLARK

S. & B. LEDERER CO., Providence, RI mark for pins, brooches, clips, necklaces, lockets, pendants, bracelets and earrings. Used since April 1941

THE BALL CO., Chicago, IL mark for jewelry. First used 1937

Slaccessories

NAT LEVY, New York, NY used this mark for costume jewelry. Since Jan. 1942

SLYDA

Mark used by the MARATHON COMPANY, Attleboro, Mass. for cigarette cases, compacts and powder cases. First used in August, 1931.

SMALL FRY

TRU-KAY MANUFACTURING, CO., Providence, RI for costume jewelry - brooches, pendants, necklaces, bracelets and pins. First used November, 1957.

Smart Set

CORO, INC., New York, NY mark for necklaces, bracelets, rings, earrings, jewelry clips, brooches, lockets and the following made of, or plated with, precious metal - beads, pins, hat ornaments, jewelry initials and jewelry made with pearls. Since January, 1935.

SMARTFIT

The TAUNTON PEARL WORKS, INC, of Taunton, Mass used this mark beginning in May, 1928 for tie-clips and other jewelry for personal adornment.

SNAP · BAR

KREMENTZ & COMPANY, Newark, NJ mark for cuff links set with stones. Since 1940.

SNAP-IT

GLAMOUR JEWELRY, INC., Providence, RI used this mark for earrings. Since April, 1956.

SOCIALITE

SOCIALITE CREATIONS, INC., New York, NY mark for finger rings, pendants, earrings and brooches. Since May 1961

SOCIALLY ACCEPTED

MORRIS, MANN & REILLY, Chicago, IL mark for ladies' costume jewelry - necklaces, bracelets, earrings, brooch pins and bead necklaces. First used July 1929

CORO mark for the usual jewelry. Used since April, 1957.

Softouch

CORO, INC., New York, NY mark for earrings. Used since March, 1959.

SOLUDA

COSTUME JEWELRY mark of RAM TOLERAM of TOLARAM INTERNATIONAL AGENCIES, Hongkong. First used in 1964 internationally.

SORET

SOMERS—ERNST CO., INC., New York, NY for all the usual types of jewelry plus 'festoons', lockets, etc. Since May 1946

Sorrento

UNCAS MANUFACTURING CO., Providence, RI, mark for jewelry since 1951.

SOUTH SEA

JOSEPH H. MEYER BROS., Brooklyn, NY mark for necklaces, bracelets, earrings and brooches with pearls. Since January, 1954.

CORO mark for the usual jewelry pieces as well as hat ornaments, cigarette boxes, compacts and comb cases. Since about 1944.

SPAULDING & COMPANY, Chicago, Illinois trademark which consists of a right angle triangle in solid color. The mark is often applied to the top left hand corner of a rectangular container for the goods. The mark was for rings, bracelets, anklets, earrings, ear clips, necklaces, pins, clips and other costume jewelry. This company also made fine jewelry and claims use of the mark since 1932.

SPANISH TREASURE

Mark of AVON PRODUCTS INC., New York, NY for costume jewelry. First used Nov. 1971

Speidel

SPEIDEL CORPORATION, Providence, RI mark for jewelry — bracelets, ornamental chains of all types, pins, clips, earrings, lockets, charms, cuff links, etc. Also jewelry findings. First used April, 1932.

Sperlyte

SPERRY MANUFACTURING CO. mark for bracelets, earrings, necklaces and brooches. Since November, 1953.

SPERRY

HELLER-SPERRY, INC., New York, NY used this mark on its jewelry as well as other versions since January, 1947.

Sperry

SPERRY MFG. CO., Providence, RI mark for jewelry for both men and women. Since January, 1947.

Spin-it

MARVELLA PEARLS, INC., New York, NY mark for charms, charm bracelets, necklaces, earrings and brooches. First used December, 1955.

Splendor

CORO, INC., New York, NY also used this mark for jewelry made with pearls, bracelets, necklaces, earrings, brooches and finger rings. Since April, 1948.

SPORTCRAFT

JULIUS LITTMAN, d.b.a. SPORTCRAFT, New York, NY mark for bracelets, cuff links, clips and buckles. Since May, 1958.

SPORTEE

ASHAWAY LINE & TWINE CO., Ashaway, RI mark for jewelry including earrings, scatter pins and tie clasps. First used about November, 1955.

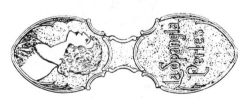

SPRINGLER, INC., Chicago, IL for pearls used in necklaces and other jewelry. The jewelry was usually tagged with this mark. First used October, 1927.

Spruce

Mark of Walter A. Dunn d.b.a. DUNN BROTHERS, Providence, RI. For jewelry. Since 1965

Mark of LEWIS M. NELSON, Camden, NJ mark for jewelry. First used about March, 1920.

Stamcor

STANDARD MERCHANDISING CORP. New York, NY mark for necklaces, bracelets, rings, earrings, clips, brooches, lockets, and tie holders. First used in 1940

Stand-Out

Theresa G. Brogan, d.b.a. J.M. HALL CO., Providence, RI for bracelets. Since February, 1948.

Mark of COLONIAL MFG. CO., INC. New York, NY for rings, earrings, brooches, bracelets, necklaces, jewelry clips and lockets. First used January, 1956.

STAR NOVELTY ★

STAR NOVELTY JEWELRY CO., INC., Chicago, IL mark for jeweled clips, pins, bracelets, buckles. Since December 1935

STUCKEY AND SPEER, Houston, TX for rings, brooches, jewelry pins, earrings, bracelets and necklaces. First used January, 1952.

Star of Persia

UNTERMEYER ROBBINS & CO., New York, NY mark for finger rings with semi-precious stones. February, 1946.

STARET

STAR NOVELTY JEWELRY CO., INC., Chicago, IL mark for jeweled clips, pins, bracelets and buckles. First used December 1935

Starjule

STAR JEWELRY CO., INC. New York, NY mark for costume jewelry, necklaces, bracelets, brooches, earrings, chatelaines, clips, lockets and pearl beads. Since June, 1946.

STARLITE

JOSEPH H. MEYER BROS., Brooklyn, NY mark for necklaces, bracelets, finger rings, jewelry clips, brooches and earrings. This mark first used January, 1944.

DAVID GRAD COMPANY, New York, NY for costume jewelry, i.e., bracelets, pendants, necklaces, earrings and fobs. Since July, 1948.

STARLORE

Mark of AVON PRODUCTS INC., New York, NY for costume jewelry. First used Oct. 1971

ROCHESTER BUTTON COMPANY, Rochester, NY mark for decorative inserts for jewelry. Since November, 1949.

STARS OF LIGHT

Mark of UNCAS MANUFACTURING CO., Providence, RI. For jewelry having simualted star stones. Since April 1971

PREMIER JEWELRY COMPANY, New York, NY used this mark for unbreakable necklace cables beginning January, 1931.

STELLA'S LUCKY STAR

Stella J. Reed d.b.a. STELLA, New York, NY for jewelry in the shape of a star or displaying a star such as necklaces, brooches, bracelets. Since January, 1956.

STERLE

MONTREAUX JEWELRY, INC., New York, NY for jewelry. Since May, 1959.

STETSON

SABIN MFG. CO., Providence, RI mark for jewelry. First used April, 1928.

STIX, BAER & FULLER CO., St. Louis, MO mark for necklaces, brooches, bracelets and earrings. Since Jan. 1962

Stocking Stuffer

Mark of CORO, INC., New York, NY for all their usual jewelry items including beads, pins and jewelry items including beads, pins and jewelry initials. Since July, 1957.

STORKETTE

LAWRENCE MFG. INC., Providence, RI, mark for its jewelry beginning August, 1944.

I. LIEBER AND COMPANY, New York, NY used this mark on its jewelry including crosses and cuff links. October, 1946.

STRAPEZE

FELCH-ANDERSON CO., Providence RI first used this mark for shoe buckles plated with precious metals in January, 1948.

STREAMLINE

COHN & ROSENBERGER, INC., New York, NY mark for strings of pearls, all the usual types of jewelry, bar pins, ornamental hat pins, pins for dress ornaments, ornamental pins and buckles for decorating hats, ornamental shoe buckles and hair ornaments. First used Feb. 1933

STRUT

Mark of ERNEST H. AUGAT, Attleboro, MA for all the usual types of jewelry as well as cigarette cases, and compacts. Used since Dec. 1945

C & G MANUFACTURING COMPANY, Providence, RI. This mark included jewelry with or without stones, Costume jewelry and pearls. Since February, 1946.

Stylecraft Gems

UNCAS MANUFACTURING COM-
PANY, Providence, RI, for brooches,
bracelets, necklaces, pins and earrings. Used
since March, 1938.

Styled to Beautify

CORO, INC. New York, NY for all the
usual types of jewelry together with pearl
jewelry of all kinds. First used December,
1938.

Stylerite

UNCAS MANUFACTURING COM-
PANY, Providence, RI mark for jewelry
such as brooches, bracelets, pins, necklaces
and earrings. First used May, 1941.

SUB-DEB

MARATHON CO., Attleboro, MA mark for
rings, bracelets, lockets, lavalieres with pendant drops, brooches, etc. First used 1931

SUB-DEB

Another mark used by MARATHON
COMPANY of Attleboro, Mass. for jewelry
as well as hand bags of precious metal and
compacts. Used since March 2, 1931.

Sublime

CORO mark for jewelry with pearls. First
used April, 1948.

SUCCESSORIES

AVON PRODUCTS, INC., New York, NY
mark for costume jewelry. First used June
1970

"SULTANA"

THE RICHTER & PHILLIPS CO., d.b.a.
CONSUMERS MERCHANDISE MART,
Cincinnati, OH mark for bracelets and other
usual types of jewelry. Since Dec. 1943

SUMMER ROSE

Mark of AVON PRODUCTS INC., New
York, NY for costume jewelry. First used
Oct. 1971

Sun-brite

GELLY G. MILLER, Oakland, California.
Mark first used June 15, 1945.

SUN-KISSED

COHN & ROSENBERGER, INC., New
York, NY mark for strings of pearls, all the
usual types of jewelry and pins for dress ornaments, ornamental pins and buckles for
decorating hats, ornamental shoe buckles and
other decorative ornaments. First used Feb.
1929

M. SICKLES & SONS, INC., Philadelphia,
PA mark for rings, earrings, brooches, pendants and bracelets. First used 1949

SUN-RAY

MAYER & MULLIGAN INC., New York,
NY for pendants. First used June, 1927.

SUNBEAM

COHN & ROSENBERGER, INC., New
York, NY for bracelets, brooches, rings, earrings, bar pins, and vanity cases. Used since
1927

SUN FROST

STAR JEWELRY CO., New York, NY for earrings, brooches, and ornamental pins. Since January, 1949.

FRED WEISS, Los Angeles, CA for cultured pearls. Since December, 1936.

SUNNYBROOK BLUE

ROYAL JEWELRY MFG. CO., INC. New York, NY used this mark for chokers, necklaces, brooches, bracelets, rings, earrings and bar pins. First used 1929

Superba

MARK DOTTENHEIM, New York, NY mark for pearl jewelry. First used October, 1919.

Supreme

CORO INC., New York, NY used this mark for jewelry with pearls, necklaces, bracelets, brooches, etc. First used April, 1948.

SWEETEEN

B.B. GREENBERG CO., Providence, RI mark for women's and children's jewelry. First used 1963

Swingband

Mark used by DAVID DAMOSA ZAKWIN, Los Angeles, California for rings, earrings, chatelaines and bracelets. Since June 25, 1946.

SYLVIA

GEMEX COMPANY, Newark, NJ mark for their usual jewelry line. Used since October, 1929.

Symblem

EISENSTADT MANUFACTURING CO., St. Louis, MO mark for charms, pendants, bracelets, brooches and rings. Since May 1918

SYMBOL OF BEAUTY

WEINREICH BROTHERS CO., New York, NY mark for pearl necklaces, pearls and other jewelry. Used since August, 1943.

SYMMETALIC

W. E. RICHARDS CO., Attleboro, MA mark for jewelry. First used December, 1936.

Synchroslide

A & Z CHAIN COMPANY, Providence, RI for wrist watch bracelets, clasps and buckles. Since September, 1932.

TRIFARI, KRUSSMAN & FISHEL INC., New York, NY mark for costume jewelry. First used 1939.

ALAN R. TENEN of TENEN BROS., New York, NY used this mark for jewelry since 1918

TREBOUR BRACELET CORP., New York, NY mark for jewelry. First used May 1962

TOWN & COUNTRY JEWELRY MANUFACTURING CORP., Malden, MA used this mark for jewelry. First used Feb. 1970

CHAS. THOMAS & SONS, INC., Attleboro, MA mark for brooches, pins, cigarette cases, combs, mirrors, etc. Since 1944

This is a fraternal jewelry mark of O.C. TANNER JEWELRY CO., Salt Lake City, UT used since January 1940

THOMAS D. GARD CO., INC., Worcester, MA used this mark for its jewelry as well as emblems. Since May, 1906.

TRIFARI, KRUSSMAN & FISHEL, INC., New York, NY mark for necklaces, earrings, brooches and the like. First used May, 1954.

Mark of TRIFARI, KRUSSMAN & FISHEL, INC., New York, NY for jewelry for personal wear. First used January, 1935.

TRU-KAY MANUFACTURING CO., Providence, RI for all types of costume jewelry. Used since February, 1946.

T-K

TRU—KAY MANUFACTURING CO., Providence, RI mark for costume jewelry. First used June, 1962

LOUIS TAMIS & SONS, New York, NY mark for all the usual jewelry types as well as vanity cases, lipstick cases cuff links, buckles, charms and perfume cases. Since June 1933

LOUIS TAMIS & SON, New York, NY mark for cigarette cases, vanity cases, compacts, watch bracelets, bracelets, earrings, cuff links, cigarette holders, and pens and pencils. First used June 1933

SERENA CREATIONS, New York, NY mark for brooch pins, charms, bracelets, rings, necklaces, earrings and clips. First used May, 1962

154

TRAUB MANUFACTURING COMPANY, INC., Detroit, MI mark for clasps, bracelets, brooches, scarf pins, lockets, lavalieres and snaps. Since February, 1917.

TABBY

CLAIRE BAXTER MARCUS, New York, NY used this mark for jewelry and for attachments to jewelry including fasteners. First used June 1940

TABU

CONSOLIDATED COSMETICS, Chicago, Illinois used this mark for costume jewelry and powder boxes since January, 1946.

TAI WINDS

Mark of AVON PRODUCTS INC., New York, NY for costume jewelry. First used Jan. 1972

CORNELL, GROSSMAN of Millburn, NJ used this mark for finger rings, bracelets, necklaces and pins. Since December, 1946.

Talisman

GROF MANUFACTURING CO., Cleveland, OH mark for both ladies' and men's rings, ornamental pins, breast pins, dress clips, brooches, earrings, necklaces, bracelets, and tie clips. First used Dec. 1947

TARA DEB

TARA DEB, INC., New York, NY mark for necklaces, bracelets, earrings, pins, rings, hair ornaments, imitation pearls and rhinestones. First used February, 1959.

Tassle Talk

CORO, INC., New York, NY mark for all the usual jewelry types plus charms and charm bracelets, pearls, beads and jewelry initials. First used 1962

TATTOO

ASSOCIATED PRODUCTS, INC., Chicago, Illinois trademark for its gold plated compacts. Since November, 1946.

TAYLOR & CO., Houston, TX mark for jewelry for personal wear. First used June 1944

TAYLOR & CO., Newark, NJ mark for all the usual types of jewelry plus cigarette cases, bangles, buttons and jewelry clasps. Since April 1940

MORRIS, MANN & REILLY, INC., Chicago, IL for women's and children's jewelry, particularly pendants and earrings. First used February, 1933.

ROCHESTER BUTTON COMPANY,
Rochester, NY mark for decorative inserts
for jewelry. Since November, 1949.

M. TECLA & CO., New York, NY assignor
to THE TECLA CORPORATION used
this mark for jewelry and jewelry with pearls.
First used about April, 1906.

TEDDY BEAR

UNCAS MANUFACTURING CO, Pro-
vidence, RI used this mark for finger rings.
First used 1959

TUCKER NOVELTY CO., INC., New
York, NY used this mark for costume
jewelry since December, 1957.

Teen-Kraft

Mark of MARATHON COMPANY, Attleboro, Mass for jewelry. March, 1946.

TEEN-O-GRAMS

CORO, INC., New York, NY mark for
jewelry initials. First used February, 1958.

Teena Little

SCHAFER-NICHOLSON INC., Utica, NY
for costume jewelry made of plastic. Since
January, 1947.

TEEN TRINKET JEWELRY of Pro-
vidence, RI mark for all the usual types of
women's and children's jewlery. First used
Feb. 1955

TEENETTE

FORSTNER, INC., Irvington, NJ mark for
bracelets, necklaces, pins and earrings. Since
May, 1958.

TEENY WEENY

ARCADIA MILLS CO., Philadelphia, PA
mark for children's novelty jewelry. First used
1965

TELLENO

HENRY TELLER & SONS, INC.,
Chicago, IL mark for jewelry. Since about
November, 1956.

TEMPLE BELLS

CORO INCORP. of RHODE ISLAND, Providence, RI mark for jewelry since June 1964.

TEMPT ME

CORO, INC., New York, NY for all the
usual type jewelry and beads, pins and
jewelry initials made or plated with precious
metal. First used May, 1963.

TEMPUS

JACOB M. SOLOWAY, New York, NY for
costume jewelry and jewel cases. First used
1941

Ten-n-Teens

ARKE INC., New York, NY for necklaces,
bracelets, barrettes, pins and fobs. First used
August, 1952.

TENDER MOMENTS

AVON PRODUCTS, INC., New York, NY mark for costume jewelry. First used June 1971

A. V. CUTT CO., INC. Tampa, FL mark for costume jewelry such as bracelets, necklaces, earrings, pins and pendants. This mark used since November, 1953 can sometimes be found on unassembled jewelry pieces.

Mark of IDEAL MANUFACTURING CO., Providence, RI for bracelets. Since May, 1921.

THELMA

GEMEX COMPANY mark for the usual types of jewelry plus buckles, fobs and charms. Since March, 1930.

CORO, INC., New York, NY mark for necklaces, bracelets, earrings, jewelry clips, brooches, lockets, and the following made wholly or partly of precious metals or plated with the same -- beads, pins, hat ornaments, holders for face powder compacts, comb cases, fancy buckles, and jewelry initials. Used since June, 1942.

Tickled Pink

CORO, INC., New York, NY mark for all their usual jewelry types. First used July, 1958.

Tie Tacks

HICKOK MANUFACTURING CO., INC. Rochester, NY for men's jewelry. First used May, 1953.

TIE-UPS

Mark of TRIFARI, KRUSSMAN & FISHEL, INC., New York, NY for costume jewelry. This mark used first August, 1957.

TRIFARI, KRUSSMAN & FISHEL, INC., New York, NY for costume jewelry since August, 1957.

Tiny Jewels

W & H Jewelry Co., Providence, RI mark for infant's and children's jewelry. Since Jan. 1940

TIVOL

TIVOL PLAZA INC., KANSAS CITY, MO mark for jewelry. First used 1958

TO A WILD ROSE

Mark of AVON PRODUCTS INC., New York, NY for costume jewelry. First used Oct. 1971

WALTER LAMPL, New York, NY mark for bracelets, rings, necklaces, lockets, barrettes and pins. In use since February, 1944.

TOGA

MAURICE GOLDMAN & SONS, New York, NY for necklaces, chokers, earrings, stick pins, bracelets of cultured pearls. Since April, 1953.

TOKEN OF LOVE

FORSTNER JEWELRY MFG. CORP., Lynbrook, NY used this mark for jewelry beginning 1965

Tootsie

Mark of the MARVEL JEWELRY MFG. CO., Providence, RI for all types of bracelets. Since January, 1948.

Top Hat Charm

WELLS MANUFACTURING COMPANY, Attleboro, Mass., mark for jewelry for personal wear, since May, 1940.

TOT-AGE

STERN & STERN, INC., New York, NY for pendants, lockets, bracelets, finger rings, brooches. Some of this jewelry was gold plated, silver plated, made of sterling silver or gold. Since February, 1955.

Towncrest

TOWN & COUNTRY DISTRIBUTORS, INC., Harrisburg, PA d.b.a. GERBUN DISTRIBUTORS, New York, NY used this mark for rings, bracelets, earrings, necklaces and pendants. First used 1962

TRAVELLING TRINKETS

COSTUME JEWELRY mark of TRAVELLING TRINKETS, INC., Woodmere, NY first used October 1970

TRAVELOGUE

CORO INC. mark for all the usual Coro jewelry. This mark first used August, 1957.

TREASURE CHEST CO., Brooklyn, NY for novelty and costume jewelry - earrings, clips and ornamental pins. First used January, 1947.

TREASURE STACK

NEIMAN—MARCUS CO., Dallas, TX used this mark for jewelry of all qualities. First used 1964

TRES BANDERAS, INC., New York, NY. Mark for simulated pearls and novelty jewelry. Since December, 1945.

TRÉZA

Mark of THE RICHELIEU CORP., Holbrooks, NY for necklaces, bracelets and earrings. First used Aug. 1964

"TRICKS for TEENS"

Mark used by George J. Hecht of CHILDREN'S PRODUCTS CO., New York, NY for costume jewelry. Since Aug., 1941

Mark of TRIFARI, KRUSSMAN & FISHEL, INC., New York, NY for perfumed brcelets made from non precious metals. First used September, 1958.

Jewels by TRIFARI

Mark of TRIFARI, KRUSSMAN & FISHEL, INC., New York, NY for earrings, pins, clips, necklaces, bracelets, gold or silver plated base metal buttons, cuff links, hair barrettes, hair combs, tiaras, belt buckles, shoe buckles, bracelet charms and hat pins. First used March, 1920.

TRIFARI

TRIFARI, KRUSSMAN & FISHEL, INC., Providence, RI for jewelry including brooches, earrings, necklaces, bracelets, etc. First used December, 1937.

TRIFARI, KRUSSMAN & FISHEL, INC., New York, NY used this mark for earrings, clips, pins, necklaces, bracelets, cuff links, tiaras, charms. Trifari also used the mark on belt buckles, shoe buckles, hat pins, hair barrettes and combs which were plated with or made wholly, or partly, of precious metal. First used December, 1937.

Jewels by **TRIFARI**

TRIFARI, KRUSSMAN & FISHEL, INC., of New York, NY, a variant mark used in the 1940s and 50s.

Costume jewelry mark of **FRED M. BIRCH CO.,** Providence, RI. First used May 1963

TRIO
TRICKS

This CORO Mark was used only on ear rings, finger rings, bracelets, necklaces, lockets, brooches and clips. Since January, 1951.

TRIQUETTE

COHN & ROSENBERGER, INC., New York, NY mark for all the usual types of jewelry as well as compacts, cigarette boxes, fancy buckles and jewelry initials. Since 1937

TRITON

TRITON was the mark used by the **AUTOMATIC GOLD CHAIN COMPANY** of Providence, RI since August, 1931.

TRU-KAY

TRU-KAY MANUFACTURING CO., Providence, RI for earrings, bracelets, pendants, brooches, necklaces, pins, etc. First used February, 1946.

TRU STAR

SKALET MANUFACTURING CO., INC., New York, NY used this mark for jewelry. First used 1960

TRULITE

WILLIAM SCHNEIDER INC., New York, NY for gold jewelry set with imitation jewels. First used January, 1956.

TRULI FINE

HARRY BALLON & CO., Providence, RI, BAL-RON CO. Inc. mark for both men's and ladies' jewelry, such as lockets, bracelets, watch bands, cigarette cases, buckles and the usual types of jewelry. First used 1944.

TUX

Mark of **MORRIS HOFFMAN,** New York, NY for all the usual types of jewelry, hair ornaments, compacts, religious jewelry, hair pins and dress pins and clips. In use since January, 1941.

Tweedbeads

CORO, INC., New York, NY used this mark for necklaces, bracelets, earrings and brooches. Beginning in 1960

TWEEN - AGE

E.K. WERTHEIMER & SON, INC. New York, NY mark for infants' and children's costume jewelry. First used July, 1939.

TWILIGHT STAR

MASSOVER BROS., INC., Chicago, IL for rings, earrings, cuff links, pins, pendants and charms. First used August, 1955.

Twin Tones

CORO INC., New York, NY mark for charm bracelets, charms and all the usual jewelry (necklaces, brooches, earrings, etc.) with pearls. Since December, 1954.

TWINKY

GOODMAN & COMPANY, Indianapolis, IN mark for rings, brooches, scarf pins, earrings, pendants, lapel buttons, all made or plated with precious metal. Since August, 1951.

THE TWIST BY RICHELIEU

JOSEPH H. MEYER BROS., Brooklyn, NY mark for necklaces, bracelets and earrings. Since 1962

Another mark of UNCAS MANUFACTURING COMPANY, Providence, RI in use since January, 1920 for jewelry such as rings, bracelets, brooches, earrings and barrettes. Both marks still active 1949.

UNCAS MANUFACTURING COMPANY, Providence, RI used this mark for rings, bracelets, brooches, earrings and barrettes. August, 1919.

UNITED JEWELRY COMPANY of Buffalo, NY used this mark on its jewelry. First used December 12, 1945.

Mark of URIE F. MANDLE CO., New York, NY mark used for costume jewelry — necklaces, bracelets, earrings, chatelaines, fobs, brooch pins and miscellaneous costume jewelry pieces in both precious and semi-precious metals. First used June, 1946.

Ultra

JOSEPH H. MEYER BROS., Brooklyn, NY for pearl necklaces, earrings and brooches. Since July, 1945.

Ultra - Cut

EDWARD GOLDSTEIN, Boston, Mass., used this mark for semi-precious, non-precious and artificial stones for jewelry. First used in December, 1928.

UNCAS

UNCAS MANUFACTURING CO., Providence, RI, used this mark on jewelry beginning July, 1959

UNCAS MANUFACTURING COMPANY, Providence, RI for finger rings. First used November, 1953.

UneeK

MORSE ANDREWS CO., Attleboro, Mass., for men's jewelry. August, 1945.

UNFORGETTABLE

Mark of AVON PRODUCTS INC., New York, NY for costume jewelry. First used Oct. 1971

UNI - FLEX

Mark of UNICORN PRODUCTS CO., INC., New York, NY for costume jewelry, bracelets, earrings, brooch pins, lapel pins, lapel clips, chokers, rings and necklaces. Used since May 15, 1946.

UNICORN PRODUCTS CO., New York, NY first used this mark in June, 1945 for costume jewelry as well as for buckles and clasps.

UNIVERSAL WATCH BRACELET MANUFACTURERS, INC., Los Angeles, CA for ornamental and watch bracelets. First used July, 1929.

Jewelry mark of VALENTINO COUTURE, INC., New York, NY. First used Oct. 1970

Mark of VOGUE JEWELRY MANUFAC-TURING CO., INC. for bracelets, pendants, earrings, rings, brooches, necklaces, chokers, bar pins, scarf pins and other jewelry. First used Jan. 1933

VARGAS MANUFACTURING COM-PANY, Providence, RI for ornamental jewelry, particularly for children, since January 15, 1947.

V-G

DAVID PFEFFER CO., INC., New York, NY mark for finger rings, pendants and earrings. First used June 1962

VT

Jewelry mark of VERIBEST JEWELRY CO., INC., New York, NY. First used 1962

VAICO

Garabet V. Chimchirian d.b.a. VENETIAN ARTS IMPORTING CO., New York, NY used this mark for costume jewelry necklaces, bracelets and earring since November, 1954.

VALCOUR JEWELRY CO., New York, NY used this mark for costume jewelry, namely, earrings, bracelets, necklaces, rings, dress clips, brooches, neck tie clasps and cuff links. First used March 1945

Valencia

ILLINOIS WATCH CASE CO., operating under the name of ELGIN AMERICAN Division of Illinois Watch Case Co., Elgin, IL mark for necklaces, finger rings, earrings, bracelets, brooches and chokers. First used September, 1950.

VALIANT

CORO, INC., New York, NY mark for pearl jewelry since July, 1948.

VALJEAN PEARL CORP. Brookly, NY used this mark for pearl necklaces and earrings. First used 1944.

VAN DELL CO., Providence, RI mark for brooches, bracelets, earrings, cameos and pendants. First used Jan. 1939

LOUIS FLEISHMANN, New York, NY mark for costume jewelry - necklaces, choker sets, bracelets, and earrings sets. First used 1949

J. VANDER ZANDEN, Green Bay, WI mark for jewelry since September, 1920.

VANITY FAIR PEARLS, INC., Brooklyn, NY mark for costume jewelry, necklaces, bracelets, earrings, buckles and accessories. First used Jan. 1949

VANITY FAIR

CORO, INC., New York, NY. Mark for necklaces, bracelets, finger rings, earrings, jewelry clips, brooches, lockets, also made of or plated with precious metals — beads, pins, hat ornaments, hair ornaments, compacts, comb cases, cigarette cases, fancy buckles and jewelry initials. This mark first used October, 1945.

VARGAS

VARGAS MANUFACTURING COMPANY, Providence, RI for ornamental jewelry, since June, 1945.

ROBERT FLEISCHER, New York, NY for costume jewelry - pins, earrings, necklaces and brooches. First used April, 1952.

COLONIAL BEAD CO., INC., New York, NY mark for iridescent costume jewelry including beads, necklaces, clips, earrings, pins and bracelets. First used Nov. 1942

VASSAR DAISY

SAMSTAG & HILDER BROS., INC., New York, NY for necklaces, bracelets, brooches, finger rings, earrings and pendants. First used about July, 1928.

HENRY STADTMAN, New York, NY for simulated pearls. First used, March, 1945.

AMERICAN PEARL CO., Providence, RI mark for ornamental jewelry - pearl necklaces. First used October, 1946.

Vendôme

CORO INC., New York, NY for charm bracelets, charms, necklaces, all other usual jewelry types and jewelry incorporating pearls. Since 1944.

BRIER MANUFACTURING CO., Providence, RI mark for all the usual types of jewelry as well as religious jewelry. First used 1958

Ver

VERITÉ JEWELS LTD. New York, NY mark for pendants, necklaces, bracelets, clips, rings, brooches, lockets, charm bracelets, charms, bead necklaces and jewelry initials. First used 1962

VERFLEX

Mark of FREDERICK M. MORIARTY, Providence, RI for bracelets. Since Nov. 1944

VERGE-CRAFT

Mark of CYRIL WOODS, New York, NY for costume jewelry. Since March, 1950.

Vibra

Wilhelm Molgedei d.b.a. VIBRA CHAIN CO., New York, NY used this mark for necklaces, bracelets, neck chains and belts. First used February, 1933.

VICOUNT

HICKOK MANUFACTURING CO. INC., Rochester, NY mark for tie bars and cuff links. Since 1957

CHARLES U. VICTOR, Chicago, IL for pearl jewelry. Since January, 1916.

VICTORIANA

Jewelry mark of WAITE, THRESHER CORPORATION, Providence, RI. Used since February, 1931.

VIKING CRAFT

ALBERT HORWIG, New York, NY used this mark for brooches, bracelets, earrings, rings, necklaces, since Nov. 1938

NOBURU HONDA of San Francisco, California, used this mark for its costume jewelry, including novelty necklaces, pendants and earrings. First used in January, 1929.

D. LISNER & CO., New York, NY used this mark for all the usual types of jewelry as well as mesh bags, ornaments and trimmings of precious metal and ornaments and semi-precious stones for handbags and pocketbooks. First used 1926

VIP

HICKOK MANUFACTURING CO., INC., Rochester, NY mark for cuff links, tie bars, tie pins, collar bars and collar pins since 1959

Mark of JOSEPH H. MEYER BROS., Brooklyn, NY for necklaces, bracelets, finger rings, jewelry clips, brooches and earrings. First used in 1938.

JOSEPH H. MEYER BROS., Brooklyn, NY mark for pearl necklaces, earrings and brooches. Since January, 1948.

PARK IMPORTING CO, New York, NY mark for artificial pearl and bead necklaces. First used 1915.

VOLUPTE, INC., Elizabeth, NJ used this mark for compacts and cigarette cases. First used October, 1926.

Mark of A.J. VAN DUGTEREN & SONS, INC., New York, NY for bracelets, brooches, rings and earrings. The mark is a facsimile of the signature of a designer for the firm. First used March 1945

J.J. WHITE MANUFACTURING CO., Providence, RI used this mark for jewelry for both men and women. First used at least as early as 1900.

WELLS MANUFACTURING CO., Attleboro, MA used this mark for costume jewelry since August 1960

Mark of ALBERT WEISS & CO., INC., New York, NY for costume jewelry namely, earrings, necklaces, bracelets, pins, tiaras, pendants and brooches. First used on or about Jan. 1951

WALLBURR, New York, NY mark for jewelry. First used July 1962

WARREN WILLIAM WELCH d.b.a. Wil-Area, Colorado Springs, CO mark for jewelry since 1961

Mark of WILBAR RING MANUFACTURING CO., INC., Buffalo, NY for rings and all the usual type jewelry. Since Jan. 1962

WEFFERLING, BERRY & CO., INC., Newark, NJ mark for jewelry. First used 1925

WILLIAM COCHRAN, Cleveland, OH mark for rings, pins, bracelets, necklaces. First used November 1948

LUDWIG SCHAPPEY d.b.a. WENDELL & CO., Chicago, IL mark for rings, charms, pins, earrings and cuff links. First used 1910

THE WILLIAMS AND ANDERSON COMPANY, Providence, RI jewelry mark. First used January, 1918.

FORSTNER CHAIN CORPORATION, Irvington, NJ for jewelry with chains. First used September, 1920.

SAMUEL WEIN of WEIN & CO., New York, NY used this mark for jewelry beginning in 1935

THE WHITEHEAD & HOAG CO., Newark, NJ mark for jewelry. Since Dec. 1923

WJT

WELDEN JEWELRY & TRADING CO., New York, NY mark for rings, bracelets, charms, necklaces amulets and other jewelry. First used 1962.

WHITE METAL CASTER'S ASSOCIA-TION, INC., New York, NY used this mark for rhinestones and rhinestone jewelry made of white metal castings. First used June, 1930.

J.R. WOOD & SONS, INC., Brooklyn, NY mark for jewelry. First used Jan. 1935

EMANUEL WINICK d.b.a. Mannie Winick, New York, NY for earrings, brooch pins, charms, bracelets, rings, necklaces, pendants, cuff links. First used 1962

WHEELER MANUFACTURING COM-PANY, INC. for jewelry. Since August, 1962.

W.R. HOOVER, INC., Buffalo, NY for finger rings, brooches, earrings, lapel buttons, charms and bracelets. Since January, 1940.

W. R. COBB COMPANY, Providence, RI used this mark on findings. It is not a jewelry makers mark. Since September, 1922.

W. E. RICHARDS CO., Attleboro, Mass., jewelry mark in use since January, 1944.

"WABBIT"

KAUFMAN AND RUDERMAN CO., INC., New York, NY for ornamental pins and brooches. Since February, 1947.

BARROWS INDUSTRIES, INC., Providence, RI mark for jewelry. First used Nov. 1954

WADSWORTH

Mark of the WADSWORTH WATCH CASE CO., Dayton, KY for compacts, cigarette cases and buckles. First used May, 1925.

COHN & ROSENBERGER, INC., New York, NY, mark for compacts and vanities. Since April 1935

WALBURT

WALTER LAMPL, New York, NY first used this mark in March, 1944 for jewelry, rings, wrist and ankle bracelets, earrings, lapel pins, necklaces, lavalieres, lockets, charms, dress clips, combs, hair ornaments and barrettes.

WALTHAM

WALTHAM WATCH COMPANY, Chicago, IL, used this mark for costume jewelry as well as fine jewelry. First used July, 1957.

WARDEN

JEWEL—SMITHS, INC., BOSTON, MA mark for rings, pins and clips. First used Feb. 1942

WED-LUCK

S & S MANUFACTURING CO., Providence, RI mark for costume jewelry of the usual types. First used 1925

WEE TOT

Mark of OTSBY AND BARTON CO., Providence, RI for jewelry. Since February, 1939.

ALBERT WEISS & CO., INC., New York, NY mark for costume jewelry products - namely earrings, necklaces, bracelets, pins, tiaras, pendants and brooches. This mark was used first beginning Jan. 1951.

Albert Weiss

ALBERT WEISS & CO., INC., New York, NY mark for costume jewelry - earrings, bracelets, necklaces, pins, tiaras and brooches. First used about Jan. 1951. (Albert Weiss being the name of the company's president).

WELDON

W. A. H. WELLS CO., INC., Providence, RI bracelets, cuff links and buttons, ornamental clasp pins and used on jewelry findings. First used July, 1924.

WELLER

E.E. WELLER CO., Providence, RI mark for shoe buckles and shoe ornaments. First used 1930

WELLS

WELLS, INC., ATTLEBORO, MA, mark for jewelry. Since 1922

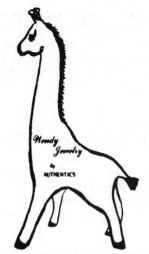

AUTHENTICS, New York, NY mark for costume jewelry, namely bracelets, necklaces, pins and earrings. First used June 1954

WERTHEIMER & LEVY INC., New York, NY for jewelry for personal wear. First used January, 1930.

WHIRLAWAY

CORO, INC., New York, NY mark for necklaces, bracelets, brooches, lockets, jewelry clips, pearl necklaces, strings of pearls, pearl brooches and pearl earrings. Since August, 1949.

WHITE COPPER BY RENOIR

RENOIR OF CALIFORNIA, INC., Los Angeles, CA used this mark for costume jewelry. Since 1958

Mark of MAURICE J. DALSHEIM, New York, NY for costume jewelry, earrings, bracelets, necklaces and brooches. First used 1939.

Mark of PARCO MFG. INC., Providence, RI for costume jewelry and jewelers findings. Since January, 1950.

WHITECO

THE WHITE MFG. CO., North Attleboro, MA mark for jewelry. Since 1928

CHAIN
WHITING & DAVIS
·CO·

WHITING & DAVIS CHAIN CO., Plainville, MA used this mark for watch chains, neck chains, decorative chains of all types, buckles, bracelets, necklaces, earrings, rings and brooches. First used Nov. 1926

WILD COUNTRY

Mark of AVON PRODUCTS INC., New York, NY for costume jewelry. First used Jan. 1972

WILLIAMSBURG

WILLIAMSBURG RESTORATION, INC., Williamsburg, VA mark for costume jewelry 1960

WINDJAMMER

Mark of AVON PRODUCTS INC., New York, NY for costume jewelry. First used Jan. 1972

WINDSOR

HARRY FARBER, Cherry Hills, NJ used this mark for "replica gems and jewelry" since Dec. 1970

WINEY

H. WEINREICH COMPANY, INC., Philadelphia PA used this mark on novelty and costume jewelry since September 28, 1939.

Mark of H. WEINREICH CO., INC., Philadelphia, PA for finger rings, earrings, bracelets, lockets, necklaces, ornamental pins, brooches, novelty and costume jewelry. Used since September, 1939.

H. WEINREICH COMPANY, INC, Philadelphia, PA for bracelets, brooches, finger rings, earrings, lockets, necklaces, ornamental pins, anklets and barrettes. First used about Jan., 1936.

 WINFIELD

ARMAND G. WINFIELD, New York, NY used this for costume jewelry - earrings, jewelry for men and watch bands. Since Sept. 1945

WINGBACK COMPANY, New York, NY mark for earrings since November, 1946.

WINGS OF GLORY

SILSON, INC., New York, NY used this mark for necklaces, earrings, clips, brooches, lockets and hat pin ornaments, hair ornaments, compacts, fancy cigarette and powder boxes, fancy buckles, cuff links and jewelry initials. First used March 1941

WINGS OF VICTORY

EVE NATHANSON, East Greenwich, RI mark for the usual types of jewelry plus compacts, dress ornaments, cuff links and collar holders. First used Sept. 1939

Wishing Bell

VERITE' JEWELS LTD., New York, NY mark for all the usual types of jewelry as well as lockets, charm bracelets, charms, bead necklaces and jewelry initials. Since 1961

WONDER WEB

Mark of JOSEPH H. MEYER BROS., Brooklyn, NY for bead and pearl necklaces. Since November, 1957.

J.R. WOOD & SONS, INC., New York, NY for jewelry. First used June, 1930.

WOOD NYMPH

Mark of CORO, New York, NY for necklaces, bracelets, jewelry clips and all the other usual jewelry types including jewelry incorporating pearls and beads, pins and jewelry initials made or plated with precious metal. First used May, 1963.

J.R. WOOD & SONS, New York, NY mark for pearls. First used April, 1923.

WOODCREST

J. R. WOOD & SONS, INC., New York, NY mark for finger rings. Since November, 1949.

WORN THE MOST FROM COAST to COAST

COHN & ROSENBERGER, INC., New York, NY used this mark for all the usual types of jewelry as well as face powder compacts, cigarette cases, comb cases, etc. First used about 1940.

Mark of L.J. WRIGHT, Hauser, OR for all forms of costume jewelry. First used May, 1951.

WRISTACRAT

LOUIS STERN CO., Providence, RI mark for bracelets and watch bracelets. Since June 1924

WURRY BEADS

MAY WHITE CORP., New York, NY mark for necklaces. First used Nov. 1960

XXX

JOSEPH H. MAYER BROS., Brooklyn, NY used this mark for pearl jewelry - necklaces, earrings, finger rings and bracelets. First used October, 1905.

EXCELL MANUFACTURING COMPANY, Providence, RI, for lockets, crosses, charms, pendants, circle pins, and jewelry findings of all types. Since March, 1916.

S. YEFFETH JEWELRY, INC., New York, NY mark for pins, earrings, pendants, rings cuff links, bracelets, jewelry clasps, chokers and other jewelry. First used 1960

YR

J. YOUNG & H. RATHAUS JEWELRY MFG. CO., New York, NY used this mark for jewelry. Since March 1962

YS

JAMES H. HALL CO., INC., Providence, RI used this mark for costume jewelry since Aug. 1964

YANKEE-ACCO-PRIDE

ACCRO MANUFACTURING COMPANY, Central Falls, RI. Mark for brooches, earrings, pins, bracelets, lockets, pendants and necklaces. Used since August, 1945.

YESTERYEAR

Mark of AVON PRODUCTS INC., New York, NY for costume jewelry. First used Oct. 1971

YOUNG AMERICA

Costume jewelry mark of JERRY DeNICOLA, New York, NY. First used Dec. 1964

YOUNGER LADY

Mark of VAN DELL CO., Providence, RI for ladies' jewelry, brooches, bracelets, earrings, cameos and pendants. Used since September, 1943.

GEORGE PHILLIPS & CO. Scranton, PA used this mark for rings, bracelets, pins, lockets, and crosses. Since Feb. 1945

Z & F

ZELMAN & FRIEDMAN JEWELRY CO., INC., New York, NY mark for bracelets, rings, brooches, and other jewelry for personal wear. Mark used since September, 1958.

ZINI

Costume jewelry mark of ISAACSON-CARRICO MANUFACTURING CO., El Campo, TX. First used 1962

ZIP

ART CRAFT WHOLESALE JEWELRY & SPECIALTIES INC., Bloomsburg, PA used this mark for costume jewelry. First used 1964

MORRIS, MANN & REILLY, INC., Chicago, Illinois mark for finger rings, earrings, lavaliers, brooches, pins, necklaces, bracelets and pendants. Since May, 1946.

Of all the unsigned rhinestone jewelry the most popular continues to be the long, dangling earrings. These are screw back, 2½" long, well made and dazzling in the 1940s fashion.   Value $75-85

2" long clip back earrings with rhinestone and purple amethyst stones in a nicely balanced composition. 1940s.   Value $75-125

In the true spirit of the rhinestone lifestyle these clip back earrings with their large dazzling stones are 4" long, articulated to sway and refract light. The stones are hand set and the clips are marked WEISS.   Value $175-225

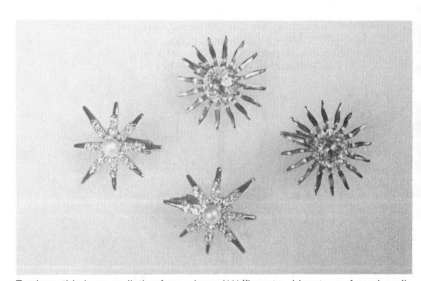

Screw back earrings with large top rhinestones, hand set, all other rhinestones pasted-in in a rather shallow silvery setting. Marked ALBION on each screw.

Value $45-55

Earrings, thin brass radiating from a large (1½") center rhinestone of good quality, clip back. Marked SARAH COV. Bought in the early 1950s.   Value $35-45
Left- earrings, clip back, starfish shape, small aurora stones ending in a solid brass tip, small center pearl. Marked EMMONS. Part of a collection of EMMONS jewelry bought in the 1950s, still worn and treasured.   Value $45-65

The collector bought these earrings as Haskell. They are by ROBERT and so marked. Small, clip back with flower heads of all rhinestone and flower heads of tiny pearls with rhinestones centers, leaves and single pearls of a large size. Silver colored metal.   Value $85-95

Kenneth Lane earrings in black plastic and small rhinestones, approximately ¾' x 1". This jewelry is not yet widely collected although sophisticates such as Dianne Vreeland have gathered pieces. Macy's New York recently had a display of the exotic Vreeland collection in its Metropolitan Museum shop. The first Kenneth Lane Boutique opened in London in 1967. Kenneth Jay Lane has recently sold the company to Ciro's.   Value $50-65

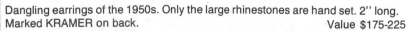

Dangling earrings of the 1950s. Only the large rhinestones are hand set. 2'' long. Marked KRAMER on back.   Value $175-225

Statement jewelry with a vengeance. Anyone wearing these earrings is bound to command attention. Almost 4'' long, articulated and with oversized faux pearls, these earrings represent a whole category of unmarked wonderful 1940s jewelry which continues to attract those with the cachet to wear it.   Value $125-$195

Dangling earrings by Kramer. Rhinestones all hand set ending in large tear drop green stones. Marked KRAMER on clip. The very light weight of these earrings adds to their delicate look.   Value $65-95

Refined, classically elegant small rhinestone earrings. Clip back these measure only 1'' long. Marked BOGOFF on clip and back of the earring itself and also with patent numbers.   Value $45-50

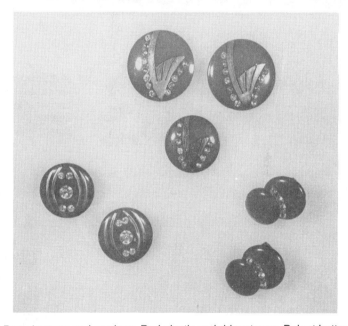

Art Deco buttons and earrings. Red plastic and rhinestones. Pair at bottom right are clip back earrings.   Buttons at left, pair $30-45
top, three $35-45
earrings $40-45

This pair of earrings are by Miraim Haskell. They belie the sometimes held belief that Haskell Jewelry is not variable in its difference. These are conventional faux pearls and pronged rhinestones in a sunrise pattern. Gilt filagree backing, each earring is marked MIRIAM HASKELL on the clip. 1½'' x 1½''.   Value $95-165

The ever popular "swinging" rhinestone earrings, 2½" long. Good quality, double, separate hoops. Clip back, unmarked. 1960s.
Value $85-100

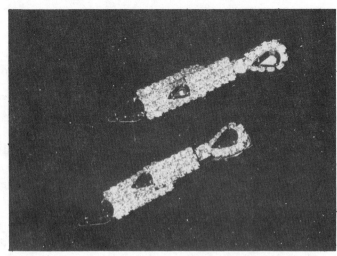

Pair of arrow-shaped drop earrings. Articulated with brilliant rhinestones and larger red stones. Marked KRAMER. 2½" long.
Value $100-150

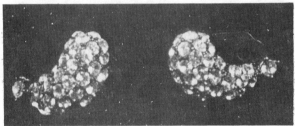

Even the back clip on this pair of small unmarked earrings is intriguing. Large purple petals with small set-in rhinestones make for a pretty pair although these were not uppper line jewelry. Early 1940s.
Value $45-65

In the manner of Haskell or Robert, these clip back earrings boast mother-of-pearl leaves, blue glass beads, a large blue hand set stone, tiny pearls and brass leaves and what looks like a strawberry. Each has one tiny rhinestone. All of these are applied to a filagree backing to which the clip is attached. 1930s. Interesting and surprisingly attractive. Not marked
Value $75-95

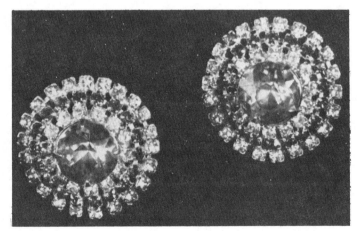

Large, round earrings with alternating rows of rhinestones and light green stones with a large center green stone. Clip back, marked on each clip HOBÉ. Not particularly unusual or imaginative but attractive color-wise. 1940s.
Value $65-85

Right:
Clip back earrings of the late 1940's. Red plastic. Rhinestones pasted in and the earrings are poor quality but typical of this popular, low-line jewelry. Plastic jewelry of this period is now the focus of many collections.   Value $35-45

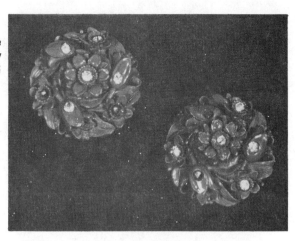

Unusual earrings, clip back. The typical Haskell pearls dangle from a half loop of steel which is set with black stones. Marked MIRIAM HASKELL Value $100-150

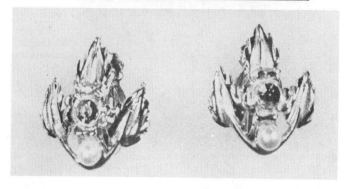

Long clip back earrings, 2'', with red stones. One earring marked HOLLYCRAFT on the clip, the other marked in three places. 1950s   Value of pair $50-85

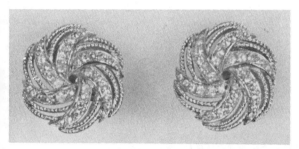

Gorgeous clip back earrings. Marked TRIFARI on each clip.
Value $85-125

Clip back earrings with large grey colored pearls with rhinestones. 1960s. One earring marked on back HAR
Value $45-55

1'' silvery clip back earrings which resemble birds in flight. Center aurora stone and one pearl on each. Marked on clip. S & G 5th Ave.   Value $30-40

Right: High quality rhinestones in these clip back earrings. White plastic with rhinestones, each earring marked on clip HOLLYCRAFT. Early 1950s.   Value $50-60

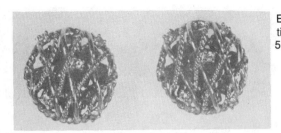

Even great designers have their off moments. These clip back earrings are attractive in a tailored way but have no particular verve. Each marked in script CARNEGIE. 5 small rhinestones in each earring.   Value $50-65

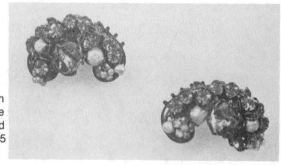

Clip back, horseshoe shaped earrings with large crystals and rhinestones set in filagree. The different sizes of the rhinestones, with small and tiny pearls, plus the filagree work and the general quality give these earrings a top line look. Marked on each clip DeMARIO, N.Y. 1930s.   Value $65-95

Small gold finish clip back earrings with a wide band of tiny rhinestones. Late 1940s. Each clip marked NAPIER.   Value $55-85

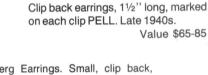

Clip back earrings, 1½'' long, marked on each clip PELL. Late 1940s.
Value $65-85

Eisenberg Earrings. Small, clip back, marked on each clip. The design of these is quite characteristic and appears on both necklaces and earrings of the same period. As with all Eisenberg the stones are clear and sparkling and it is the obvious quality of the piece which makes these rather small earrings successful.
Value $65-85

1950's rhinestone, screw back earrings in the shape of stemmed flowers.
Value $25-28

A choice example of costume jewelry in this earring by MAZER. Single earrings of this quality can be made into attractive brooches.   Value $20-25

A single IKE earring made for the Eisenhower presidential campaign and distributed as a souvenir. Screw back. Also of interest to political memorabilia collectors.   Value $35-55

Screw back earrings, black with rhinestones. Marked Coro in script.   Value $35-45

174

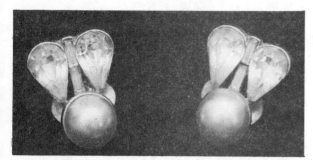

Clip back earrings of the late 1940's. Rhinestones and simulated pearls.
Value $35-45

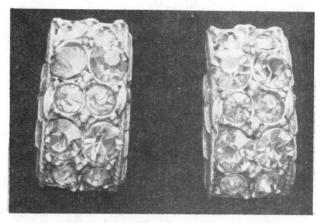

Clip back earrings, large purple stones, early 1950's.
Value $45-65

Pair of rhinestones on polished brass earrings of the 1940's. Neither card nor earrings has any manufacturer's identification.   Value $55-75

Rhinestone and pearl bell earrings, clip back. Bought during the Christmas season in the 1950's. Probably a seasonal item. Value $30-45

Screw back earrings bought in the early 1950's. Black enamel petals outlined in silver, clusters of rhinestones. Marked CORO. Value $55-75

Rhinestone, clip back earrings. 1950's   Value $65-85

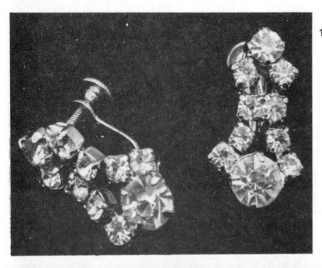

1940's rhinestone earrings, screw back, ¾ inch long.   Value $30-40

Rhinestones and black glass stones set in gilt metal. Clip back earrings of the 1940s. Dramatic fashion accents. Value $65-95

1940's rolled earrings with rhinestones and clip back. Somewhat unusual design. Rhinestones on front and both sides.   Value $45-65

Late 1940's earrings. Blue stones and rhinestones pasted in gilt metal. Lower line of jewelry of the period.   Value $25-35

1930's brass and filigree screw back earrings. Center stone pronged.

Value $45-65

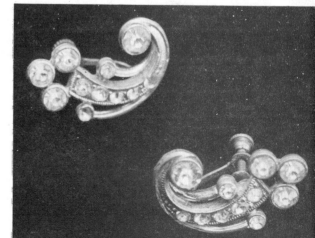

Screw back earrings, rhinestones in base metal. Early 1940's.   Value $25-35

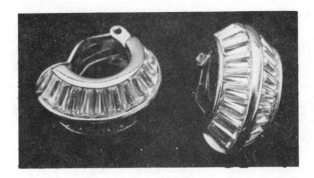

1950's clip back half-hoop earrings. Well made but unmarked.
Value $40-50

Green glass ('stone') earrings of the 1940's. Large 'stones' dangle from chain which is attached to brass screw back finding.
Value $40-50

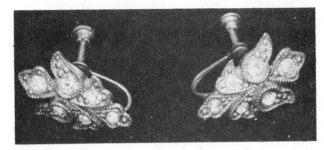

1930's screw back earrings, set in gilt metal.   Value $40-45

Blue enamel and cluster rhinestone clip back earrings.
Each earring clip marked CINER.   Value $45-55

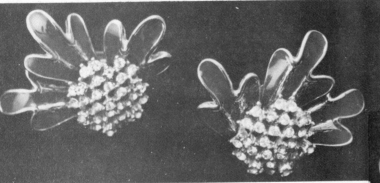

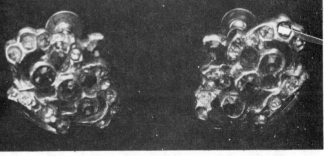

Gilt earrings in the shape of crown. More difficult to find than brooches with same motif. Screw back, red and lavender stones are pasted in. Early 1940s.
Value $40-60

Clip back earrings, 1950's. Multi-colored stones in shades of blue and green. Hand set. Marked KRAMER.   Value $60-75

Earrings. 1940's pearls and blue stones, set in prongs. Unusual clip back. Well made. Marked Pat. Pend. **Probably Kreisler** Value $55-80

Earrings. Early 1940's. Deep blue stones set in frames of gold wash over sterling silver. Screw back. Value $50-75

1950's clip back earrings, large (1½'' long, 1½'' wide). Imitation topaz stones with aurora borealis. Value $35-45

An interesting and attractive pair of earrings from the early 1940's. Brass and vivid red stones, clip backs. Value $45-55

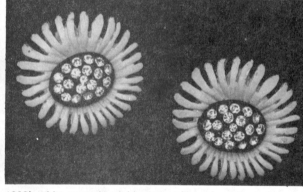

1960's white enamel and rhinestone clip back earrings. Pretty design. Marked BSK © Value $25-40

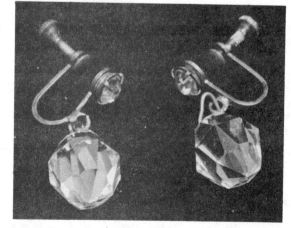

1950's rhinestone earrings, good quality but unmarked. Even at this time many companies were not signing their costume jewelry. 2''. Stones are hand set. Value $55-85

Screw back earrings of rhinestone and crystal. 1930's. Value $55-65

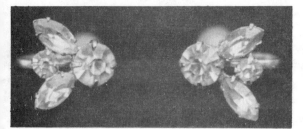

Small earrings, screw back, multi-colored stones which are hand set and still sparkling. 1940's.   Value $35-45

Small rhinestone earrings. Marked with the trademark of VARGAS MANUFACTURING COMPANY. 1948.
                                    Value $45-50

Pretty diamond shaped earrings with pink stones in thin brass frame. For pierced ears.   Unusual.   Value $40-50

1930's screw back earrings. Clusters of beautifully sparkling rhinestones attached to finding. Marked on back MADE IN CZECHOSLOVAKIA.
                                    Value $75-95

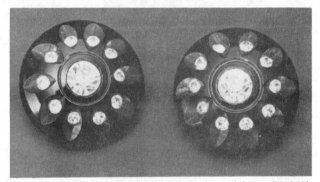

Black plastic and rhinestone clip back earrings of the early 1940's. Interesting design work in that the rhinestones set around perimeter seem much larger because of the clear cuts.   Value $32-38

Realistic drop earrings, each with its single rhinestone to simulate a diamond. For pierced ears.   Value $30-40

1940's earrings. An example of the good design work on these inexpensive pieces. Rhinestones, black glass and thin brass.   Value $40-45

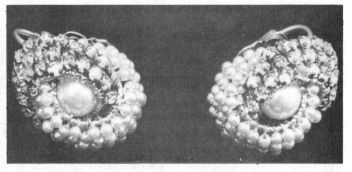

Rhinestone and pearl earrings, clip back. Pearl necklace completes the set and has a closure which matches the earrings. Obviously better costume jewelry, but unmarked. 1940s.
                    Set Value $145-200; Earrings, Value $50-65

179

Multi-colored stone earrings in an unusual combination of colors, screw back, late 1930's - early 1940's.   Value $50-65

Earrings, screw back, 1950's, sparkling blue stones, hand set.   Value $45-55

Very large clip back rhinestone earrings. 1¾'' round. 1940's.
KRAMER   Value $85-100

Early 1930's soft plastic with rhinestones. Brass rosette, screw back earrings. Rare.   Value $45-65

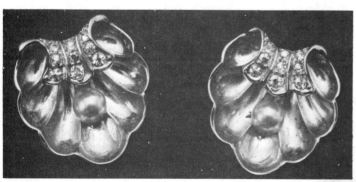

Elegant shell shaped earrings with clip backs. Rhinestones and center simulated pearl. Gold wash on sterling. Unmarked. 1940's.
                                              Value $55-75

Copper and rhinestone earrings, an unusual combination.
Screw back, marked but unreadable. 1940's .   Value $50-75

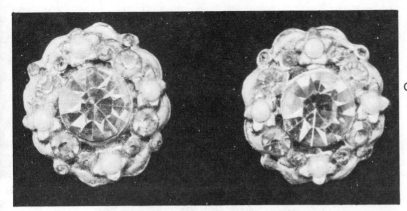

Clip back blue stone and seed pearl (simulated) earrings. 1940's.
Value $45-50

1950's long drop earrings (1⅓ inches) with clip backs. This type is spectacular and often commands higher prices than the unmarked older pieces. Value $145-195

Screw back earrings, late 1930's. Hand set pink stones with center rhinestone. Gold wash over sterling. Unmarked. Value $65-85

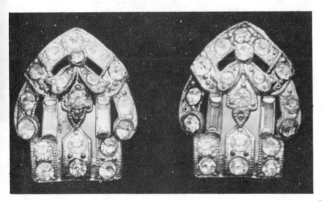

Earrings with unusual clips. Rhinestones and gilded base metal. 1930's. Value $50-60

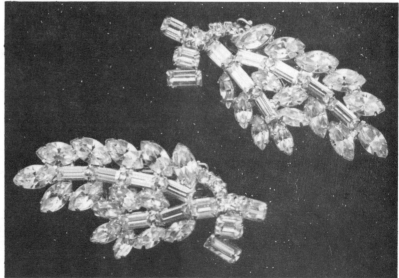

Pair of clip back earrings in the 1950's spectacular fashion. Approx. 2½'' long. Baguette and pear shaped rhinestones all hand set. One of these earrings has been worn frequently as a lapel clip. Value $145-185

These small dainty sunburst earrings with their red stones, pearls and fancy brass 'rays' are unsigned but representative of so much jewelry design of the late 1940s. Wearable and always in fashion. Bought very early in the 1950s. Value $85-150

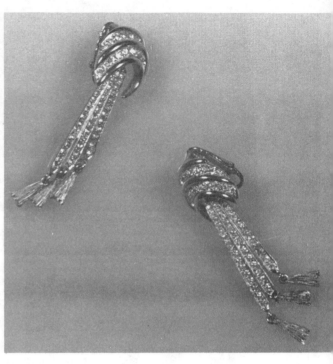

A striking pair of earrings, 2½'' long. The tassels are gold metal, framing the baguette rhinestones and the rows of smaller rhinestones is silver metal giving each earring the ambience of very upscale chic. Each earring marked POLCINI, a company originally founded in 1896, whose name was changed to LEDO in 1949 and again to POLCINI in 1960. Value $175-200

LAGUNA EARRINGS, clip back with pink glass beads. A very attractive mobile. The beads glow differently in different light. Marked LAGUNA on each clip. Value $50-75

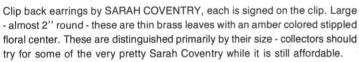

Clip back earrings by SARAH COVENTRY, each is signed on the clip. Large - almost 2'' round - these are thin brass leaves with an amber colored stippled floral center. These are distinguished primarily by their size - collectors should try for some of the very pretty Sarah Coventry while it is still affordable. Value $35-45

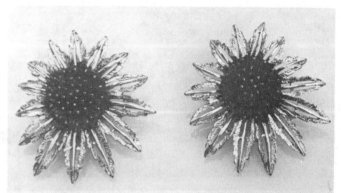

MARVELLA displays consistently good design work. These essentially simply designed earrings exude good taste while showcasing the pearls and rhinestones which were (and are) the company's trademark. These are clip back, marked on the back of each earring, (not the clip) and are of silvery metal. Lovely. Value $75-95

These clip back earrings by HOBÉ are pearl and rhinestones set in gilt metal. Marked on each clip HOBÉ. 1½'' long.   Value $100-135

The unusual color combinations rivet attention on these beautiful drop ear--rings. 2'' long and signed on back ART the pendant drops are a myriad of fascinating colored stones shading from pale blue to deep blue to green with large topaz colored stones, aurora borealis light blue, clear, darker blue and all set in gold colored metal. The metal becomes part of the background and is unobtrusive. A lovely pair. 1960s   Value $100-145

Rather unimaginative large clip back earrings redeemed by the exquisite colors of the stones and the quality of manufacture. Light green accented by opaque pale green stones and pearls, these clip back earrings measure 2'' x 1¾'' and are marked SCHIAPARELLI in script on the clip. Value $300-400

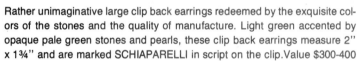

The newest rage - faces on jewelry. This category continues to attract sophisticated collectors but is becoming unaffordable. These large (2'') round clip back earrings are framed with brilliant orange colored stones around stipple gold colored metal. Very well defined face in center. Marked on each clip. JUDY LEE. Not for everyone but certainly stunning.   Value $55-75

Eisenberg earrings in original box. The earrings are large and each is marked on the clip. The box itself is marked EISENBERG JEWELRY, EXCLUSIVE HERE. The owner says "Almost all the Eisenberg jewelry in this area was bought through Younkers, a local department store. Older ladies remember getting it at Younkers and paying high prices (for the times) 1930s

Value in original box $600-800

The ever desirable long dangling earrings. These 1940s beauties are 3¼" long and are marked E in script on each clip. Eisenberg.   Value $250-300

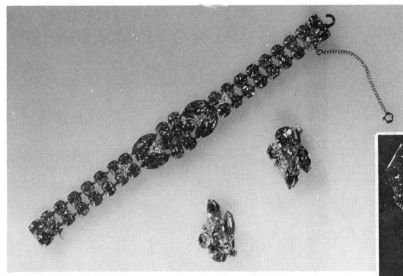

A beautiful set - bracelet and earrings in the ever-popular light blue stones, highlighted rhinestones. The EISENBERG craftsmanship is immediately apparent in the brilliance of the stones, the unusual closure, the safety catch, the overall look of high quality and the weight. One end of each catch is marked COPYRIGHT, the matching end is marked EISENBERG ICE US PATENT. The matching earrings are marked EISENBERG ICE. 1940s.   Value of set $300-450

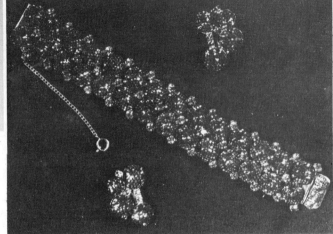

This highly unusual bracelet and earring set is by Kramer. The bracelet is 1" wide, dark topaz stones covered with netting, both earrings are made in the same way, pronged stones covered with brown netting. The gilt metal backing of the bracelet is marked on a disc KRAMER OF N.Y. Each clip on the earrings is marked in script KRAMER OF NY.
                                        Value $300-450

"Clunky", "chunky", "bizarre" in the best sense, this bracelet and earrings are heavy, gilded over base metal, unmarked but very well made. Stones of all shapes and colors, blue, pink, topaz light green, pink and rhinestones make a pleasing whole. Simulated small pearls just to prove that this jewelry had everything. Square shape of the earrings match the square of color in the center of the bracelet.

                                        Value of set $300-350

A lovely bracelet and earring set by Lisner. Its silvery metal blends well with the pink, green blue, yellow stones to give a beautiful effect to this narrow, well-made choker. Each matching earring marked LISNER on clip. The choker is unmarked.   Value of set $200-275

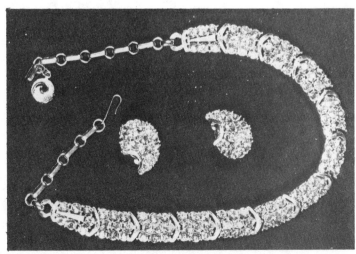

Bracelet and earring set. The beauty of this rigid bracelet and 1½'' earrings set with irridescent stones in shades of red is outstanding and gives rise to new conjecture as to why jewelry of this quality was not signed as late as the 1950s. Value $200-250

Bracelet and earring set. Blue stones with rhinestones on a link bracelet, safety catch. This unmarked set has an expensive look, although it is in the same general style of much of the 40s jewelry.

Value of set $200-275

3 piece set, bracelet and matching clip back earrings. Molded blue plastic flowers with white enamel leaves and rhinestones on gold filled metal; c.1948. This type was considered 'summer jewelry'. Marked CORO.

Value, set $195-250

A striking set of earrings and brooch. The green center stones are complemented by the silver colored metal and tiny rhinestones. Marked EMMONS. 1950s. Value $150-195

Pin and matching earrings. Thin brass settings, lightweight but dainty. Tiny black enamel leaves surround the hand set rhinestones. Marked AUSTRIA.   Value of set $85-125

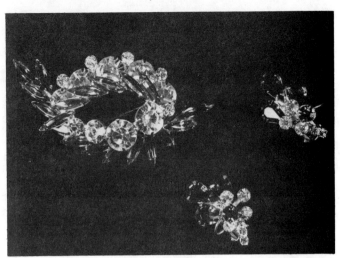

Pin and earring set. In the 1940s topaz colored stones were very popular. This brooch and earrings have topaz colored stones and rhinestones in differing shapes which lend interest. The pieces are very well made and the whole is characteristic of the 1940s. Unmarked. Brooch is 3½" long.   Value $150-200

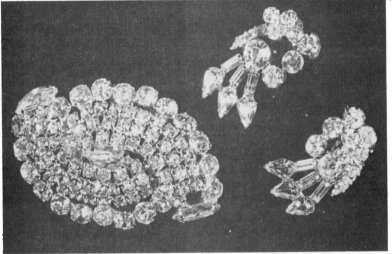

3" Brooch in the spectacular, attention-getting 1940s style. Nice balance of small and large, differently shaped stones, all of which are of excellent brilliance. Unmarked. Matching clip back earrings are 1½" long.   Value of set $350-450

This pretty set of earrings and pin is gilt with aurora borealis stones in shades of topaz and bluish-green. Probably 1960s. Pin marked in two places - on MADE IN AUSTRIA, on an applied disc KARU, ARKE, INC. Each earring is marked AUSTRIA on the clip and each bears the mark on the disc. Unusual and attractive. Value of set, $145-$195

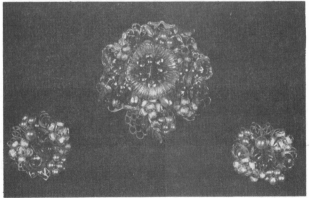

Brooch and earring set similar to much of Haskell's work. Small pearls, stones in blue, green, pink, all on a gilt filagree backing. The earrings are unmarked. The brooch is marked ROBERT de MARIO, N.Y.C. on a disc. Value $125-145

This irridescent brooch and earring set is in the highly favored deep blue color which shades to green in some light. Weiss. Each earring marked WEISS in a disc. The pin is unmarked.
Value $200-250

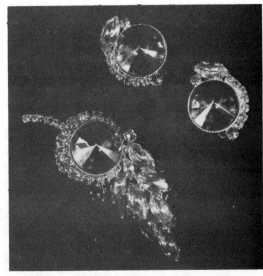

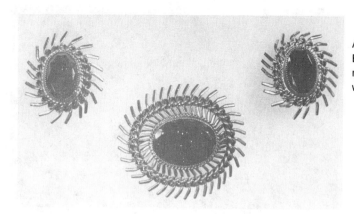

A rather bizarre set of earrings and brooch by DANECRAFT, marked Sterling. Black center stones in frames of silver with asymmetrical silver 'spikes'. Since most collectors associate DANECRAFT with tailored sterling silver jewelry without stones, this is a good example of other work.   Value $165-200

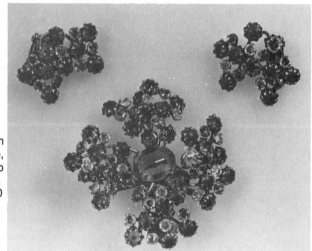

This pin and earring set is somewhat less than beautiful but the color combination is typical of the period - brown, topaz, orange and rhinestones. The brooch is large, 3''x3'' and has an open feeling. The stones are all hand set and the pin and clip back earrings (1½'') is each marked on a disc SCHRIENER, NEW YORK. 1940s.
Value $195-250

A museum quality set of brooch and earrings. The heavy sterling silver base of this 3'' brooch is covered with turquoise colored small beads with red accent stones. The frame is tiny rhinestones with 8 tiny red stones. The large center cabachon is mirror like. All pieces are marked STERLING with a patent number and MOSELL.
Value of set $800-120

A monumental set - earrings and pin. Bees with rhinestones hold the large swinging pearls. The matching pin/brooch is framed in gold colored metal, the large pearl has its own resident bee. Each part of this set is magnificently crafted and the whole is representative of the best of fashion jewelry. The earrings are 2½'' long, the pin 2½'' wide. Each piece marked on back HATTIE CARNEGIE.
Value of set $800-1500

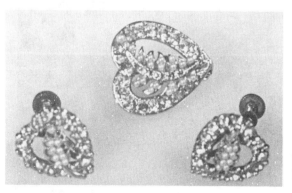

Pin, 1'', small pearls and rhinestones. Matching screw back earrings. Nicely done. Marked EMMONS. 1950s.   Value $100-150 set

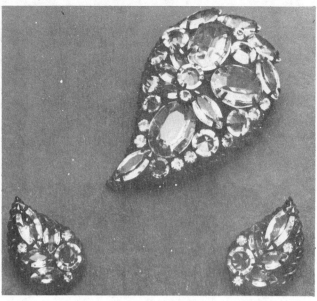

Excellent quality cyrstals hand set in black metal. This is a very fine set, 1950's, but unsigned. The matching earrings are approx. 1¾''. Set $175-225

Red and purple stone set of the late 1940's. Clip back earrings. Brooch measures 2½'' by 3'' and earrings 1½''. This set is certain to command attention. Unmarked.
Value $195-250

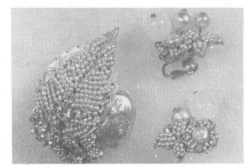

Pin and earrings by Miriam Haskell. The usual many tiny seed pearls, larger baroque pearls and hand set rhinestones. Value $300-500

This dainty set of pin and screw back earrings has light blue stones and rhinestones. Marked STAR-ART 1/20 12K G.F. The earrings measure only ¼'' long and each is marked on the screw with star and 1/20 21K G.F. The pin measures 1½''.

Value $150-175

Striking brooch and earrings set with blue stones. Marked KRAMER OF NEW YORK on applied metal disc on back of brooch; KRAMER on each earring clip. Square shape gives this set an extra appeal.
Value $200-300

A magnificent set of brooch-pin and earrings. Blue and green stones with rhinestones. Incredible that jewelry of this quality should be unsigned by maker. Brooch is 3" x 3". Probably 1950's.   Value $400-650

An outstanding set by TRIFARI. Earrings are 3¼" long, brooch is 2" round. In spite of their size, the pieces all seem light and elegant which is the result of good design and workmanship. All pieces are marked.
Value $800-1000

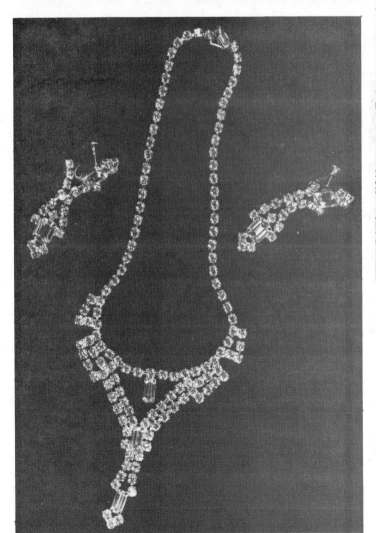

Light blue stones in this necklace and dangling earrings in this set make it very desirable. The earrings are almost 2½" long and the necklace somewhat more elaborate than many in the 1940s sets. Very wearable.   Value $250-350

These clusters of vari-colored beads and pearls in several shapes and sizes are typical of much of the work of Miriam Haskell. A heavy necklace/choker on a thin chain, well made and attractive. Shades of pink glass beads blend with the pearls to make a delightful addition to a collection. The rhinestone and pearl clasp of the necklace is unmarked, each earring is signed MIRIAM HASKELL on a round disc.
Value $600-1200

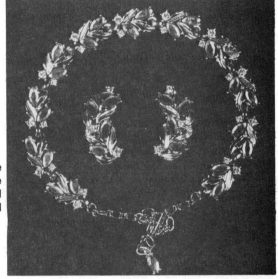

Necklace and earrings by SARAH COVENTRY. An interesting combination of pale blue stones and silver, blending almost without contrast. The clip-back earrings are 1½" long and each is marked in 2 places. The necklace is marked Sarah Cov. Well made, this jewelry has not yet reached major collectible status; is still available and affordable and represents an unusual opportunity.   Value of set $125-155

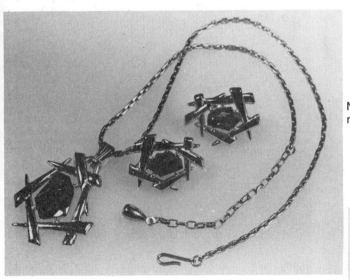

Necklace and clip back earrings of unusual design. Earrings marked on clip, necklace also marked SARAH COV. Irridescent blue stones in silver metal. 1950s.
Value $150-195 set

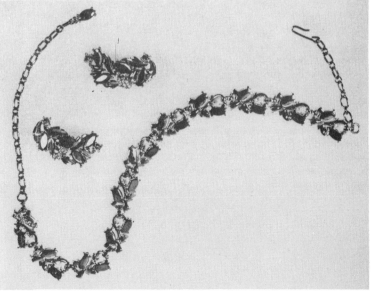

Choker/necklace in silver metal with blue stones and rhinestones. Matching earrings which bear an unreadable date. Marked SARAH COV. 1950s.   Value set, $135-165

Van Dell necklace and earring set in the original box. Dark blue stones and rhinestones with light airy elegant touch of Van Dell jewelry. Necklace is on a thin chain and both earrings and necklace are marked VAN DELL 1/20 12KGF. Purchased at fine jewelers in Syracuse, New York, 1950. Value of set in box **$400**-**700**

Elegant, expensive-looking Eisenberg. This choker/necklace with matching earrings have the trademark sparkling stones and well crafted settings of all Eisenberg. The pieces are heavy, the necklace is unmarked, but each earring is marked on the clip back EISENBERG. Blue stones with rhinestones and nicely detailed this set is from the late 1940's.   Value $500-600

The classic beauty of KREMENTZ. Serpentine chain ending in tasteful rhinestone flower and leaf motif. Matching earrings. Earrings and necklace each in own original box with standing tag which reads '14K ROLLED GOLD OVERLAY' with Krementz mark for this quality jewelry. Inside of each box marked KREMENTZ but none of the jewelry itself is marked. 1950.

Value of set in original boxes $800-1000

Very attractive chain necklace with pendant which can be detached and worn as a pin. Rhinestones with large center green stone. This has a delicate air. 1940s. Matching screw back earrings.

Value, set $250-275

1940s necklace and earrings set. Snowflake pendant is part of the rhinestone necklace itself. Matching earrings are screw back and none of the pieces is marked. The stones are good quality and hand set. Value $200-275

Necklace of deep green stones and myriad tiny rhinestones, all hand set. 11'' long. A fabulous early Kramer, marked KRAMER, N.Y. on the intricate clasp. An exciting example of why Kramer has become so collectible. Value $800-1000

Green stone necklace and earring set. The ingenuity of the designers is evident in the continual variations on the basic form, especially in these sets. Late 1940s. Gold colored metal to blend with stones. Value $250-275

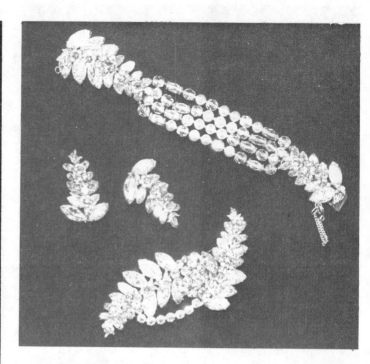

A very beautiful set of bracelet, pin and earrings by Robert. This designer is still underrated. Crystals, irridescent beads, small flower heads with pearl centers. The varying shapes and sizes of the stones lend exquisite balance to these large pieces. Bracelet has safety catch, and small gold spacers. It is signed on the back as is the pin ORIGINAL BY ROBERT with palette. The earrings are signed on the clips 'Robert'. This set represents all that was excellent in 1940s rhinestone jewelry.   Value of set $500-600

Varying shades of yellow highlight the gilt metal of this necklace and earring set. An unusual color in these sets. 1940s. Iridescent crackle stones and rhinestones.   Value $250-275

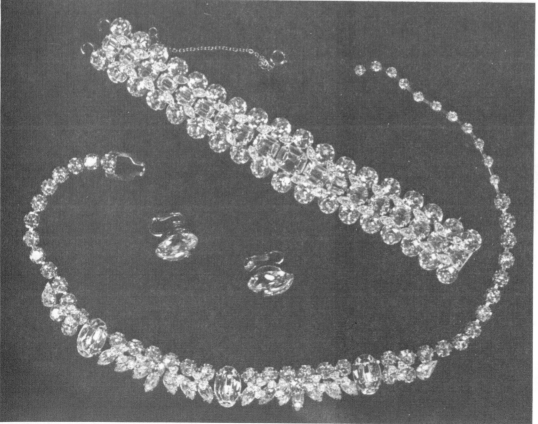

This EISENBERG necklace, bracelet and earrings comes replete with the original box. The three largest stones in the necklace measure ½''. Usual Eisenberg quality and impact, which is to say stunning. Marked EISENBERG ICE.

Value as set in original box - $800-1200

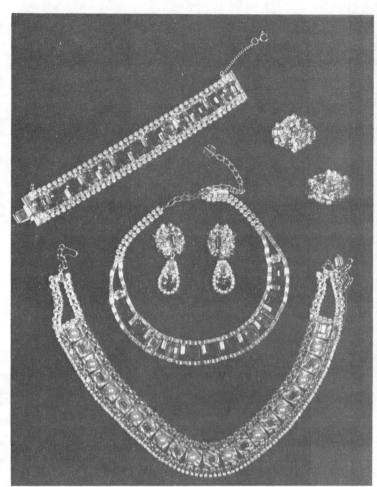

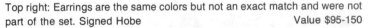

'Jewelry by Hobe' has a lovely ring to it. The older Hobe has an elegant, refined air. These pieces are all signed Hobe - the bracelet and choker set (top and center) have purple and amethyst stones channeled by rhinestones. Gold colored metal. Marked Hobe in an oval.   Value of set $500-700

Top right: Earrings are the same colors but not an exact match and were not part of the set. Signed Hobe   Value $95-150

Matching set of necklace, earrings, bracelet and ring. It is unusual enough to find such a complete set including the original box but also the matching ring - any collector would be transported to Rhinestone Heaven. Then, imagine this - the set would have been made by Hobé. It even has a fascinating provenance - that Maureen O'Hara supposedly wore all this in the film 'Wings of Eagles'. The necklace/collar with its three center tassel drops is 22'' long, and measures almost 2'' at its widest. The backing metal is gold colored, the stones are yellow, gray, and rhinestones. The ring is overall smoky grey stones in gold metal. The original tag reads COSTOMERY JEWELS by HOBÉ. William Hobé did custom jewelry work for theatrical personalities. Aside from its beauty, a set such as this is an awesome find. Value of set in original box $2000-3500

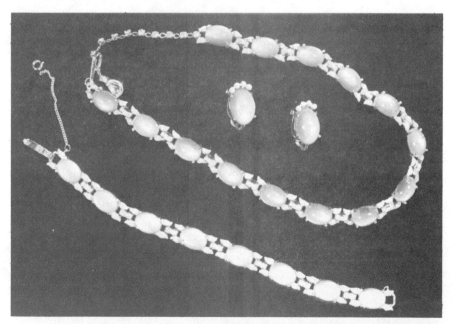

Matching necklace, earrings and bracelet of absolutely typical styling of the early rhinestones period. Light blue opaque stones with rhinestones. Choker is 16'', clip back earrings. All set in silvery metal. Signed JOMAZ on necklace clasp, earrings on clip, bracelet is not signed.   Value $145-175

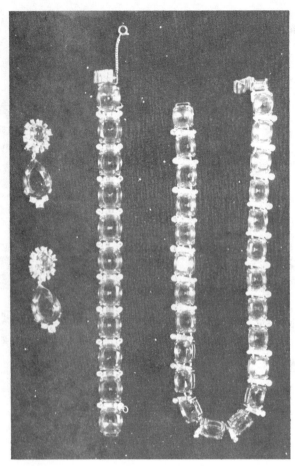

A JOMAZ set. Deep blue stones are mounted in silver metal with rows of rhinestones as separators. The quality of the stones, the color, as well as the superior design and workmanship give this set its importance. Only the earrings and necklace are signed JOMAZ.

Value of set $300-400

Any true lover of spectacular jewelry is already familiar with the name KRAMER. To see this set is to cause such a collector to salivate. Kramer can always be depended upon to produce jewelry which not only looks marvelous but is certain to be of high quality. This set is no exception. The very desirable deep red stones are framed by narrow bands of small rhinestones on all the pieces. The five pendant drops match the necklace exactly and move independently to flash vivid fire when the wearer moves. At rest, they hug the body and give an impression of brilliant mass. The matching bracelet is narrow, the earrings are clip back. Bracelet marked KRAMER of NY on the clasp, earrings are not signed. Necklace is 18'' long.   Value of this set is $1000-1200

This stunning set by SCHIAPARELLI is a good example of typical 1940s design work as well as esoteric combinations of colors and shapes used during the period. The look became so definitive it has become a generic one. This adds value and wonder at the beauty achieved within these parameters. This 16'' choker in silvery metal has clear blue and gray-green stones with irridescent purple leaves which shimmer with movement.

All pieces are marked - The wide bracelet with its safety catch is marked on the back near the clasp. Each earring bears a patent number and is also signed SCHIAPARELLI. 1940s.   Value of set $850-1200

196

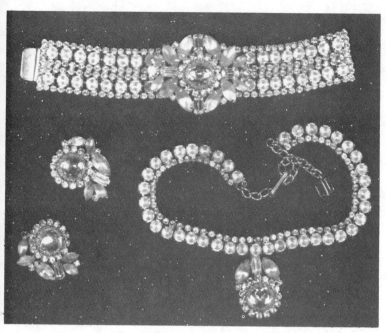

Complete sets of earlier HOBÉ are very difficult to find and one such as this is guaranteed to make any collector's heart flutter. The opaque stones are irridescent, the rhinestones are large and impressive and the exciting aurora borealis center stones are all set in gold tone metal. This sparkling array is quite breathtaking. Signed HOBÉ in an oval.   Value of set $1200-1500

This set is of silver colored metal set with turquoise colored stones. The necklace of three strands of stones descends from a chain set with the same stones. Different sizes and shapes are repeated in the fringe pendant. The matching earrings are 2½" long and are screw back. The wide flexible bracelet has a safety catch. A gorgeous set, marked WEISNER only on the earrings.

Value $800-1000

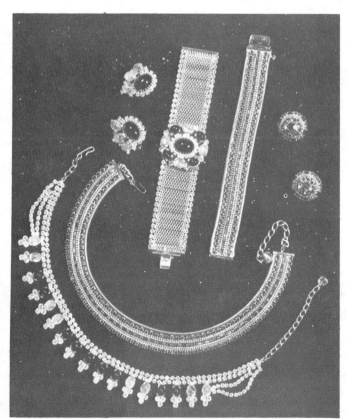

First set: Hobé choker (bottom), earrings (top left), and bracelet (center left). To add interest to a design quite common to the 1940s Hobé has alternated the drops of the choker - 2 pink, then 2 black, suspended from a double strand of rhinestones. The centerpieces of the wide gold metal mesh band edged with rhinestones has the large black stone and the same motif as the necklace. The earrings add greatly to the set.

Value of set $600-850

2nd set: Exquisite color marks this set. Delightful cranberry colored stones are mixed with grayish rhinestones. The wide mesh bracelet (center right) and earrings (top right) match this elegant choker. Signed Hobé 1950s.

Value $450-650

These two sets exemplify the diversity of SCHIAPARELLI jewelry which varies not only in materials but in feeling and execution. The set at left - bracelet, earrings and necklace has opaque yellow and clear crystal stones set in gold tone metal. The spacers have a touch of aurora borealis. Both bracelet and necklace are on chains. The necklace is 16". All pieces are signed - earrings on the clips, bracelet and necklace on back.
Value of set $500-800

Right side of photo illustrates another set by Schiapparelli. The necklace and earrings have yellow and gray opaque stones set in gold tone metal, with decorative rhinestones. All the pieces are signed.
Value of set $450-650

A lovely set by Trifari. The rhinestone drop necklace with its fine chain is gold tone metal, as are the earring frames. During this era of TRIFARI (the 1940s) the jewelry the company made is easy to recognize. This set reflects that TRIFARI touch. The necklace is not signed, the earrings are signed with the crown above the T. The gold tone bracelet with its quality stones and beautiful design is signed TRIFARI pat. pend.
Value of necklace and earrings $300-400
Value of bracelet $250-350

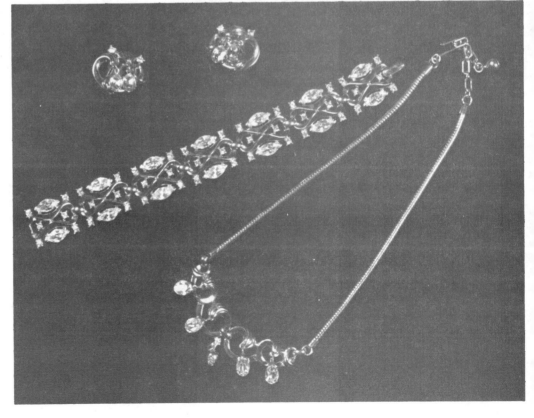

An Eisenberg choker in the popular light blue stones which are set in rhodium. 16" long. Marked EISENBERG on the catch. 1940s.   Value $300-350

A 16" necklace of great splendor. Unusually clear large stones (each measures ¾" x ¾"). This example is one of the finest I have seen. Heavy, gives an impression of great affluence. Marked on back of center pendant stone with a script E. 1940s.   Value $1500-2000

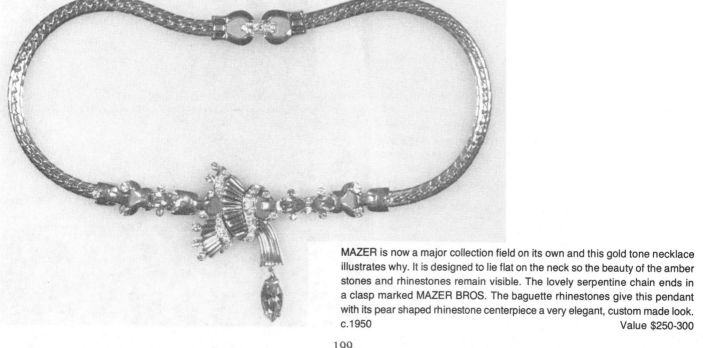

MAZER is now a major collection field on its own and this gold tone necklace illustrates why. It is designed to lie flat on the neck so the beauty of the amber stones and rhinestones remain visible. The lovely serpentine chain ends in a clasp marked MAZER BROS. The baguette rhinestones give this pendant with its pear shaped rhinestone centerpiece a very elegant, custom made look. c.1950   Value $250-300

199

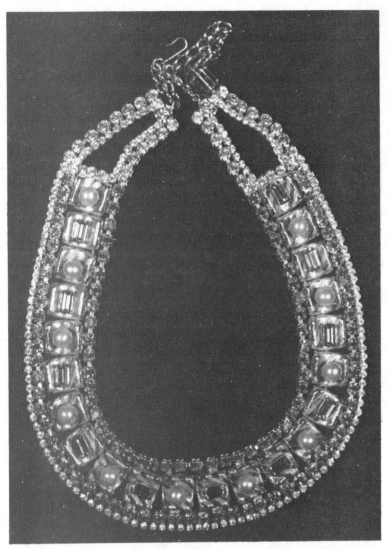

This 18" choker by HOBÉ is truly impressive with its aurora borealis stones, pearls and alternating irridescent stones. Wide, very well done and with its varied stones, this modified collar is eminently wearable, collectible and desirable. Gold colored metal, purple and amethyst stones. Marked Hobé in an oval.

Value $750-1000

THE HATTIE CARNEGIE touch is evident in the clasp of this crystal and pearl necklace. The many strand necklace regained popularity in the 1980s and early 1990s. This 16" example is timeless. The many small rhinestones which make up the endearing bow clasp are set in gold tone metal. A lovely piece of jewelry. Signed HATTIE CARNEGIE on the clasp. 1940s.

Value $450-650

This 16" necklace has irridescent stones, yellow stones, and smokey/gray rhinestones all set in gold colored metal. All the lines of stones are of the same size. The large pronged stones are of exceptional quality. Signed HOBÉ. This beautiful necklace has that rare, expensive gem-like quality common to much of the earlier HOBÉ.

Value $600-800

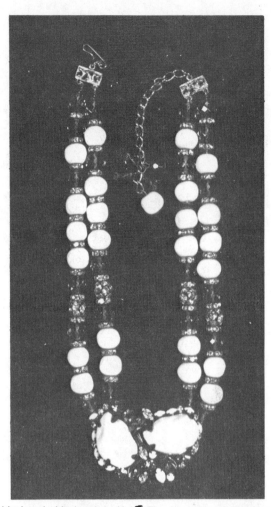

This 28'' long necklace of rhinestone studded rectangles separated by chain rings has an overall rhinestone pendant which measures 2½'' x 2½''. The effect of the many small rhinestones against the gilt metal chain projects an air of pageantry and certainly foreshadowed the heraldry jewelry of recent years. The length of this necklace gives it added importance. Marked HOBÉ in an oval.

Value $200-350

An 18'' choker of black and white beads by Hobé. The rhinestone spacers lend drama to the stark black and white. 2½'' wide at the center drop. Signed Hobé in an oval. 1950s.

Value $150-195

A cascade of golden blossoms hang from a line of pearls and rhinestones and lighten the look of this necklace/choker by SARAH COVENTRY. A piece such as this should alert collectors to the possibilities of this maker's jewelry. Feminine and pretty. Marked SARAH COVENTRY on closure disk.

Value $100-150

KENNETH LANE necklace. A double bright gilt chain supports 3 tiers of round white opaque beads and a center transparent glass ball. Each of the three tiers supports an undulating dragon with a red stone eye. Heavy and clunky.
Value $150-195

This black glass necklace is highly dramatic. The rhinestones accentuate the stark black beads, the clasp is small, pretty and shows the attention to detail by these jewelry designers. c.1940s. Marked on back of center drop with a raised oval MIRIAM HASKELL.   Value $300-350

This necklace has to be experienced in person. It is 'Oscar' jewelry but if you are up for an 'Emmy' you could probably make do with this necklace of large black cabachon stones and rhinestones which drop in graduated lengths. Each pendant has one or more wide bands of pronged rhinestones ending in a 1'' apple green stone surrounded by rhinestones and pear shaped green stones. The 'drops' range from 3'' to the 5'' center. Unmarked. A daring if not unduly creative rather wonderfully garish necklace which deserves a signature. Much lighter in weight than an older similar piece would be. Gilt metal.
Value $350-500

This VENDOME choker has a pretty rhinestone clasp but otherwise is composed of a double strand of irridescent purplish and green glass beads, tiny pink glass beads, wood separators and plastic squares. Interesting. Marked on clasp VENDOME.   Value $125-165

This SARAH COVENTRY pendant on a rather heavy chain has a Byzantine look. Beautiful large, round stones in brown and canary colors are set in a dramatic frame of gold colored metal. 1960s.   Value $95-150

A beautiful classically designed pendant on a fine chain. 2'' long. Unmarked but elegant and the kind of jewelry which cries out for an appraisal it looks so real. Late 1930s, early 1940s. Unsigned but a necklace to drool over.   Value $300-500

These cabachon red stones framed in gold tone metal have all the fire required of the real thing. Choker length, this is signed TARA. The rhinestones surrounding the stones are good quality. 1950s jewelry produced more jewelry with red stones than some earlier periods. This passionate color makes the necklace very effective.   Value $150-185

This NETTIE ROSENSTEIN necklace reflects the influence of genuine gemstone jewelry. This important piece with its slender band of round and pear shaped rhinestones and its pearl and rhinestone pendant is 18'' of silver metal and flashing stones. The free form floral effect of the pendant was a dominant theme in costume jewelry. This is a wonderful necklace. Signed NETTIE ROSENSTEIN. 1940s. Value $1200-2000

MIRIAM HASKELL, 18'' red glass beads, rhinestone rondels. Marked MIRIAM HASKELL on attached disc. Value $250-295

Right in photo - 16'' necklace distinguished by the gold spacers and trademark Haskell pearls. The lapis blue colored adds interest. The 2½'' drop is marked on back with an oval. Early 1940s. Value $300-350

A very elaborate necklace whose original inspiration can be traced almost to antiquity. Gold metal frames green stones on individual drops connected by a series of short chains with rings. c.1940. Marked BARCLAY on clasp. Value $300-350

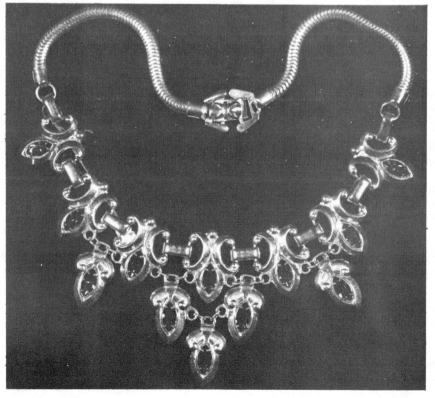

This necklace could be described as "incredibly beautiful" and no photograph can do justice to the clarity and brilliance of the stones and intricate workmanship. Small simulated pearls, crystals and rhinestones hand set in thin brass, all on nicely embossed chains. Unsigned. 1940s.
Value $450-600

Early 1940s necklace by CORO. The gorgeous deep blue stones and the flower head of small rhinestones with a tiny deep blue stone center are attached to a thin chain. The simple design work here is impressive.   Value $225-275

An unsigned beauty. The crescent shape of this gold metal collar can be traced to the Byzantine of the 17th century. Design is almost always influenced by what has gone before and never is that more obvious than here. This beautifully executed piece has multi-colored stones - amber, light green, yellow, brown, shades of blue, orange and purple. It is 16" long and 6" at its widest. 1940s.   Value $500-650

An elaborate long necklace of the 1940s. Signed VOLUPTE. Scarce Mark.   Value $225-275

This is an unusual necklace, heavy and impressive. The brilliance of the stones and the weight of the piece immediately classifies it as Eisenberg. The mark EISENBERG is on the clasp. The stones are all hand set and the rhinestone triangles are attached in a flexible way so the necklace will lie flat.   Value $300-400

This bangle boasts a single charm, a delightful flower cart has moveable wheels, multi-colored stones and a center pearl. These bracelets are becoming increasingly popular consequently more expensive, although originally they were inexpensive jewelry. Unmarked CORO. Fun to own and wear. These 1940s whimsies have a special appeal. Value $85-125

1930's necklace plum colored glass and crystal beads on chain. Value $250-350

A very dramatic necklace in the popular topaz stones of the 1930s. The large center stone is faceted. An unusual combination of designs, somewhat Victorian in feeling with definite Deco touches. Even the chain shows the care which went into the making of this jewelry. Not signed. Value $300-350

Right:
A finely crafted and well thought out necklace of the 1930s. The large center glass stone is surrounded by gold tone flower heads with topaz colored stone centers reaching part way up to the chain. Value $200-300

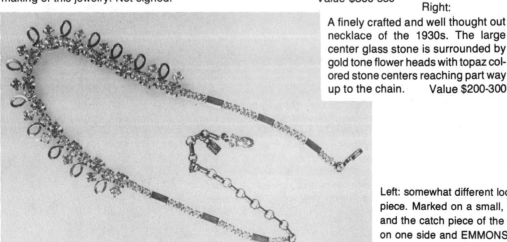

Left: somewhat different look to this well made choker. Handsome piece. Marked on a small, free-swinging metal square EMMONS, and the catch piece of the closure is marked with a large script E on one side and EMMONS on the other. Value $200-250

Necklace/choker, brass leaves, pearls, rhinestones, seed pearls, supported by three strands of pearls, tiny rhinestones, long metal separators with a well defined rhinestone clasp. Brass filagree back with ORIGINAL BY ROBERT on a disc. Quite beautiful.   Value $350-500

The clustered effect of the high quality rhinestones makes for a highly theatrical choker and earrings set. The differing shapes and sizes of stones not only add interest but project a mass of opulence and glamor. A very desirable set of the 1950s made by Hattie Carnegie. Necklace is signed HATTIE CARNEGIE, earrings CARNEGIE. Beautiful set. c.1948-1950   Value $1500-1800

An exquisite necklace of rhinestones, white beads, the pendant large stone is yellow with flecks of darker gold surrounded by rhinestones and different shaped stones in colors of blue, pink, topaz and with three pendant drops of vari-colored stones. A stunning piece of jewelry. Unsigned.   Value $250-325

A particularly elegant example of the kind of rhinestone necklace which is now so much sought after. 21 pear-shaped, hand-set rhinestones are set in rhodium.
Value $225-300

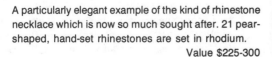

207

Unmarked rhinestone necklace with lavaliere type drop. $85-95

1930s deep set rhinestones in base metal. Stones are pasted in. This necklace has the distinctive look of the 1930s and because this type was relatively inexpensive originally many have been discarded and are now found in poor condition. In spite of original cost it is beautifully designed and should be a prime target for collectors.   Value $350-400

Leaf choker/necklace of silvery metal and rhinestones. Each leaf measures 2''. Marked on clasp WEISS. Unusual. 1940s.

Value $500-600

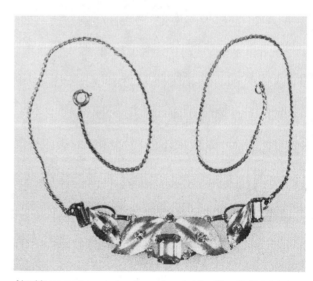

Necklace and screw-back earring set by Van Dell. Light blue stones and rhinestones in a leaf motif. Sterling silver. 1950. The usual light elegant touch that marks much of the Van Dell jewelry. Necklace and earrings marked VAN DELL. A beautiful set.
Value $300-350

Short length rhinestone necklace. 1940's. 15 inches.   Value $85-95

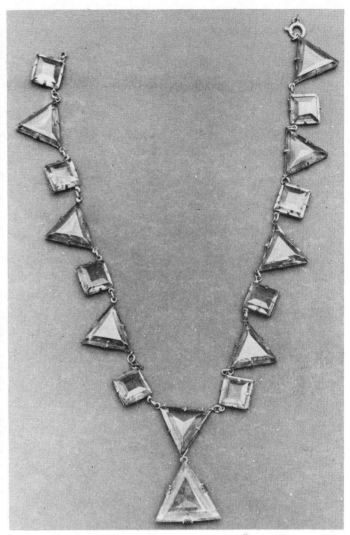

Blue glass necklace. Each piece set in thin brass frame and held by prongs, connected by rings. 1929.   Value $250-275

Beautifully designed and executed 1950s rhinestone necklace. Unmarked. Necklace curves gracefully away from the large center stone.   Value $75-95

This necklace not only has the deep blue stones which are so popular, the design is intricate and appealing. Marked HOLLYCRAFT on the back it has the additional distinction of being dated - COPR. 1952. Dated jewelry is rare.   Value $145-195

One of the prettier of the late pearl pieces is this necklace of pearls, rhinestones and irridescent crystals, on chain 15'' long.   Value $200-300

Long rope of pearls on chain with green and gold beads and rhinestones. 29 inches long. About 1940. An exciting necklace.   Value $250-325

This necklace of green glass pendants on a thin, delicate chain was purchased in 1929. It is a much sought after type Value $200-295

Absolutely typical necklace/choker of the 1940s except for the color of the stone These rhinestones are made to appear a smoky color which lend interest to an oth wise rather run-of-the-mill piece. Also as usual, remarkably good quality. Not marke
Value $100-1

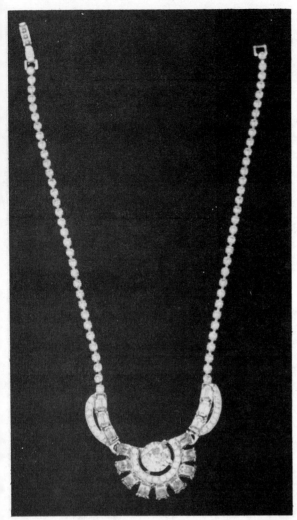

Lovely rhinestone and blue stone necklace. Either 1949 or 1950. Blue stones are ever popular, especially in this light color.
Value $145-175

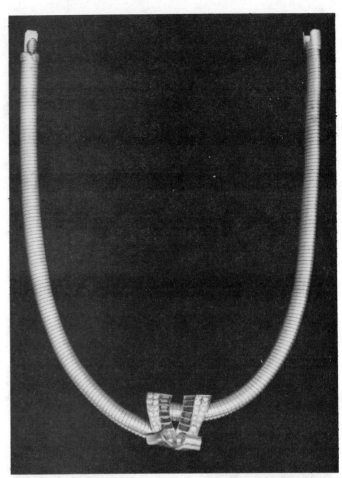

Necklace of unusual design. Flexible necklace is in two sections and the red stone and rhinestone pieces are also attached separately. Initially a more expensive piece.
Value $200-300

The green stones in this long necklace are completely striking. The chain is nicely decorated. Quality workmanship. A stunning piece of jewelry. 12" long. 1930s.
Value $350-450

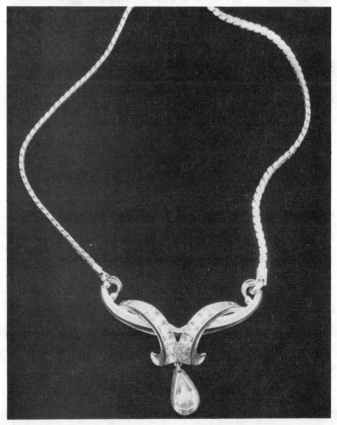

Gold plated necklace with square blue stones and large blue stone drop. Marked CORO.
Value $175-200

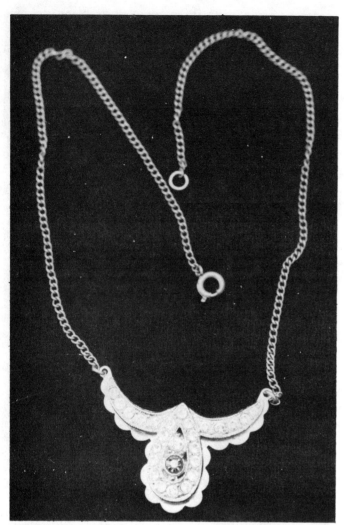

1930's necklace on chain, brass backing to rhinestone pendant which has green center stone.   Value $150-200

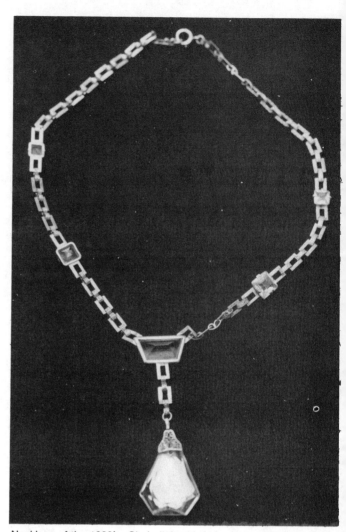

Necklace of the 1930's. Chain link with blue stones and blue stone pendant.   Value $150-200

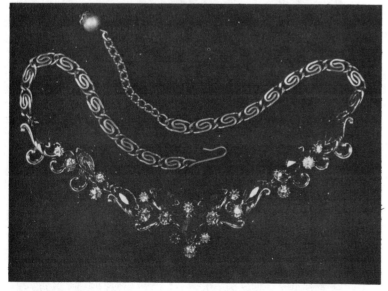

A nicely crafted choker of the 1940s. Aurora Borealis stones in shades of blue and rhinestones on an intricately worked chain. Gilt over base metal.

Value $195-250

The Victorian look of this necklace is often found on 1920s jewelry. This necklace might be considered 'crowded' with various colored stones and pearls - pale green, aqua chips, raised 'cut diamond' rhinestones. the center stone turquoise colored surrounded by pearls, pale violet - the whole surpasses the parts and the necklace is attractive and old fashioned looking. It was bought in New York in the 20s.

Value $200-275

1930's necklace. 13'' long. Pink glass beads on chain, faceted pink stone pendant. These are much coveted types.   Value $300-$350

Multi-colored stones and rhinestones in thin metal. Double chain with rhinestone clasp. 1920's. Rare.   Value $400-600

An exquisite necklace of faux pearls and small rhinestones set in 'gold'. Each reticulated segment boasts a flower tremblant and the drop segment incorporates a bird tremblant. 1940s.   Value $350-450

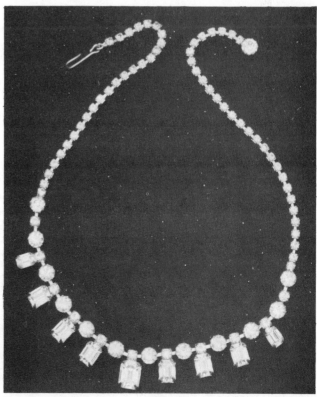

Beautifully simple necklace, pink pronged stones set in gold finish, marked Weiss.   Value $200-300

213

A single rhinestone drop on this rhinestone necklace of simple design. Bought in 1948.

Value $65-85

A heavy necklace on an equally heavy double chain, ending in a lovely little round clasp of topaz colored stones. Vari-sized topaz colored stones decorate the necklace itself. 'Clunky' but effective, well made and a good example of how companies which listed themselves as makers of 'chains' and 'chain jewelry' were involved with the rhinestone manufacturers. Gilt. Late 1930s. Unmarked.   Value $350-500

Mesh choker with rhinestone accents. Gold tone. 1950's.   Value $75-95

This short necklace shows design work of a superior kind. Rhinestones and blue stones it is marked BOUCHER and numbered 537. A rather difficult name to find but always worthwhile.

Value $300-450

Rhinestone necklace. Stones hand s 1940's.   Value $75-10

214

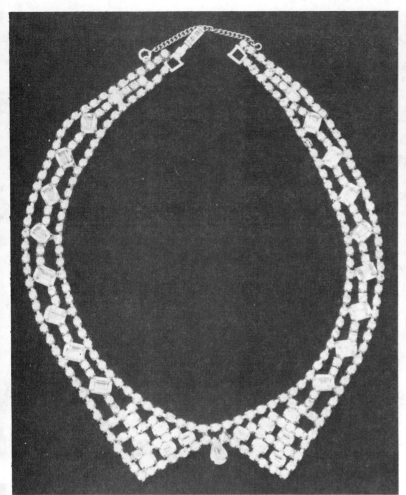

Choker length rhinestone necklace. Simpler than most. 1940s. 13'', adjustable.   Value $85-95

Outstanding rhinestone necklace of the 1940's. Wide (Approx. 1'' widening to 1½'' at points.) This is rigid to give collar effect and lay perfectly flat. Not marked. Safety chain.
Value $150-175

Necklace/choker, brilliant scintillating tear drop pendant drops each attached separately to the body of the necklace. Stones are all hand set. Extravagant piece. Marked KRAMER. 1940s.   Value $350-500

Short necklace of the 1940s. Gold plated chain with 5 metal flowers, each with rhinestone centerpiece.
Value $95-125

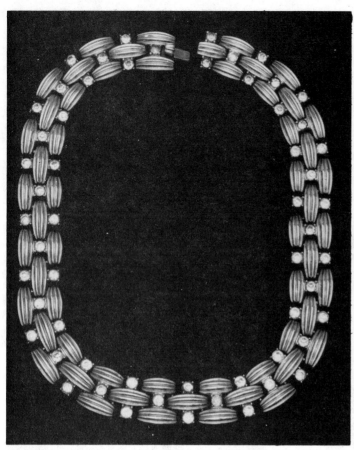

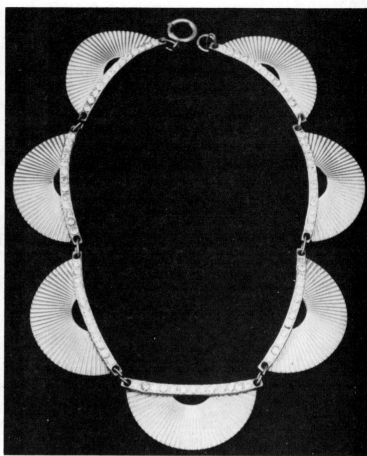

Necklace, ¾'' wide. A beautiful piece by Trifari. Bought about 1943. This necklace cost $55 when purchased from Lambert Bros. Jewelers in New York and is in original retailer's box. Marked 'crown' TRIFARI and DES PAT. PEND. The styling is timeless.

Value $400-600

Gorgeous Art Deco necklace. Copper with antiqued white finish and rhinestones. Each fan with rhinestone band is a separate link. 1930s.

Value $500-750

Left: Necklace, 1940s, unmarked but of the kind sold in better jewelry stores. Gold plate over sterling with three sizes of rhinestones.

Value $200-250

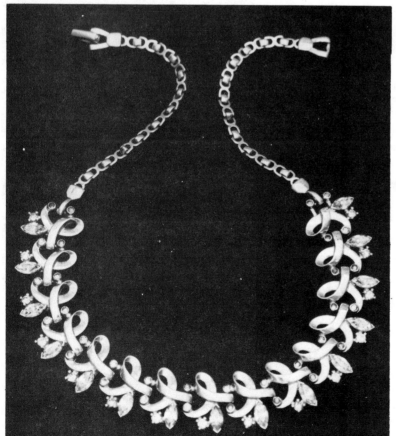

Pearls have made a strong fashion comeback and the pearls and rhinestones of the 1940s have a rich, nostalgic look which lends them added attraction. The quality is usually good and they are still a bargain. The double strand necklace is a pretty example of the combination with its channelled stones and good length. The clasp is silver metal with large rhinestones.

Value $45-75

The matching barrette is dainty and very feminine. These earlier barrettes often are overlooked although they are quite endearing.

Value $35-45

216

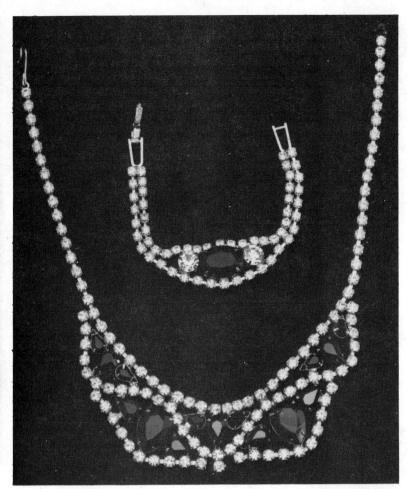

Striking set of rhinestones and black stones. Necklace is 2'' wide at bottom, the bracelet is 1'' at its widest. Value $195-250

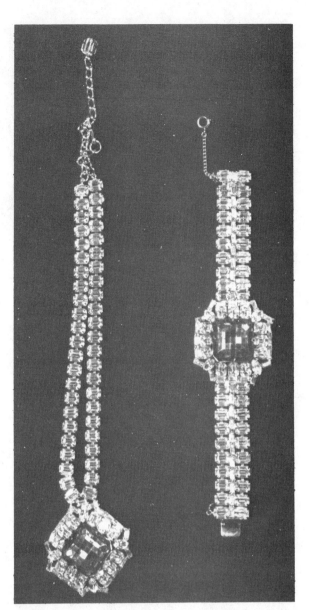

The design work of earlier Hobé tends to be either highly creative and imaginative or firmly rooted in the classic work of the great masters of fine jewelry. This necklace and bracelet fall into the latter category. Magnificently simple one might say. This 22'' necklace centers upon a large stone of varying shades of pink, green, lavender, yellow and blue surrounded by rhinestones. This is suspended from a line of emerald cut rhinestones, all of the same size. The bracelet matches exactly. Silvery metal. A wonderful Hobé set.

Value $500-750

A spectacular set - necklace/choker, earrings and bracelet. Stones of lavender and purple with smaller blue stones are set in a collar made up of five separate parts. The 1½'' bracelet has the same colored stones in two rows. Superb quality. This is the kind of remarkable costume jewelry which takes the right attitude to carry off. Heavy, beautifully crafted with a high fashion, expensive look. Only the dangling earrings intended for pierced ears are signed BOUCHER and the number 5671.

Value $1000-1500

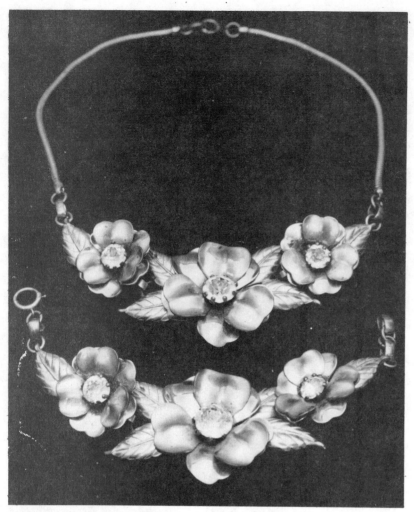

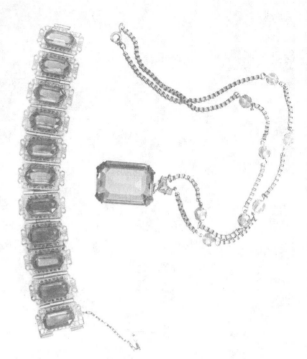

A classically beautiful necklace and bracelet. The large topaz stone pendant is attached to a fine chain with topaz glass beads. 18'' long. The bracelet is equally exquisite. Cut topaz stones, each set in its own filagree frame of high quality thin brass. Each segment moves independently to give the bracelet flexibility. Safety catch. Both bought in the same jewelry shop in 1927 and always worn together by the owner but this is probably not an exact matching set. But close enough certainly. Very desirable.

Necklace and matching bracelet. Large rhinestone centers in each plated brass and copper flower. Serpentine chain. c. 1939. Glamorous set.

Value $400-500

Value of necklace $300-400
Value of bracelet $250-300

Superlative is the only word to describe this KRAMER set. Silver colored metal frames fine quality red stones and rhinestones. The collar choker hugs the neck, the bracelet is rigid, and hinged. Marked KRAMER, NY

Value of set $800-1000

218

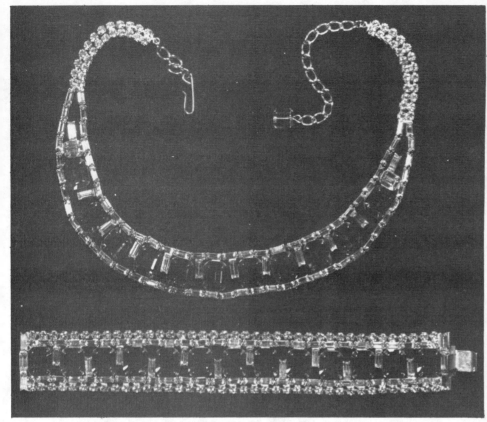

Choker and bracelet by HOBÉ. Purple and amethyst stones bordered with rhinestones. Gorgeous set. 1940s   Value $350-500 set

Multi strand necklace and earring set. This very effective 24" strand chain necklace with its pearl-look opaque beads, and tiny crystal spacers has a beautiful rhinestone and gold metal clasp which measures 1½" and with its pearls and large rhinestone exactly matches the earrings. Necklace signed HOBÉ in an oval.   Value of set $400-600

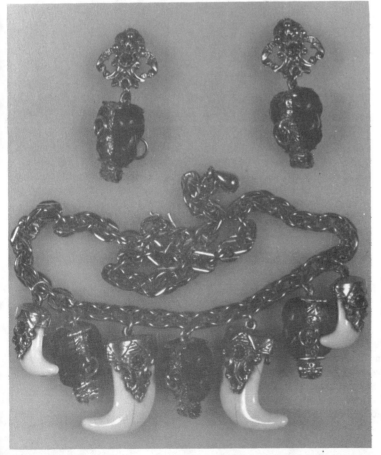

This bizarre necklace and earrings set fits into a category on its way up into the financial stratosphere. The chain dangles 4 faux 'claws' and 3 African heads. The silvery metal fittings create a unique setting with their vivid red stones. The clip back matching earrings with their own dangling African heads are marked SELRO CORP. on back of each clip. While most of the 'faces' jewelry is unmarked that made by SELRO often carries their name. To add interest for the dedicated collector the clasp is marked JAPAN. This type of 1950s jewelry has risen rapidly from minimal price. (my first pieces cost $8 for the set) to the low hundreds.
Value $150-250

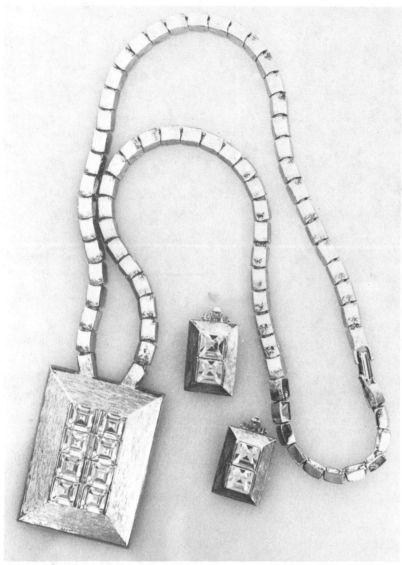

EISENBERG necklace and earring set. A departure for Eisenberg and quite arresting. Silvery metal link necklace with a square pendant with 8 magnificent square cut rhinestones. This necklace is 18" long and the pendant is marked E on the back on an applied metallic square. The earrings are miniatures of the pendant and equally brilliant. Each earring is marked E. 1972, original price of necklace $12.50, earrings $5   Value $300-450

An Alice Caviness necklace and earring set. This continues to be a rather elusive signature. Turquoise beads, pale amethyst beads, dark blue, light blue beads with small silver spacers between each bead give this set an effervesence it would otherwise lack. The clasp is a thing of beauty by itself. Both the earrings with their pale blue centers and the necklace are signed.
Value $350-500

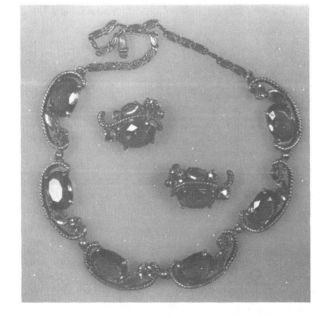

The luscious blue shade of the stones in this necklace give the piece its reason d'etre. The frame is silver colored metal, narrow and restrained to point up the faceted stones. The small blue toned irridescent stones add interest. A fine chain supports the 6 large and 12 smaller stones on the necklace. The clip back earrings are large and match the necklace exactly. Each earring is signed on its clip - SCHIAPARELLI and the necklace is signed on the back of the frame.

Value of set $400-500

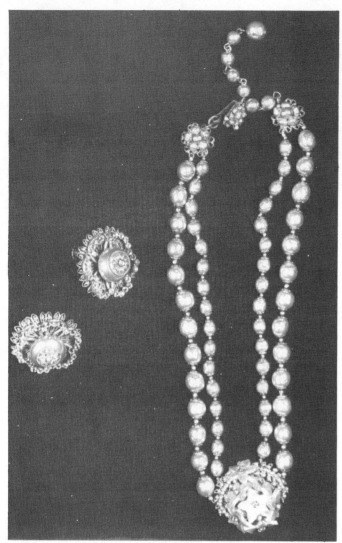

An intriguing necklace. The design is much more complicated than a cursory inspection would indicate. There are 7 irridescent stars set into gold colored filagree metal, highlighted with the characteristic seed pearls and center rhinestones. This choker is 17'' long and is well signed - on back of the center drop and again on the clasp - MIRIAM HASKELL. 1940s.   Value $300-400

The earrings on the left side of photo show the same general design approach but are not a match to the necklace. Gold tone metal with a large center pearl surrounded by rhinestones. The filagree frame gives the earrings a light feeling. Signed HASKELL.   Value $125-195

Right:

Patience is a highly prized attribute in any collector. About 7 years ago I purchased this necklace of white opaque beads with its pretty pendant of white glass leaves, attractive brass accents and twinkling center rhinestones. It is marked on the back DeMARIO, NY. Recently I found the matching earrings in a shop far from home. Each is marked DeMARIO, NY, each measures 1½''. This summer type jewelry does not have the popularity of other more glamorous types, consequently it is still underpriced. It is also thoroughly charming, and exudes a kind of innocence.   Value of set $175-225

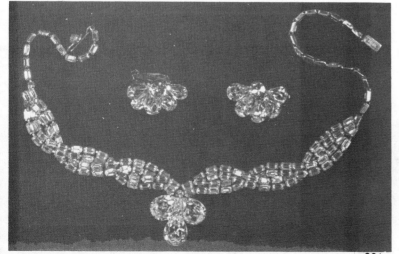

The twisted effect in this necklace enhances the openwork baguette rhinestones and narrowing to feature the three large rhinestone pendant. Framed in silver metal. The necklace is 18''. Matching clip back earrings. This stunning set is by WEISS, marked on back of pendant.   Value of set $400-500

The irridescent of these large pearls coupled with the flashing rhinestone spacers tends to rivet attention on the wearer. As a skilled designer, Nettie Rosenstein was aware of this function of jewelry. The choker is not signed, the matching earrings themselves (not the clips) are marked NETTIE ROSENSTEIN in script on a raised oblong bar. Sets such as this where not all pieces are signed point up the necessity for sellers NEVER BREAKING SETS.   Value of set $500-650

Christian Dior necklace and matching earrings. Blue and green stones with pearls on a fine silver metal chain. 20'' long. All pieces signed. A traditional elegant set by a famous designer name. c.1960s   Value $250-350

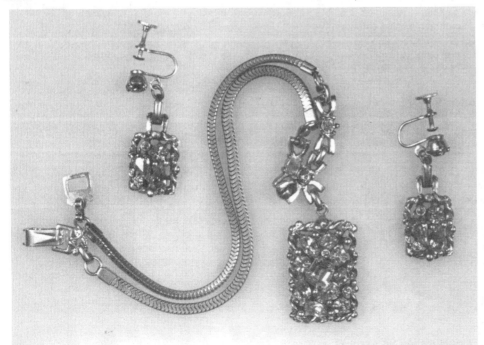

Necklace and screw back earring set by BARCLAY. Multi colored stones of blue, green amethyst and rhinestones set in gold tone metal. The serpentine chain and square shapes make this set somewhat unusual. Signed BARCLAY on the necklace only. 1940s.   Value $300-400

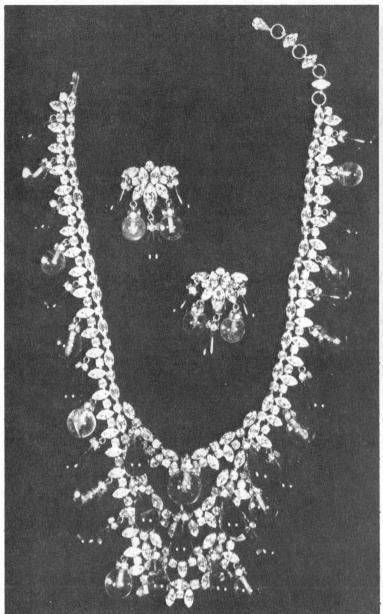

A line of 5 pendant drops of clear green stones with white shadings mounted in gold tone metal and framed with rhinestones are attached to ovals which form part of the chain necklace. These are separated by exquisite rhinestone bows. The antique-inspired design does not need the NETTIE ROSENSTEIN signature to give it validity although the designer name adds to the value. It is quite stunning. Necklace is 19'' long and is signed on a raised oval at the back of the center pendant.

Value $1200-1800

Centered in this outstanding necklace is a beautifully simple blossom by the same designer. A signed NETTIE ROSENSTEIN rose.

Value $350-400

This necklace is 24'' long. Its 2 strands of overall rhinestones of varying cuts and sizes support green red and blue glass tear drops mixed with round glass ball drops. Matching earrings. This set is wondrous - the dazzling stones, the multi colors of the drops and the intricate design combine for splendor. Incredibly it is signed only with the infamous "pat pend."   Value $500-600

The numbers of the WEISS collecting cult have been increasing steadily since the first edition of this book was published. Understandable in view of the beautiful jewelry WEISS produced. A good example is this necklace and pin. The pin measures 2'' x 1½'', the necklace 16'' long, 3'' at its widest. Both pieces are signed WEISS.   Value set $600-800

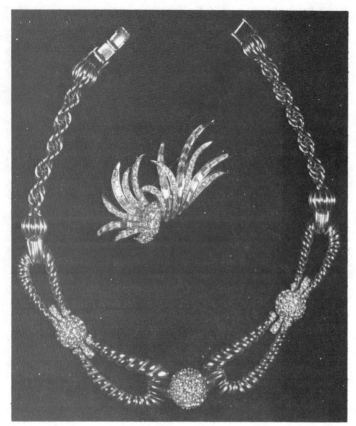

Magnificent wide bracelet with its cluster of blue shaded stones. Unmarked. Gilt metal. Value $225-295

This heavy short - 14'' choker by BOUCHER features gold colored metal, a woven chain and 3 clusters of outstanding quality small rhinestones.
Value $400-500

This bird with his magnificent wingspread which seems to be in motion is composed of small rhinestones and baguette set rhinestones set in silver metal. Signed BOUCHER and numbered. Value $250-300

From its large center blue stone, guarded by two small topaz stones and yellow and blue enamel work this bracelet of filagree is so well made it commands instant respect and exclamations at its beauty. Its owner inherited this, specially mentioned in a will. Value $400-500

This lion head bracelet is a real eye-catcher. The colored stone eyes and well defined head with its open mouth lend an air of excitement to this wide, rigid, gold-tone bracelet. Safety catch. Marked HHC CO.
Value $300-400

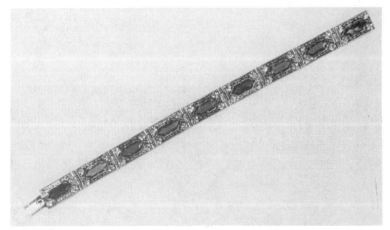

This is the type of jewelry which requires your friendly neighborhood expert in tow before purchase. The amethyst stones are each set in heavily embossed, hinged gilt metal squares cornered by pronged rhinestones. Unmarked. 1930s.
Value $350-500

A slightly different look in expandable bracelets. This has alternating rows of gilt metal and hand set pink stones. This was bought in 1940s.
Value $195-250

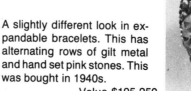

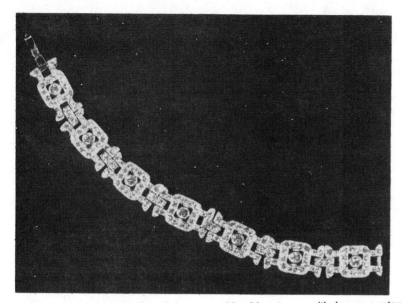

Bracelet, 1½" wide, separate links, pasted-in rhinestones with larger center rhinestone. 1930s. Very attractive.   Value $200-250

The pasted-in rhinestones on this wide (approx. 1½") bracelet blend too well into the gilt metal and become obvious only in artificial light. Marked CORO 1940s.
Value $200-250

This bracelet looks like the real thing. Rigid gold filled with tiny blue stones and rhinestones across the top. Marked CAM & CO.   Value $300-450

1940's rhinestone bracelet. Well made and ever popular.
Value $75-125

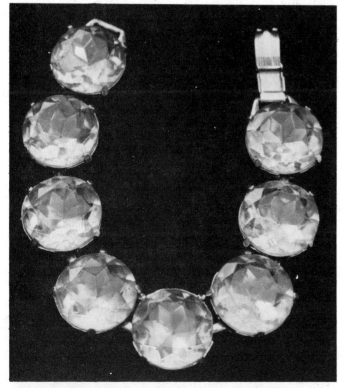

Heavy bracelet with light blue stones pronged and set in white metal. Stones 1" across. Chrome clasp 1930's.   Value $125-175

Bracelet, white metal, 1940s, 2 attached but separate bands of rhinestones with the wider diamond shaped centerpiece. Band is approx. 1" at its widest. Unsigned as are most of these bracelets.   Value $100-145

Many of these bracelets with the their beautifully faceted and channeled rhinestones seem to have been made by the same manufacturer and all I have seen are unmarked. The quality is outstanding. Notice the detail in the inside of the bracelet. The embossing around the outside is equally fine.   Value $400-500

A delicate narrow rhinestone bracelet whose workmanship is obvious, although it is unsigned. Unusual swing catch. Probably early 1940s.   Value $400-450

This is the kind of bracelet everyone who collects this jewelry should be seeking. It has large, hand set, high quality rhinestones, each in a separate bezel, which is channeled into the frame. Unsigned, but confronted with this quality and beauty marks become unimportant. Early 1940s.   Value $500-650

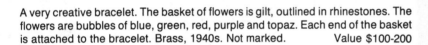

A very creative bracelet. The basket of flowers is gilt, outlined in rhinestones. The flowers are bubbles of blue, green, red, purple and topaz. Each end of the basket is attached to the bracelet. Brass, 1940s. Not marked.   Value $100-200

This is one of the showy, well made pieces of 1940s jewelry which is so often unmarked. This bracelet is approx. 1½'' wide at its center, the rhinestones are hand set and the whole is pleasing.   Value $175-250

A beautiful rigid bracelet, pull apart closing. Hand set rhinestones channeled all around, large brilliant stones at top center. Unsigned. 1940s. ½'' wide.
Value $300-450

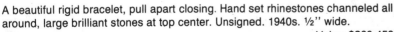

Two rigid bracelets of the slip-on type. One in gold colored metal, one silver. The silvery bracelet has rhinestones all around, the gold has deep green stones. Although the basic bracelet is the same in each case, these are not a pair. The rhinestones are much larger than the green stones. All stones are hand set and both are good quality. 1950s.   Value $95-125 ea.

Bracelet with large clusters of rhinestones connected by links. Safety catch. Elegant. Marked BARCLAY in script.
                    Value $300-400

A fairly pedestrian bracelet, design-wise, but well made and a nice blend of aurora stones in shades of blue and silvery metal. Marked LISNER on the clasp. Late 1950s.   Value $145-165

Jewelry by Mosell, the maker of this magnificent bracelet, is scarce. The design work is always superior and the craftsmanship so wonderful that a collector of Mosell calls it "gasp" jewelry. "I always gasp with amazement when I see a new piece," she says. Understandable because Mosell is almost always gorgeous and innovative. This bracelet is 2" wide with four rows of deeply bezeled rhinestones on a bed of gilded, simulated bamboo. It is heavy and wraps the wrist comfortably. Marked MOSELL on a disc.   Value $1000-1500

Rhinestone bracelet with bow shaped center. Length 7 inches. 1940's.
                    Value $65-95

Bracelet, 1940's. Rigid center piece with rhinestones, blue stones and pearls and two long metal links.
Value $200-250

Slightly different rhinestone bracelet of the 1940's. Narrow single band of nicely faceted hand set rhinestones.
Value $95-150

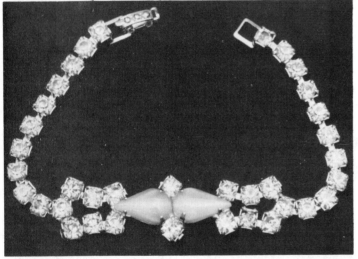

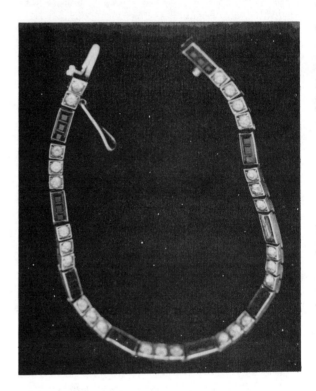

Bracelet. Late 1940's. Blue stones with irridescent blue glass center stones, probably part of a set.
Value $65-100

1930's rhinestone and blue stones set in sterling silver. Narrow bracelet with safety catch. Unmarked but fine quality.
Value $250-300

1930's rigid bracelet, green painted wood with green stones pasted in.
Value $100-150

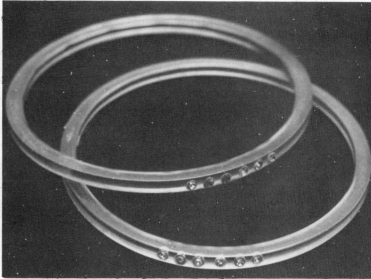

Narrow celluloid bracelet with six green stones. 1930's. Value $95-150
Narrow celluloid bracelet with six red stones. Value $95-150
These were usually worn in twos or threes.

Bracelet. Typical narrow band of rhinestones with large center detail.
In this case one large center stone and smaller surrounding stones.
Band is ⅛''. Value $60-85

Quite different wide bracelet of white metal with rhinestones. ¾'' wide.
Late 1930's or early 1940's. Value $150-200

1930's bracelet. Alternating round and square blue stones set in sterling
silver. The simplest possible approach to jewelry. Value $125-175

Rhinestone and blue stone bracelet, 1949. In original retailer's box, ¾ inch
wide, safety chain. Value $125-250

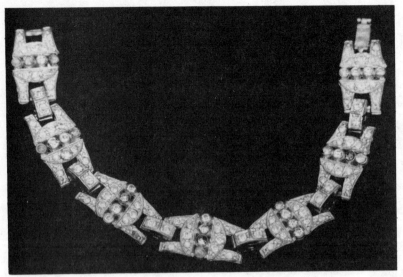

1930's bracelet. Inexpensively made but entirely characteristic of the period. ½ inch wide.   Value $100-175

Flexible bracelet with rhinestones. These are easy to wear and are now prime collectors items. Early 1940s.   Value $175-195

Wide 2¾'' bracelet with clusters and bands of rhinestones. 1930's. Celluloid   Value $250-300

Rigid white metal bracelet of the 1930's with safety chain. Center row of bright green stones between rows of rhinestones. These bracelets are highly desirable.   Value $300-400

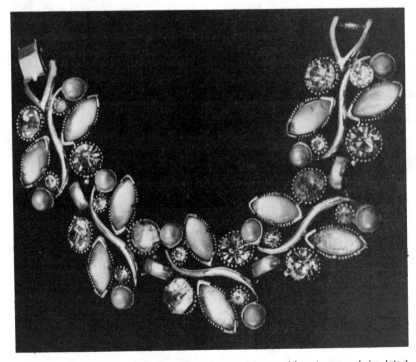

Wide (Approx. 2½ inches) bracelet of imitation moonstones, blue stones and simulated pearls. Marked on clasp SELRO CORP. This manufacturer is still doing business as The Selro Corp. and is located in New York.   Value $195-225

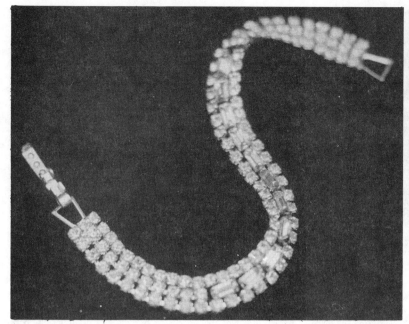

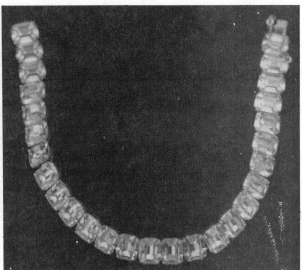

Bracelet 7'' long with safety chain. 27 faceted pink stones, hand set. Good quality.   Value $150-200

Another narrow bracelet with a look of fragility. The eleven baguette stones in the center give the piece an expensive air. 1940's.   Value $125-175

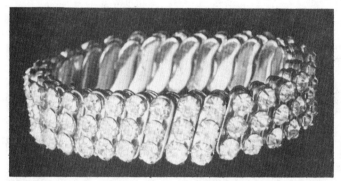

Flexible bracelet with three rows of rhinestones. These are all more or less the same and are rarely seen with colored stones.

Value $150-175

Unmarked 1940's bracelet. Rhinestones with center row of opaque white stones, probably part of a set.   Value $65-85

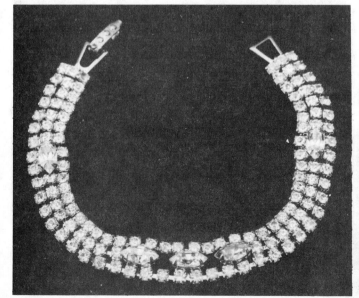

Dainty maroon rhinestone bracelet of the late 1940's or early 1950's. These smaller bracelets are becoming more difficult to find than the wider type.   Value $75-95

1930's base metal bracelet with safety chain. Bands of rhinestones and black glass stones. Bracelet is ⅜ inch wide.   Value $200-300

Well made bracelet of imitation pearls and rhinestones. Guard chain and rhinestones on clasp. As with much of this jewelry which has such visual appeal the designer was obviously influenced by the jewelry designs of the 18th century. Very fine quality but unsigned. Value $100-150

Charm bracelet with framed devil faces interspersed with blue and amber discs with silver heads glued on each. Silver colored base metal. Not only are charm bracelets rising in popularity but those such as this one with human, mythological or even devilish subjects are developing into a whole subcategory of collecting. 1950s. Marked FLORENZA on back of each of framed face. Value $150-200

1930s bracelet. Each metal link has rhinestone center with cuts radiating out from stone. Most interesting snap closure is marked FISCHERS PAT, SNAP. William Fischer produced jewelry in New York as early as 1922. I have seen similar necklaces with the snap and mark and with different colored stones. This is an attractive and wearable piece. William Fischer, NY since 1922. Value $135-195

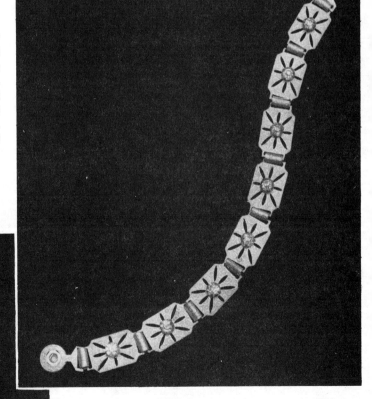

Very attractive 1" wide bracelet by Coro. Signed in script on clasp. Separate links, each of two clusters of pink stones and rhinestones. Value $135-175

This bracelet, earrings and pin set is part of the world of fascinating 'faces' jewelry. Rather eclectic design work but of great interest and a departure from the traditional work of the time. The various colors and shapes of the stones alone would command attention, the faces are well detailed and invite closer attention. Which is after all, the role of jewelry. This kind of jewelry is rising very rapidly in price. Not signed, few of these types are.
Value of set $200-300

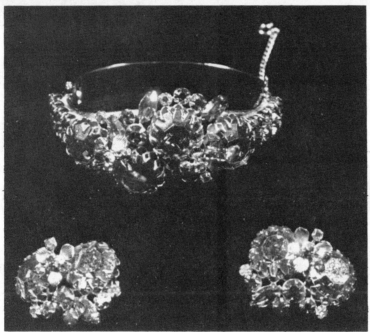

An outstanding bracelet and earrings by Alice Caviness Gold tone metal. The rigid bracelet and matching earrings have aurora borealis stones in shades of purple. All pieces are signed. Value $450-650

Pearl and rhinestone set by MIRIAM HASKELL. 4 strand gray strand bracelet with its flower head clasp set with the usual Haskell tiny rhinestones and seed pearls and a large round pearl center. Clip back earrings match this clasp. Gold colored metal. Simple and beautiful. Signed MIRIAM HASKELL. Value $400-500

233

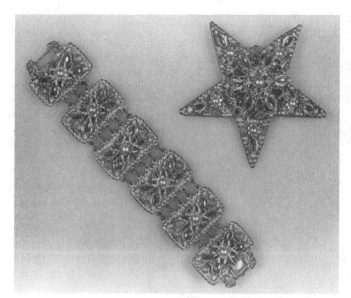

A theatrical looking set of bracelet and pin by ALEXANDER KORDA. The wide bracelet of gilded base metal has pearl centers with radiating star points made up of flower heads on open work metal. The small pearl centers are surrounded by colored stones - red, green blue, purple and blue enamel accents. The nicely detailed catch has a red stone. Back of bracelet is marked in two places - THIEF OF BAGDAD KORDA. Alexander Korda directed this famous film .
A few pieces of this jewelry is beginning to surface, almost all made in the same way, but the mark is rare enough to excite intense interest and consequent price rises.   Value $1000-1800

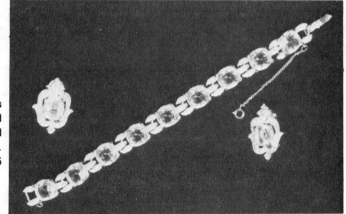

Jewelry bearing the JOMAZ name is usually well done. Although the mark is not too easily found, it is well worth searching for. This bracelet is composed of articulated sections, each with a clear yellow stone set in silvery metal and framed with rhinestones. Both clip back earrings and bracelet are signed. JOMAZ.   Value of set $250-295

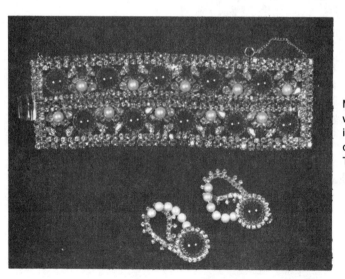

Matching bracelet and earrings. This wide (2½'') bracelet features black stones with rhinestones, tiny pearls and aurora borealis stones, each line of which is flanked by rows of rhinestones and aurora borealis. The earrings, which are certainly of an original design, are signed HOBÉ. The bracelet is not signed. These wide bracelets are achieving real status. 1940s. Value $600-750 set

Wide (1½'') bracelet by HOBÉ. White opaque stones banded with separate circular rhinestones and baguette bands of rhinestones. Outer lines have the white stones and rhinestones. Signed HOBÉ. These wide bracelets can be very flattering to the wrist. 1940s.   Value $200-250

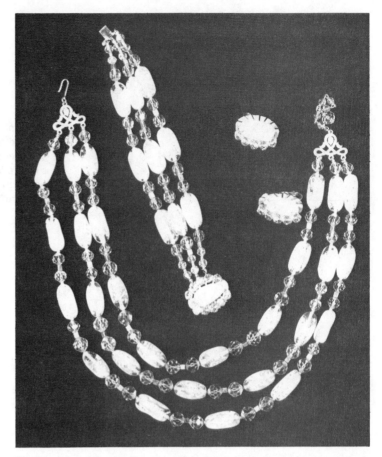

The owner/collector calls this set 'sweet'. It does have a particularly pretty look with its green enamel leaves and pink stones. The design too is delicate looking yet frothy. Very appealing. An early 1940s design by Katz for CORO.

Value of 3 piece set $350-450

Bead jewelry of the great costume jewelry period is becoming increasingly popular. This triple strand of pink glass beads intersperced with opaque long pink beads combines with the matching bracelet and earrings to make a pretty, very feminine statement. Only the bracelet and earrings are marked TRIFARI. Late 1940s.

Value of set $300-350

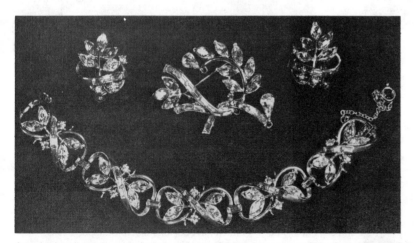

A typical well made and charming set by CORO from the 1940s. Topaz and light green stones highlight the bracelet, earrings and pin.

Value $300-450

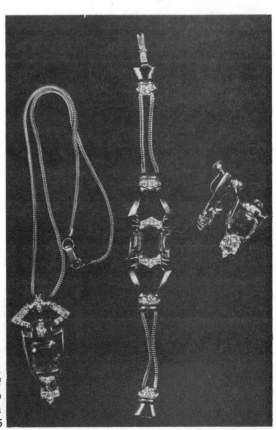

This necklace, bracelet and earring set, although unmarked is high quality jewelry. The design work is classic, the stones are fine quality. The moveable pendant of the necklace is carried on a chain, the bracelet strap is a double chain joined in two places with rhinestone studded gold bars, the center stone on all four pieces is a large faceted blue. The earrings are screw back.

Value of set $200-275

235

A floral pin and earrings set of obvious quality. Light red stones cunningly set in curled gold-wash sterling silver petals which hold the stones in place. The gold over silver gives the brooch a lovely buffed 'rose gold' finish. This set is most effective for its coloration, design work and upscale execution rather than originality. Stamped PENNINO STERLING. Early 1940s. The Pennino signature is not easy to find on jewelry.   Value $450-500

A rather grand pin and earring set. The pin measures 2½'' x 2'' with the usual impressive stones set in rhodium. Each piece is marked EISENBERG. 1940s.
Value $450-650

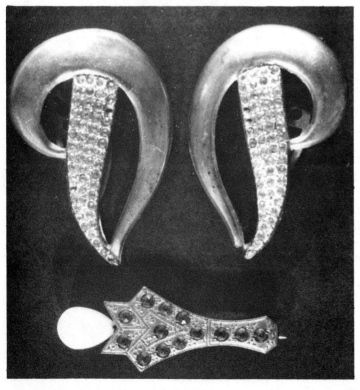

A pair of dress clips and a rather bizarre pin all of the 1930s. The dress clips are fairly effectively simple and with the lead looking-finish metal of the time. The tiny rhinestones are still intact and in good condition. These matching clips have gilt clips, unusual since the clips nearly always match the body of a piece. Stamped J.N.C. 2½'' x 2''.

The pin at the bottom of the photograph has the typical flat look of the 1930s, the rhinestones are still twinkling and all intact and all would have been fine had the designer left well enough alone. The opaque white bead at the top seems totally incongruous. Unmarked 2½'' x 1''.   Value dress clips $175-225
Pin/Brooch $100-150

Eisenberg set, pin and earrings. Each is marked Eisenberg. Pin measures 2" x 1½" and has the stones set in rhodium. 1940s.   Value $450-650

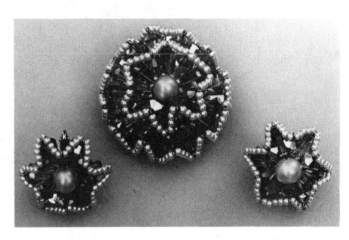

This pin and clip back earrings are reminiscent of the older crochet doilies with their starched and ruffled edges. Very pretty 2" pin of lilac beads with small pearls outlining the ruffled edge. Matching clip back earrings are 1½" and like the pin have a large round pearl center. All pieces are marked VEN-DOME   Value of set $145-185

SCHIAPARELLI set, pin and matching earrings. An amazing combination of colors on this 2½" pin - orange, red and clear. The stones are molded in such a way as to throw back bright irridescent flashes when the brooch or earrings move on the body. The clip back earrings have a large orange stone with white effects and red stones. Signed SCHIAPARELLI in script on oblong disk on back of pin and on clip of each earring.   Value $400-500

This extravaganza in rhinestones is by SCHIAPARELLI. The pin with its crystal drop is 4" long, silvery metal and signed on back of the large top rhinestone on a raised disc. Each earring consists of two family-sized rhinestones and each is marked on the clip back with the SCHAPIARELLI name. 1940s.
          Value of set $600-700

This set, pin and earrings, is not only pretty and well done, it is in its original box. The pin has a full complement of brass leaves, a fall of baguette rhinestones balanced by a line of circular pronged topaz stones. The earrings are screw back and each is marked. The pin is marked 1/20 12KG with an arrow through the letters CA. The box itself is a lovely green velvet and it bears a label reading CA GUARANTEED QUALITY WORKMANSHIP AND FINISH. A lightweight, delicate set.   Value of set in original box $300-400

This stylized flower head with its center clear blue stone set in gold wash sterling silver is marked MAZER and STERLING. The matching earrings are centered with the same blue stone and have the same gold wash over the sterling silver. Earrings are marked only STERLING. 1940s.   Value of set $300-350

This snake bangle bracelet depicts a two headed creature with green stone eyes and green stones for trim. Cabachons on the heads are an orange-peach shade. The bracelet itself is realistically 'scaly'. Matching clip back earrings. This set is marked TRIFARI and again the imagination of the designer is evident. Snakes as a jewelry motif have always been popular which is certainly surprising given the general antipithy to the reptiles   Value $200-400

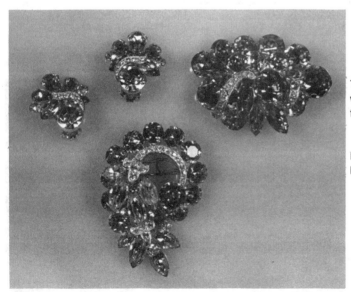

Top: Eisenberg jewelry in colors is finding a separate niche in the collecting world. These stones are deep pink, lighter pink, and lavender set in rhodium-finish metal. Marked in block letters EISENBERG on both pin and earrings.   Value $400-600

Pale yellow and lavender stones with rhinestones. 2½'' x 1¼'' pin is marked EISENBERG and numbered.   Value $300-500

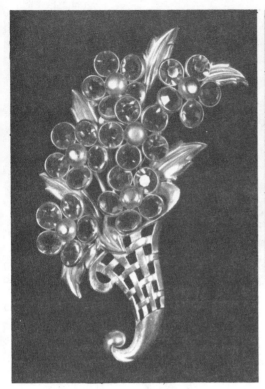

This unsigned matching bracelet, earrings and brooch/pin set has all the properties of very upscale jewelry. This is the kind of set which even though unsigned has virtually disappeared by nature of its visual appeal and excellence of manufacture. Even lacking a well-known name it is a desirable and collectible set. Value $600-800

At a social evening you could probably fool your friendly neighborhood jeweler with some BOUCHER. Good taste above all is always evident, restraint, excellent workmanship design and quality are almost always present in signed Boucher. The bracelet is composed of 5 links featuring outside rows of baguette rhinestones enclosing the single row of red stone baguettes. Silver metal, safety catch. Signed BOUCHER center back. Value $300-400

This pin has stones of a particularly lovely shade of cranberry. The metal is gold colored, it has a rhinestone stem. Signed BOUCHER and numbered. Value $200-250

This BOUCHER pin features cascading scrolls of rhinestones set in silvery metal contrasting with the vivid red baguette stones. A classic design. Signed BOUCHER and numbered. Value $200-250

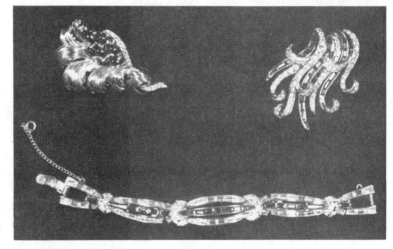

Miriam Haskell. Top - matching pin and earrings. Gold tone pin (measures 4'' x 2'') is overall tiny seed pearls with larger center pearl. The earrings are marked on the clips with the old horseshoe mark. Value $400-500

Lower right of photo - Haskell pin measures 3'' x 1¾'', gold tone, old horseshoe mark MIRIAM HASKELL. c.late 1930s.

Value $275-325

239

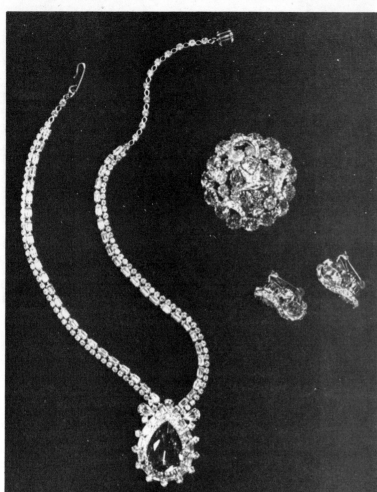

This 20'' necklace has a 1'' pink/purple stone in its center drop which is suspended from a double strand of rhinestones. Signed HOBÉ in an oval on back of pendant. Silver colored metal. A classic jewelry design

Value $200-300

Right: Matching pin and earrings, amber colored stones with rhinestones. Pin measures 2'' x 2'', clip back earrings are 1''. Gold colored metal. Only the earrings are signed - Hobé .

Value, set $125-195

Pin and earrings set. Green irridescent stones on filagree background of gilt metal. Signed STANLEY HAGLER, N.Y.C. A scarce mark. Value, set $95-125

Upper right: A pin which manages to catch the movement of a streaking comet. Red, lavender pale blue and rhinestones with irridescent stones in the center make for a very pretty, expressive bauble. Signed FLORENZA. This is an excellent example of some of the good jewelry Florenza made, we are more familiar with their work on accessories. 1950s. Value $85-95

Was this a happy design accident or was it really intended to be the all-seeing eye? One of the imponderables of the fashion jewelry world. It is certainly 'eye-catching'. The large pink opaque center stone is embedded in small rhinestones and the baguette stones are framed in silver toned metal. An interesting pin. Signed Mazer Bros. 1940s.

Value $95-125

240

Gold overlay chain and pendant with light topaz colored stone. Very fine workmanship. Value $75-100

Blue stone pendant on silvery chain, 1942. Value $45-65

A rather spectacular unmarked pendant, originally on a thin chain. Gilt backed sprays of rhinestones descend from the pendant through a circle of bright red stones. All the stones are hand set. 3" long. Mid 1940s. Value $75-125

An overall rhinestone locket, somewhat difficult to find these. Interior brass frames for two photographs. Wearable and pretty. 1940s.
Value $125-165

1930's lavaliere originally attached to chain. As with much of this early, less expensive jewelry it has a primitive look but is actually well designed and made. Value $75-150

Lavaliere rhinestone and gilt with center rhinestones and three drops. To be worn on a chain. 1940's. Value $45-55

A charming California souvenir item, probably 1930s. Rhinestones frame the convex glass sided brass pendant. One side pictures a fisherman hooking his fish looking remarkably like genuine gold, the reverse pictures two horses heads. Interesting.
Value $85-125

A lovely locket with frames for two pictures. Gold filled with "brilliants" and heavy embossing. Although these pieces do contain rhinestones they, in fact, predate the true rhinestone era and are generally considered late Victorian jewelry. The owner's grandmother bought this from a Sears catalog c.1902.
Value $120-155

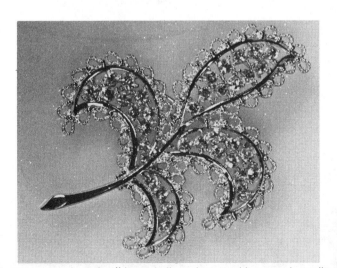

Pin, approximately 4" long, 4 silvery leaves with aurora borealis stones. Marked EMMONS, a scarce mark. Early 1950s. Value $135-175

This rhinestone and birds-on-nest pin has outstanding workmanship and design. Obviously expensive when first sold it bears no markings, and many collectors who do not collect unmarked pieces would neglect it. This jewelry is proof positive that quality is where you find it, regardless of signature. This brooch is cleverly designed; the birds hover over a nest full of faux pearl eggs and with the spray the piece is nicely balanced. Value $175-200

Finely crafted and elegant, this is a large, 4"x3", brooch by Hattie Carnegie. Heavy, brightly gilded and restrained in the manner of much Hattie Carnegie jewelry, this is definitely statement jewelry. In the center of each flower are clusters of tiny rhinestones. Very effective either for day or evening wear.   Value $350-450

A wonderful example of why collectors should not limit themselves only to signed jewelry. This is not marked, but is magnificent - dazzling jewels, tiara shaped bouquet of flower heads and 11 pendant drops to entice attention. A fantastic large brooch.   Value $400-650

Leaf pin by Trifari. Interesting "free-standing" rhinestones form the center of each leaf which is then framed by smaller rhinestones. Signed on back. Value $165-195

Two large rhinestone flower heads are surrounded by large rhinestone leaves. This spray is elegant and marked MAZER.   Value $195-250

When worn this brooch seems about to jump off the garment. It is an exciting pin perhaps intended to represent a dandelion with the same light, airy feeling of that little plant. Gold colored metal with brilliant hand set rhinestones.

Value $135-16

Outstanding double clip in the shape of a bow. Rhinestones outlined with a red stone border, gilt. 3¼" long, marked with 3 different patent numbers – the joining piece and clips have been patented separately from the jewelry design. No manufacturer's mark. Probably 1930s. Value $150-225

Spectacular rather understates the visual impact of this brooch. Although its size, 5" x 4¼" and its brilliant large green stones, and equally brilliant large rhinestones should make it seem garish, it is in fact one of the most gorgeous of the 1930s pins. The bow literally ties it all together. Unmarked. Value $195-250

Because this brooch looks so genuine it defies detection, this is the kind of rhinestone jewelry which requires a bodyguard should you decide to wear it. Set in filagree are stones varying from tiny to small, all deeply set in the frame. The design is classic with its central flower motif. A refined, genteel piece not altogether in keeping with the mood of the period, but decidedly lovely. Unmarked. 1930's 3"x2". Value $175-300

This brooch measures 3"x3" and is by KRAMER. It is overall rhinestone and all the stones are hand set. Quality jewelry. Marked KRAMER OF NEW YORK on a disc. Value $150-250

This elephant is a fun piece, stylized and certainly not like any elephant you are likely to see. Gilt with blue stones, red stripes and rhinestone trunk, a tiny red stone surrounded by rhinestones on his tail, green and red stones to liven up his bulk. 1960's, unmarked and probably for the collector of elephants or whimsy or those who are now legion - collectors of jeweled animals. Value $40-65

This ferocious creature with green glass eyes, red enamel tongue and white enamel teeth is a harmless brooch made in the 1970s. The black enamel stripes and high gilding make it attractive to the collector of costume animals.   Value $40-55

Right - This clip is so stupendous it is almost priceless. Almost 4'' long, the quality of the stones and the setting is marvelous. Very heavy with the clip marked EISENBERG ORIGINAL. After all these years, the effect is mezmerizing, with no loss of brilliance. A Florence Nathan design of 1942   Value $1000-1500
This is a beautifully designed and executed pin of the 1940s by Eisenberg. Marked EISENBERG ICE on the back it is indeed lovely, but much lighter than the old clip and very different in attitude. This was bought from a dealer in 1986 for $55. 2½''x2¼''   Value $145-250

Rhinestone rooster, 1940's.
Value $40-50

These whimsical animals and birds decorated with rhinestones and colored stones have become popular with collectors of other manifestations of those creatures. The pins are worn as a badge. The owl is heavy, 2½'' long with a large center blue stone and purple stone eyes. The gilt on the base metal is somewhat worn. 1930s.
Value $35-45
Center - The early 1970s stylized owl is bright gilt and black enamel with tiny rhinestones surrounding the eyes. This small pin is marked A 1261.
Value $25-35
The parrot on the right has a folk art look as he sits on his perch. Overall tiny, pasted-in rhinestones with a red stone for the eye. This is a 1930s pin. The mark is a four leaf clover.   Value $40-50

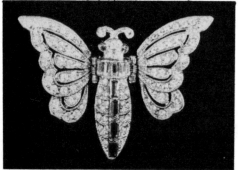

Insect pin of the early 1940's. Multi-colored stones.
Value $45-65

This butterfly clip of rhinestones and green stones is well designed and exhibits the fine detail of excellent workmanship as well as the typical flat look of the 1930s. The wings are on tiny springs.   Value $95-150

This mythic creature with his crown and wings decorated with large stones is unusual and artistic. The brooch exhibits a sense of life and livliness and is, in general, a rather surprising piece of jewelry. It is a wonderful example of the wit which some early designers showed.   Value $175-225

This pin shows the usual Trifari excellence. 2'' long, deep blue pear-shaped stones border 3 rhinestone flower heads centered with small blue stones. Marked on stem. Designed by Alfred Philippi in 1940
                    Value $195-250

Brooch pin. This is an actual mesh purse with hand set amethyst and pink stones. Purse to top of clasp is 3½'' long. Unmarked and unique. Purchased at Neiman-Marcus, Dallas in the early 1940s.   Value $135-195

Beautifully designed and executed spray pin with rhinestone flowers. Possibly KREMENTZ but unmarked. Rhodium.
                    Value $150-200

Well made pin, silvery white metal, 1948.   Value $125-185

Starfish shaped pin, greenish-blue stones set in black metal. Approx. 3'' wide, late 1940's. Signed MANDLE.
Value $65-95

Rhinestone bar pin of the 1930's. 1½'' across.
Value $75-100

Magnificent circular pin-brooch by Hobé. Marked on back HOBÉ Because of the excellence of the designs and the quality of the jewelry Hobé is a sought after name for collector.
Value $350-500

Two heart-shaped matching pins. 1¼'' long and wide, overall rhinestones. Unmarked. Late 1940's.
Value $85-125 each

Appealing and well made key pin. Blue stones, approx. 1½'', unmarked, good detail. 1950's.
Value $30-40

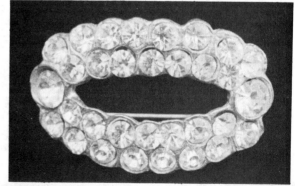

Brooch-pin of the early 1940's. Rhinestones pasted in shallow cups. 1½''.
Value $40-50

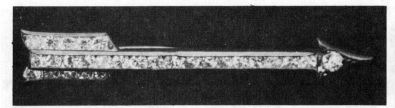

1930's arrow pin. Small rhinestones in sterling silver. Excellent quality stones.
Value $75-95

Pin-brooch. Typical 1930's style highlighted by good quality center square stone. 2½'' across.　　　　Value $95-145

Massive looking brooch with blue stones in center; tentacle-like thin brass frames holding hand-set yellow stones; large red stones and silvered simulated pearls in a baroque shape. Brass filigree around red stones. A good illustration of the often bizarre but intriguing jewelry of the period. Marked on disc on back SCHREINER, NEW YORK. When laid flat this brooch reaches 1¼'' off the surface. It is approx. 3⅛'' round.　　　　Value $300-400

A striking pin. Eye-catching blue stones are secondary to the message – What? Who? Where? When? 1950s. Weiss.
Value $150-195

Brooch in silvery metal, pink stones, rhinestone center, pearl drop, 1940s.
Value $45-65

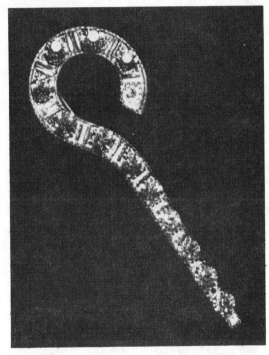

This 1930s question mark is part of a large collection of nothing but rhinestone and colored stone question marks. This is 3'' long with Austrian stones hand set in thin brass. It is a pin with a long shaft on back.
Value $145-195

A rather strange combination of colors and materials in this brooch. Overall patterned green glass with smaller purple stones with one small green stone in each cluster. 2¾'' x 2½''. Marked on disc on back SCHREINER, New York. Late 1940s.

Value $150-195

247

CORO brooch. 2½'' free form thin brass with large center rhinestones. Marked CORO in script.   Value $75-125

A spectacular rhinestone brooch which can be worn as a pendant. Female nude figure pouring from a container. Bronze. Marked OR.   Value $300-400

One of the many type initial pins in rhinestones. Novelty items were made by most manufacturers. This is on the original card and is by Nemo of New York. Poor quality but interesting. Its value is enhanced by its definite attribution.   Value $40-50

Circular pin-brooch, gold wash over sterling, rhinestones. Rather simple design for its time. 1930's.   Value $100-145

Brilliant well made brooch of the 1940's. Interesting use of variously shaped rhinestones all of which are hand set.   Value $150-200

Pin brooch marked MADE AUSTRIA. Beautifully faceted hand set crystals. Fine quality.
Value $165-245

Rather primitive, heavy bow pin of the 1930's set with bluish green stones. Gilt worn but a good example of early, lower line jewelry.
Value $40-60

Elegant floral pin by Hattie Carnegie, 1940's. Flower head is small amber colored stones. Disc on back reads HATTIE® CARNEGIE. 2½''.
Value $200-275

Circular pin-brooch, pink stones, 1950s, 4¼'',
Value $45-65

Elephant pin. Brown finish over silvery metal, white enamel tusks, red stone eye and rhinestones in the trunk and head. 1960s.　　Value $35-50

Brooch of sterling silver. Interesting design, the two drops of chain and rhinestones lend a sense of balance to the heavy goldtone metal top. Marked ''sterling'' in two places. Another example of how different sized stones lend appeal to a piece, this combines 8 different size rhinestones.

Value $135-195

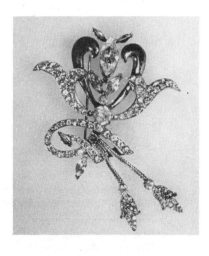

Large, blantantly fake brooch of the 1930s. The large stones are deep blue with rhinestone accents. Base metal. This has the simple approach of folk art, direct and colorful.

Value $145-195

The Art Deco Period with its vivid, striking colors is exemplified here. The red enamel trunk of this lush rhinestone-studded tree is an impressive piece of work, both in design and execution. The small rhinestones are deeply bezeled with occasional touches of green and blue. Highly imaginative and beautifully finished. Unmarked. 1930s. The brooch measures 3½'' x 2¼'' and is set in sterling. Unique. A Pilippe design for Trifari.

Value $500-800

A stunning piece of jewelry. Overall hand set rhinestones in a magnificent setting. The original paper label reads FOR THE WORLD'S BEST MR. JOHN COUTOURIER JEWELS. This brooch has never been worn. Jewelry by Mr. John is rarely found. Unless the labels or boxes are intact the jewelry itself is not marked.

Value $600-1000

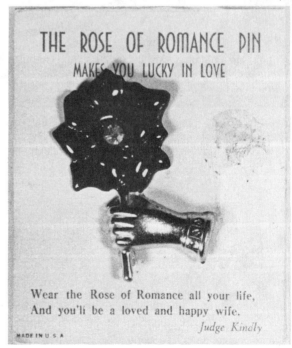

The card on which this hand pin is displayed is almost as valuable and captivating as the brooch itself. Except for the notation, itself almost an anachronism MADE IN THE USA the jewelry is unmarked. Part of a collection of hands, the black enameled pin boasts a large rhinestone in its center.

Value of pin on card $65-85

Pin alone $40-50

250

Unmarked Deco pin. Pink stones. Unusual.   Value $75-100

Brooch of tiny seed pearls, rhinestones and large faux baroque pearl. Large size 2½" x 2" and fairly heavy. Signed on disc on filagree back, MIRIAM HASKELL.   Value $200-300

A most unusual and decorative pin. A large vase of flowers with a clear pink stone as the container, green enameled leaves, multi-colored flowers with small pink, blue and rhinestone centers and large clear blue and topaz colored stones. Brass, well made, imaginitive but unmarked. 1930s.
Value $400-450

3" brooch in free form style: Gold wash over sterling with rhinestones and red stones. Marked STERLING BY GLAMOUR on an applied disc. This is a Coro mark.
Value $95-150

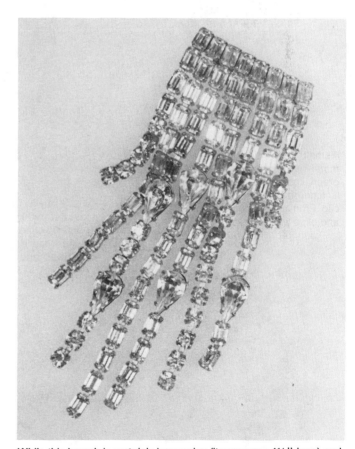

While this brooch is certainly impressive (it measures 4½" long) and its differently shaped rhinestones attractive, the design work seems somewhat incomplete. Here is a case where the piece will command many more dollars than is warranted because it is by LILY DACHE. Marked on back. Lily Dache jewelry is scarce.

Value $400-600

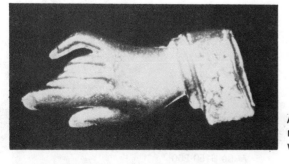

A tiny graceful hand cuffed with equally tiny rhinestones. This engaging pin measures only 1¼". 1940s. This has vast appeal, not only to collectors of rhinestone whimsies but also to many collectors of hands, in whatever guise. Value $65-95

251

This brooch which measures 1¼"x1" is too realistic to be worn comfortably without a guard. The design is classic, the rhinestones small and of superior quality. The restraint shown here is uncharacteristic during this period of manufacture. It is elegant and Opera Opening wearable. c. 1923-24. Sterling silver. Not marked.   Value $300-350

A small (1½") dress clip. Gilt over base metal. Rhinestones pasted in. Red, green, blue and topaz accent stones. Enamelled center star. Ladies Auxiliary clip. From a collection of fraternal pins and clips with rhinestones. 1930s.
Value $50-85

Eagle and stripes in this World War II pin. Gold wash over sterling, the gold shows some wear. The eagle has a red stone eye and rhinestone wings. This pin has added value as a military collectible.   Value $75-100

Blackamoor Pin. Turban with red stone and top rhinestones. V neckline outlined in red stones, rhinestones at top and bottom of V. Unsigned, a fairly common form during the 1930s. This is of a somewhat later period. Value $60-80

A high quality fraternal dress clip of the very late 1930s or early 1940s. All over rhinestones of varying sizes with a small white enamelled center with a blue star and a narrow blue border AMERICAN LEGION AUXILIARY. No maker's mark   Value $100-125

The large, light green stones surrounded by darker, smaller green stones enhance an otherwise mundane pin by Celebrity of NY. The pin is marked with a small applied medallion. Gilt metal.
Value $65-85

The restrained elegance of TRIFARI in this brooch. A lovely cluster of hand set rhinestones seems to tie the ribbon. Marked crown/TRIFARI on back.
Value $150-200

The whimsy which is evident in many of Adolph Katz' designs is exhibited in this piece. Here is his "doorknocker" brooch, marked CORO in script on the back. It can only be categorized as wonderful. Gilded brass is enhanced by a top blue stone and a blue stone in the circle below. A green stone and a bottom rhinestone complete harmonious touches of color on the nicely decorated metal. The knocker can be raised.
Value $175-225

This floral spray brooch is 3½" long, gold wash over sterling, distinguished by the ingenuity of the way the pasted-in rhinestones are set in embossed base metal to give the flowers an expensive look. Each center is a green stone. Late 1930s, very early 1940s.
Value $95-145

Three clips by TRIFARI. The workmanship is superb and the characterizations so lively and compelling, this trio really does stop pedestrian traffic. Enameled, colored stones and rhinestones.   Value set of three $450-650
A Philippi design of Jan. 1945

Right:
A 1930s pin, 3½''x2½'', signed on disc on back REINAD, N.Y.C. which immediately adds to the interest of this unusual brooch. A veritable multi-colored stone bouquet rises out of the rhinestone container. Blue green topaz and rhinestone give the pin a focus, while not detracting from the overall rhinestone effect.   Value $300-400

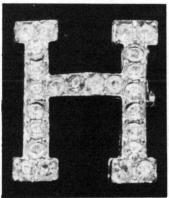

Rhinestone initial H. All letters of the alphabet were produced by many companies as initial pins. This is rather poor quality but certainly is clear in its intention.   Value $20-30

Brooch of the 1930's. 2½'' long, purple center stones, rhinestones, in base metal.
Value $75-100

Very heavy brooch with purple stones and rhinestones. Brass. Marked McCLELLAND BARCLAY on back. 1930s. One large purple stone has small chip but piece is rare.
Value $150-200
If perfect $400-500

Pin. Late 1930's. Rhinestone and square blue stones pasted in except for center stone. Good quality.   Value $60-80

253

Brooch of the 1930's, 2½'' long. A nice example of the form.
Value $145-195

1950's pin. Two shades of blue stones in open design which gives the piece an airy feeling.
Value $60-80

1930's pin-brooch, rhinestone and deep blue stones in various shapes. Marked ''H Pomerantz & Co., N.Y.'' A worthwhile addition to a collection.
Value $150-185

1930s brooch, heavy and with several obviously replaced stones. Entirely typical of the period and a desirable piece. Large purple stones have open backs. The underside of this brooch is nicely finished. 4'' long.

Value $60-75
If perfect $135-175

Brooch by LISNER. Red stones in gilt metal. Marked LISNER on back. Brooch is 2¼'' long. Lisner also carded some of its jewelry.
Value $100-135

254

Small pin by Coro made particularly attractive by its combination of colored stones, blue, green and rhinestones. A neat little bouquet. Marked CORO in script on back.   Value $75-145

One of the typical brilliant, flashing styles of the 1950's is this pin with most of its rhinestones hand set. Almost 2'' round.   Value $125-145

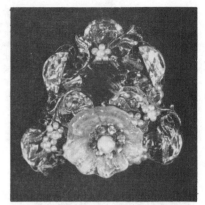

Brooch by Miriam Haskell. Marked with the applied disc on back, it has the typical combination of seed pearls, multi-colored stones - pink, lavender, green, clear and rhinestones - on a rather small piece of jewelry. These often daring, unorthodox combinations of colors and material, together with some of the somewhat unusual design work are what makes Haskell so collectible.   Value $150-195

Left:
A very effective crystal and rhinestone pin which shows to advantage in daylight as well as artificial light. 2'' round, it is by VENDOME. Marked on a disc on a filagreed silvery back.   Value $100-150

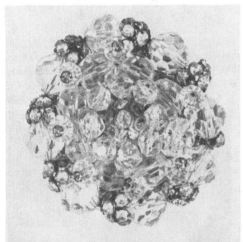

Early 1940's pin-brooch. App. 1½''. Stones are hand set.   Value $45-60

Set of matching pins. Dainty rhinestone and pearl. Late 1940's. Approx. ½'' ea.   Value $40-50

A stunning set of brooch-pins. Open centers to allow color of costume to highlight the rhinestones. Stones are fine quality Czechoslovakian and well set. Probably 1920s.   Value each, $125-195

Magnificent clip by EISENBERG. Marked EISENBERG ORIGINAL. Beautifully designed and executed in spite of the base metal setting. 3½'' x 2½'', 1930s. Pieces of the size and quality are rare and choice. 1942.
Designed by Florence Nathan   Value $850-1500

255

Small (approx. 1¼'') pin. Rhinestones in white metal. 1930's. Value $40-50

Elegant feather brooch-pin, rhinestones in sterling, by Trifari. Also marked PATENTED: 1940's. Value $200-250

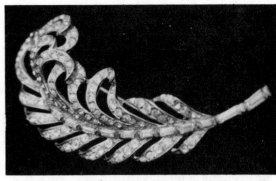

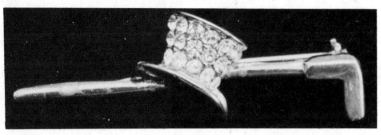

Whimsical pin of the 1930's. Top hat with rhinestones, gilt walking stick. Value $50-75

Square brooch-pin, 12 red stones separated by rows of rhinestones. Approx. 1¾'' by 1''. Marked on back KRAMER OF NEW YORK. This pin has matching earrings. 1940s. Value of brooch, $150-175 Vlaue, set $225-250

Impressive 1960's pin. Lavender and purple stones and small rhinestones in gilt metal. Value $60-75

1940's pin. Deep red stones and small pearls. Outer stones and center stone hand set. Although this is nicely crafted and has the fairly uncommon red stones, the basic design was widely used with variations. Value $50-65

Left: 2¼'' long dress clip in the characteristic design of the period. Deeply bezelled center stone, the other rhinestones pasted-in but still in excellent condition. Marked DOCTOR DRESS on the clip. Rare. Value $750-1000

Right: Finding original carded jewelry is a challenge. Almost always lower line and lower priced this was expendable and consequently is scarce. Plastic with rhinestones, the original price and maker's name and logo are a tremendous asset to a definitive collection. The pin itself is unmarked. Lisner. Value $45-50

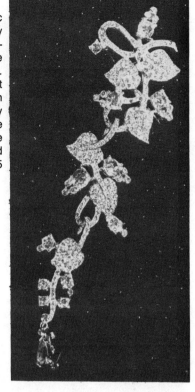

Right:

A wondrous pin. 1940's in a classic style, it has many small, good quality stones deeply set in. Made in three sections it was deliberately made to move with the body and so catch the light. This long, lovely brooch has its lowest section fitted with a separate pin which keeps the whole in line. A beautifully thought out and crafted brooch, a piece to point up the mistake collectors make when they pass up unmarked period jewelry.   Value $150-175

Left:

A brooch/pin of the 1930s. Striking with its 1¼'' center red stone and its original rhinestones pasted into the gilt finish over base metal frame.

Value $95-150

Star shaped pin with blue stones, outer ones hand set. Brass, 1939.

Value $40-50

Multi-colored 'stone' flower heads on spray. Marked 'Coro'. 1940's.

Value $40-50

Well designed pin which can also be worn as pendant. Gold wash over sterling with a large cluster of rhinestones opening to a peacock's tail of metal, blue stones and baguette rhinestones. 1940s unsigned.

Value $50-60

Novelty jewelry of the 1950's. Bicycle pin. Rhinestones pasted in.

Value $30-35

1940's pin brooch. Bright red stones. The design shows influence of military decorations.

Value $60-75

257

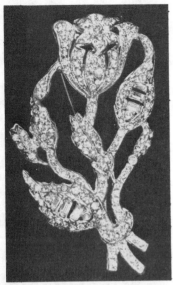

Circular pin with blue center stones. Marked CORO in rhomboid with Pegasus alongside on jewelry itself and CORO on pin back. Mid 1940's.   Value $55-75

Brooch of the 1930's. These are becoming difficult to find in good condition. Although this is the usual heavy piece it has a deceptive look of lightness. Rhinestones are pasted-in but the design is attractive. 4" long.
Value $145-195

Circular pin-brooch, pink stones. 1950's. $45-65

A very pretty pin by DeMario, 2½" long. Yellow plastic, gilt leaves and green stones with mother of pearl accents. Both the colors and tasteful combination of materials blend very well in this originally inexpensive piece of jewelry. 1940s.
Value $165-195

EISENBERG green stone and rhinestone pin. 1940's. Marked on back 'Eisenberg'.   Value $150-195

1930's brooch pin, unmarked. Large (3½" long) and showy.   Value $175-250

Brightly gilded angel by Hobé. Stylized pearl head surrounded by tiny rhinestones, rows of handset rhinestones comprise the body. Lovely pin, 2" long, marked on a disc HOBÉ and dated 1965.   Value $55-85

Dynasty jewelry. Lapel watch 4" long. Rhinestones all hand set but piece is not signed. Probably late 1940s or early 1950s. Watch in running condition.
Value $250-295

As intriguing a dress clip/pendant as ever was made. Mirror in frame with multicolored stones set deeply into bezels. Marked on back of clip AT 180 112. Probably late 1930s.
Value $195-250

258

This dashing brass hat with its large hand set rhinestones is a conversation piece brooch. 1940s.   Value $55-85

Brooch by MIRIAM HASKELL. The seed pearl, large baroque pearls, gilt metal accents and imaginative design work which characterizes much of Haskell. Marked on disc on filagree back.   Value $275-350

To the intelligent collector and researcher jewelry found in original boxes or cards is often more facinating than the jewelry piece itself. Such is the case with this carded pin of rhinestone and catalin. 1930s.

Value on original card $100-150

Snowflake   pendant, rhinestone and pearl, ruby colored   stone   center. 1940's.

Value $45-65

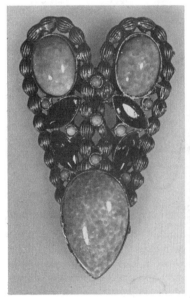

This little pin with its disparate elements is surprisingly pleasing. The blue stone in the star tops a rhinestone framed long-haired nude. Unmarked. 1940s. Gilt.   Value $75-95

A rather staggering, funky, clunky dress clip of the 1930s. It is 3½'' long with spotted opaque pinkish stones, large purple stones and smaller pink and turquoise stones. To the serious collector, this is an astounding, exciting acquisition. Heavy. Marked on back with a patent number.   Value $250-350

All early Eisenberg has to be seen to be truly appreciated. The size and refractive quality of the stones is unbelievable. Each of the large hand set faceted stones here is ¾'' long. The dress clip itself is the usual 3'' long. Marked EISENBERG ORIGINAL. At a recent antique show Eisenberg Original pieces were costing $600-700.

Value $600-800

Lower line jewelry initial. These were made by many companies and Coro manufactured them almost from the beginning. Unmarked. 1940s. Still worn by original owner who bought it in New York City.   Value $35-45

A pendant/pin of the 1940's distinguished by its classic design which makes it eminently wearable. Gold wash on sterling, 2½'', it has the ubiquitous 40's pearls and small rhinestones. Marked 'sterling'.

Value $95-125

259

One of the features of the 1930's rhinestone jewelry is the really wonderful enamel work on some of these older pieces. This impressive brooch is 2½" around, excluding the length of its five pendant drops. The seven large faceted, pronged rhinestones within the frame are fine quality and the back of the whole is gilded. This kind of jewelry is sophisticated and sought after but scarce. Value $350-500

A large and distinguished brooch. Gilt over base metal with 8 large faceted purple stones, hand set, separated by small flowers with pearl centers. Large faceted purple stone, hand set, measures 1¼". Overall dimensions are typical of the 1930s. 3½" x 3".

Value $350-450

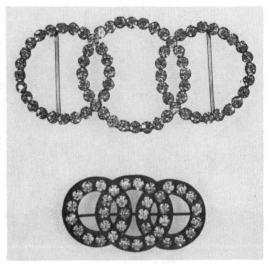

Typical Czechoslovakian pieces. Top is a long belt buckle, bottom is a pin/brooch, both have all hand set rhinestones of the usual superior quality, both are brass and both are from the 1930s.

Value of buckle $125-150
Value of pin $95-125

Pink plastic and rhinestone pin in a tasteful gold frame. Marked on disc in back ALICE CAVINESS. Her jewelry is scarce. Value $85-150

Thin brass setting for the magnificent old rhinestones. Czechoslovakia. 1930s pin. Value $65-85

A highly decorative pin with its gilt finish, 2 Peking glass beads, part of the costume covered in rhinestones the shirt partially enameled. 3" long and 3" wide it makes an impressive display. Unmarked. Being a collector is partly detective work which this pin proves - I own two exact duplicates made in sterling silver with no rhinestones and with silver balls instead of beads. One of the silver pins is marked MEXICO another I own is a silver colored base metal with sterling silver balls. This pin was designed by Louis Mark for Rice-Weiner & Co. in 1941.

Value $200-250

An unusually attractive souvenir pin, another growing segment of the rhinestone collecting field. Only 1¼", it has a surprising impact. Eiffel Tower on a background of mother-of-pearl surrounded by light green stones which are pasted in. Value $60-75

This bee pin measures 2½". The wings are on springs to give the effect of flight and add immeasurable interest. The quality rhinestones are enhanced by the shaded gold finish. Marked on tail back HATTIE CARNEGIE.

Value $300-400

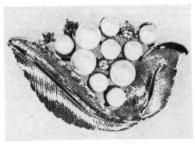

Tailored pin; gilt, pearls and rhinestones, marked with a star.

Value $45-55

260

One of Katz' inimitable designs, this bonnet is marked CORO in script. Lower line but charming. The bonnet sports green stones in the wreath of flowers and blue stones on the edge trim. Only 1¾'' long, this little bonnet has the usual attention to small details of all Katz' work.   Value $50-75

A small (¾''x¼'') rhinestone pin which spells out GOP. A man's lapel pin. Supposedly a convention souvenir.
Value $55-85

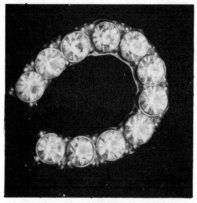

Rhinestone horseshoe pin crudely made but stones of good quality. 1930's.
Value $40-45

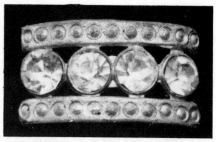

A rather primitive example of a 1930s brooch. Four large rhinestones pasted in unfinished white metal. A good example of the lowest line in this depression era jewelry.   Value $35-50

Remarkable shading in the large stones of this brooch. Lavender to opaque white. Approximately 2½'' round, it is wearable and lovely. Stones hand set. Marked KRAMER OF NEW YORK on disc.   Value $200-300

This Space Needle brooch is a souvenir of the World's Fair held in Seattle in 1962. It was inexpensive but certainly definitive since this was a centerpiece of the Fair. This pin was bought at the Fair but many are now turning up in thrift shops and other sales. This is not part of a rhinestone jewelry collection, although it certainly qualifies, but is much at home in a collection of World's Fair Memorabilia.   Value $30-50

Very early 1930s pin. Rhinestones and green stones set in gilded base metal with large celluloid pendant depicting traditional proposal scene. This pin has a little bit of everything and has enormous funky appeal.
Value $225-275

The vivid green of the stones of this floral spray are tied with a rhinestone band. The hand set stones are pronged with silver metal which gives added contrast to the deep color of the stones. A classic, timeless design beautifully constructed. The piece is unmarked but it bears the paper label of Mr. John. Rare. Value $400-600

261

The cameo did not escape the rhinestone craze, although the cameo on the left pre-dates the peak rhinestone period. Plastic, in silvery metal, the lovely lady has a rhinestone ear bob and another rhinestone at the neckline. 1920s. Rare. This is from a collection of cameos with rhinestones and portraits in frames which fit into such a collection.   Value $200-295

The portrait on the right is framed in thin brass with 4 poor quality rhinestones although the picture itself is signed and is under thin plastic. Very early 1930s.
Value $250-325

Early 1930s brooch. Rhinestones with one large square green stone at top of frame. Gilded base metal, a traditional romantic scene. The owner has in the last 3 years collected about 15 of these, all with different scenes, although they are difficult to find.   Value $200-250

Crown by Trifari. Sterling with multi-colored stones and an unusual plum pair at either end, blue stones etc. Marked Trifari. Designed by Alfred Philippe in 1944.
Value $175-225

Multi-colored stone crown pin. Unmarked and lower line. 1940's. This same design with slight variations was made by almost every manufacturer in different sizes. This pin is 1¼'' across and 1'' high to top of blue stone in crown.
Value $25-30

Crown by CORO. A complete collection of costume jewelry crowns could be made and this is one of many similar types. Marked in script and PAT. PEND. Designed by Katz. early 1940s   Value $65-95

This unsigned crown can also be worn as a pendant. Excellent quality. 1940s.
Value $60-80

Seven crowns from a large collection showing the diversity in size, quality and design work. Top crown from the 1950s, extreme right crown is better jewelry, bottom crown is older and poorly made. These vary in price from $25-85. None is marked.

Another of the crowns by CORO. 2" long with multi col-ored stones and rhinestones. This brooch has had the floral motif added to the bottom of crown which gives it a different look. Marked CORO.   Value $125-175

Selection of Christmas tree pins from a very large collection. These pins are now an important part of rhinestone collecting and have many devotees. Prices are rising accordingly. Almost any Christmas tree pin will now have a begin-ning price of $25 and the range is wide.

Christmas pin in the shape of stylized tree. Multi-colored stones with rhinestone at top. Excellent simple design. Early 1960's.   Value $40-60

Two recent pins by HOBE. These are small and marked only by the attached paper label. These Christmas tree pins are issued annually but once the season has passed are almost impossible to find. At issue, price was around $12.

BOUCHER PINS. This 'golden' hummingbird has a pearl head, a red stone eye and rhinestones on his wing. The sensation of motion here is uncanny. Signed BOUCHER and numbered. $250-300

LEFT: The peacock at his dazzling best. Turquoise and blue stone body and tips of feathers. Gold tone metal. This pin has a three dimensional look and has the lively aspect of most of Boucher's creatures.   Value $200-300

BOTTOM: Boucher's attention to detail and quality is expressed here in the genuine pearl being held by the gold tone squirrel. No wonder he looks so enthusiastic. The rhinestones on the chest and tail are accents. Marked BOUCHER and numbered.   Value $200-275

RIGHT: This very attractive golden head has a cranberry and blue necklace and headband trim. The large stone at neck is turquoise colored. Jewelry of this particular genre is becoming a passion. The creature pins are also becoming a huge part of the collecting world. Signed BOUCHER and numbered
                                                    Value of head $250-300

This 1930s flamingo renounced his pink heritage to parade in the typical shades of the time period in which he was made, black and white. The pose is still characteristic and he looks happy. This fur clip was bought in Albuquerque, New Mexico, not exactly flamingo territory. His body is entirely rhinestone covered, his plumage is black and white enamel, his feet are black enamel, his beak is yellow enamel with a black accent line. One red glass eye. A delightful unsigned creature. Flamingo collecting is in full flight and has risen with the ascendancy of collectibles of the art deco period as well as things of the 1950s. 2¾" long. A very desirable bird.   Value $300-500

As butterflies become endangered in nature we collectors are doing our passionate best to keep them safe in their costume jewelry incarnation. This magnificent specimen with its 4" wing spread, large and small rhinestones and red stone eyes not only inspires and delights us but could easily enchant us into believing it is ready to fly off. An unbelievably beautiful brooch. Signed Staret. Late 1930s
                                                    Value $1800-2500

EISENBERG ORIGINAL fur clip. Gold metal flower head centered with a very large rhinestone surrounded by smaller rhinestones. Six large rhinestones pop out among the curling leaves. 4½" x 3".   Value $600-800

Crescent pin of silver filagree metal with pearls and blue stones. 3½'' long and 3'' wide this brooch is large and arresting in the theatrical way of the jewelry made during the period of Alexander Korda's famous film the Thief of Bagdad in 1940.

Marked on back THIEF OF BAGDAD, KORDA. This pin is one of the many pieces of jewelry made in conjunction with the release of the film. Scarce mark.

Value $850-1000

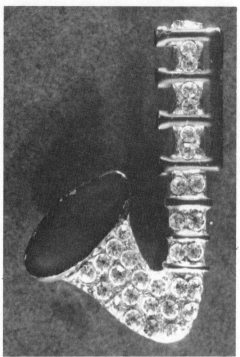

This early saxaphone pin of black, gold and rhinestone is a good example of a fast rising genre of rhinestone collection - music. Amazingly though the black enamel shows enough wear to uncover the gilt finished metal, the pasted-in rhinestones are still all in place. 2½''x1''.

Value $100-150

This large (3''x3½'') gold metal star has its center composed of many tiny massed rhinestones which are pasted in. Marked CAPRI on the back. The folded pattern of the gold metal gives this pin a rich look but the overall design is pedestrian. A coming collectible mark, however.

Value $65-85

HATTIE CARNEGIE at her best. The long stemmed rose brooch has a dew crusted rhinestone stem ending in a gold tone leaf. The brooch is 5'' long with a 1'' bee nestled in a bed of rhinestones on the mother-of-pearl rose petal. Looking into the rose itself discloses a pearl and the base of the petals also has tiny seed pearls. The body of the bee, which is very well done, is overall rhinestone. The bee was a favorite device of Carnegie's. This pin could be the subject of a fine arts poster. It is signed in an oval on back of large leaf HATTIE CARNEGIE in script.

Value $500-600

This floral spray has 8 deep blue and 8 light blue large pear shaped stones fanning out from the 1'' deep blue center stone. The stem is formed with baguette stones of deep blue and circular rhinestones. All set in a bright silver metal. Marked on back C. PELL. A graceful brooch.

Value $200-250

Top - Small daisy pin has white enamelled leaves with yellow tips and center and two large green leaves. The pin itself is interesting being a large brass safety pin which is original to the piece. Not signed.   Value $30-35

Left - This large (3'' around) daisy pin also has white enamel leaves with a yellow center (the designer knew his botany) and is effective because it is utterly simple and straightforward and is exactly what it purports to be - an appealing flower. These summer jewelry pieces are wonderful costume accents. Not marked in any way.   Value $65-85

Right - Orange flowers are emphasized by the canary and smoke colored stones on this spray pin. The stones are excellent quality and tend to validate the WEISS signature.   Value $150-175

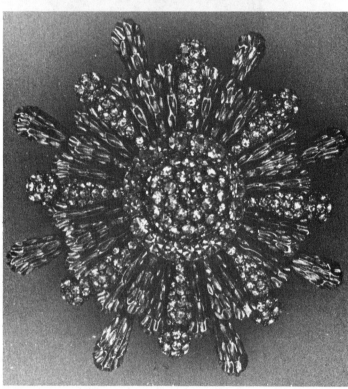

A classically designed tailored brooch by NAPIER. Gold tone metal with pearls.   Value $150-200

A heavy elaborate sunburst brooch by CINER. Of gold colored metal, the rays radiate from a rhinestone cluster center. As with all designs from all companies at certain periods, there was considerable variation on the basic themes. In the 1940s period sunbursts were being made in countless variations. This pin reflects a different approach from most and is heavier both in aspect and actuality than most of its contemporary types. Signed CINER Value $200-300

COROCRAFT pearl drop pin purchased new in 1964. The antiqued-finish gold metal, together with the circular rhinestones set in deep bezels, the differing types of pearls, give the brooch a very old fashioned look. Nicely done. Signed on back. 3½'' long, 2½'' wide.   Value $75-125

266

Left: Studying this remarkable brooch/pin reinforces the conclusion that because jewelry is unsigned it should not command any less attention than a signed piece. This tree is reminiscent of the trees so prominent in Victorian paintings, except it is infinitely more cheerful. It is so true to life the designer must have gone directly to the forest for inspiration. The blue, yellow, red and green stones are mixed with small pink and blue enamelled petals, the trunk seems to be swaying as the well laden branches bend in the wind. There is even an endearing knot hole. Never pass up unsigned jewelry which appeals to you, in fact keep looking diligently for unsigned pieces of costume jewelry of this quality and grace. This was designed by Alfred Philippe of TRIFARI in the early 1940s.   Value $400-600

Right: This unsigned basket of flowers is colorful and attractive but lacks the light touch of the designer of the tree. The rhinestone container is done in the early style, the bouquet has green leaves with bright green, blue and red center stones, the twisted handle has inset rhinestones. Altogether charming. Late 1930s   Value $200-225

A three inch long enameled leopard. A very fashionable animal sporting white enamel spots, a fancy rhinestone bow and startling green eyes. This dress clip is quite heavy, is backed with gold tone metal and is signed on back KENNETH LANE on an applied oval. Leopard shown lying on his original home - a leatherette red and black bag. 1970s. Value $150-200

A lovely sterling silver pin in its original box. Unusually light weight because of its filagree silver background. Instead of the rhinestones being overpowered by the silver as one would expect, they simply sparkle among the leaves. Signed Am Lee in script on the back, the box is marked "By Am Lee Sterling Silver on the top inside and the silver and blue label reads "HAND MADE STERLING SILVER." 2¼ round.   Value $250-350

A massive looking brooch in the early style. Overall quality rhinestones pasted i 4" across and straight forward in its approach. Signed POMERANTZ & CO., NY 1930s
Value $400-50

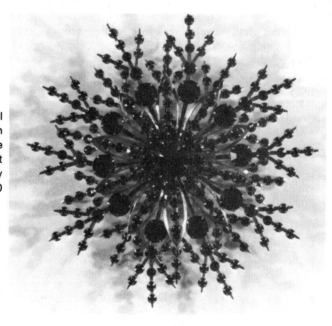

This startling sunburst pin is 4½" round with vivid red stones of various sizes, all hand set. It certainly lives up to its name both in size and effect but the very thin brass frame renders the pin lightweight and airy. Spectacular but unsigned. The sunburst motif should be on everybody's mind, it was a dominant motif throughout the late 1940s and into the 1950s. It can be breathtaking jewelry. This certainly is.
Value $300-400

Hattie Carnegie must surely have been inspired by the whirling skaters at Rockefeller Center in New York. The sense of motion communicated by this little pin is amazing. It will certainly revive memories in anyone who has seen or participated in this winter ritual. A plus indeed for a small piece of jewelry. The pin is 2½" overall, gilt metal accentuated by tiny rhinestone accents on the costumes, the headpiece and each skater has rhinestone eyes. The circular base is scored to simulate a skating rink. Delightful. Signed on an applied disc on base HATTIE CARNEGIE in script.
Value $125-175

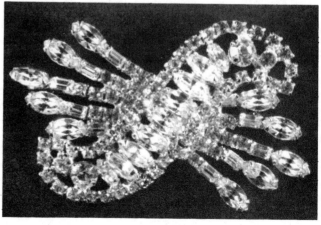

A 1950s KRAMER brooch. 3" long x 2". The usual high quality stones, pear shaped and pronged on the ends, baguette, pear shaped center line enclosed in bands of smaller rhinestones. Silver colored metal, signed KRAMER in script on an applied disc.
Value $175-250

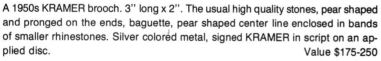

An unusual floral pin. Sterling silver, the two flower heads are opaque glass with silver leaves and large pronged blue stones. The larger silver leaves on the stem have a subdued finish to contrast with the shiny leaves above. Interesting, somewhat different. Stamped on back STERLING CA with arrow.   Value $150-250

CORO collecting could easily become one's life work (and probably even beyond) as this rich looking gilt and rhinestone brooch attests. The collector originally assumed it was high priced designer jewelry but CORO is such a surprising company. It is impossible at first glance to tell where the name will appear. Here the gold metal separates the rows of fine rhinestones in a free flowing way unusual in such pins. The nicely designed stem also gives an impression of life. This is truly an impressive brooch. Marked CORO in script on the stem.   Value $300-350

EISENBERG larger than life and in the same way, intensely interesting and compelling. This bow motif has been used by jewelers since at least the 16th century, it is still popular. Eisenberg uses the large brilliant rhinestones characteristic of the company, sets them in sterling silver measuring 3¾" x 2", signs the piece EISENBERG ORIGINAL and voila - a true gem. Designed by Florence Nathan. 1942.
Value $800-1200

A 3¼" x 2" oval brooch which illustrates the versatility of its maker CORO. The brilliant amethyst stones are large enough to suggest Eisenberg rather than CORO and the pin has a center line of cabachon opaque blue stones. Small pearls outline the frame. Quite lovely. Signed CORO in script.
Value $350-400

TRIFARI quality is evident in this small pin. The 1920s style female head is only 1½" long but has well defined features and a pretty rhinestone bandeau which blends nicely with the gold colored metal. Marked TRIFARI. Value $75-95

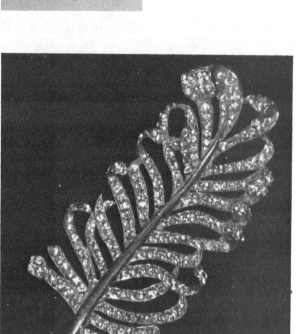

'Dancing Natives' brooch in black and gold. The sharp rise in ethnic jewelry is phenomenal adding value to pieces such as this. These fairly recent danci natives with their elaborate accoutrements including the rhinestone studded shi are a good addition to a collection of this type jewelry. The exuberance the portrays is a plus. Not signed.   Value $55-

This feather brooch is about as classic as jewelry design can get. Almost 5 inches long it is elegantly simple. Overall small rhinestones emphasizing the curled metal edges of the pin, this has as they say 'great lines' and will never go out of fashion as a jewelry accent. Not signed but a quality piece.

Value $225-300

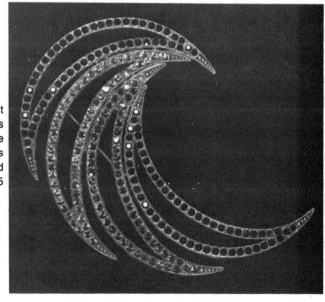

This 'wing' brooch is remarkable design work. Is it a wing? Is it a bird? At first glance, a wing but study reveals a bird's head. Two bands of black stones at top, two bands of rhinestones, 2 bands of red stones and again 2 black stone bands at bottom. Signed PELLINI. This pin is quite light in weight and excites the imagination. It also illustrates how red stones can dominate multi-colored stone jewelry.   Value $200-225

1930s jewelry has never been better defined than in this small oval pin. Celluloid, enamelled in red, black and gold with rhinestones on goldstone, it epitomizes an era. Certainly inexpensive when made and originally sold it is now a very desirable piece. Not marked in any way.   Value $250-350

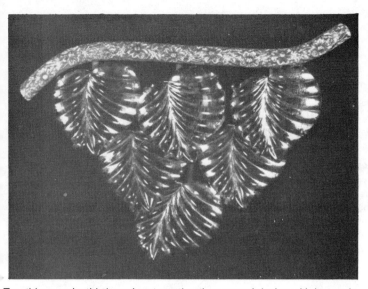

Two things make this brooch noteworthy, the unusual design with its spark-ling green leaves dangling from a gilded branch and its signature KANDELL & MARCUS, NY on an applied disc.   Value $600-750

A clip from the early period. The porportions are so balanced and lively this piece resembles a jabot which was a common dress fashion of the time. The exquisite round stones are each set in a deep bezel, the baguettes and small stones are matched and brilliant. A remarkable brooch. Signed on back MASTERCRAFT.   Value $1000-1500

This cornucopia with its magnificent collection of colored stones - purple, red, blue, green and yellow was obviously made by the same manufacturer as the set illustrated, but this, too, is unsigned. Nevertheless a goodly overflowing of riches. Large and effervescent. Perhaps the symbolism of the cornucopia gives this brooch its happy feeling. 1940s.   Value $400-500

A variation of the sunburst design. This pin is very attractive with massed pink stones interspersed with tiny blue opaque stones and a large center stone. A thin brass frames set off the stones. 2½''. Marked BSK Value $145-195

A departure from much of the design work of EISENBERG ORIGINALS is this elegant clip with its five pendant pearls and its 6 round pearls set in a bed of gorgeous rhinestones of typical Eisenberg quality. A 'forever' piece of jewelry. Marked EISENBERG ORIGINAL on the clip.   Value $1500-2000

This silver metal fur clip is part of a collection of jewelry with faces, heads and claws. It is getting more difficult to build this type collection, examples have never been abundant and this outstanding clip has the added fillip of being scarce, sought after and bearing a desirable signature - ALEXANDER KORDA. The African head is magnificently detailed. Blue opaque stones trim a headpiece out of which rises a faux boar's tusk. The long earring is a well crafted snake from which a blue/green bead dangles. 4" long. Marked ALEXANDER KORDA on back. This is the kind of jewelry which requires flair to wear but which is now a prime collecting area. 1940s   Value $1200-1700

This maiden stops traffic wherever she goes. An early clip by CORO she has black braids, a rosy complexion and she wears enamel feathers, a rhinestone headband and a rather alluring expression. This design was by Adolph Katz for COHN and Rosenberger in 1942.
Value $600-800

A fur clip by EISENBERG. Customary large size, usual wonderful quality stones, and the traditional concern for design incorporating various sized stones in an exciting way.   Value $1700-2200

Dagger of a high quality. Sterling silver, 3¼" long. Large topaz stone forms the handle, small rhinestones the ferrule with a deep green stone for contrast. A band of rhinestones pasted in edges the dagger itself. Many of the large companies made dagger jewelry, this could very well be TRIFARI. It is unsigned.
Value $200-300

Frog collectors abound. This jumping amphibian has character as well as pebbly green 'skin' with 5 rhinestones and moveable legs. Unsigned, the owner 'thinks' it was bought in the 1960s. These jeweled creatures attract many collectors. They are still inexpensive, whimsical and can be worn or collected on their own or can be fitted into major collections of animals. Many collectors would jump at the chance to own this endearing creature with the pink eyes
Value $25-40

Right:

The Duchess of Windsor certainly had no monopoly on flamingo pins. This amusing bird is nicely proportioned, posed characteristically as most of them seem to be in costume jewelry and somehow altogether loveable. His beady black stone eye is set in a head and neck of tiny rhinestones and pink stones and he surveys the world over an imposing pink stone beak. His tail feathers of small rhinestones balance the scaly legs and rhinestone feet. The body of gilt metal is 'feathered'. This pin is from the CLASSIC rhinestone years and is a treasure. This fellow who was made by H. Pomerantz of New York is definitely not CARTIER but valuable nonetheless.   Value $600-800

As with most older EISENBERG if the word 'spectacular' weren't already in the dictionary, it would have to be invented for this brooch. It is simply too imposing to be termed a 'clip'. 4½'' x 3'' its stones are as brilliant as when they were first set in the 1930s. This brooch/fur clip is an EISENBERG ORIGINAL, its styling timeless with the curves of the frame giving the stones added sparkle as they refract from the differing arcs. An amazing and truly beautiful sight. All Eisenberg of this age and quality is now museum status jewelry.
Value $1000-1500

Bees which are the bane of picnickers everywhere were a minor passion with almost all jewelry designers. This piece is saved from the obscure by the meticulous rendering of that insect poised on the green stone, the leaves are thin brass. Marked JOSEFF in script on a round applied disc on back. Made after 1969.   Value $150-225

One of a good-sized collection of newish 'city and country' pins. These are all contemporary, bought within the last 15 years and are part of a travel souvenir collection. All the pins with rhinestones spelling out either the city or country name visited have been bought by the collector in those places. London, Rome, Paris, San Francisco, Italy, USA and many others are all represented. A new rhinestone collectible and a memorable, wearable travel souvenir. The cost of this pin when bought in 1980   Value $25-35

A 1940s pin by Eisenberg. 2"x1½", marked Eisenberg. Canary colored and clear stones are set in Rhodium. Pretty if not sensational.

Value $300-400

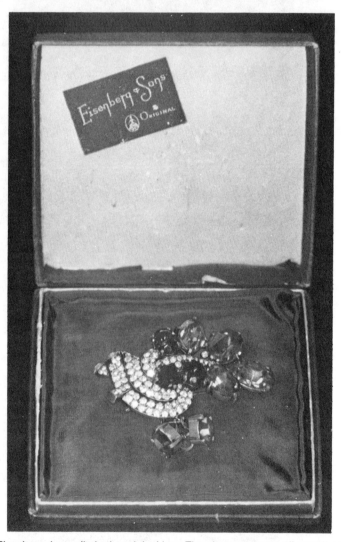

Eisenberg dress clip in the original box. The piece measures 3" x 1½" and is marked on the body of the piece. The matching earrings are not marked. The stones shade from light pink to darker pink with the end stone measuring ¾". Smaller rhinestones highlight this gorgeous clip. The box read EISENBERG SONS ORIGINAL. 1930s   Value in original box $1500-2000

Another monumental Eisenberg dress clip measures 3"x2¼" and is marked on the back, EISENBERG ORIGINAL. The huge stones range from light pink to darker pink to red. Gold wash on sterling. The slight wear on the gold gives the clip a lovely patina and seems to accentuate the still dazzling rhinestones. This clip was bought in West Virginia, Eisenberg really got around. 1930s.

Value $800-1000

A good example of the Eisenberg use of stones to make the statement, rather than intricate, confused design. A relatively simple but amazingly effective dress clip. Clip measures 2½'' x 2'' and is marked on the clip - EISENBERG ORIGINAL STERLING. The large clear stone is beautifully cut and measures 1¼'' x ¾''. 1930s.   Value $1200-1500

The particular talent of Eisenberg is evident here. Good design made magnificent by the use of large, extraordinary quality stones. This fur clip is an EISENBERG ORIGINAL, marked on back. It measures 3¼'' x 2'', is sterling silver and its stones are very light, clear blue which blend well with the metal and in themselves are traffic stoppers. This wonderful clip is part of an Eisenberg Original collection. 1930s.   Value $1000-1500

A deceptive large Eisenberg clip. It's gigantic measurements (4'' x 3'') are belied by the design. The openwork of the sterling silver with its rhinestone accents gives this clip an airy, lightweight feeling. Any good collection of early Eisenberg illustrates the dramatic approach the company took to this jewelry while never sacrificing good taste. Marked on back EISENBERG sterling
Value $1500-2000

Pin by EISENBERG. Sterling with gold wash with beautiful large blue stones. The pin measures 3½''x3'' and is marked on back EISENBERG ORIGINAL STERLING. A lovely jewelry accent. 1930s.   Value $1200-1500

275

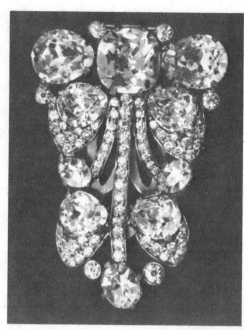

Dress clip, 2½'' x 1½''. Canary colored stones in a characteristic clip of the period. Marked EISENBERG ORIGINAL on clip. 1930s. Value $1500-2000

This pin measures 3'' x 2¼'' and has varied-sized stones set in sterling silver. The floral spray approach, so prevalent, is slightly different here. Marked on back of pin EISENBERG ORIGINAL STERLING 1930s. Value $1000-1500

Horizontal pin with shades of bright blue stones and rhinestones. 3¼'' long x 1½''. 1930s Eisenberg Original. Marked on back. Value $1000-1200

A very pretty traditionally styled dress clip. Large impressive stones with smaller rhinestones. 2½'' x 2''. Marked on clip EISENBERG ORIGINAL. 1930s. Value $1000-1500

Dress clip with topaz colored stones so popular in the 1930s. Gold wash over sterling. This clip measures 4'' x 3'' and is marked EISENBERG ORIGINAL on back. Value $1800-2500

This large bow is relieved from boredom by the brilliant colors. Large pink stones, small pink stones and rhinestones. The overall effect is one of great beauty. 2½'' x 2½''. Marked on back of pin EISENBERG ORIGINAL. This bow was purchased in West Virginia.   Value $1000-1500

Another example of Eisenberg's wondrous way with stones. The design is classic and simple and instead of the very large stones Eisenberg favored these are all smaller except for two. Although the dimensions of the pin - 3¼'' x 2½'' seem substantial, when worn this piece of jewelry is open to the cloth underneath and has a graceful look. Marked EISENBERG ORIGINAL on back. 1930s.   Value $1200-1800

This Eisenberg dress clip is a brilliant assemblage of close-packed stones. It is a minor departure in design work for EISENBERG and is almost royal in its approach. The stones as usual are of excellent quality and the variations in coloration lend interest to the mass. An interesting EISENBERG ORIGINAL. Marked on back. 3'' x 2''. 1930s   Value $1500-1800

Stones shading from pink to purple distinguish this pin. The shape is not unfamiliar but the gloss of the stones becomes paramount. Marked EISENBERG ICE. 1940s. 2¼'' x 2¼''. Set in Rhodium.   Value $500-600

When we use the word 'typical' in relation to Eisenberg it seems dismissive but this clip is indeed typical. The shape of this dress clip plus the magnificence of the large stones is definitive of the 1930s Eisenberg work. This clip measures 2¾" x 2" and is marked EISENBERG ORIGINAL.   Value $1500-2000

A stunning pin. Round rhinestones, square rhinestones and smaller stones all set so that they seem to float separately from the frame. 2¼"x2¾". Marked on back EISENBERG ORIGINAL. 1930s.
Value $1500-1800

When Eisenberg Original was at its zenith the clothing of the period demanded dress clips. The variety of these clips seems boundless. Here is one 2¾" x 2" with the finest large stones of various types with a graceful elegant look. Marked EISENBERG ORIGINAL on back. 1930s.   Value $1500-2000

Again the simplicity of the design is enhanced by the use of the wonderful stones. This dress clip is sterling silver with a gold wash. It's rows of small rhinestones are balanced with clear stones. 2¼"x2¼" Marked EISENBERG STERLING on back and STERLING on clip. This clip was bought in Nebraska.
Value $1500-2000

The four pieces above were designed by Florence Nathan.

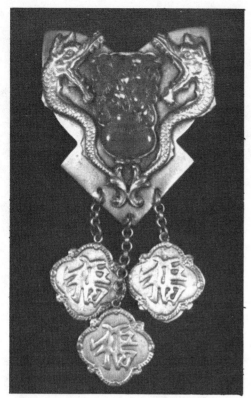

This profile 'devil' pin illustrates the talent of the designer and mold maker. Only 2½'' long and only 1½'' wide the face projects such expression as to seem sculptural. The rhinestone beard and tail and the red stone eye add zest to the total look of this happily diabolical demon. An amazing piece of workmanship in such a small pin. Gold colored base metal. Unsigned.

Value $125-175

A carved agate stone of vase and flowers is supported on gold-toned finish brass by fierce dragons. From the body of this pin dangle three 'Chinese coins' Unique costume jewelry. Not signed. 1940s   Value $150-185

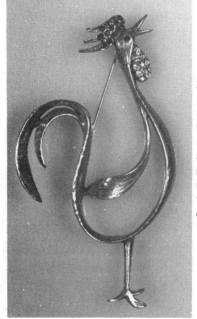

A sprightly rooster of gold colored metal. Unusual combination of the abstract and folk art approach in this minimal treatment but sophisticated in its use of stones and expression. 4½''x2½'', red stones in the comb match the single visible eye. Tiny rhinestones from the wattle. Signed JEANNE on an applied oval disc on back.

Value $65-75

Pair of matching pins. Concept is certainly unusual. What seems to be a pair of branches with rhinestone leaves could suggest birds in flight to the imaginative. The two pins are well made and matching pins or clips are always a desirable fashion accent. Abstract art on one's jacket? Hattie Carnegie would probably be surprised. Signed on applied round disk-HATTIE CARNEGIE. Each pin is 2'' long.   Value of pair $350-500

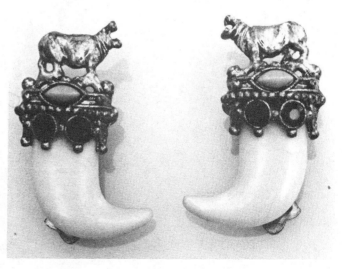

This pair of dress clips confound the observer with their realistic faux tusks and gold colored metal ferrules bearing 2 bright red stones topped by opaque turquoise colored stones, and standing over all this opulence a pair of open-mouthed hippopatomi. Incongruous but fascinating. Unsigned.Value $150-225

A wonderfully whimsical pin. The green enamelled frog with his bulging green glass eye and yellow spots sits in a bed of rhinestone lily pads with rushes and yellow spotted cattails. The enamelling is superior, the frog completely life-like. The whole is enchanting. This is marked CORO CRAFT STERLING.
Value $200-250

The subtle design work here is provocative. The use of the tiny gold flowers strewn among the large green, clear and topaz stones as well as the unexpected blue stones and the delicate rope work gives this combination brooch/clip a feeling of massed precious gems while still maintaining its flamboyant JOSEFF style. It measures 2¼"x2" and is marked on the back JOSEFF HOLLYWOOD in an applied rectangle.
Value $1200-1500

Top-A selection of extraordinary Eisenberg. A classic openwork fur clip which measures 3"x2". Marked with a script E and 'sterling'.
Value $800-1000

LEFT: An EISENBERG ORIGINAL fur clip with the large stones set in sterling silver 3½"x2½" Value $800-1200

RIGHT: Matching pin and earrings set. Both pieces signed EISENBERG in script. Rhodium finish. Value $350-500

BOTTOM: Sterling silver mounting holds a center stone which measures 1¾". Overall size of this fur clip is 2½"x2". The center stone is a pale citrine color. Signed EISENBERG in script. Value $800-1000

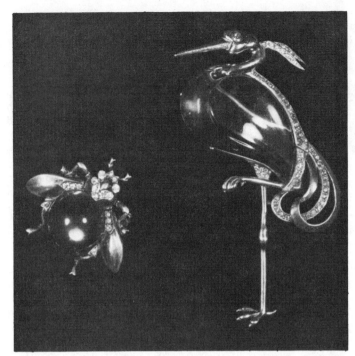

Left: These wonderful creatures are 'jelly bellies' by TRIFARI. The jelly belly bee has a rhinestone head and rhinestones on the wings. Signed TRIFARI and also marked STERLING. The large clear glass body is a surprising touch and has turned pieces such as this into a separate collecting category. They are scarce and expensive. Gold wash over sterling.   Value $500-750

Right: This TRIFARI jelly belly stork is 3½'' tall and 2½'' wide. He has a red eye, rhinestone back and tail feathers and is a sensational piece of jewelry. He manages to be rather subdued and totally flamboyant at the same time - a great talent Alfred Phillipe had with jewelry. Signed TRIFARI. c.1945
Value $1200-1750

Four impressive TRIFARI pins.
TOP: Asymmetrical branch of green stone baguettes, pearl and rhinestone flowers set in gold tone metal. Signed TRIFARI and pat pend.
Value $150-175
LEFT: A true TRIFARI pin in silver metal - pin, blue and purple stones, clear rhinestones at top. Signed TRIFARI.   Value $195-250
RIGHT: A gorgeous pin in the basket design done by so many makers but nowhere better than this. Gold wash over sterling silver, flowers are in shades of amber and yellow. The handle and body of basket set with baguette rhinestones. 2½'' wide x 2¼'' long. Probably Kramer.
Value $200-250
BOTTOM: A typical TRIFARI use of the silver metal to display rhinestones in this 1940s pin. Direct and very wearable. Signed. Value $195-250

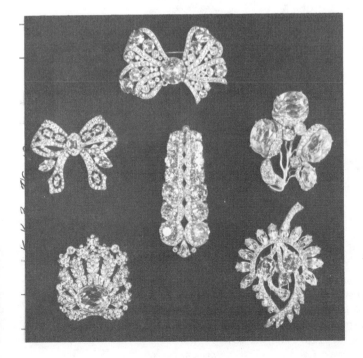

A selection of fine Eisenberg pins which clearly illustrates the emphasis the company put on showcasing large, magnificent quality rhinestones. The bow at top measures 3¼'' x 2''. It has one super size center rhinestone and descending sized rhinestones enclosed in the ribbons. Marked EISENBERG ORIGINAL, STERLING. Designed by Florence Nathan 1942
Value $1000-1500
Left Center: This entirely different kind of bow is a fur clip. Its antique styling with the openwork large rhinestones has a special appeal today. Signed, Sterling and EISENBERG ORIGINAL. Designed by Florence Nathan, 1942
Value $1000-1500
This Eisenberg waterfall clip is typical work and possibly the most sought after of all the jewelry of the period. These can be truly spectacular, this one is 4'' by 1½'' and is set in base metal. Signed EISENBERG ORIGINAL and numbered. Designed by Florence Nathan, early 1940s   Value $900-1200

The stones in this fur clip measure 1'' each. The pin itself 3'' x 2½''. This is a beautiful accent piece. SIGNED EISENBERG ORIGINAL and numbered. 1940s   Value $800-1000

Lower left: EISENBERG ORIGINAL dress clip, base metal, large 1'' center stone, other size rhinestone in different shapes. Almost tiara or crown shape. Signed EISENBERG ORIGINAL. 1940s   Value $700-1000

Lower right: Another large 3½'' x 2½'' base metal fur clip. The openwork center opens up the pin to the colored material beneath and gives the whole piece a lightweight feeling. Wonderful quality rhinestones. Signed EISENBERG ORIGINAL and numbered. 1940s.   Value $800-1200

LEFT TOP: This brooch has everything without being totally overwhelming. Basically gilt filagree metal with a light chain 'fringe' beard, it is almost 4½'' long and 4'' wide. This interpretation of a Chinese mask has lace-like filagree work and fine quality small rhinestones. The swords are rhinestone studded and balance the triangular helmet which has among other things - birds, flowers. This is a costume jewelry copy of a well known Deco piece designed by Georges Fouquet. Fine craftsmanship and a stunning costume accent. Rare.

Value $800-1200

The American Indian is a most desirable form in jewelry. In costume jewelry beautifully crafted pieces such as this are scarce and eagerly sought after. This brass clip has a magnificently molded face and head dress with its thin brass filagree headdress. Three deep blue stones set in bezels are precisely placed to attract attention to the face. This kind of jewelry is almost art and could be collected if enough could be found to form a collection for a wall or series of frames. The whole is compelling. Unsigned. 2½''x2½''.Value $600-800

This clip and earrings set bears only a patent number. A most interesting set, not only for its obvious attractions but because of the way it is constructed. The exquisite faces of painted metal were made separately and attached to the brass frames. The coiffures with long curling locks and the top plumes are accented by rhinestones and small red stones in a most attractive way. The profiles are cameo-like in the purity of the lines and this set is an important one although unsigned. 1940s.

Value $1000-1700

One of the most exquisite pieces of costume jewelry ever conceived. This large (approx. 4'' x 3'' encrusted with varying shades and sizes of excellent quality pink stones. Tiny round pearls enhance the dainty feeling and round pearls define the antennae. A rather remarkable piece which should look and feel heavy given its size and quota of gems but instead seems fairly-like and utterly feminine. Applied palette on back is signed ORIGINAL BY ROBERT.

Value $750-1000

One of the prettiest of the Christmas tree pins. Multi-colored stones. Christmas tree pins of good design continue to rise in price regardless of attribution.

Value $45-85

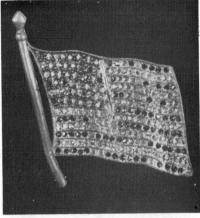
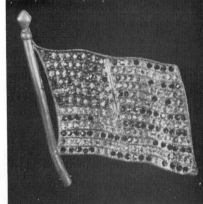

Santa Claus pins. Since Santa has become a collectible in the most expensive sense, the pins are an inexpensive way to satisfy your passion but they have a great future. The one on the left is bright gold with a large red stone on his low belt, rhinestones on hat, hem and hands. 1960s. Value $45-65
The pin on the right has a Santa face with his silvery beard, topped by a Christmas tree with colored stones, with a rhinestone top star. Santa pins with colored stones or rhinestones are more difficult to find than the trees, but are not yet widely collected.
Value Value $40-65

Within the general category of rhinestone collecting, the smaller categories have risen in importance. Such a collectible is the American Flag. There now exist large and comprehensive accumulations of various styles and ages of flags. This example is late 1920's - early 1930's. It is surprisingly bright with only 4 tiny rhinestones missing. Prices are rising accordingly in this field. Value $95-145

American flag brooch in stones of red, white and blue. Each small stone is hand set. 1960s.
Value $40-45

Two recent EISENBERG Christmas tree pins. Although these annual issue pins were not marked for many years, Karl Eisenberg says the company has begun marking them again. These are marked EISENBERG on the back. I have had so many requests for sources to buy these pins at issue time and price - Marshall Field's in Chicago or Nordstrom's Seattle are my own sources $14.25 at issue price in 1987. The pins now range from about $15 to about $90.

This NIXON pin is from a small collection of rhinestone political pins. The owner disclaims partisan politics but many pieces in the collection seem to reflect the Republican party. Such a collection of political memorabilia has great potential.
Value $125-195

Crossed flags, these are not so common as the singles. Colorful and collectible.   Value $75-95

A pair of treasured early Eisenberg dress clips in the original box. 1930s heavy metal, the clips have a surprising light feeling, the stones still sparkling saucily.
Value $400-450

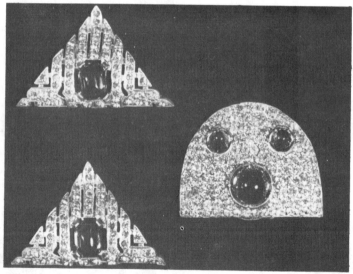

Two triangular dress clips and one rounded dress clip. A very interesting trio, could almost be a set but the difference in quality betwen the smaller triangular shaped clips and the other are obvious. Both the smaller and larger have rhinestones pasted-in and similarly colored larger red stones. The rounded edge clip is an earlier piece and the rhinestones are better quality. The triangular clips are early 1940s. All un-marked. Set on left $65-85
Right $65-95

Rare dress clip by Eisenberg, one of the great names in Fashion Jewelry. This spectacular clip is in its original box marked EISENBERG & SONS ORIGINAL and boasts magnificent large Austrian stones and coral. 1930's. Also marked on clip EISENBERG ORIGINAL. Approx. 3½'' x 2½''

Value $1800-2200 with box

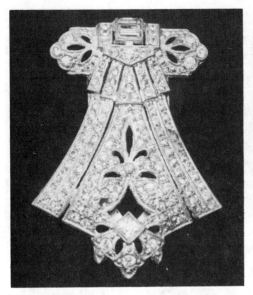

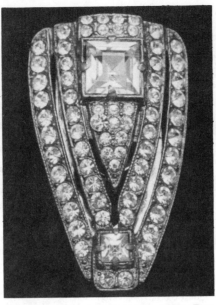

Dress Clip, 1930's. Gilt over white metal. Value $40-50

Excellent example of a good quality, graceful dress clip of the 1930s. Many of the clips show great attention to detail, not only with the stones and setting, but with the embossing on the clip itself.   Value $175-200

Better quality lady's dress clip. 1930s. Two square rhinestones complemented by smaller stones; back of clip is nicely embossed.   Value $195-250

Cheaply made but tasteful small dress clip of the 30s.   Value $35-45

Dress clip, 2¼ inches long, of the 1930's. Rhinestones with large center green stone which is slightly damaged but the piece is a perfect example of its type, which was worn at the base of a V-neckline dress. The stone was probably chipped through careless storage.   Value $60-75
If perfect $150-195

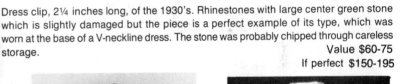

Another spectacular 1930s dress clip of massive size and Eisenberg styling and quality although it is not marked. 3''x2''. Value $250-300

Lovely Deco dress clip. Rhinestones and ivory colored plastic. 2¼'' long, 1930s. Value $150-175

Lovely small, dainty, well-made dress clips of the 1930's.
Difficult to find in this size.   Value $125-165

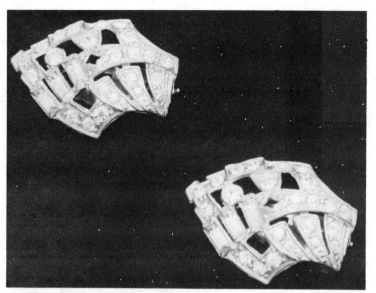

Dress clip of the 1930's. Rhinestones in white metal with well faceted center stone. Value $145-200

Pair of gilt over base metal dress clips. The dress clips of gold colored metal are much more difficult to find than in white metal of the period. 1930's. Very attractive.
Value $95-150

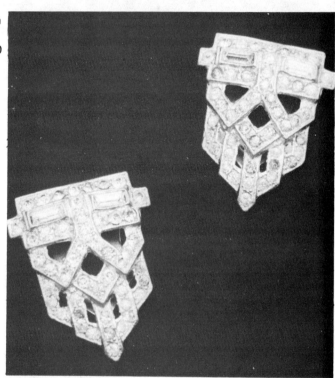

1930's heavy base metal dress clip with large blue stone which was set separately and soldered to rest of piece.
Value $95-145

Dress clip, white metal, interesting design. 1930's.
Value $50-85

Pair of rhinestone dress clips of the 1930's in the more restrained smaller size, white metal. Value $145-225

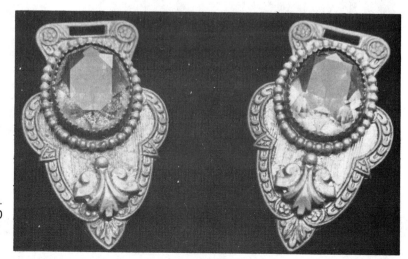

Unusual and finely detailed dress clips of the late 1930's. Large blue center stones. Value $195-250

Dress clip marked with crown and Trifari, older piece. **Value $165-200**

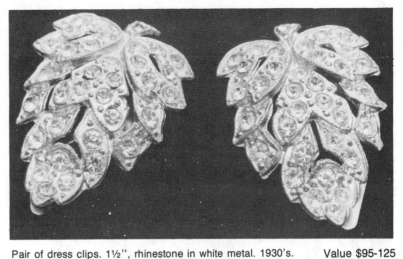

Pair of dress clips. 1½'', rhinestone in white metal. 1930's. **Value $95-125**

Dress clip in a somewhat different design. c. 1940. **Value $75-145**

This 5'' long dress ornament is a stunning example of fine quality stones and beautifully worked flexible frame. The original dress was velvet. 1930s. **Value $95-145**

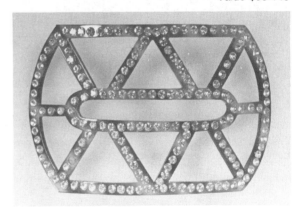

A large plastic decorative piece, 4½''x3''. Rhinestones pasted in. **Value $40-45**

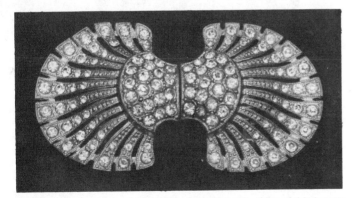

Elegant lady's dress buckle, 1930's. Sometimes buckles of this beauty are soldered together and made into brooches. **Value $200-250**

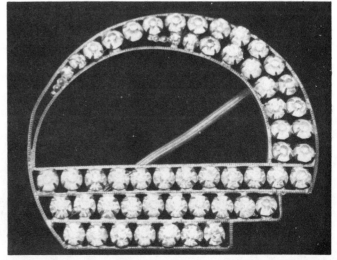

Fabulous 1930s dress buckle. Marked on back CZECHOSLOVAKIA. This type jewelry is scarce and eagerly sought by collectors. An interesting design and a good illustration of the old Czech rhinestones. **Value $175-200**

287

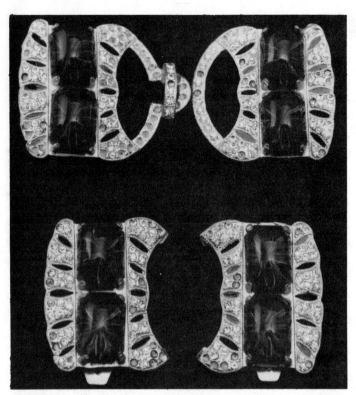

Deco dress buckle with large red molded glass stones and 2 matching dress clips. These sets are unusual enough to interest the collector even though many small rhinestones are missing. White metal. 1930s. Value as is $65-85
If perfect $150-225

Pretty belt buckle but in the way of much lower line 1930s jewelry the backing is rather crude. Marked ARTCR T.   Value $50-85

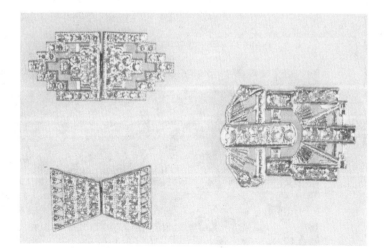

Three belt buckles of the 1930s. Unfortunately for the vintage clothing collector these were removed from their original belts, and the belts discarded. Inexpensive when originally sold, they reflect the poor quality but good design work of much of the jewelry of the period.   Value of each set $65-75

Three outstanding examples of dress ornaments of the 1930s. Top left a belt buckle, right was stitched to a dress, bottom a two part belt buckle. All of these are brilliant in the characteristic way of pieces marked CZECHOSLOVAKIA.
Value left $75-95
Right $135-165
Bottom $75-100

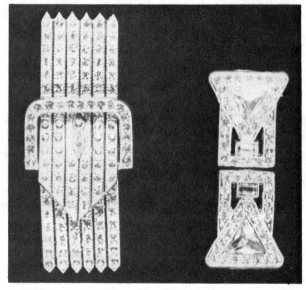

Belt buckles. Left is typical in buckles of the 1920s - early 1930s period, nicely made, good quality rhinestones, pasted-in. 3" long.
Value $75-100
Right: belt buckle, 2" long, stones pasted in, pretty overall effect especially on the original dark belt. Large triangular rhinestone in center of each part. 1930s.

Value $75-100

A stupendous belt buckle. It measures 6½" x 4". Beautifully worked brass with 7 large, hand set rhinestones of superior quality. Fantastic 1930s piece. Marked on disc on back KANDELL & MARCUS, N.Y. Value $500-750

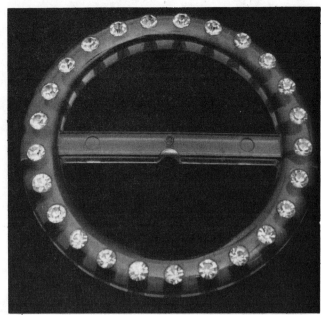

Large (3") circular buckle, clear plastic with 25 rhinestones, numbered '6'. Value $30-35

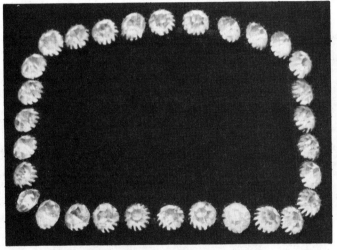

An example of French paste. Hasp on this buckle needs replacing. Value $200-300

Belt buckle. Decals on celluloid set in thin brass and framed with rhinestones. Originally on black velvet belt for lady's evening gown. 1920's-early 1930's. Value $125-195

1950's belt buckle, 2 pieces, rhinestones and aurora borealis. Garish but effective. 2½" high, 2½" wide. Value $75-100

Belt buckle with large rhinestones pasted in base metal with silvery finish. Brass hasp. Very effective piece. Late 1930's. Value $95-125

Belt Buckle. One of the razzle dazzle early pieces of wonderful costume jewelry. Brass with hand set beautiful Czechoslovakian rhinestones.

Value $145-185

2 piece belt buckle, topaz colored stones in brass filagree. Late 1920s, 4¼". Value $195-250

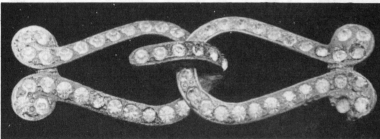

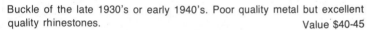

Lady's belt buckle, 1930's. Most of the stones are still bright but metal has lost its lustre. Value $95-125

Buckle of the late 1930's or early 1940's. Poor quality metal but excellent quality rhinestones. Value $40-45

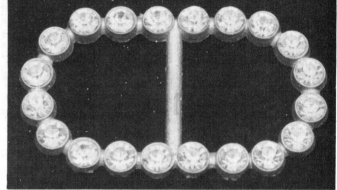

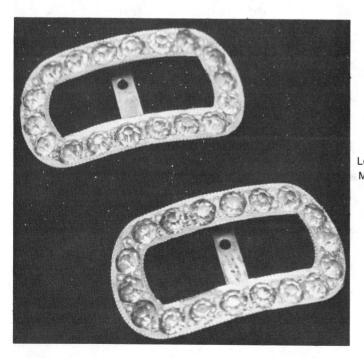

Lovely small size shoe buckles of the 1920's. Rhinestones in base metal. Marked B.A. Co. on back of each buckle. 1½" long. Value $60-65

Highly desirable type of 1920's shoe buckles. Square, rhinestone borders, original satin backings. Curved. 1½'' x 2''.
Value $100-125

Beautiful small size shoe buckles won over T-strap in 1928. This type can be more difficult to find than the larger sizes.
Value $75-85

The desirable small size shoe buckles worn in the late 1920's and early 30's with T- strap shoes. White metal with fine rhinestones which are deeply set in.
Value $95-125

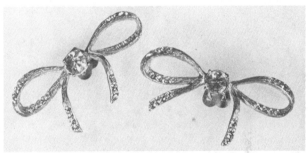

Shoe buckles, lightweight and light in feeling. Simple bows outlined in small pasted-in rhinestones set into the base metal. Large good quality center rhinestone. Marked shoe buckles are difficult to find - each of these is stamped c.MUSI.
Value $40-45

Heavy, large shoe buckles of the 1930's. Marked on clip back EVERGRIP in broken diamond and PAT APPLD FOR F B N CO. 2 x 1½''.
Value $95-125

These shoe buckles from the 1920s do not have back clips. They were meant to be sewn onto the shoe. Signed but unreadable.
Value $125-175

Shoe buckles, clip on type, double clips, each buckle marked on clip MUSI,
Value $45-50

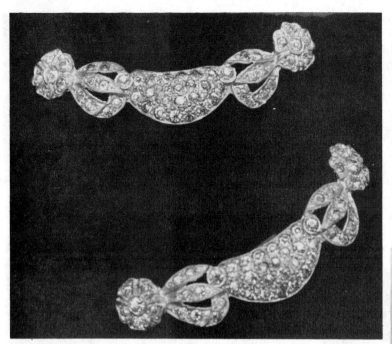

Shoe buckles, single clip back. Late 1920's or early 1930's. Known to have been worn in 1932.   Value $100-145

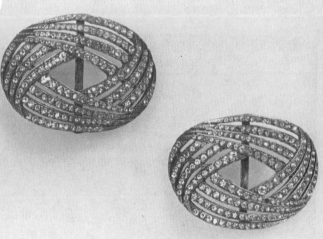

Oval shoe buckles of the 1950s. Steel with pasted in rhinestones. No markings.   Value $50-65

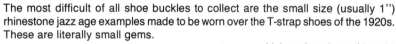

2 piece Art Deco black glass and rhinestone buckle. 1930's.   Value $195-250

The most difficult of all shoe buckles to collect are the small size (usually 1'') rhinestone jazz age examples made to be worn over the T-strap shoes of the 1920s. These are literally small gems.

Value of each set $95-125

Shoe buckles, 1950s, Rhinestones pasted in very shallow settings.
Value $30-35

1930's shoe buckles. Rhinestones in white metal. An unusually large size. 2½'' x 2'' and heavy.
Value $100-155

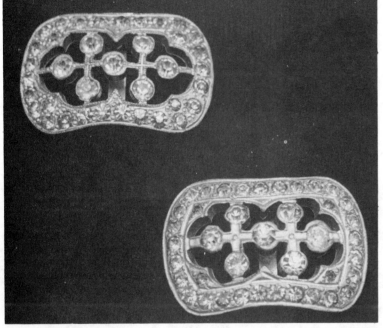

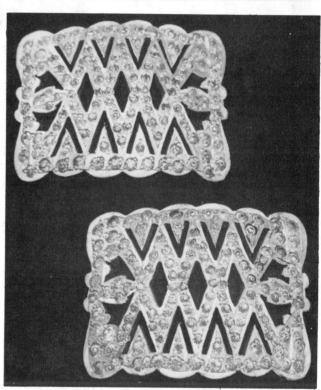

Very desirable buckles of the late 1920's. 1'' by 1¼'' and although rhinestones are pasted in they are set deeply enough so that wear has not loosened them. Worn in 1929 and in the early 1930's.
Value $95-145

Very heavy shoe buckles of the 1930's. Well designed. Original leather backing. Rhinestones in white metal.
Value, pr. $100-145

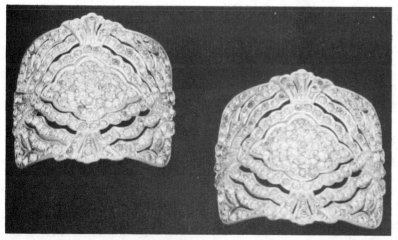

Nicely designed shoe buckles of the 1930's. Curved. These older small rhinestones blend with the white metal to make an impressive display under lights. Marked DEAUVILLE.
Value $95-125

This refined pair of shoe buckles is in the very desirable small size - 1¼'' x 1¾''. Quite beautiful with their still sparkling rows of fine quality rhinestones pasted in. Original padded satin box marked JOHN WANAMAKER, New York, Philadelphia, Paris, London. 1930s. All shoe buckles are still way undervalued.
$125-175 in original box.

Late 1950's shoe buckles, single clip back. Grosgrain bows with rhinestones.   Value $25-35

Rhinestones in white metal shoe buckles of the late 1920 - early 1930 period. Single clip back, small size 1½''.   **Value $95-125**

Large oval rhinestone shoe buckles, 3'' across, double clip backs, unmarked, open centers. 1950's.
                              Value $45-55

Very beautiful shoe buckles of the 1920s. Black backing on one to show the way it highlights the buckle itself. The cluster effect of the many rhinestones gives a definite effect of diamonds.
                              Value $125-165

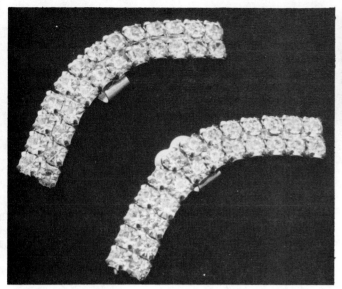

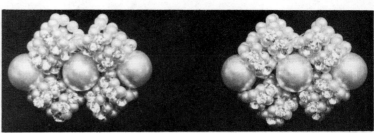

Shoe buckles. Single clip back is glued to a thin sheet of plastic which is applied to the rhinestones and pearls. 1950s, unmarked. These buckles exactly match a pair of earrings but were not bought at the same time. A good example of how the industry made use of a single design for different pieces of jewelry.
Value $30-35

Crescent shaped double row rhinestone shoe buckles. Single clip back. 1950's.
Value $40-45

These 1920s shoe buckles are large, heavy, curved and boast a 1½'' center faceted stone. These are intact on the original shoes. The pasted in rhinestone on the base metal do not show the sophistication of workmanship and design as some buckles but the pair is unusual and striking.
Value $135-175

Late 1920s base metal rhinestone shoe buckles. 2½'' x 1¾'', rhinestones all hand set. One of the great collectibles, shoe buckles are still undervalued.
Value $135-195

These 1930s shoe buckles still have the original satin backing and the original shoes are part of the collection. Heavy white metal, rhinestones pasted in. The shoes show much use so the way the rhinestones have retained their sparkle and are still intact is a tribute to the maker. Design has great proportion and interest. Shoe buckles are still undervalued.
Value $135-195

1950s plastic and rhinestone shoe buckles. Imitation tortoise shell, with a rather severe addition of rhinestones, these are a good example of the extensive use of rhinestones during the period.
Value $35-45

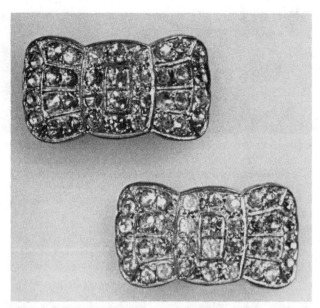

These marvelous shoe buckles from the late 1920s (a relative wore these in 192[...] were remarkably sturdy for all their beauty. These are 2½"x1¾", slightly curve[d] rhinestones are pasted in base metal with a single bezeled rhinestone raised a[...] a centerpiece. Back clip. The buckles are marked but the mark is not readable[...]
Value $145-19[...]

Shoe buckles worn in 1930, probably dating somewhat earlier. 2" long, slightly curved in the ubiquitous bow design, hand set rhinestones all intact and good quality, single clip back, marked PAT APPLIED FOR. A real find for the shoe buckle collector.
Value $145-195

Shoe buckles, 1930s. Marked on back clip HOLFAST, PAT. APPL FOR. One of the most interesting things about these buckles is the great variety of the clips. Value $100-145

A late 1930s ring with a large blue stone. The quality of the stone and the finely detailed and well constructed setting make this a choice costume ring.
Value $150-185

Early blue glass costume ring. Non-expandable band. Open back.
Value $45-65

Magnificent rhinestone ring. If the word 'spectacular' did not exist, it would have to be created for this jewel. Although its effect is of fine jewelry, it completely fulfills the raison d'etre of all costume jewelry - to attract attention in a way that is blatantly fake. Who do you know who could possibly afford this? Unmarked.
Value $195-250

This marvelous costume ring of baroque pearls, chunky "gold" and tiny rhinestones measures 1¼". Signed VENDOME.   Value $125-150

A treasure. This impressive ring with its five faceted quality rhinestones is marked EISENBERG ORIGINAL and STERLING. Rare.   Value $900-1500

Heavy KENNETH LANE costume ring. Coral colored with 2 bands of small rhinestones channelled in gold metal. The ring band is rigid and wide, the inner band is adjustable. Not for the small women, it rises 1½'' from the band. Signed KENNETH LANE on a round disc. Value $150-200

The ultimate treasure - an Eisenberg ring. Large (each is ¾'' x ½'') stones set in sterling which is marked is script E. 1940s $1500-2000

Ring by VENDOME. Overall green stones with two bands of rhinestones. Frankly costume with the square silvery band Vendome used on many of its rings. These rings are fun and not yet costly. Value $55-95

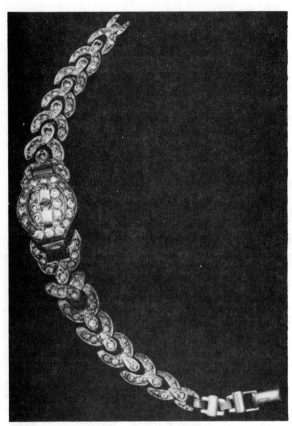

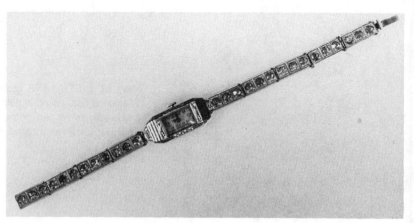

This narrow watch with its rhinestone band is dated 1932. Working condition.
Value $300-500

Rhinestone watch cover and bracelet. 1930's.
Value $350-500

A stunning rhinestone covered watch. The cover snaps open at a touch and when the watch is worn the rhinestones are positioned so they display to advantage on the most visible side of the wrist. The watch face is marked ORLOFF 7 Jewels. This was bought in 1948 at John Wanamaker's, Philadelphia at the sale price of $12. Perfect running condition.
Value $300-450

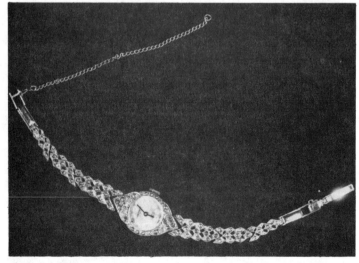

A watch bracelet destined to fool anyone not carrying a loupe. The small, fine stones, the safety catch and the styling make this an important acquisition for the collector. The watch bracelet was the province of many manufacturers and setting good quality watches into them was common practice - where have they all gone? The value of this watch and bracelet is
Value $350-500

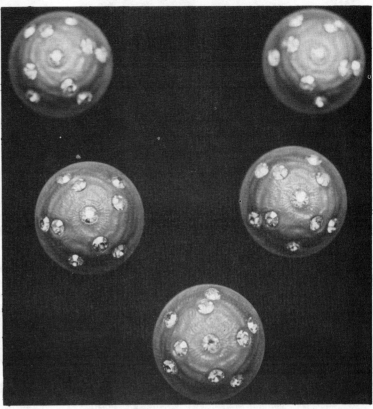

Fabulous set of 3 rhinestone buttons. Although the stones are pasted in, the buttons have outlived their original velvet jacket. Base metal very heavy. Value, ea. $40-45

1950's set of 5 buttons of red plastic. Aurora borealis stones are pasted in. Value, set $35-45

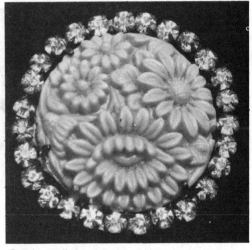

1940's button, dome shaped covered with rhinestones pasted in base metal. Value $15-18

Button. Base metal set with rhinestones. Value $15-25

Button, 1½" round, hand-set rhinestones surround molded plastic flowers simulating coral. Metal back. Late 1930's. Value $40-50

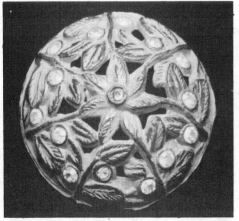

Very heavy metal button from 1930's dress, one of a set of 4 which must have required some stamina to wear. Small stones pasted in. Not particularly attractive but of interest to the collector. 1½" across. Value, each $10-20

Pair of lovely brass and aurora buttons which would make attractive earrings. 1950's.   Value $32-38

Pair of plastic buttons of the 1960's set with blue stones.   Value $10-20 ea.

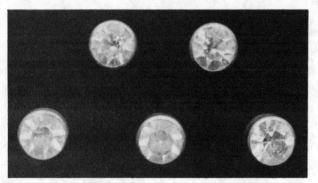

Set of five rhinestone buttons from 1930s dress. Deeply set in bezels so that despite heavy wear stones have never loosened. Nicely faceted rhinestones.   Value, set $45-75

Clear plastic button of the 1950's with large rhinestones.   Value $10-15

Button. Black metal set with sparkling green stones. 1930's.   Value $15-2?

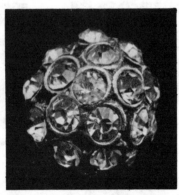

Small, star-shaped button, 1940's. Unusual enough to appeal to the rhinestone button collector.   Value $12-15

Heavy, base metal button of the 1930's. Rhinestones.   Value $15-18

1930's rhinestone button. Originally on black satin dress.   Value $20-28

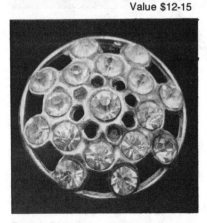

An example of a man's tie clasp by SWANK. Red stone. Marked SWANK on back. 1940's. These were often part of a set and can still be found in the original boxes. This clasp is still used regularly.   Value $25-35

Button. Rhinestones in gilded metal set within a circular frame. 1940's.
Value $10-15

Rhinestone and clear plastic lady's cuff links. 1940s. Value $15-25

1940's ladies tie-tacs. Pearl and rhinestones. Marked with Pat. number on back. ½ inch.　　Value, pair $35-45

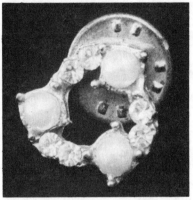

Pearl and rhinestone tie-tac. 1940's.
Value $20-30

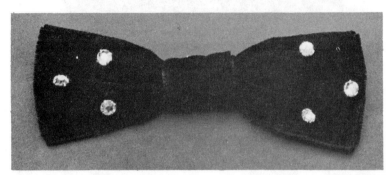

Velvet Bow Tie with rhinestones originally had elastic band.　　Value $20-25

Man's shirt studs of the 1920s. Set of three in silvery colored metal with rhinestone. These look remarkably like their more expensive counterparts when worn. Two with gilt finish.
Value, each $15

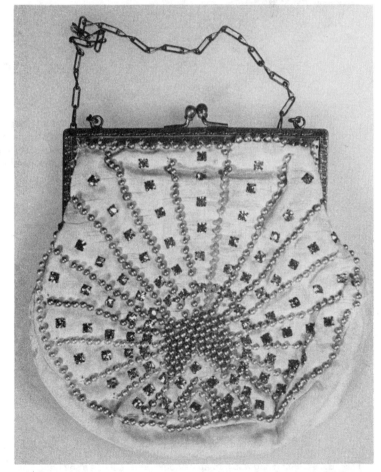

The marriage of pearls and rhinestones is a happy one in this bag. Chain handle, lovely shape, this bag was used in 1929 at a wedding.
Value $175-225

301

A different styling in the rhinestone bag category. This is gold mesh with the angle of the deco period outlined in rhinestones. Chain handle. Bag shows signs of wear but worthy of being in a collection. 1930s.   Value, imperfect condition $95-1

Fine gold mesh bag, chain handle, hand set rhinestones in top frame. 1960s.   Value $100-125

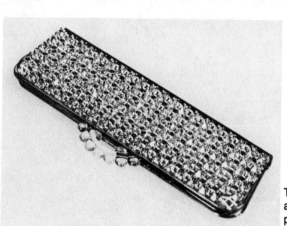

This is another well made purse accessory by SCHILDKRAUT. The paper label is almost obscured and if it is destroyed identification would be impossible. The comb pulls out of a rhinestone-strip covered gilt case by a delightful small plastic handle. The back is mirrored. A charming piece.   Value $45-50

This 1930s evening bag was probably a home project. It has a self handle on the back and an inexpensive, rather primitive zipper pull. The whole is very typical of the 1930s, however, its condition is good and it is a difficult to find, worthwhile, useful addition to a collection. Canny collectors look for these less than designer type rhinestone objects from the early years.

Value $150-195

1930s velvet evening bag, fold over top with excellent quality large rhinestone clasp. The clasp is much in style of brooches of the period. Self handle of velvet on back. A perfect representation of the period with its black velvet backless dresses.

Value $225-250

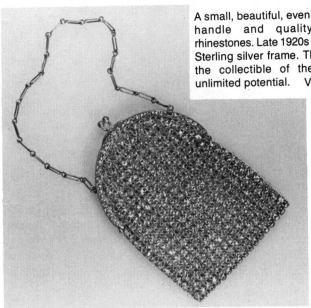

A small, beautiful, evening bag, chain handle and quality hand set rhinestones. Late 1920s or early 1930s. Sterling silver frame. These bags are the collectible of the future with unlimited potential.   Value $200-295

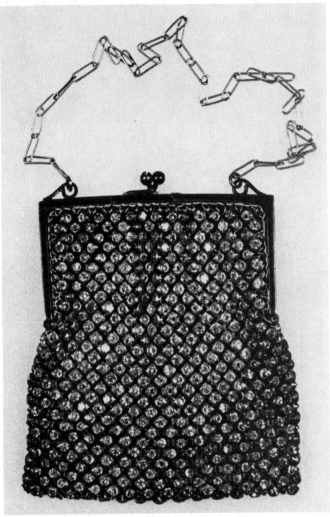

One of the finest of the 1920s evening bags. Each sparkling rhinestone is set deeply into its individual bezel, each attached to another and all forming the body to the bag itself. The silk lining shows signs of wear, the frame is marked MADE IN FRANCE. 4½'' x 3½''.
Value $225-300

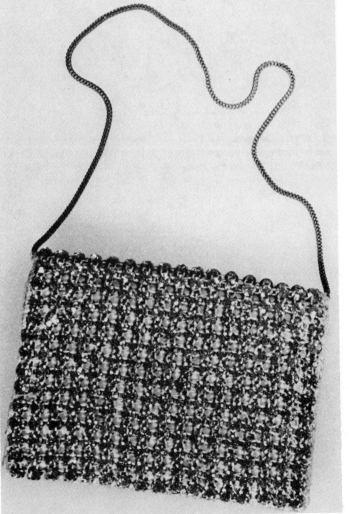

1930s envelope evening bag, chain handle, hand set rhinestones overall. The lining is in perfect condition but the clasp area shows signs of wear. 3½'' x 4½''.   Value $145-195

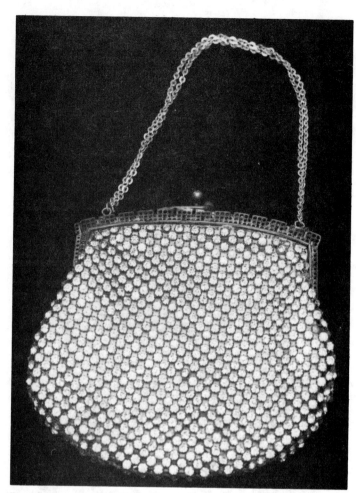

An exquisite powder compact. Thin with mother of pearl cover with hand set pink stones and rhinestones. Not marked and original puff is missing on which the manufacturer's name probably appeared. 1940s.   Value $45-50

Fine quality overall rhinestone evening bag. Silk lined. Made in France and used in late 1920's and early 1930's. Double chain handle.
                              Value $165-195

Square powder compact with unusual closure. The entire line of red stones set into triangles pulls down to open the case. Unused condition. Marked VOLUPTE U.S.A. on the inside cover.   Value $35-45

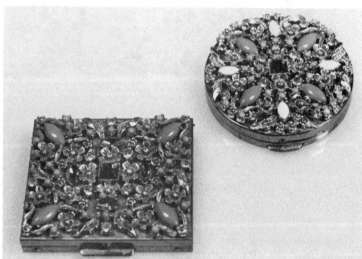

Two powder compacts with identical decorations on the top, the square example has opaque blue with dark blue center stone and smaller blue stones with silver metal and flowers. The original puff is marked with a crown and S.F. CO., 5th Ave., Unused.   Value $30-40
The round compact has the blue opaque and center blue stone with opaque white stones for accent. Made exactly the same way as the square compact but this has the overall floral powder puff and is unmarked in any way.   Value $30-40

Almost wafer thin this elegant compact has a corner square of rhinestones with one larger blue stone and radiating lines in the gold colored metal. Marked on the inside cover VOLUPTE, U.S.A.   Value $45-55

A thin powder compact highlighted by the ever-popular crown.
Unused, not marked in any way.   Value $40-45

Powder compact, late 1940s, early 1950s, white enamel with applied
white metal decoration with blue center stones. Marked only "Made in
U.S.A."   Value $40-45

A fairly common powder compact, which was made
with a variety of different color dominant stones. This
has pink opaque with aurora borealis stones, with
very ornate metal work. This has the original powder
and the puff is overall floral.   Value $35-40

Large metal evening case, an enlargement on the
basic compact. There is space for powder, lipstick,
cigarettes, etc. By Volupte', a well known maker.
Rhinestone trim. 1955.   Value $85-95

The bright silvery finish compact is topped by pearls and blue stones. Many of these
1940s powder compacts have never been used. This is in unused condition. Marked
on the powder puff handles EVANS and also on the inside cover. Value $45-55

Novelty item of the early 1940's or late 1930's. Metal rouge compact with clock face and moveable hands. Hours are marked with rhinestones.　　Value $45-65

Powder compact, oval with hand set rhinestones. Marked MAJESTIC on the handle of the original powder puff. Gold colored metal.
　　Value $50-75

Powder compact with mirror. Top covered in one strip of rhinestones. This has a small interior paper label reading "styled by Schidkraut" 1940s. These labels are rarely found intact, but Schildkraut made many such accessories.
　　Value with label, $60-75

Novelty purse mirror with swing cover and double check design. One check set with rhinestones. 1940's.　　Value $40-55

A restrained, almost perfect example of the timeless design of some of the 1930s jewelry. This compact is black enamel with a cluster of fine rhinestones, hand set and brilliant, at its closure. Marked in script ELGIN AMERICAN, MADE IN U.S.A. Compacts are still available and still under-priced.　　Value $75-95

Another example of the use of the ubiquitous decorations achieved by using strips of rhinestones is this lipstick case. Such purse accessories were very popular during the 1940s. Top flips open.　　Value $40-45

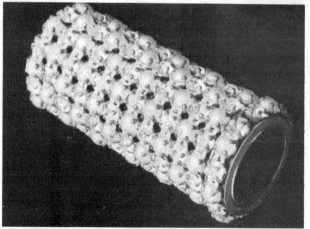

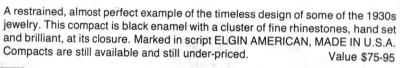

Lipstick case covered with rhinestones and pearls applied from a solid strip. 1940's.
　　Value $35-45

Lipstick holder from the 1940s. Gilt with tiny opaque white beads, rhinestones and deep blue stones. Pull apart type. Marked on bottom in script REVLON. This company known mainly for its cosmetic line produced many lipstick holders with colored stones and rhinestones. Many of the designs were originated by Lurelle Guild of New York and Henrietta P. Manville of Connecticut, many of whose mid-1950s creations with the nipped-in centers are easily identified and quite striking. This holder from the 40s is valued at $40-50.

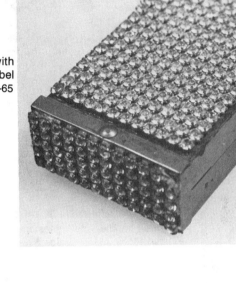

Case for a full package of cigarettes. Brass with hinged top cover. Covered with rhinestones on strips and pasted on. The inside of the cover bears the label MARKHILL FASHIONED ON FIFTH AVENUE, N.Y.   Value $50-65

Cigarette case, 7''x8'', gilt metal aurora borealis stones. 1950s.   Value $75-95

A rounded purse cigarette container. Black enamel with a brass mesh top embedded with rhinestones. Never used. Beautifully lined with satiny brass.   Value $65-85

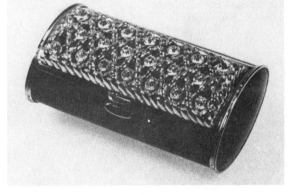

Cigarette holder of late 1930's or early 1940's. Small rhinestones. Chic.   Value $75-95

Purse ashtray. Brass with filagree top decorated with four colored stones - one blue, one topaz, one red and one green. Tiny pearls at each corner. Handle. 1940s.
Value $30-40

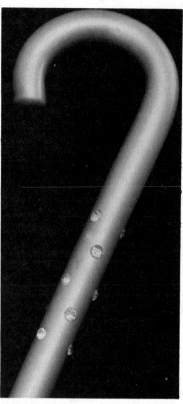

Tiara of gilt filagree studded with hand set rhinestones. Highly unusual and capt vating in a fairy princess way. In a collection of over thirty tiaras this example i unique. 1930s.
Value $85-10(

Umbrella handle with rhinestones. Plastic, 1950s.　　Value $35-50

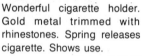

Wonderful cigarette holder. Gold metal trimmed with rhinestones. Spring releases cigarette. Shows use.
Value $75-95

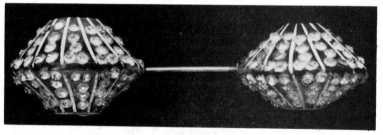

Tiara of rhinestones, metal band. Supposedly worn by June Haver in one of her films.
Value $75-85

1930's plastic and rhinestone hat ornament.　　Value $45-65

This small tiara is meant to encircle gathered hair at the top of the head. These are not easy to find. Hand set rhinestones. 1940s.
Value $75-100

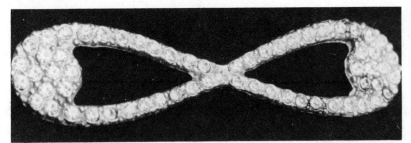

Hat or dress ornament, rhinestones in gilt metal. $30-35

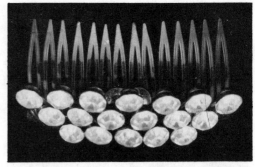

Plastic side comb of the 1940's. Has 18 rhinestones.
One of a great variety of rhinestone combs of the period.
Value $30-45

Plastic comb, rhinestone crown accent. 1940's. $30-38

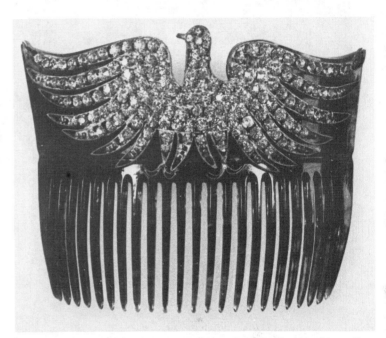

A monumental comb, a museum quality piece. About 5½'' wide, 4'' long. Tortoise shell with a rhinestone eagle. Faceted rhinestones hand set in a brass frame. This is from the era of "brilliants". Unique.   Value $325-395

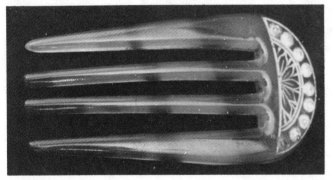

Tuck comb. 9 brilliants, etched design. 1920's. Combs of this type, especially those with squared tops can be found with varying colored stones.   Value $40-55

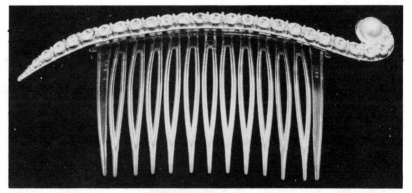

Plastic comb with rhinestone and large pearl top accent.   Value $35-40

Clear plastic side comb with silvery metal and rhinestone tiara-like decoration, hinged to lie flat for easy storage.   Value $35-50

Comb in brass case covered with rhinestones. Found in French rhinestone evening bag, but stones are differently set and of a different quality so probably not original to bag.

Value $45-60

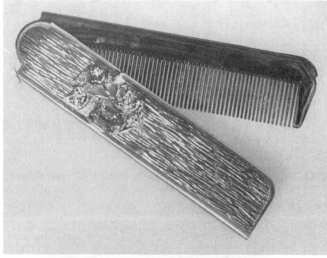

This comb and case has the very bright silvery finish of late pieces. The floral spray holding one large square rhinestone blends almost too well into the metal and is almost obscured. These make an interesting collection. Not marked.   Value $30-35

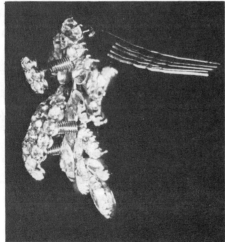

Small, highly decorative comb with silver, rhinestone flower head centerpiece "en-tremblant" to move with the motion of the head. Ingeniously designed. Well made but not signed.   Value $55-95

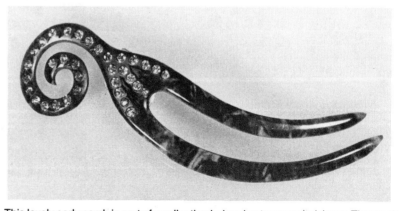

This lovely early comb is part of a collection belonging to a peacock lover. The mock tortoise shell has some wear on the gilding but all the rhinestones which are pasted-in are good quality and intact. The shape of the comb reflects the bird motif without being overdone. This is shown in a photograph dating from 1918. Value $45-55

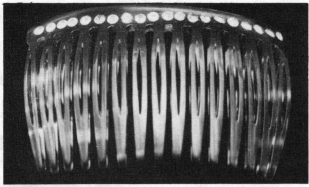

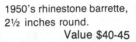

Comb, plastic in imitation tortoise shell, line of rhinestone along top is decidedly uneven. Marked MADE IN SWITZERLAND.   Value $15-20

Hat pin of the early 1940's. Rhinestone and pearl. Approx. 4''.   Value $40-45

1950's rhinestone barrette, 2½ inches round.
       Value $40-45

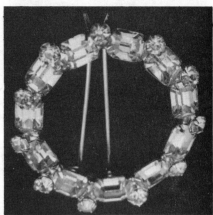

1930's Stick Pin. Blue center stone surrounded by small rhinestones. Brass.
          Value $35-40

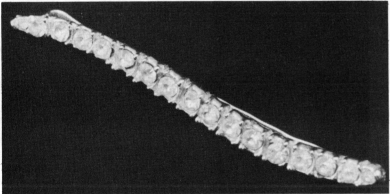

Rhinestone hairpin of the late 1950's.   Value $30-42

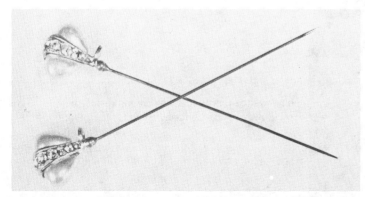

Hat pins of the 1940s. Pretty matching pair of pearls and rhinestones.
          Value of each, $45-50

Right: Scarf pin with hand set blue stones and larger opaque blue stones. 1940s. 3'' long.   Value $45-55

Left: Hat ornament of the 1930s. Base metal with rhinestones and two greenish stones at bottom. Imitation pearl drop.   Value $50-55

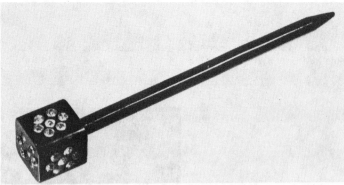

This hair decoration is a great beginner's collectible. Still inexpensive they are not abundant but can be found with some ease. Black plastic with good rhinestones pasted in. This was bought in a novelty shop in the 1960s.   Value $15-35

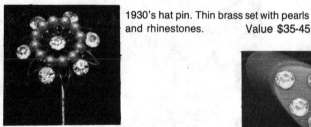

Hat pins of the early 1940s. Similar in shape but vastly different in quality. The pin on the right was originally a less expensive example. These are coming into their own as older hatpins and stickpins become so costly.

Value left $50-60
Right $55-75

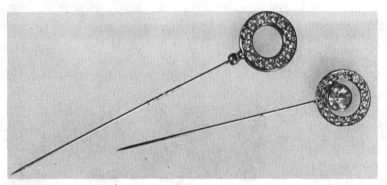

1930's hat pin. Thin brass set with pearls and rhinestones.   Value $35-45

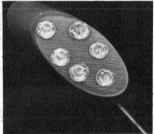

1930's hat ornament Bakelite and rather large rhinestones.   Value $50-75

Hatpin with 9½" shaft. Rhinestone framed porcelain plaque of romantic scene.   Value $175-195

Stickpin or scarf pin. Early 1940's. Simulated pearl surrounded by rhinestones. Brass.   Value $35-45

Stickpin with one large center rhinestone. Brass. 1920's.   Value $35-45

Vinyl eyeglass case. Metal studs and rhinestone trim. Dowdy Optical Company, St. Petersburg, Fla.   Value $20-40

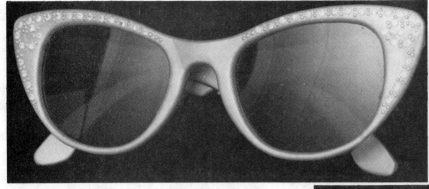

Sunglasses, 1950's, blue plastic frame with rhinestones. Marked GRANTLY U.S.A.   Value $35-45

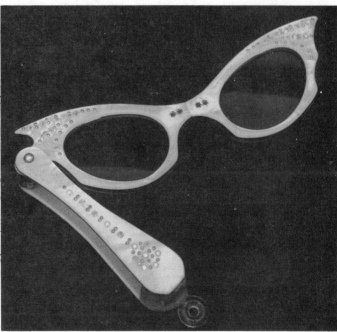

Small size lorgnette, entire frame set with rhinestones and it has a twisted handle which ends in rhinestone design. Pink plastic.   Value $75-100

Boudoir Clock, black enamel with rhinestone framed face which is marked BLACK FOREST. This little alarm clock has been in use since the late 1940s and while it shows signs of wear, the pasted-in rhinestones have never needed replacements.   Value $95-125

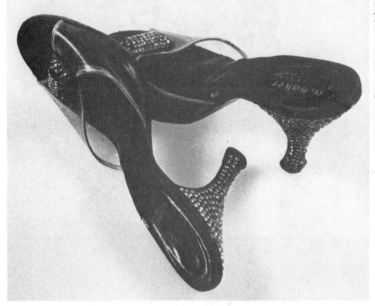

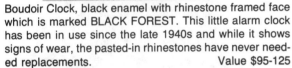

Folding lorgnette, rhinestone studded handle and butterfly frame, plastic. 1950's.   Value $75-95

These shoes are a testimony to the well-made but well-worn and still effective shoes with rhinestone studded heels and buckles of the early 1940s. Later shoes do not have the verve and depth of the rhinestones and the knowledgeable collector can tell the difference at a glance. A new collectible has also resulted - beautiful pairs of high heels, detached from the worn shoe and sold as a pair are now surfacing and being added to shoes or collections. These shoes were bought in California, are black with the usual plastic front band with its rhinestone and black plastic buckle stapled on.   Value $100-125

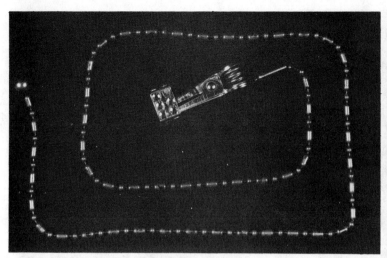

An ingenious device for pulling zippers, it is ornamented with aurora borealis stones and marked NEW ZIP AID, PAT. PEND. The spring gripper is on a chain.

Value $45-55

Novelty jewelry of the period.
Marked: KING'S KEY FINDER/LOS ANGELES/REG. U.S. PAT OFF. Clip and key ring. Green stone centerpiece. Unusual.

Value $20-40

Perfume bottle with atomizer. The bottle is removeable from the filagree brass stand which is decorated with round pearls and small hand set rhinestones. Bought in 1938.

Value $300-325

This kind of piece which was relatively inexpensive in its heyday has a sculptured look. This bouquet of flowers in its stand is made entirely of thin filagreed brass. The leaves are shaded and the flowers are made of red stones, each on its individual wire. Unusual and very decorative. Bought in 1940. Not signed, 4'' tall.

Value $150-200

Sweater grip in original box by Coro. Pearls and rhinestones on gilt metal. The piece itself is unmarked so once the box had been discarded positive identification would be almost impossible. Late 1940s.

Value $35-45

One of the appealing whimsies of the 1940s. The bracelet composed of faux pearls on a chain, the box opens and on its face is a telephone mouthpiece of green stone attached by a chain to the earpiece on the side. The dial is tiny multi-colored stones surrounding a pink stone.

Value $85-125

One of the great assets of the rhinestone jewelry period was the fact that designers imaginations were given free rein. Here is a whimsical set of binoculars which are in fact two perfume bottles joined by a thin brass frame. The vision adjuster is a hand painted enamelled rose center encircled by pasted-in rhinestones. Delightful. Early 1940s.

Value $55-75

These novelty holders were made with both pens, as in this case, and pencils. The filagree work over the brass case is well done, the stones are blue, green and red and there is a small chain to be carried or attached to a bag or belt. This was bought in 1939 but these were made into the 1940s.

Value $40-45

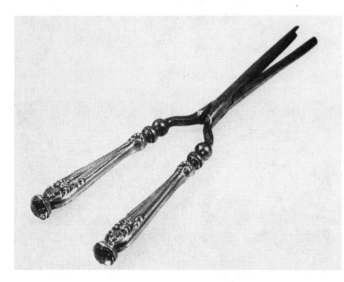

Curling iron with handles of sterling silver with large green faceted stone at end of each handle. Unique and beautiful. 1920s.

Value $125-185

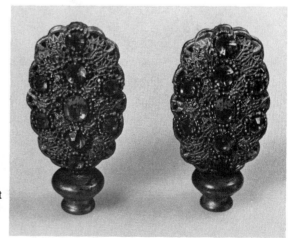

A tremendous find. Lamp finials of the 1920s. 3½'' tall, heavy with blue stones set into the old gilt filagree.

Value of pair $300-400

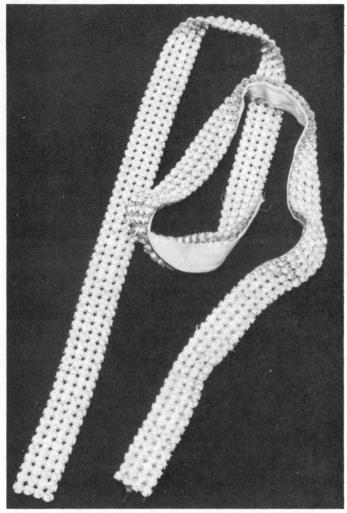

Long strip of dazzling rhinestones (1'' wide, 25'' long) of the type used for shoulder straps or other trim on gowns. This piece has the original pink silk and ribbon lining. 1930s. Value $200-250

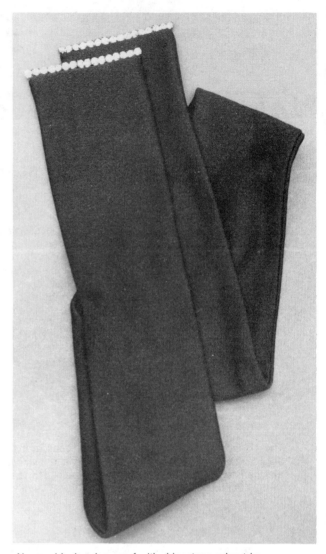

Narrow black nylon scarf with rhinestone edge trim.
Value $45-55

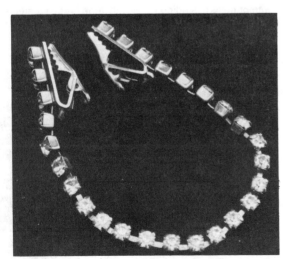

Rhinestone sweater guard, 1940s with hand set stones. Period sweater guards are a whole new collecting category. Value $40-45

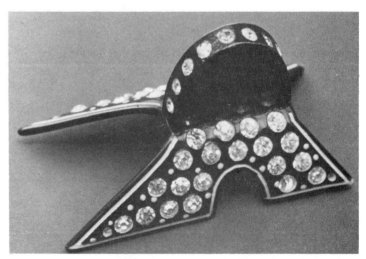

Bakelite and rhinestone whimsy. Probably a scarf tie. 1930's.
Value $50-60

Pair of gilt hands joined together by a spring. Cuffed and braceleted in small rhinestones, chain with somewhat unusual closure for hanging. 2¼'' long, large topaz colored stones on each side of bracelet. This is part of a collection of hands, an example of how this wonderful jewelry fits into other collections. Not signed. 1940s.   Value $50-60

Novelty item of the 1940's. One of the many kinds of musical instruments made during the period. Saxophone with multi-colored stones for keys.
Value $38-65

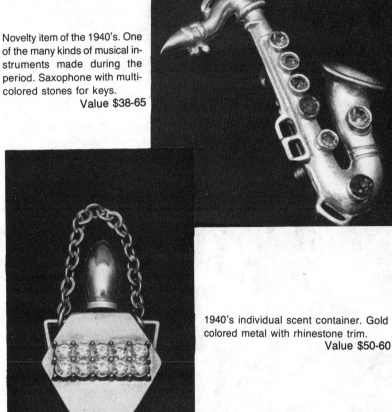

Black enamelled wooden dice set with rhinestones, the only such pair I have ever seen. The original case is leather covered metal. Tremendous collector's item and conversation piece. Early 1920s.   Value $200-250

1940's individual scent container. Gold colored metal with rhinestone trim.
Value $50-60

Standing picture frame 2½'' by 1¾'' for two photos. 1960s. Enamelled white metal with aurora borealis stones in red and rhinestones. Marked FLORENZA and paper label. Velvet back. Scarce.
Value $55-85

Pink plastic desk accessory which now holds bobby pins and small safety pins. Two small drawers, top lifts for pad underneath. Metallic ornamented top with flower centered with a large rhinestone. 1940s   Value $40-45

1940s plastic container for body powder. Pale blue with floral decor and surrounding rhinestones it was part of a complete dresser set. It sits on brass ball feet and has a hinged lid, inside of which is a compartment for a large powder puff. These colorful dresser accessories are coming collectibles. Bought in 1947   Value $45-50

Lucite handbag of the late 1940s. Rows of good quality rhinestones are pasted on the bag to frame an endearing print of adorable kittens. Rigid handle.
          Value $95-125